W9-DGD-024

Analyses in the Economics of Aging

**A National Bureau
of Economic Research
Conference Report**

Analyses in the
Economics of Aging

Edited by   **David A. Wise**

The University of Chicago Press

Chicago and London

DAVID A. WISE is the John F. Stambaugh Professor of Political Economy at the John F. Kennedy School of Government, Harvard University. He is also the Peter and Helen Bing Senior Fellow at the Hoover
Institution and director of the NBER Program on Aging. Among the
many titles he has edited in this area are the recent *Themes in the Economics of Aging* and *Perspectives on the Economics of Aging.*

The University of Chicago Press, Chicago 60637
The University of Chicago Press, Ltd., London
© 2005 by the National Bureau of Economic Research
All rights reserved. Published 2005
Printed in the United States of America
13 12 11 10 09 08 07 06 05   1 2 3 4 5
ISBN: 0-226-90286-2 (cloth)

Library of Congress Cataloging-in-Publication Data

Analyses in the economics of aging / edited by David Wise.
        p.   cm. — (NBER conference report)
     Papers presented at a conference held in Carefree, Arizona, in May
2003.
     Includes bibliographical references and index.
     ISBN 0-226-90286-2 (cloth : alk. paper)
     1. Aging—Economic aspects—Congresses. 2. Older people—
Economic conditions—Congresses. 3. Older people—United
States—Economic conditions—Congresses. 4. Retirement
income—Congresses. 5. Older people—Medical care—Costs—
Congresses. 6. Medicare—Congresses. I. Wise, David A. II. Series.

HQ1061 .A63 2005
305.26—dc22

                                                    2004062822

Relation of the Directors to the
Work and Publications of the
National Bureau of Economic Research

1. The object of the NBER is to ascertain and present to the economics profession, and to the public more generally, important economic facts and their interpretation in a scientific manner without policy recommendations. The Board of Directors is charged with the responsibility of ensuring that the work of the NBER is carried on in strict conformity with this object.

2. The President shall establish an internal review process to ensure that book manuscripts proposed for publication DO NOT contain policy recommendations. This shall apply both to the proceedings of conferences and to manuscripts by a single author or by one or more co-authors but shall not apply to authors of comments at NBER conferences who are not NBER affiliates.

3. No book manuscript reporting research shall be published by the NBER until the President has sent to each member of the Board a notice that a manuscript is recommended for publication and that in the President's opinion it is suitable for publication in accordance with the above principles of the NBER. Such notification will include a table of contents and an abstract or summary of the manuscript's content, a list of contributors if applicable, and a response form for use by Directors who desire a copy of the manuscript for review. Each manuscript shall contain a summary drawing attention to the nature and treatment of the problem studied and the main conclusions reached.

4. No volume shall be published until forty-five days have elapsed from the above notification of intention to publish it. During this period a copy shall be sent to any Director requesting it, and if any Director objects to publication on the grounds that the manuscript contains policy recommendations, the objection will be presented to the author(s) or editor(s). In case of dispute, all members of the Board shall be notified, and the President shall appoint an ad hoc committee of the Board to decide the matter; thirty days additional shall be granted for this purpose.

5. The President shall present annually to the Board a report describing the internal manuscript review process, any objections made by Directors before publication or by anyone after publication, any disputes about such matters, and how they were handled.

6. Publications of the NBER issued for informational purposes concerning the work of the Bureau, or issued to inform the public of the activities at the Bureau, including but not limited to the NBER Digest and Reporter, shall be consistent with the object stated in paragraph 1. They shall contain a specific disclaimer noting that they have not passed through the review procedures required in this resolution. The Executive Committee of the Board is charged with the review of all such publications from time to time.

7. NBER working papers and manuscripts distributed on the Bureau's web site are not deemed to be publications for the purpose of this resolution, but they shall be consistent with the object stated in paragraph 1. Working papers shall contain a specific disclaimer noting that they have not passed through the review procedures required in this resolution. The NBER's web site shall contain a similar disclaimer. The President shall establish an internal review process to ensure that the working papers and the web site do not contain policy recommendations, and shall report annually to the Board on this process and any concerns raised in connection with it.

8. Unless otherwise determined by the Board or exempted by the terms of paragraphs 6 and 7, a copy of this resolution shall be printed in each NBER publication as described in paragraph 2 above.

Contents

Preface

This volume consists of papers presented at a conference held in Carefree, Arizona, in May 2003. Most of the research was conducted as part of the program on the Economics of Aging at the National Bureau of Economic Research. The majority of the work was sponsored by the U.S. Department of Health and Human Services, through the National Institute on Aging grants P01-AG05842 and P30-AG12810 to the National Bureau of Economic Research. Any other funding sources are noted in the individual papers.

Any opinions expressed in this volume are those of the respective authors and do not necessarily reflect the views of the National Bureau of Economic Research or the sponsoring organizations.

Introduction

David A. Wise

This is the tenth in a series of volumes on the economics of aging. The previous volumes were *The Economics of Aging, Issues in the Economics of Aging, Topics in the Economics of Aging, Studies in the Economics of Aging, Advances in the Economics of Aging, Inquiries in the Economics of Aging, Frontiers in the Economics of Aging, Themes in the Economics of Aging,* and *Perspectives on the Economics of Aging.*

This introduction provides a summary of the papers and draws heavily on the authors' own language. Analyses in prior volumes have included discussion of the saving effect and the spread of personal retirement accounts, especially 401(k) plans, and of the effect of defaults on the 401(k) saving decisions of employees. This volume includes introductory work on evaluations of risk in 401(k) plans and continues work on defaults with theoretical discussion of optimal defaults. There are papers on the growth of Medicare cost and on the efficiency of Medicare. Three papers consider different aspects of disability and the consequences of health shocks.

There is a paper on the evolution of, and the relationship between, health, wealth, and living arrangements as people age. The volume also includes papers on saving in other countries compared to the United States. Prior volumes have included many papers on aging issues in other countries. This tradition is continued in this volume with a paper on population aging and the plight of widows in India.

Finally, modern surveys like the Health and Retirement Study and the

David A. Wise is the John F. Stambaugh Professor of Political Economy at the John F. Kennedy School of Government, Harvard University, and the director for Health and Retirement Programs at the National Bureau of Economic Research.

Asset and Health Dynamics among the Oldest Old survey ask respondents to provide estimates of subjective probabilities of survival and other uncertain outcomes. Specific features of the responses limit the usefulness of the data. A paper in this volume provides a method to obtain useable distributions of survival probabilities based on the survey responses.

401(k) Plans: Risk and Optimal Defaults

The shift from employer-provided defined benefit pension plans to employee-controlled personal retirement accounts in the United States has drawn increased attention to the effect of participants' asset allocation decisions on their retirement resources. In "Utility Evaluation of Risk in Retirement Saving Accounts" James M. Poterba, Joshua Rauh, Steven F. Venti, and I begin research to evaluate the implications of asset choices in personal accounts. In this paper we develop a stochastic simulation algorithm to evaluate the effect of holding a broadly diversified portfolio of common stocks compared to a portfolio of index bonds on the distribution of 401(k) account balances at retirement. We compare the alternative distributions of retirement wealth both by showing the empirical distribution of potential wealth values and by computing the expected utility of these outcomes under standard assumptions about the structure of household preferences. Our analysis highlights the critical role of other sources of wealth, such as Social Security, defined benefit pension annuities, and saving outside retirement plans, in determining the expected utility value (based on a constant relative risk aversion utility function) of holding equities in the retirement account.

Given the historical pattern of returns on stocks and bonds, a household that is not highly risk averse would achieve a higher expected utility by holding a portfolio of stocks rather than bonds. We have explored the robustness of this finding to reducing the expected return on corporate stocks by 300 basis points per year. While this shifts the distribution of retirement balances to lower values and reduces the expected utility of holding stocks, we still find that only highly risk-averse investors would choose not to hold corporate stocks.

First, we present "pictures" of the distribution of wealth outcomes for different investment allocation rules. This approach is closely related to the techniques used by many financial planners, who show clients the set of outcomes that they might achieve under a given set of assumptions about future returns and investment strategy. It is also the approach that we, and others, have used in past studies that considered the returns to different investment strategies. Second, we tried to synthesize the information in the distribution of wealth outcomes by computing an expected utility measure corresponding to each distribution. This approach allows for the possibility that the marginal utility of wealth declines with wealth, so that a given increment to wealth is more valuable when wealth is at a low level than when it is high. We conclude that both approaches to the evaluation of risk can be important and that the appropriateness of each is likely to depend on the specific goal of the evaluation.

Given the apparent inconsistencies between standard behavior and the predictions of standard utility functions, we hope to gain a better understanding of individual preferences over uncertain levels of future retirement assets by developing a set of survey questions designed to elicit respondent preferences over alternative wealth outcomes. We hope to include these questions on household surveys like the Health and Retirement Study and other surveys.

In the previous volume in this series, James J. Choi, David Laibson, Brigitte C. Madrian, and Andrew Metrick reported evidence on the effect of plan defaults on 401(k) participation and contribution rates. Based on this and other research, they conclude that defaults have an enormous effect on employee choices. In "Passive Decisions and Potent Defaults" in this volume, they develop a theory of optimal defaults based on these considerations: Defaults matter because opting out of a default is costly and these costs change over time, generating an option value of waiting. In addition, people have a tendency to procrastinate.

In a world of saving preference, the authors conclude that it may sometimes be optimal to set *extreme* defaults that are far away from the mean optimal savings rate. This effect arises for two reasons. First, a default that is far away from an employee's optimal savings rate may make that employee *better off* than a default that is closer to the employee's optimal savings rate. Intuitively, if an employee suffers from a procrastination problem, then a "bad" default—that is, one that is far from the consumer's optimal savings rate—will be more motivating than a better default. Hence, sometimes bad defaults make people better off than better but imperfect defaults. Second, their theory implies that optimal defaults are highly sensitive to the actual distribution of optimal savings rates. In particular, optimal defaults are often associated with the modal optimal savings rate and not the mean optimal savings rate. Since these modes are sometimes extreme (e.g., minimum or maximum contribution rates), optimal defaults will sometimes be extreme as well.

At the end of their paper Choi, Laibson, Madrian, and Metrick calibrate their model and use it to calculate optimal defaults for employees at four different companies. For two of these companies, the optimal default is close to the mean optimal savings rate, whereas for the others the optimal defaults are extreme: 0 percent and 15 percent, respectively. Their analysis suggests that optimal defaults are likely to be at one of three savings rates: the minimum savings rate (0 percent), the employer match threshold (typically 5 percent or 6 percent), or the maximal savings rate (around 15 percent in their sample of companies from the late 1990s).

Medicare Cost Growth and the Efficiency of Medicare

The increasing cost of Medicare is an ongoing concern. In "Characterizing the Experience of High-Cost Users in Medicare" Thomas MaCurdy and Jeff Geppert provide new insights into the source of cost growth over the past decade. Their study reveals several valuable insights into the growth of Medicare expenditures in recent years, both in projecting aggregate trends and in discovering the extent to which the concentration of spending on high-cost users contributes to overall expenditures. Considering the growth in Medicare program payments from 1989 to 1999, they attribute 20–30 percent of total growth to an increase in the participation rate, 50–60 percent to an increase in average program payments per service recipient, and the remainder to higher enrollment.

In sharp contrast to the first half of the 1990s, total Medicare costs fell in the late 1990s. Whereas the lower percentiles of the expenditure distribution continued to increase throughout the period, expenditures fell for the highest-cost users for Medicare services. Published statistics extending beyond their sample period suggest that this was only temporary; starting in 2000, the overall growth in Medicare expenditures reverted to its previous rate and may have accelerated. Annual Medicare spending is highly concentrated among a small segment of the beneficiary population, and the share of spending attributable to high-cost users has remained remarkably stable over the 1989–99 decade even though growth rates have varied considerably during the period. Those beneficiaries classified in the top 2 percent of the annual expenditure distribution account for about one quarter of total expenditures, and those in the top 5 percent cover almost half of annual expenditures. Considering spending by months only reinforces this picture of concentration. The top 2 percent of months with spending during a year account for around two-fifths of total annual expenditures, and the top 5 percent of months cover nearly two-thirds of yearly Medicare expenditures. While high-cost episodes account for a large proportion of total spending during any year, the majority of the elderly experience such episodes at some point over a decade, implying far less concentration in expenditures when viewed over lifetimes. Three-fifths of beneficiaries experience at least one 95th-percentile month in the decade, and two-fifths realize one or more 98th-percentile months. Knowledge of the incidence of 95th-percentile months alone explains nearly two-thirds of Medicare spending over the decade, and spending accumulated for those in the 98th-percentile months comprises almost four-fifths of total decade expenditures.

MaCurdy and Geppert emphasize that a major challenge faced by researchers involves identifying intense users of health care services along with the factors leading to the incidence and duration of their utilization. Such a task requires a detailed understanding of the patterns of medical care for periods much shorter than a year to adequately capture the onset of health events and relationships linking the persistence of costs in both the short and long runs. Many surmise that restricting attention to those in their last year of life identifies most high-cost users, but existing work shows that the majority of the most intense users measured by accumulating expenses annually live beyond a year after incurring their high expenses. Further, previous work has met with limited success in associating large fractions of the highest-cost users with particular diagnoses or chronic conditions. The availability of the monthly longitudinal Medicare data greatly enhances options for improving our understanding of the sources of high-cost utilization.

The United States spends more on health care in per capita terms and as a percentage of gross domestic product (GDP) than any other developed country. This can be interpreted in two ways. One is that the elevated spending is symptomatic of failure in the health care system. Money is wasted through administrative overhead, the overuse of fully insured health care, or the provision of expensive tertiary but only marginally useful technology. A different view is that U.S. citizens demand, and get, a higher quality level of health care than anywhere else in the world. It may be expensive, but the technological advances provided in the United States have led to dramatic improvements in functioning and life expectancy. In "The Efficiency of Medicare," Jonathan Skinner, Elliott S. Fisher, and John E. Wennberg use the idea of "natural randomization" to evaluate the efficiency of the Medicare program.

The authors attempt to test whether the Medicare program is broadly consistent with the efficiency criterion commonly used in public economics, where the marginal social value of the last dollar spent on specific types of health care (in each region) is equal to the marginal social benefits of the dollar that could have been spent for other worthy causes. They used data on survival rates, Medicare expenditures, and health status measures across 306 hospital referral regions in the United States to test these hypotheses. Their best estimate of the incremental value of Medicare spending with regard to effective care suggests that spending for these types of services is too low, especially considering how this type of care is associated with overall Medicare expenditures. On the other hand, the supply-sensitive dimension of care is a major factor in explaining overall Medicare expenditures—roughly 20 percent annually—but does not show any impact in terms of improving survival rates across regions. These results, the authors conclude, suggest that the inefficiency inherent in the Medicare program is as much as 20 percent of total Medicare expenditures.

A Focus on Disability and the Implications of Health Shocks

Substantial recent evidence shows a reduction in disability among the elderly in the United States, on the order of 25 percent in the past two decades. The major issue raised by these findings is why disability has declined. In "Intensive Medical Technology and the Reduction in Disability" David M. Cutler investigates the role of intensive medical technologies in the decline in disability. Using data from the National Long-Term Care Survey, he documents that increased use of intensive procedures might be associated with some reduction in disability but probably does not account for the majority of the decline.

Cutler presents preliminary evidence on the role of increased medical procedure use in response to acute episodes of disease. These procedures consist largely of major surgical operations—open-heart surgery for people with cardiovascular disease and hip replacements for people with fractures or severe arthritis, for example. Use of these procedures has diffused widely, in many cases doubling or tripling over a decade, suggesting they could play a large role in improved health.

Cutler documents two facts about procedure receipt and disability change. He shows that most of the reduction in disability is not from people having fewer disabling conditions. The share of people with a stroke, fracture, or other serious condition has increased over time. Rather, reduced disability is because fewer people who have these conditions become disabled. Since intensive medical care is most important after a person has an acute event, this suggests the potential role of increased utilization of medical services in reducing disability.

Examining specific technologies shows that receipt of intensive procedures is associated with some, but not a large, reduction in disability. People with musculoskeletal problems and circulatory diseases are much more likely to get surgery now than in the past, and disability for people with these conditions has fallen. But this does not account for a large share of the total decline. Other medical and nonmedical interventions are more important in aggregate. Cutler speculates about what other factors might be relevant, but he does not provide conclusive evidence.

Self-reported health status (SRHS) is an imperfect measure of nonfatal health, but it allows examination of how health status varies over the life course. Although women have lower mortality than men, they report worse health status up to age 65. The SRHS of both men and women deteriorates with age. There are strong gradients, so that at age 20, men in the bottom quartile already report worse health than do men in the top quartile at age 50. In the bottom quartile of income, SRHS declines more rapidly with age, but only until retirement age. These facts motivate Anne Case and Angus Deaton to study the role of work, particularly manual work, in health decline with age, as reported in their paper, "Broken Down by Work and Sex: How Our Health Declines."

Case and Deaton start from the observation that SRHS worsens with age and that it does so much more rapidly among those at the bottom of the income distribution, who also start their working lives with lower health. They originally expected that, because manual work involves more wear and tear on the body, the health of manual workers would decline more rapidly than that of nonmanual workers, thus offering an explanation for their starting facts. The data from the National Health Interview Survey (NHIS) show that the health of manual workers does in fact decline more rapidly during the working years than does the health of nonmanual workers, in spite of the existence of health-based selection out of manual work, which artificially inflates the health of those who remain. The authors do not find this result at all implausible. Instead, the implausibility lies in the health repair technology that is routinely assumed in the health economics literature.

The authors find that manual workers have worse health than do nonmanual workers, and although their health declines more rapidly, the major factor accounting for the differences in health and health decline in different parts of the income distribution is whether or not people are in the labor force, a mechanism where causality runs from health to income, not the reverse. Even so, both income and education have independent protective effects on health for those who are in work, and these effects are reduced but not eliminated by controlling for occupation. With only a few exceptions, Case and Deaton find a marked similarity in all of these results between men and women.

Considerable analysis has been directed to understanding and disentangling the multiple ways in which socioeconomic status (SES) may influence a variety of health outcomes. Much less attention has been directed to the impact health may have on SES. In "Consequences and Predictors of New Health Events," James P. Smith aims to estimate the effect of new health events on a series of subsequent outcomes that are both directly and indirectly related to SES. These outcomes include out-of-pocket medical expenses, labor supply, health insurance, and household income.

The analysis is based on the HRS and AHEAD surveys and thus considers persons first observed when they were between ages fifty-one and sixty-one. The author concludes that among people in their preretirement years, feedbacks from health to labor supply, household income, and wealth are realities that should be neither ignored nor dismissed as of secondary importance. Working is the critical link in this chain, with out-of-pocket medical expenses of lesser importance. The negative income and wealth consequences of new health shocks appear to decay with age and are much smaller in an already retired population. What these consequences would be ten or twenty years earlier in age is an important and yet unanswered question. The evidence in this paper, along with that available in other studies, shows that we can say with confidence that health has quantitatively strong consequences for several dimensions of SES, particularly financial, in certain age groups.

Smith observes that only tentative conclusions are warranted with respect to the effect of SES on the future onset of disease. Household income never appears to predict any future onset over the horizon of about a decade. However, even after controlling for an extensive list of baseline health conditions, education is a strong predictor if the future onset of disease.

Health, Wealth, and Living Arrangements

Health, wealth, and where one lives are important indicators of living conditions. In "Healthy, Wealthy, and Knowing Where to Live: Trajectories of Health, Wealth, and Living Arrangements among the Oldest Old," Axel Börsch-Supan, Florian Heiss, and Michael D. Hurd investigate the joint evolution of these three conditions as persons age. The elderly reach their early postretirement years in an initial status that is characterized by housing wealth, nonhousing bequeathable wealth, annuity income, health status, and family connections. The broad goal of the paper is to describe the trajectories of health, wealth, and living arrangements as people age; to understand how the trajectories of health status, wealth position, and living arrangements are interrelated; and to be able to predict how health and living arrangements would evolve when economic and other conditions change.

The authors reproduce the finding that wealth and health are strongly related to each other. Wealthier persons live longer and are healthy longer. This interaction is moderated by where elderly persons live. Remaining in the lowest wealth quartile is most likely when an elderly person lives in a nursing home, and it is least likely when this person lives with others. The reverse pattern is true for the probability of remaining in the highest wealth quartile. For the initially wealthy, living with others decreases the expected future wealth relative to living alone. This is consistent with the notion that cohabitation implies intrafamily transfers to the needy. For those who remain living independently, home ownership declines, but the speed of reduction is slower than it is for financial wealth. The authors emphasize that the results in the paper are descriptive and imply no causality. Further research will apply more sophisticated econometric methods to attempt to identify patterns of causality.

Saving: The United States Compared to Other Countries

In addition to relying on public retirement provisions, households prepare for retirement through tax-sheltered and after-tax savings. They may invest these funds in a wide variety of assets, including housing, stocks, bonds, savings accounts, and so on. These asset types differ in their risk, return, and liquidity characteristics as well as in their fiscal treatment. Economic theory postulates that households allocate their portfolios according to their risk aversion, time horizon, uncertain out-of-pocket medical expenditures, income risk, informal (family) risk sharing arrangements, and the like. Both testing and quantification of the theory are hampered by the fact that important variables do not exhibit sufficient variation within a country to establish their relative importance for portfolio choice or, more generally, for retirement saving and investment. This gap is partially filled by Arie Kapteyn and Constantijn Panis in "Institutions and Saving for Retirement: Comparing the United States, Italy, and the Netherlands."

In this paper, they consider retirement saving and portfolio choice in three countries with widely varying institutional arrangements for retirement income: the United States, Italy, and the Netherlands. The authors emphasize that the number of countries considered and the data are limited. Nonetheless they propose these implications:

- Americans should save more for retirement than the Dutch or the Italians.
- Americans should save more due to more exposure to uninsurable income and consumption risk.
- Italians should save more due to severe borrowing constraints in their country.
- The Dutch should have relatively low stockholdings due to the low level of private wealth.
- Stock ownership in the United States should be higher than in Italy because of the more developed capital markets in the United States.

The authors emphasize that while each of these implications is borne out by the data, it is in general not possible to establish the relative magnitude of factors influencing wealth accumulation or portfolio choice. For instance, both low replacement rates at retirement and higher consumption and income risk in the United States imply that Americans should save more than Europeans.

In "Household Saving in Germany—Results of the First SAVE Survey," Axel Börsch-Supan and Lothar Essig take a fresh look at the saving behavior of German households. They use the first wave of the SAVE panel. It is a preliminary look, since many aspects of saving can only be understood using longitudinal data. The authors take this paper on German saving behavior as both a comparison with and a contrast to the large literature on the saving behavior of U.S. households.

Germany is an interesting country in which to study household saving behavior since it appears to contradict the familiar textbook version of the life-cycle theory of consumption and saving. First, there is little borrowing by young households. More striking is that nearly everyone—whether in the middle income bracket or richer—saves substantial amounts at older ages. Only in households that earn less than 25 percent of average income between the ages of 60 and 75 is there dissaving.

Overall, the findings show a savings pattern that is extraordinarily stable. Germans save regularly, in a manner that is planned and often with a clearly defined purpose in mind. German households appear not to save in order to balance out transitory income fluctuations. Rather, they appear to save out of income components that are stable in the long run. German labor income has less individual variation than labor income in the United States. This should reduce the precautionary savings motive, all else being equal, relative to the United States. In addition, German public pension replacement rates are much higher than those of the U.S. replacement rates. This should reduce the savings motive for old-age provision relative to the United States. The findings on German savings motives, however, contradict these predictions: The authors find that precaution and old-age provision are the two most important savings motives in Germany. Less developed credit markets may explain the high saving rate relative to the United States.

Aging Issues in India

The elderly are a very large and rapidly growing population in India. The well-being of widows in particular has attracted considerable attention. In his paper, "Caste, Culture, and the Status and Well-Being of Widows in India," Robert Jensen pursues two issues. The first is how norms, attitudes, and practices vary across groups in India and how they affect the well-being of the elderly. He first examines the influence of caste on well-being. Caste is a social organization prevalent in India that creates a well-defined social ordering. The objective is to examine the consequences for widows, using indicators for individual nutritional status and health, rather than relying on household income or expenditure per capita. The second issue is whether social and cultural institutions and the status of widows have any underpinnings in economic factors. In particular, Jensen explores whether the production of crops for which women and the elderly are able to make larger economic contributions leads to improved status of widows.

Jensen draws two primary lessons from his paper. The first lesson is that issues of intrahousehold allocation are essential for assessing individual well-being, especially for the elderly. While this has been widely appreciated in economics for some time, very little is done about it in practice, and most studies focus only on household per capita measures in assessing living standards. This observation also has implications for studies on the relationship between SES and health. Further, the results also show that the relationship between SES and health or nutrition in India is more complex than simply the purchasing power potentially implied by income or expenditure. In particular, other factors, such as the treatment of individuals within the household, mediate this relationship. Jensen finds that widows are much better off in forward-caste households when measured in terms of per capita expenditure, but in using body mass index (BMI) as a crude proxy for consumption of the elderly, forward-caste persons are no better off than lower-caste households, suggesting the share of household resources is not measured well by expenditure per person.

The second lesson is that the status, treatment, and well-being of widows have a foundation in potential economic value, either through bargaining power within households or through a cultural underpinning to the evolution of cultural norms. The claim is not that economic factors are the only, or even the largest, determinant of "culture" or to argue that factors such as history and lineage are not important. However, the evidence indicates that economic factors appear to play at least some role in the well-being and status of widows. The implication is that programs (such as microenterprise ventures) that expand economic opportunities for women or the elderly attempt to minimize age or gender discrimination in private-sector employment, or gender- and age-sensitive hiring schemes for public projects, especially in places where the state employs a significant number of people, may improve women's and widows' status.

Using Survey Responses on Subjective Probabilities

Many economic models are based on the forward-looking behavior of individuals. Although it is often said that expectations about future events are important in these models, it is the probability distributions of future events that are contemplated in the models. For example, an individual's consumption and saving decisions are assumed to depend on future interest rates, the likelihood of dying, and the risk of substantial future medical expenditures. According to typical theories, individuals have subjective probability distributions about these and other events and use these subjective distributions to make decisions about their saving practices. In "Individual Subjective Survival Curves," Li Gan, Michael D. Hurd, and Daniel McFadden use responses from HRS and AHEAD survey data to estimate individual subjective survival probabilities.

The HRS and AHEAD surveys ask individuals for their expectations on the probability of given future events. On average, the subjective probability of a future event is consistent with the observed probability that the event does occur. For example, in general, the averages of individual survival probabilities reported by survey respondents are consistent with those from life tables.

However, at the individual level, the subjective probability responses in HRS and AHEAD suffer serious problems of focal responses at 0.0 and 1.0. Consequently, applications of subjective probabilities will be extremely limited if "true" subjective survival probabilities are not recovered.

In this paper, the authors suggest a Bayesian update model to account for problems caused by focal responses of 0.0 and 1.0. As a result, individual survival curves derived from the model do not suffer the problems of focal responses. The authors also propose two approaches to model individual heterogeneity in subjective survival curves. One approach modifies the life table hazard rates while another approach models the subjective aging process, which is different from the life table aging process. The model is estimated from the observed survival information in the sample the authors use. From the estimated model, they construct several optimistic indexes for each individual and conduct a test that is based on out-of-sample prediction. These optimistic indexes are used to create individual subjective survival curves that have considerable variation and are readily applicable to economic models that require individual subjective survival curves.

1

Utility Evaluation of Risk in Retirement Saving Accounts

James M. Poterba, Joshua Rauh, Steven F. Venti, and David A. Wise

The last two decades have witnessed a remarkable shift in the structure of retirement saving in the United States. In 1980, most workers with pension plans participated in defined benefit plans, with benefits determined by the worker's earnings history, years of service, and age at the time of retirement. The investment allocation of assets in defined benefit pension accounts was determined by professional money managers or corporate executives, and the worker controlled his retirement benefit only through the choice of retirement age and job change decisions.

Over the 1980s and 1990s, the U.S. pension system shifted toward a defined contribution structure, with 401(k) plans growing particularly rapidly. In the late 1990s, about 85 percent of pension plan contributions were directed to defined contribution personal retirement accounts. This shift transferred responsibility for investment decisions, contribution rates, and ultimately the draw-down of retirement assets from firms to workers. It replaced the link between retirement income, job change, and final earnings, which were important sources of worker risk, with a link between retirement account balances and the uncertain return on invested assets. The

James M. Poterba is the Mitsui Professor of Economics and the associate head of the economics department at the Massachusetts Institute of Technology, and the director of the Public Economics Research Program at the National Bureau of Economic Research. Joshua Rauh is an assistant professor of finance at the University of Chicago Graduate School of Business. Steven F. Venti is a professor of economics and the DeWalt Ankeny Professor of Economic Policy at Dartmouth College, and a research associate of the National Bureau of Economic Research. David A. Wise is the John F. Stambaugh Professor of Political Economy at the John F. Kennedy School of Government, Harvard University, and the director for Health and Retirement Programs at the National Bureau of Economic Research.

We are grateful to Constantijn Panis and Robert Willis for helpful comments and to the National Institute on Aging (grants P30 AG12810 and P01 AG05842) for research support. Poterba also thanks the National Science Foundation for support.

risk that workers bear as a result of fluctuations in the value of assets in retirement accounts has attracted considerable attention in the popular press, often with the claim that workers are now facing riskier retirement prospects than in the past.

This paper presents new evidence on the risk of different investment strategies when evaluated in terms of retirement wealth accumulation. We use two different approaches to describe the risk of investing 401(k) assets in a broadly diversified portfolio of common stocks, compared to a portfolio of index bonds. The first involves computing the empirical distribution of potential wealth values at retirement resulting from different investment strategies, and then making explicit comparisons of the wealth distributions. If the average return on one asset class, such as corporate stock, is substantially greater than the average return on another asset class, such as bonds, this approach shows that over long horizons, the higher-return asset class will outperform the lower-return asset class with very high probability. One criticism of this approach is that it does not adequately consider the potential cost to a retiree of the low levels of wealth at retirement that might emerge from the riskier, but higher-expected-return, strategy.

Our second evaluation approach is designed to address this issue. We assume that the value that the retiree assigns to the consumption stream after retirement can be parameterized using a simple utility function, in which utility is a function of the stock of wealth at retirement. We then use simulation methods to compute the distribution of wealth at retirement that might emerge under different portfolio investment strategies, and to evaluate the expected utility of this distribution. Comparing the expected utility, which recognizes the potential cost of a small probability of very unfavorable outcomes, provides an alternative to comparing the distributions as a method for evaluating different investment strategies.

We compare the distribution of retirement wealth and the expected utility of retirement wealth for three different investment strategies. The first involves holding only index bonds, the second holds only a portfolio of common stocks similar to the Standard & Poor 500 index (S&P 500), and the third invests in a fifty-fifty mix of index bonds and common stocks. We conduct our analysis at the household level, recognizing that retirement plan investment decisions have implications for all household members. We also treat the evaluation of risk as a collective household decision. To make the retirement wealth calculations as realistic as possible, our simulations are run through the lifetime profiles of Social Security earnings records for each of 759 Health and Retirement Survey (HRS) households. This allows for realistic variation in age-specific labor income flows. We also calculate the level of non-401(k) wealth holdings for these HRS households. We find that the expected utility of retirement wealth is very sensitive to the value of wealth held outside the defined contribution plan, including both liquid wealth and annuitized wealth such as prospective Social Security benefits or defined benefit plan payouts.

The paper is divided into seven sections. Section 1.1 describes our basic framework for evaluating the risks associated with the accumulation of retirement saving. The second section discusses our use of earnings histories for a subset of HRS households. These earnings histories are the basis for contribution flows into our hypothetical 401(k) account. Section 1.3 describes our decomposition of the wealth holdings of HRS households near retirement age. The wealth data provide the benchmark against which we evaluate the level of 401(k) assets. The fourth section describes our assumptions about the returns to both stocks and index bonds that are available for the retirement saver, and it outlines our simulation algorithm for generating the distribution of plan assets at retirement. Section 1.5 presents our results on the distribution of retirement plan balances and shows the stock of retirement wealth under different assumptions about portfolio allocation. The sixth section reports our expected utility calculations, focusing on different asset allocation strategies during the accumulation phase. A brief conclusion summarizes our findings and suggests several directions for future work, particularly the comparison between the risks of defined contribution and defined benefit retirement plans.

1.1   A Framework for Modeling Retirement Wealth Accumulation in Self-Directed Retirement Plans

To analyze the risk associated with the accumulation of retirement assets in defined contribution pension plans, we need to model the path of plan contributions over an individual's working life and to combine these contributions with information on the potential returns to holding 401(k) assets in different investment vehicles. We need to decide whether the unit of observation is the individual or the household and to specify the age at which contributions begin and end. For the initial analysis reported in this paper, we focus our attention on married couples. We do this because we suspect that this group is more homogeneous than nonmarried individuals, some of whom are never married and some of whom have lost a spouse. Married couples represent about 70 percent of individuals reaching retirement age. We assume that a fixed fraction of the household's earnings is contributed to a defined contribution plan. We do not address whether the contributions are due to one or both members of the couple participating in a defined contribution plan. We follow Poterba, Venti, and Wise (1998), who report that the average 401(k) contribution represents roughly 9 percent of contributing household earnings, including both employer and employee contributions.

We assume that the couple begins to participate in a 401(k) plan when the husband is twenty-eight and that they contribute in every year in which the household has Social Security earnings until the husband is sixty-three. Households do not make contributions when they are unemployed or when both members of the couple are retired or otherwise not in the labor force. When the husband is sixty-three, we assume that both members of the household retire, if they have not already, and that contributions cease.

We denote a couple's 401(k) contribution at age a by $C_i(a)$, where we index each couple by i. A household's contribution $C_i(a) = .09 \cdot E_i(a)$, where $E_i(a)$ denotes Social Security covered earnings at age a. We express this contribution in year 2000 dollars. To find the 401(k) balance for the couple at age sixty-three ($a = 63$), we need to cumulate contributions over the course of the working life, with appropriate allowance for the returns on 401(k) assets at each age. Let $R_i(a)$ denote the return earned on 401(k) assets that were held at the beginning of the year when the husband in couple i attained age a. The value of the couple's 401(k) assets when the husband is sixty-three is then given by

$$(1) \qquad W_i(63) = \sum_{t=0}^{35} \left\{ \prod_{j=0}^{t} [1 + R_i(63 - j)] \right\} C_i(63 - t).$$

We in turn assume that $R_i(a)$ is determined by the returns on stocks and index bonds. The couple may hold a portfolio of all stocks, in which case $R_i(a) = R_{\text{stock}}(a)$; all index bonds, in which case $R_i(a) = R_{\text{bond}}(a)$; or a fifty-fifty mix of the two asset classes, in which case $R_i(a) = .5 \cdot R_{\text{stock}}(a) + .5 \cdot R_{\text{bond}}(a)$. We discuss presently our calibration of the distribution of risky returns associated with holding stocks.

We report the distribution of $W_i(63)$, averaged over the 759 households in our sample, for the three different investment strategies. These three distributions provide some evidence on how each investment strategy might affect the retirement resources of households that pursued them. The difficulty with this approach, however, is that it does not capture the cost of low payouts in the event of unfavorable returns. To allow for differential valuation of wealth in different states of nature, we evaluate the wealth in the 401(k) account using a utility-of-terminal-wealth approach. We assume that the household's preferences over wealth at retirement (which we now write as W, dropping the household subscript for ease of notation) are described by a constant relative risk aversion (CRRA) utility function,

$$(2) \qquad U(W) = \frac{W^{1-\alpha}}{1 - \alpha}$$

where α is the household's coefficient of relative risk aversion. The utility of household wealth at retirement is likely to depend on both 401(k) and non-401(k) wealth, and thus we need to modify equation (2) to allow for other wealth:

$$(3) \qquad U(W_{401(k)}, W_{\text{non-401(k)}}) = \frac{(W_{401(k)} + W_{\text{non-401(k)}})^{1-\alpha}}{1-\alpha}.$$

The difference in the utility associated with different levels of 401(k) wealth is likely to be very sensitive to the household's other wealth holdings, so in the empirical analysis that follows, we summarize the balance sheets of retirement-age households in the HRS.

To determine the expected utility associated with various investment strategies, we generate hypothetical thirty-five-year 401(k) return histories associated with the all index bonds, fifty-fifty bonds or stocks, and all stock investment strategies for each household in our sample. Each return history, denoted by h, generates an associated 401(k) wealth at age sixty-three, $W_{401(k),h}$ (63), and a corresponding utility level, U_h, where

$$(4) \qquad U_h = \frac{(W_{401(k),h} + W_{\text{non-401(k)}})^{1-\alpha}}{1-\alpha}.$$

We evaluate the expected utility of each portfolio strategy by the probability-weighted average of the utility outcomes associated with that strategy, and we denote these expected utility values EU_{SP500}, EU_{Bonds}, and $EU_{\text{50-50}}$, respectively. These utility levels can be compared directly for a given degree of risk tolerance. They can also be translated into certainty equivalent wealth levels (Z) by asking what certain wealth level would provide a utility level equal to the expected utility of the retirement wealth distribution. The certainty equivalent of an all-equity portfolio, for example, is given by

$$(5) \qquad Z_{\text{SP500}} = [EU_{\text{SP500}}(1-\alpha)]^{1/(1-\alpha)} - W_{\text{non-401(k)}}.$$

We present certainty equivalent calculations of this form to summarize our findings. Note that when the household has non-401(k) wealth, the certainty equivalent of the 401(k) wealth is the amount of 401(k) wealth that is needed, *in addition to the non-401(k) wealth,* to achieve a given utility level. We treat non-401(k) wealth as nonstochastic throughout our analysis.

1.2   Earnings Profiles for Current Retirees

Calibrating the expected utility of various 401(k) portfolio strategies requires information on both the earnings histories and the non-401(k) wealth held by these households. We obtained these data for households in the 2000 wave of the HRS. The HRS is a longitudinal study of the economic and health status of older Americans. In the first wave of the study (1992), in-home interviews were conducted for respondents in the 1931–41 birth cohorts and their spouses. Follow-up surveys were administered by telephone every two years. The fifth wave of the survey was completed in

2000, and the core final data for this wave were released in September 2002. This wave provides the most recent and complete source of information on the balance sheet of U.S. households around retirement age.

Table 1.1 shows the relationship between the number of households in various waves of the HRS and the corresponding household counts for the U.S. population. There were 7,580 households in the first wave of the HRS, but various factors, the most important of which are death or voluntary termination of survey participation, reduced the sample size in subsequent waves. By the 2000 wave, respondents from only 6,074 of the original households remained. After accounting for household splits due to divorce and excluding five observations with missing birth years, we had a sample of 6,195 households in 2000. The sampling probabilities for these households suggest that they represent 16.7 million U.S. households. Among these households, 4.3 million had a household head, which we define as the husband in the case of married couples, with less than a high school education; 8.6 million had a household head with maximum education attainment of high school or some college; and 3.8 million had a household head with a college or postgraduate education. Because lifecycle earnings profiles differ for households with different levels of education, we present separate earnings histories for these three groups.

We construct an earnings profile for each household using data from the Social Security administrative records file. These data are available for 4,233 of the 6,195 households in the 2000 wave of the HRS and contain Social Security earnings from 1951 to 1991. Appendix table 1A.1 provides a detailed breakdown of the number of sample households in the HRS that satisfy our further data requirements and are included in our sample.

Table 1.1   **Sample composition and education attainment, Health and Retirement Survey (HRS)**

	Survey households	Population counterpart
HRS Wave 1 (1992)	7,580	18.6 million
HRS Wave 5 (2000)	6,074	n.a.
Excluding households with missing birth years and accounting for household splits (Wave 5)	6,195	16.7 million
Head < high school	1,823	4.3 million
Head high school or some college	3,103	8.6 million
Head college degree or more	1,269	3.8 million
With Social Security earnings history	4,233	11.6 million
Head < high school	1,228	3.0 million
Head high school or some college	2,123	6.0 million
Head college degree or more	882	2.7 million

Note: n.a. = not available.
Source: Authors' tabulations from HRS.

Throughout our analysis, we deflate historical nominal wages by the Consumer Price Index (CPI) to construct real wages at each age. For years after 1991 in which a member of the household was still working, we multiply reported HRS wage and salary earnings by a scaling factor equal to the ratio of Social Security administrative earnings in 1991 to reported HRS earnings in the same year. We thereby construct a proxy for Social Security earnings for 1993, 1995, 1997, and 1999. We assume that in even-numbered years for which we do not have a survey response, earnings remained at the same level as in the previous year.

We want to base our simulations on households who have completed their working lives, and potentially to consider their wealth at retirement relative to their final earnings. We therefore construct a measure of final earnings that we view as representative of household labor earnings near retirement. This measure is defined as household earnings in the year before the household's reported retirement year. In dual-earner households, this is the year in which the first retirement takes place. Retirement of either the primary or the secondary earner can therefore trigger the final earnings calculation.

A number of the HRS households reported that all members of the household were still working in 2000, so that we could not define final earnings for them. Extrapolating the HRS data to the nation as a whole using HRS weights, out of 16.7 million households in the survey, 9.0 million had at least one member of the household working, and 2.6 million had two earners. Another group, 0.9 million households, contained someone who reported both working and being retired. These individuals are presumably working part-time or have partially reentered the labor force. Out of 2.1 million couples for whom we could compute final earnings, and in which the husband was aged sixty-three to sixty-seven, 1.3 million had at least one person working, 0.5 million had both working, and 0.2 million had at least one person claiming to be both retired and working.

Table 1.2 presents summary information on the median earnings profiles for households in our sample, including years with no earnings because of unemployment or retirement. The table also reports the number of HRS households that are used to estimate the earnings profiles. We present tabulations for four different sets of households in the HRS universe. The first, in the first column, is the earnings profile for all HRS households with Social Security earnings histories, regardless of their household structure and whether they had left the labor force by 2000. The second column shows the earnings profile for households with at least one labor force leaver and for which it is therefore possible to compute final earnings—this represents 3,749 of the 4,233 households with earnings profiles. The third column further tightens the selection criterion by limiting the analysis to married couple households at the time of the 2000 HRS survey. This reduces the sample size to 2,275 households. Finally, in the last column we restrict the

Table 1.2   Average income trajectories for Health and Retirement Survey households in 2000

	Median including zeros				Mean including zeros			
Age range	Households with SS histories	Households with final earnings	Couples with final earnings	Couples with final earnings, male 63–67	Households with SS histories	Households with final earnings	Couples with final earnings	Couples with final earnings, male 63–67
	Less than high school education ($ thousands)							
25–27	9.8	12.3	21.2	18.6	13.0	14.2	19.5	17.6
28–30	14.4	16.9	25.4	24.4	15.8	17.1	23.7	21.5
31–33	17.3	20.3	26.8	28.2	18.1	19.7	26.9	26.8
34–36	19.9	22.9	29.5	33.1	20.6	22.4	30.4	30.7
37–39	21.7	24.8	34.4	34.9	22.8	25.0	34.3	34.0
40–42	22.8	26.3	37.6	42.1	24.5	27.1	37.4	38.2
43–45	21.6	26.1	40.0	42.3	25.2	28.0	38.9	40.4
46–48	20.8	24.7	42.0	41.2	25.7	28.6	40.3	39.4
49–51	19.8	24.2	40.0	41.2	25.1	28.2	39.6	40.1
52–54	17.6	21.7	38.4	40.1	24.2	27.3	38.4	38.7
55–57	13.8	18.7	32.7	33.7	21.7	24.7	34.6	34.9
58–60	6.1	11.8	25.8	29.2	17.9	20.6	28.8	31.1
61–63	0.0	1.1	6.6	11.6	11.3	13.3	18.1	20.3
64–66	0.0	0.0	0.0	0.0	4.2	4.9	7.3	4.2
	High school degree and/or some college ($ thousands)							
25–27	20.4	21.8	26.5	26.4	18.8	19.6	26.3	25.2
28–30	24.9	25.7	28.3	26.8	21.5	22.4	30.0	27.9
31–33	26.3	26.7	33.6	34.6	23.8	24.9	33.1	33.9
34–36	28.4	30.2	36.4	36.3	26.7	28.0	36.8	36.4
37–39	32.9	34.0	41.2	41.5	30.0	31.7	41.4	41.0
40–42	34.0	35.6	45.6	47.5	32.5	34.4	44.8	45.8
43–45	34.7	37.0	48.0	49.7	34.3	36.3	47.4	48.3
46–48	34.9	38.0	50.6	51.6	35.8	37.9	49.9	48.6
49–51	33.7	36.7	51.2	50.7	35.8	38.1	50.3	49.1

Age								
52–54	31.0	33.9	49.0	50.3	35.2	37.5	49.8	49.5
55–57	26.0	29.1	44.7	44.3	33.2	35.6	46.8	48.0
58–60	15.0	18.6	32.8	37.3	27.4	29.6	39.1	46.5
61–63	0.0	0.1	4.6	19.9	15.7	17.0	22.8	33.5
64–66	0.0	0.0	0.0	0.0	6.2	6.8	9.3	8.6

College degree and/or some postgraduate ($ thousands)

Age								
25–27	20.9	22.4	24.8	24.8	19.5	20.3	23.6	22.1
28–30	26.2	26.5	28.7	26.8	23.5	24.5	29.0	26.4
31–33	27.4	29.1	33.6	32.5	26.2	27.7	32.5	30.8
34–36	34.0	34.7	37.0	36.0	30.2	31.9	37.0	33.5
37–39	36.6	37.7	42.5	41.1	34.3	36.4	42.2	39.4
40–42	41.9	43.7	48.4	48.1	38.7	41.2	47.9	47.1
43–45	46.2	47.3	54.5	53.8	42.7	45.5	52.8	51.2
46–48	49.0	51.8	59.1	58.1	46.7	50.0	58.5	53.8
49–51	53.0	56.9	63.1	62.7	48.6	52.0	60.5	56.6
52–54	51.7	56.0	63.5	65.5	50.7	54.4	63.5	59.4
55–57	46.5	51.2	62.0	59.8	53.0	56.9	64.4	59.4
58–60	24.2	30.2	40.8	44.8	40.3	43.2	49.6	55.0
61–63	0.0	0.4	3.1	21.7	23.4	25.2	30.3	45.4
64–66	0.0	0.0	0.0	0.0	11.0	11.8	14.9	12.8

Sample size information by education group

Less than HS	1,228	1,027	595	180	1,228	1,027	595	180
HS/some college	2,123	1,912	1,116	390	2,123	1,912	1,116	390
College/postgraduate	882	810	564	189	882	810	564	189
Total	4,233	3,749	2,275	759	4,233	3,749	2,275	759

Weighted sample size by education group (millions of households)

Less than HS	3.0	2.5	1.5	0.4	3.0	2.5	1.5	0.4
HS/some college	6.0	5.4	3.2	1.1	6.0	5.4	3.2	1.1
College/postgraduate	2.7	2.5	1.8	0.6	2.7	2.5	1.8	0.6
Total	11.6	10.4	6.4	2.1	11.6	10.4	6.4	2.1

sample to married couples in which the husband was between sixty-three and sixty-seven in 2000. This limits the sample to only 759 households. This is a relatively homogeneous sample that we use for much of our subsequent analysis. The earnings trajectories for this subsample display a smaller education premium than those for the larger sample. This might be because less-educated workers who have already retired have above-average lifetime earnings trajectories. In future work we plan to explore these subsample differences in further detail, and to generalize our procedures to the sample of all households.

The entries in the columns of table 1.2 track median earnings for each of the education groups and subsamples that we consider. Not surprisingly, there are very substantial differences in the level, and the shape, of the earnings profiles across subgroups. The peak earning level for couples in our sample is up to 6 percent higher than the peak earning level for all couples with final earnings and up to two times higher than that of all households with earnings histories (including singles). The ratio of peak median earnings to salary early in life is highest for the group with the highest education levels. Median earnings of couples in which the better-educated spouse has at least a college degree are up to a third higher around age sixty than those in couples in which neither has a college degree. The better-educated households have lower earnings than the less-educated groups, however, between ages twenty-five and thirty, when the highly educated group is presumably still accumulating educational human capital.

For comparison, panels A and B of figure 1.1 show the age-earnings profiles for couples with final earnings and a husband between the ages of sixty-three and sixty-seven in 2000. These figures exclude years in which a household has zero earnings. Panel A of figure 1.1 shows median income relative to age twenty-eight earnings, and Panel B of figure 1.1 shows median income in year 2000 dollars. All three educational groups show a decline in the last third of the working life even excluding household-year observations with zero earnings. The shape of the age-earnings profile matters for our computations of 401(k) balances at retirement, and it also affects the interpretation of financial magnitudes that are normalized by final earnings. We therefore analyze the three education groups separately in our simulation of 401(k) balances at retirement. We include years of zero earnings in our simulations to account realistically for work interruptions and retirement.

1.3   Household Balance Sheets and Non-401(k) Wealth for HRS Respondents

We now consider the household balance sheet, to calibrate the non-401(k) wealth that affects the expected utility of retirement wealth. We classify total household wealth into seven categories: the present discounted value of Social Security payments, the present discounted value of

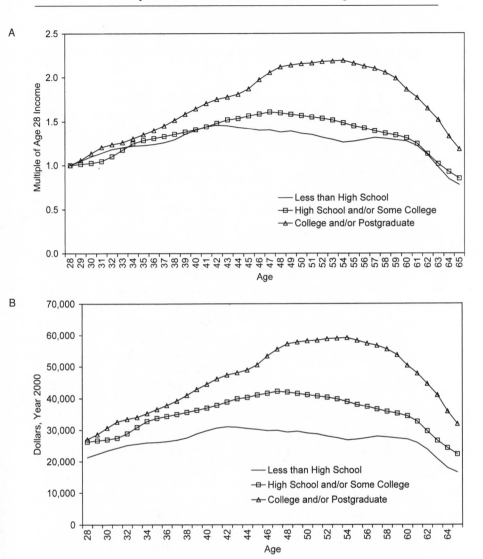

Fig. 1.1   *A,* **Median household income in the HRS relative to age twenty-eight earnings, three-year moving average;** *B,* **median household income in the HRS in year 2000 dollars, three-year moving average**

defined benefit pensions, the present discounted value of other annuities, the current value of retirement accounts, all other net financial wealth, housing equity, and all other wealth.

The retirement account category includes individual retirement accounts (IRAs), 401(k)s, and other defined contribution (DC) accounts. Data on DC plan balances were collected for each respondent in the employment module of the HRS, and then aggregated to the household level.

Amounts classified as DC wealth include the balances of workers at their present job, plus any balances that workers or retirees left to accumulate in the plans of former employers. "Other net financial wealth" includes stocks, equity mutual funds, bonds, fixed-income mutual funds, checking and saving accounts, money market mutual funds and certificates of deposit. We refer to this category below as "financial wealth" despite the fact that it excludes annuitized wealth and retirement account assets. Net housing wealth equals gross home value less mortgages and home loans on the primary residence. The other wealth category includes the net-of-debt value of real estate other than household's principal residence, the value of businesses or farms net of any outstanding debt, all assets held in trusts not otherwise classified, vehicles, and all "other" HRS wealth, which includes jewelry and expected repayment on personal loans.

The present discounted value (PDV) of Social Security wealth is calculated based on the reported current Social Security payments for members of the household already receiving Social Security, plus reported expected Social Security payments for other members not yet receiving Social Security. We do not use actual Social Security earnings histories to compute expected or accrued Social Security payments for individuals still in the labor force in 2000. Actual earnings histories end in 1991, and there is uncertainty about the date of retirement for individuals still in the labor force. We used cohort mortality tables for individuals born in 1930 to value Social Security payment streams. Distinct mortality probabilities for men and women were taken from the Social Security Administration (SSA) life tables for the U.S. Social Security area, as reported by Bell and Miller (2002). The SSA's intermediate-cost scenario discount rates (3.0 percent real, 6.0 percent nominal) were applied to discount future payments, and payments were assumed to be indexed using an expected inflation rate of 3 percent. In these calculations, we take the joint-and-survivor properties of Social Security into account. We assume that as long as both members of the couple are alive, each respondent receives his or her current or projected Social Security benefits. When only one member of the couple is alive, we assume that the household receives benefits equal to the maximum of the two spouses' benefits.

Of the 6,195 observations represented in HRS wave 5, 2,293 reported receiving a defined benefit (DB) pension, while 478 reported expecting to receive a DB pension at some future date. Thus, out of the 16.7 million represented households, 7.7 million received or were expecting to receive DB pensions. To determine the PDV of reported DB wealth, we took a similar approach to our valuation of Social Security wealth and valued the annuitized payment streams using the same mortality tables and discounting assumptions. Although some DB plans have cost of living adjustments, most are not indexed to inflation. We therefore assume that all DB pensions have a fixed nominal payout. We make the same assumption for any other annuities owned by household members.

Table 1.3   **Household balance sheets, Health and Retirement Survey households in 2000 ($ thousands)**

Wealth component	All households	Households with SS histories	Households with final earnings	Couples with final earnings	Couples with final earnings, male 63–67
Medians					
Social Security	159.9	162.1	172.3	222.3	242.0
DB pension	0.0	0.0	0.0	27.6	35.4
Other annuity	0.0	0.0	0.0	0.0	0.0
Retirement accounts	4.5	4.6	8.0	24.5	30.0
IRA	0.0	0.0	0.0	8.0	11.0
401(k) and other DC	0.0	0.0	0.0	0.0	0.0
Other financial wealth	30.0	29.0	35.0	70.0	88.8
Housing equity	15.0	15.0	16.0	26.0	30.0
Other wealth	15.0	15.0	16.0	26.0	30.0
SS + DB + other annuity	215.3	218.4	225.9	285.4	316.4
+ other financial	286.3	285.5	300.1	405.3	460.6
Total (excl. retirement accts)	422.0	414.5	436.6	582.4	652.3
Total	454.8	447.6	470.7	636.4	713.2
Final earnings			35.1	48.2	45.8
Means					
Social Security	160.7	163.2	170.8	207.2	228.9
DB pension	136.3	145.8	145.0	195.3	182.6
Other annuity	5.0	5.2	4.8	5.2	5.1
Retirement accounts	94.3	94.5	101.4	135.0	154.3
IRA	66.0	65.6	69.4	92.5	106.8
401(k) and other DC	28.3	28.9	31.9	42.5	47.5
Other financial wealth	181.6	187.6	200.3	253.3	287.2
Housing equity	104.2	95.5	97.8	121.3	123.7
Other wealth	129.5	108.0	113.3	141.9	141.6
SS + DB + other annuity	302.0	314.3	320.5	407.8	416.6
+ other financial	483.7	501.9	520.8	661.1	703.8
Total (excl. retirement accts)	717.4	705.4	732.0	924.3	969.1
Total	811.7	799.9	833.3	1,059.3	1,123.4
Final earnings			44.6	56.0	55.1
Sample size					
No. of households	6,195	4,233	3,749	2,275	759
Weighted size ('000s)	16,709.5	11,648.1	10,390.1	6,403.2	2,084.4

Source: Authors' tabulations from 2000 wave of the Health and Retirement Survey.

Table 1.3 presents information on mean and median wealth levels for the four groups of HRS households whose earnings histories were shown in table 1.2. The Social Security earnings history sample is slightly less wealthy than the sample consisting of all households, but the households generally become wealthier as we move from the entire HRS to our most restricted sample of couples with husbands between the ages of sixty-three and sixty-seven in 2000. We focus on this group in the subsequent analysis, since this is the group that is at, or slightly older than, the typical age of retirement in the most recent HRS survey wave. For this group, we find the median value of a DB pension of $35,400. The mean value, $182,600, is much greater, reflecting the right skewness of the distribution of pension values. For Social Security wealth, the median ($242,000) is actually greater than the mean ($228,900), which reflects the upper limit on Social Security benefits.

Table 1.3 also shows several wealth aggregates. First, we compute annuitized wealth as the sum of the present discount values of Social Security, DB pensions, and other annuities. We also present the sum of annuitized wealth and all other financial wealth, as well as aggregates reflecting all wealth and all wealth excluding retirement account assets. When we calibrate our simulations with individual households' non-401(k) wealth, we focus on two wealth components: annuitized wealth and all wealth excluding retirement account assets. We do not wish to include retirement account assets in the calibration of non-401(k) wealth on the grounds that we are using our simulations to construct values of retirement accounts. By using the observed values of these wealth components from the HRS, and treating them as nonrandom when we evaluate the expected utility of 401(k) retirement balances, we are implicitly assuming that changes in 401(k) wealth values do not affect other components of wealth. In future work, we plan to allow for correlation between the returns on assets in 401(k) accounts and the returns on other components of the household balance sheet.

Table 1.3 also shows final income for the various HRS subsamples. Presently we report the ratio of the wealth components to final income, so the variation in final income is of independent interest. In the upper panel of table 1.3, the ratio of median Social Security wealth to final income is a little over five, while the ratio of broadly defined net financial wealth to final income is about three. These statistics suggest the importance of recognizing wealth sources other than DC plans in analyzing the risks of portfolio strategies.

Although table 1.3 shows net housing wealth as a balance sheet component, its role in providing resources for retirement consumption is not clear. Several studies, such as Venti and Wise (2001a, 2004) and the references cited therein, suggest that retired households do not typically draw down their housing wealth to finance nonhousing consumption. This work suggests focusing only on nonhousing wealth as we consider the wealth available to support retirement spending. One way to conceptualize this approach is to assume the utility from housing consumption as additively separable from all other consumption in the household's utility function and to further assume that owner-occupied housing generates only housing consumption. The difficulty with this approach is that it is possible that households view their housing equity as a reserve asset that can be tapped to support other consumption in the event of financial difficulty. In this case, housing equity should be combined with financial assets in calculating the household's assets outside defined contribution plans. To allow for this possibility, we present results in which we consider housing as well as other financial assets as the household's non-401(k) wealth at retirement.

Table 1.4 presents information on wealth holdings across different education subsamples. The results suggest that there are important differences across groups. The table focuses on the subsample of HRS couples that have earnings records and in which the husband is between sixty-three and

Table 1.4   **Household balance sheets, Health and Retirement Survey households with final earnings, males aged 63–67**

	All education levels	Less than high school degree	High school and/or some college	College and/or postgraduate
Medians				
Social Security	242.0	217.0	248.5	248.8
DB pension	35.4	0.0	46.6	100.0
Other annuity	0.0	0.0	0.0	0.0
Retirement accounts	30.0	0.0	29.0	126.1
IRA	11.0	0.0	9.5	80.0
401(k) and other DC	0.0	0.0	0.0	0.0
Other financial wealth	88.8	8.1	71.0	328.0
Housing equity	91.0	60.0	87.0	130.0
Other wealth	30.0	18.0	25.0	70.0
SS + DB + other annuity	316.4	240.8	323.6	375.5
+ other financial	460.6	257.3	441.2	838.9
Total (excl. retirement accts)	652.3	362.3	601.7	1,102.4
Total	713.2	378.7	673.6	1,303.4
Final earnings	45.8	35.7	46.2	56.8
Means				
Social Security	228.9	206.8	234.4	235.0
DB pension	182.6	57.2	112.6	416.7
Other annuity	5.1	1.1	5.7	7.1
Retirement accounts	154.3	39.5	114.2	321.4
IRA	106.8	31.2	89.0	200.0
401(k) and other DC	47.5	8.3	25.2	121.4
Other financial wealth	287.2	68.9	180.4	665.1
Housing equity	123.7	71.9	106.7	197.1
Other wealth	141.6	78.0	92.9	286.2
SS + DB + other annuity	416.6	265.1	352.7	658.8
+ other financial	703.8	334.1	533.1	1,323.9
Total (excl. retirement accts)	969.1	484.0	732.7	1,807.2
Total	1,123.4	523.5	846.9	2,128.6
Final earnings	55.1	37.5	55.0	68.7
Sample size				
No. of households	759	180	390	189
Weighted size ('000s)	2,084.4	428.8	1,097.7	557.9

sixty-seven in 2000. The summary statistics show the clear link between education and wealth, measured both in absolute dollars and relative to final income. Annuitized wealth alone is $240,800 for the median household with less than a high school education and $375,500 for those with at least a college degree. The dispersion here is mostly due to the disparities across education categories in the level of DB pensions. The PDV of Social Security benefits varies relatively little. It is $217,000 for those who never finished high school and $248,800 for those with at least a college degree. Other financial wealth, which excludes annuitized wealth and retirement account assets, displays a high degree of dispersion, with $8,100 for the median household with less than a high school education and $328,000 for the median household with at least a college degree. These findings suggest that in evaluating 401(k) plan risk, the effect of accounting for non-401(k) assets will vary across education groups.

Table 1.4 summarizes the average wealth holdings of the different education groups, but it does not characterize the dispersion of wealth within these groups. Table 1.5 offers further detail on such distributions, showing the 20th, 40th, 60th, and 80th percentiles of the distribution of each wealth component relative to final income. Consider, for example, financial wealth. For households with high school and/or some college education but no college degree, the 20th percentile value of the ratio of financial wealth to final earnings is 0.1 while the 40th percentile value is 1.0 and the 80th percentile value is 7.4. Patterns like this emerge for each of the asset categories, with very substantial dispersion between the lowest and the highest percentiles. These tabulations suggest that one household having a higher educational attainment than another does not guarantee a higher ratio of any given financial asset class to labor income. In particular, the ratio of Social Security wealth to final earnings decreases with education. Venti and Wise (2001b) emphasize the wide range of asset accumulation within like lifetime earnings groups, at all lifetime earnings levels.

The entries in table 1.5 show the ratio of wealth components to final earnings. Final earnings vary systematically across education group, however, which makes it difficult to identify the underlying differences in wealth holdings. To facilitate such analysis, table 1.6 presents information on the wealth distribution with all entries measured in year 2000 dollars. For the median household in each education group, the results suggest a substantial amount of non-401(k) wealth already in place. The 40th percentile value of total wealth excluding retirement assets for couples in our sample with less than a high school degree is $311,800, compared with $527,700 for those with at least a high school degree and $1,007,700 for those with at least a college degree. For the 60th percentile these values are $424,900, $708,600, and $1,393,900, respectively. The households in the 60th percentile of the distribution of those with less than a high school degree correspond to those near the 30th percentile in the group with a high

Table 1.5   **Distribution of household balance sheet items as a ratio to final earned income: HRS married households with final earnings and males aged 63–67 in 2000**

	All education levels	Less than high school degree	High school and/or some college	College and/or postgraduate
20th percentile				
Social Security	3.0	3.6	3.2	2.1
DB pension	0.0	0.0	0.0	0.0
Other annuity	0.0	0.0	0.0	0.0
Retirement accounts	0.0	0.0	0.0	0.2
IRA	0.0	0.0	0.0	0.0
401(k) and other DC	0.0	0.0	0.0	0.0
Other financial wealth	0.1	0.0	0.1	1.5
Housing equity	0.8	0.3	0.8	1.2
Other wealth	0.2	0.1	0.2	0.4
SS + DB + other annuity	4.2	4.5	4.2	3.5
+ other financial	5.8	4.9	5.8	7.4
Total (excl. retirement accts)	8.1	6.7	8.1	10.7
Total	8.6	6.8	8.8	12.4
40th percentile				
Social Security	4.4	4.9	4.6	3.4
DB pension	0.0	0.0	0.2	0.0
Other annuity	0.0	0.0	0.0	0.0
Retirement accounts	0.2	0.0	0.2	1.4
IRA	0.0	0.0	0.0	0.7
401(k) and other DC	0.0	0.0	0.0	0.0
Other financial wealth	1.1	0.1	1.0	4.5
Housing equity	1.6	1.2	1.5	2.2
Other wealth	0.5	0.3	0.5	1.0
SS + DB + other annuity	5.2	6.3	6.3	6.1
+ other financial	7.2	6.8	9.1	13.8
Total (excl. retirement accts)	12.6	8.9	12.3	19.2
Total	13.5	9.1	13.5	22.8
60th percentile				
Social Security	5.7	6.7	5.9	4.9
DB pension	1.7	0.3	1.7	2.8
Other annuity	0.0	0.0	0.0	0.0
Retirement accounts	1.3	0.1	1.2	3.5
IRA	0.7	0.0	0.7	2.3
401(k) and other DC	0.0	0.0	0.0	0.0
Other financial wealth	3.3	0.6	3.0	9.2
Housing equity	2.5	1.8	2.3	3.1
Other wealth	1.3	0.9	1.0	2.5
SS + DB + other annuity	8.8	8.3	8.6	9.7
+ other financial	13.7	9.3	12.7	20.9
Total (excl. retirement accts)	18.3	12.9	17.4	28.3
Total	21.2	13.4	19.9	33.3

(*continued*)

Table 1.5   (continued)

	All education levels	Less than high school degree	High school and/or some college	College and/or postgraduate
80th percentile				
Social Security	9.2	9.8	9.4	7.6
DB pension	4.6	2.9	4.4	7.3
Other annuity	0.0	0.0	0.0	0.0
Retirement accounts	4.6	1.0	3.8	11.2
IRA	3.3	0.5	2.9	6.6
401(k) and other DC	0.5	0.0	0.3	2.0
Other financial wealth	9.1	2.9	7.4	19.3
Housing equity	4.8	4.3	4.3	8.6
Other wealth	4.0	2.3	3.0	6.6
SS + DB + other annuity	14.0	11.8	13.2	17.3
+ other financial	23.0	15.7	20.1	46.5
Total (excl. retirement accts)	32.5	21.2	26.9	59.0
Total	38.9	22.7	30.9	63.8

school degree and/or some college education, and to those near the 10th percentile in the group with at least a college degree.

1.4   Asset Market Returns and Equity Premium

Our simulation methodology is designed to calculate the 401(k) wealth at retirement for households with any given earnings profile while accounting for uncertainty in the distribution of financial market returns. We treat the other components of the household balance sheet as nonstochastic, although as we further develop the simulation algorithm that we describe here we will include a more complete analysis of the uncertainties associated with non-401(k) wealth.

We assume that households have two investment choices in their 401(k) accounts. One is an index bond, with an assured real return of 2.8 percent per year. The current term structure of yields (April 22, 2003) on U.S. Treasury Inflation Protection Securities is upward sloping. For bonds with a maturity of between five and six years, real interest rates are less than 2 percent. At a maturity of almost thirty years, the yield is between 2.7 and 2.8 percent. Since retirement saving accumulation takes place over long horizons, and to err on the side of generosity in the assumed return on bonds, we assume that investments in index bonds earn a return of 2.8 percent each year, net of inflation.

Index bonds deliver a net-of-inflation certain return only if the investor holds the bonds to maturity. Investors who sell their bonds before maturity, however, are exposed to asset price risk. If real interest rates rise between

Table 1.6   **Distribution of household balance sheet items ($ thousands): HRS married households with final earnings and husbands aged 63–67 in 2000**

	All education levels	Less than high school degree	High school and/or some college	College and/or postgraduate
20th percentile				
Social Security	151.2	138.5	176.4	136.3
DB pension	0.0	0.0	0.0	0.0
Other annuity	0.0	0.0	0.0	0.0
Retirement accounts	0.0	0.0	0.0	11.0
IRA	0.0	0.0	0.0	0.0
401(k) and other DC	0.0	0.0	0.0	0.0
Other financial wealth	2.0	−1.0	4.8	94.0
Housing equity	39.0	7.0	44.0	80.0
Other wealth	10.0	2.8	10.0	16.0
SS + DB + other annuity	199.7	151.2	214.1	229.3
+ other financial	241.1	148.6	253.7	455.7
Total (excl. retirement accts)	347.5	202.0	374.7	675.2
Total	357.5	203.1	384.7	718.4
40th percentile				
Social Security	216.5	194.2	224.8	215.4
DB pension	0.0	0.0	8.9	0.0
Other annuity	0.0	0.0	0.0	0.0
Retirement accounts	11.0	0.0	12.0	93.0
IRA	0.0	0.0	0.0	40.0
401(k) and other DC	0.0	0.0	0.0	0.0
Other financial wealth	40.0	1.0	39.0	242.0
Housing equity	78.0	45.0	73.0	105.0
Other wealth	20.5	10.0	20.0	47.0
SS + DB + other annuity	272.3	217.9	277.4	320.7
+ other financial	374.5	229.6	376.3	729.5
Total (excl. retirement accts)	536.3	311.8	527.7	1,007.7
Total	575.4	313.6	565.0	1,097.2
60th percentile				
Social Security	261.1	235.7	265.1	284.6
DB pension	84.8	10.4	84.8	192.0
Other annuity	0.0	0.0	0.0	0.0
Retirement accounts	59.0	4.0	50.0	185.0
IRA	34.0	0.0	31.0	133.0
401(k) and other DC	0.0	0.0	0.0	0.0
Other financial wealth	156.0	18.0	124.5	411.3
Housing equity	105.0	75.0	100.0	175.0
Other wealth	51.0	28.0	40.0	114.5
SS + DB + other annuity	353.9	277.0	358.7	477.4
+ other financial	599.5	311.9	496.7	945.3
Total (excl. retirement accts)	812.5	424.9	708.6	1,393.9
Total	882.5	430.6	811.5	1,641.8

(continued)

Table 1.6   (continued)

	All education levels	Less than high school degree	High school and/or some college	College and/or postgraduate
80th percentile				
Social Security	311.7	277.0	309.7	327.4
DB pension	221.4	132.0	191.2	389.0
Other annuity	0.0	0.0	0.0	0.0
Retirement accounts	220.0	36.0	180.0	448.9
IRA	150.0	19.5	106.9	310.0
401(k) and other DC	20.0	2.0	13.0	104.5
Other financial wealth	400.0	90.0	285.8	960.0
Housing equity	170.0	110.0	150.0	300.0
Other wealth	147.0	90.0	127.0	295.0
SS + DB + other annuity	504.4	364.5	462.0	660.4
+ other financial	888.4	440.9	707.9	1,754.9
Total (excl. retirement accts)	1,212.8	657.6	1,001.0	2,299.5
Total	1,422.4	772.3	1,134.4	3,312.0

the time that index bonds are purchased and the time they are sold, the price of the bonds can decline, leaving the investor with a capital loss. Similarly, a decline in real interest rates would generate a capital gain. When investors do not know the precise timing of their withdrawals, as they may not when they contemplate retirement with an unknown life span, purchasing an index bond is not riskless. These bonds nevertheless seem like the least risky long-term investment available to retirement savers.

The alternative investment in our simulations is a diversified portfolio of large capitalization U.S. stocks. We assume that the uncertain real return on this portfolio is represented by the empirical distribution of returns during the 1926–2001 period. Ibbotson Associates (2003) reports the annual return time series, which has an annual average real return of 9.4 percent and a standard deviation of 20.4 percent. Figure 1.2 presents a histogram of real returns.

In an earlier simulation analysis of 401(k) wealth accumulation, Poterba, Venti, and Wise (2004) considered investments in nominal bonds and corporate stock. We consider investments in index bonds rather than corporate bonds in the current project because they are likely to provide a less risky source of long-term returns and, therefore, to provide a more natural benchmark for analyzing the risks of corporate stock from the vantage point of retirement income accumulation.

On each iteration of our simulation algorithm, we draw a sequence of thirty-five real stock returns from the empirical return distribution. The draws are done with replacement, and we assume that there is no serial correlation in returns. We then use this return sequence to calculate the real

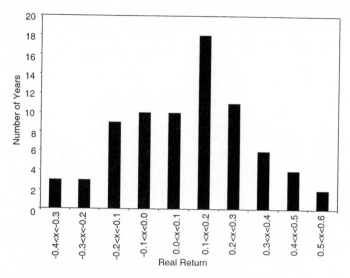

Fig. 1.2   Empirical distribution of real S&P 500 equity returns

value of each household's retirement account balance at age sixty-three, assuming that their contributions are determined by their earnings history. We consider the full thirty-five-year working life for each household, and we evaluate both a 100 percent equity investment case and a fifty-fifty stocks and index bonds case. Since the goal of our procedure is to generate reasonably precise estimates of the distribution of possible wealth outcomes for a given contribution history, we need to repeat our basic iteration many times. We found that with 200,000 replications, we could obtain estimates of the outcome distribution that did not vary substantially from one simulation to another. For each one of the 759 households in our sample, therefore, we simulate their 401(k) balance at age sixty-three 200,000 times. We then summarize these 200,000 outcomes either with a distribution of wealth values at retirement or by calculating the expected utility associated with this distribution of outcomes.

1.5   The Distribution of 401(k) Account Balances under Different Portfolio Strategies

Table 1.7 shows the distribution of 401(k) plan balances in thousands of year 2000 dollars, averaged across the 759 households in our sample. Households are stratified by education group. The first row in table 1.7 shows the results associated with a 100 percent index bond investment. Since the real bond return is certain, there is no uncertainty about the final wealth in this investment scenario. The value of 401(k) wealth varies somewhat across education categories: $172,700 for those with less than a high

Table 1.7	Simulated distribution of 401(k) balance at retirement in thousands of year 2000 dollars		
Investment strategy/percentile	Less than high school degree	High school and/or some college	College and/or postgraduate
100% riskless bonds	172.7	230.4	248.2
50% riskless bonds, 50% large-cap corporate stocks			
1	54.6	75.5	83.4
5	162.9	217.9	233.4
10	188.4	251.3	267.8
20	225.1	299.2	316.9
30	256.0	339.7	358.1
40	286.0	378.8	397.9
50	317.2	419.7	439.2
60	352.0	465.1	485.1
70	393.6	519.3	539.7
80	448.7	591.2	611.8
90	538.1	707.9	728.6
Mean	345.8	456.9	475.8
100% large-cap corporate stocks			
1	15.8	22.8	26.4
5	127.7	172.0	185.4
10	171.5	229.6	244.8
20	246.6	328.2	345.7
30	321.7	426.6	445.4
40	404.6	535.1	554.7
50	502.1	662.6	682.5
60	623.8	821.7	841.2
70	787.8	1,035.9	1,053.8
80	1,036.2	1,360.8	1,374.7
90	1,517.0	1,989.7	1,992.8
Mean	730.1	960.9	972.9
50% riskless bonds, 50% large-cap stocks (risk premium reduced by 300 basis points)			
1	41.8	58.4	65.7
5	120.4	162.0	176.4
10	138.7	186.0	201.5
20	164.8	220.3	237.0
30	186.9	249.2	266.8
40	208.2	277.1	295.5
50	230.4	306.1	325.2
60	255.0	338.2	358.1
70	284.4	376.6	397.2
80	323.3	427.3	448.6
90	386.3	509.4	531.7
Mean	250.3	331.9	350.8

Table 1.7   (continued)

Investment strategy/percentile	Less than high school degree	High school and/or some college	College and/or postgraduate
100% large-cap stocks (risk premium reduced by 300 basis points)			
1	10.0	14.8	17.9
5	70.8	96.8	107.7
10	93.4	126.8	139.6
20	131.7	177.3	192.7
30	169.6	227.1	244.4
40	211.1	281.4	300.5
50	259.5	344.8	365.5
60	319.6	423.3	445.5
70	400.2	528.4	552.0
80	521.7	687.0	711.4
90	755.5	991.9	1,016.2
Mean	369.4	487.8	506.6

school degree, $230,400 for those with high school and/or some college, and $248,200 for those with a college degree. As all three groups are assumed to have the same contribution rates out of earnings, these disparities reflect differences across groups in age-earning profiles. The assumption that all households contribute 9 percent of their earnings to their 401(k) account is a critical determinant of the overall magnitudes of the final account balances. Account balances could be scaled up or down for alternative assumptions about the contribution rate.

The next two panels of table 1.7 show the distribution of 401(k) balances when half, and then when all, of the 401(k) account is invested in corporate stock. The table shows the value for every tenth percentile of the distribution. For households with a high school education, simulated 401(k) wealth is $299,200 at the 20th percentile, and $591,200 at the 80th percentile when the 401(k) account is invested 50 percent in corporate stock.

Panel A of figure 1.3 shows the ratio of 401(k) wealth to final earnings for households with a high school or some college education, for the all-index bond, the mixed, and the all-stock portfolio strategies. Over most of the distribution of possible stock returns, the ratio of wealth to final earnings is higher when the portfolio is half in corporate stock than when it is completely in index bonds. The figure shows that if a household holds the all-equity portfolio, the chance is slightly greater than 10 percent that the wealth outcome at retirement will fall below the outcome for the index bond portfolio. The scale of panel A of figure 1.3 illustrates why we focus on dollar amounts of the simulation in our tables and analysis. Some households' earnings decline before retirement, resulting in very low final earnings and correspondingly very high ratios of 401(k) balances and other wealth components to final earnings. The mean of such a distribu-

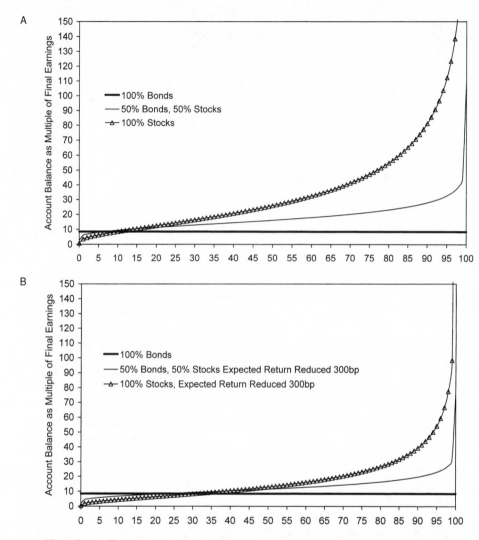

Fig. 1.3 *A,* Cumulative density functions of 401(k) wealth relative to final earnings for households with high school or some college education; *B,* cumulative density functions of 401(k) wealth relative to final earnings for households with high school or some college education, stock return reduced by 300 basis points

tion is very sensitive to these extreme values. To highlight this issue, panel A of figure 1.4 shows the same data as in panel A of figure 1.3, but with dollar amounts instead of ratios to final earnings.

One potential difficulty with our simulation procedure is that the historical period over which we measure equity returns may have been abnormal. Mehra and Prescott (2003) discuss this possibility along with other poten-

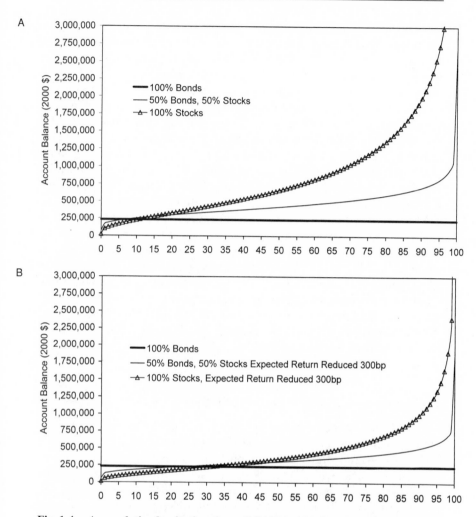

Fig. 1.4 *A,* cumulative density functions of 401(k) wealth for households with high school or some college education; *B,* cumulative density functions of 401(k) wealth for households with high school or some college education, stock return reduced by 300 basis points

tial explanations for the "equity premium puzzle." To allow for the possibility that the historical distribution of equity returns may overstate the prospective returns on stocks, we also consider a reduced equity return scenario, in which we reduce the expected return on corporate stock by 300 basis points, while leaving the dispersion of returns the same as in the base case. The results of this modification, for both half and all of the 401(k) account invested in corporate stock, are shown in the lower two panels of table 1.7 and in panel B of figures 1.3 and 1.4. The results indicate that with a lower equity return, the index bond investment strategy looks more attractive relative to the equity investment strategy. Even with the reduced equity return, however, there is still a relatively low probability that the all-index bonds strategy will outperform a fifty-fifty mix of index bonds and corporate stock. With the reduced equity return, the retirement wealth in the all index bonds case for a household with high school and/or some college education falls at around the 22nd percentile of the outcome distribution for the fifty-fifty mix of index bonds and stocks. It falls at around the 31st percentile in the outcome distribution with only stock investment, which attests to the greater volatility, as well as the greater average return, from holding all stocks rather than a fifty-fifty mix. Similar patterns emerge in the retirement wealth distributions for the other educational groups.

Evaluating the absolute magnitude of retirement assets as reported in table 1.7 is complicated by the fact that assets in the 401(k) account are measured on a pretax basis. Withdrawal of these assets would trigger income tax liability for the beneficiary. Simple corrections for this, such as multiplying by $(1 - t)$ where t is a plausible estimate of the marginal tax rate on ordinary income, are not sufficient, because if the assets remain in the 401(k) account for many years after the head of household turns sixty-five, the effective tax burden may be relatively low. Poterba (2004) presents illustrative calculations on the conversion between balances in taxable and tax-deferred accounts.

1.6   Certainty Equivalent Measures of the Cost of Uncertain Returns

Table 1.7 and panels A and B of figure 1.4 are examples of the use of the entire distribution of retirement wealth outcomes to describe the effects of different portfolio strategies. They present information on how different portfolio strategies will affect the average level of retirement wealth, as well as its dispersion. The fraction of retirement wealth outcomes in the all-stock or fifty-fifty stock/index cases that fall below the outcome in the all-index-bond case provides some insight on the risks associated with the various strategies. Results similar to these are a key component of "outcomes-based" financial planning software that enables clients to determine the probability of reaching retirement wealth goals. These software programs are based on Monte Carlo simulations of future wealth accumulations, and their results provide a picture of the risk associated with different investment strategies. Presumably, different investors with different tolerances for risk would prefer different investment strategies.

Results that portray the "picture" of retirement wealth risks provide no a priori way to describe how households or groups of households might evaluate these two distributions and thereby decide which portfolio strategy to pursue. At the heart of this difficulty is the question of how households evaluate small probabilities of low retirement plan balances. The picture approach does not attempt to evaluate the cost to a household of a retirement wealth outcome below the all-bonds level.

The last part of our analysis is directed to this issue. We compute the expected utility generated by the distribution of retirement resources for each portfolio strategy, using a standard household utility function. We then convert this expected utility to a certainty equivalent wealth measure to value the potential outcomes of different portfolio strategies. Table 1.8 presents these results assuming that the 401(k) balance is the household's only wealth. By excluding other wealth and assuming that the household is dependent on 401(k) wealth only, these calculations exaggerate the true level of risk faced by the household. Since household consumption risk during retirement is tempered by the existence of non-401(k) wealth, we relax this counterfactual assumption below.

The values in the first panel in table 1.8 are based on linear utility ($\alpha = 0$) and are thus the expected values of each investment choice represented

Table 1.8   Certainty equivalent wealth in thousands of year 2000 dollars for different portfolio allocation rules and expected stock returns, assuming no wealth other than 401(k)

Investment strategy/risk aversion (alpha)	Less than high school degree	High school and/or some college	College and/or postgraduate
alpha = 0			
100% riskless bonds	172.7	230.4	248.2
50% bonds, 50% stocks	345.8	456.9	475.8
100% stocks	730.1	960.9	972.9
50% bonds, 50% equity return reduced 300bp	250.3	331.9	350.8
100% stocks, equity return reduced 300bp	369.4	487.8	506.6
alpha = 1			
100% riskless bonds	172.7	230.4	248.2
50% bonds, 50% stocks	317.8	420.7	440.4
100% stocks	506.2	669.3	690.3
50% bonds, 50% equity return reduced 300bp	230.9	306.9	326.2
100% stocks, equity return reduced 300bp	262.7	349.6	370.8
alpha = 2			
100% riskless bonds	172.7	230.4	248.2
50% bonds, 50% stocks	292.3	387.7	408.0
100% stocks	355.5	473.3	498.0
50% bonds, 50% equity return reduced 300bp	213.2	284.1	303.5
100% stocks, equity return reduced 300bp	190.1	255.5	276.6
alpha = 4			
100% riskless bonds	172.7	230.4	248.2
50% bonds, 50% stocks	248.1	330.4	351.4
100% stocks	186.1	252.8	276.4
50% bonds, 50% equity return reduced 300bp	182.4	244.3	263.8
100% stocks, equity return reduced 300bp	106.0	146.0	164.0

in table 1.7. The second panel shows that for a household with no wealth outside the retirement account, and whose preferences over wealth are given by $U(W) = \log W$, which implies $\alpha = 1$ the certainty equivalent value of a portfolio invested in the large-cap equity portfolio is nearly three times as great as the value of the all-index-bond portfolio for a household with a high school education. For a fifty-fifty index bond and stock portfolio, the certainty equivalent is between 80 and 85 percent larger than the value of the all-index bond investment strategy. As risk aversion rises, the certainty equivalent value for the stock portfolio declines relative to the value of the index bond portfolio. When the household has a relative risk aversion of two, for example, the certainty equivalent of the all stock investment declines to about twice that of the all index bond portfolio, while the certainty equivalent of the fifty-fifty portfolio falls to around 70 percent of the value of the index bond investment. At a risk aversion of four, the certainty equivalent of an all-stock portfolio allocation is only slightly greater than that of an all-index bond allocation, but the value of a fifty-fifty portfolio remains considerably larger in certainty equivalent terms.

Figure 1.5 shows the cumulative distribution of the *utility values* of the wealth outcomes in the simulated distribution for four different levels of risk aversion. These are transformed values of the constant relative risk aversion utility function in equation (2) for each of the simulated outcomes. The utility values are scaled using a linear transformation, such that zero is the worst empirical outcome and one is the best outcome for each value of α. When $\alpha = 0$, so that the household is risk neutral, the plot of the cumulative distribution function (CDF) for utility levels is the same as the cumulative distribution of the values of wealth at retirement. The 90th percentile outcome is less than 10 percent of the level of the best possible outcome, reflecting the very long upper tail of the empirical distribution. The cumulative density function for the risk-neutral household is convex. As risk aversion increases, the distribution of utility diverges more and more from the distribution of wealth, and it becomes clear that raising risk aversion puts more weight on the negative outcomes in the left tail of the potential retirement wealth distribution. The second derivative of the CDF rises as risk aversion increases. When $\alpha = 4$, the CDF is highly concave, as the low retirement wealth outcomes generate very low utility outcomes. As a result, by the 5th percentile of the utility outcome distribution, household utility is already 99 percent of the level of the best utility outcome.

Panels A and B of figure 1.6 show the distribution of certainty equivalent wealth values, measured in dollars at age sixty-three, for different levels of risk aversion and for each of our investment strategies. We restrict attention in these figures to households with a high school education. The three sets of figures differ in the assumptions that they make about the household's non-401(k) wealth at retirement.

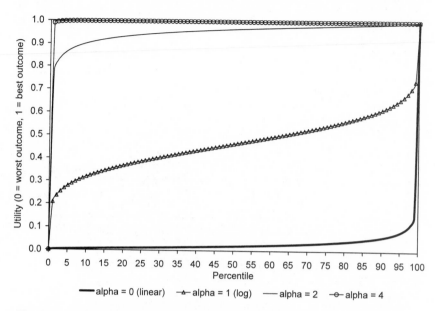

Fig. 1.5   Cumulative density functions of different utility functions for households with high school or some college education

Notes: This figure shows the cumulative distribution of the utility values of the wealth outcomes in the simulated distribution for four different levels of risk aversion. The scale of the utility values depends on the risk aversion parameter. In this figure, all utility values are scaled so that 0 is the worst outcome, and 1 is the best outcome, for a given alpha. The Von-Neumann Morgenstern (VNM) utility function over which expected utility is calculated is unique up to an affine transformation. The linear transformation necessary to put each utility value on a 0–1 scale is therefore a legitimate transformation that preserves the VNM function's properties. Furthermore, since the actual utility magnitudes of outcomes across different alphas are not comparable, the scale on which we represent the distribution of outcomes can be arbitrary as long as the VNM ordering is preserved.

Panel A of figure 1.6 shows that an all-stock portfolio is preferred to an all-index bond portfolio by investors with risk aversion (α) below approximately 4.25. This is not surprising, since the empirical distribution of historical stock returns has a much higher mean than the index bond portfolio. Thus, only a small number of 401(k) wealth outcomes under the partial- or full-equity strategies fall below the value of the index bond portfolio. The variability of returns on corporate stock does not create enough low utility outcomes to lead households with modest risk aversion to choose index bonds over a portfolio with some equity exposure. A fifty-fifty mixture of stock and index bonds is preferred to an all-bond portfolio by investors at all levels of risk aversion shown in the figure. The value of α that would make a household indifferent between the all-index-bonds portfolio strategy and each of the equity exposure strategies can be found at the intersections of the various curves. A value of α greater than eight is

A

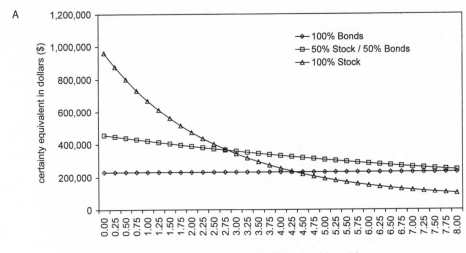

alpha = coefficient of relative risk aversion

B

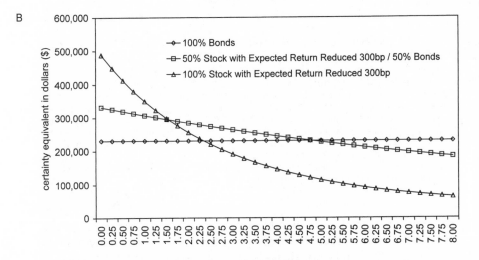

alpha = coefficient of relative risk aversion

Fig. 1.6   *A*, Certainty equivalents and risk aversion for households with high school or some college education, baseline equity returns, and no wealth other than 401(k); *B*, certainty equivalents and risk aversion for households with high school or some college education, reduced equity premiums, and no wealth other than 401(k)

needed for a household to prefer all index bonds to a fifty-fifty index bond–stock mix. For $\alpha > 2.75$, a household prefers the fifty-fifty mix to an all-stock portfolio.

Panel B of figure 1.6 shows that the certainty equivalent of the 50 percent and 100 percent equity allocations declines if the expected return on corporate stock is assumed to be 300 basis points lower than historical returns. The effects are most pronounced at high levels of risk aversion. For $\alpha = 4$, for example, the certainty equivalent of an all-stock allocation falls substantially *below* that of the all-index-bond portfolio when the expected equity return is 6.4 percent, while it is just under 10 percent higher than the certainty equivalent of the bond portfolio with an average equity return of 9.4 percent, the historical mean. Even with $\alpha = 2$, however, the expected utility of following the all-stock investment strategy exceeds that of the all-index-bond strategy when the expected equity return is 6.4 percent. When we reduce the average return by 300 basis points, the levels of α for which stocks and the fifty-fifty mix are preferred to the index bond portfolio are lower. Investors with $\alpha < 2.25$ prefer the all-stock portfolio strategy over all index bonds in this case, and those with $\alpha < 4.5$ prefer the fifty-fifty mix to the all-index-bond portfolio even when the expected return on stocks is reduced.

The results in table 1.8 and both panels of figure 1.6 assume that the 401(k) balance is the only wealth that the household accumulates to provide for retirement support. A sequence of stock market returns that delivers a very low retirement wealth is therefore very costly in terms of household utility. Yet the summary statistics in our earlier tables show that essentially all households have Social Security wealth and a large fraction of households have other wealth as well. To explore the importance of these other sources of retirement income, we repeated our stochastic simulations, taking account of other wealth. In table 1.9 and panels A and B of figure 1.7, we assume that each household holds non-401(k) wealth at retirement equal to the present discounted value of their Social Security wealth, DB plan wealth, and income annuity wealth. In table 1.10 and panels A and B of figure 1.8, each simulation household receives non-401(k) wealth at retirement equal to its total net worth—including Social Security wealth, DB wealth, and income annuity wealth—but excluding the value of retirement account assets that they report.

Table 1.9 thus presents findings like those in table 1.8, but from simulations that account for the presence of Social Security, DB wealth, and other income annuities, in addition to simulated 401(k) wealth. The first row of each panel in table 1.9 shows that for a couple with a high school education, the index bond portfolio generates the utility level associated with $230,400. This is identical to the index bond portfolio certainty equivalents in table 1.8, and it is independent of α, as there is no uncertainty associated with this simulated investment strategy. Comparing the other results in table 1.9 with those in table 1.8 shows that the certainty equivalent from holding a risky stock portfolio is larger when the household has other sources of financial support than when it does not. For example, households with a high school education and with log utility ($\alpha = 1$) have certainty equivalent wealth equal to $669,300 for the stock portfolio in table

Table 1.9   Certainty equivalent wealth in thousands of year 2000 dollars for different portfolio allocation rules and expected stock returns, assuming non-401(k) wealth = Social Security + defined benefit + other annuities

Investment strategy/risk aversion (alpha)	Less than high school degree	High school and/or some college	College and/or postgraduate
alpha = 0			
100% riskless bonds	172.7	230.4	248.2
50% bonds, 50% stocks	345.8	456.9	475.8
100% stocks	730.1	960.9	972.9
50% bonds, 50% equity return reduced 300bp	250.3	331.9	350.8
100% stocks, equity return reduced 300bp	369.4	487.8	506.6
alpha = 1			
100% riskless bonds	172.7	230.4	248.2
50% bonds, 50% stocks	328.7	435.1	455.7
100% stocks	562.0	743.6	772.9
50% bonds, 50% equity return reduced 300bp	239.9	318.6	338.4
100% stocks, equity return reduced 300bp	301.5	400.8	425.5
alpha = 2			
100% riskless bonds	172.7	230.4	248.2
50% bonds, 50% stocks	313.4	415.5	437.5
100% stocks	454.0	603.9	641.4
50% bonds, 50% equity return reduced 300bp	230.4	306.6	327.1
100% stocks, equity return reduced 300bp	256.3	342.6	370.0
alpha = 4			
100% riskless bonds	172.7	230.4	248.2
50% bonds, 50% stocks	287.2	381.9	406.0
100% stocks	330.1	443.3	485.6
50% bonds, 50% equity return reduced 300bp	214.0	285.7	307.1
100% stocks, equity return reduced 300bp	200.8	270.9	299.5

1.8, where we assume no non-401(k) wealth. But the certainty equivalent of the 401(k) account rises to $743,600 when Social Security, DB pension wealth, and other income annuity wealth are included as non-401(k) wealth as in table 1.9.

Including another nonstochastic wealth component for non-401(k) wealth raises the certainty equivalent of the 401(k) account still further, as shown in table 1.10, where all nonretirement account assets reported in the HRS are included in the utility evaluation for each household. For the household with a high school education and log utility, the all-stock portfolio now has a certainty equivalent of $779,600. Therefore, relative to the all-index-bond case, where the certainty equivalent is $230,400, the all-stock investment generates a certainty equivalent that is 2.9 times greater if there is no wealth; 3.2 times greater than the case with Social Security, DB, and other annuity wealth; and 3.4 times greater than if non-401(k) wealth consists of all HRS wealth excluding retirement accounts. This in-

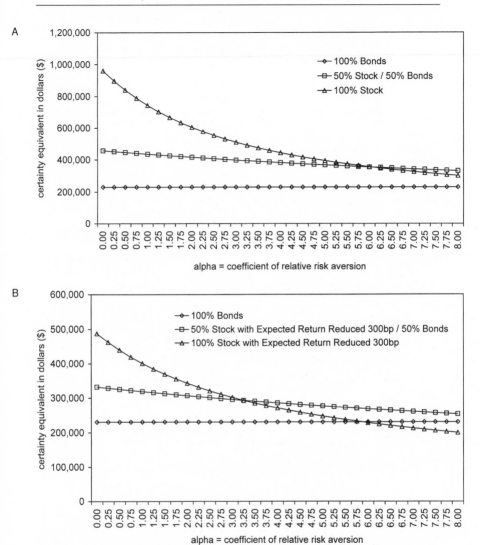

Fig. 1.7   *A,* **Certainty equivalents and risk aversion for households with high school or some college education, baseline equity returns, and SS + DB + annuity wealth;** *B,* **certainty equivalents and risk aversion for households with high school or some college education, reduced equity premiums, and SS + DB + annuity wealth**

crease in certainty equivalent wealth with larger levels of nonstochastic wealth is a feature of the constant relative risk aversion utility function.

At higher levels of risk aversion, the assumptions that we make about non-401(k) wealth are more important than at lower risk aversion values. The all-stock strategy has a certainty equivalent of $252,800 for $\alpha = 4$ when we assume households have no non-401(k) wealth, as in table 1.8.

Table 1.10   Certainty equivalent wealth in thousands of year 2000 dollars for different portfolio allocation rules and expected stock returns, assuming non-401(k) wealth = all HRS wealth excluding retirement accounts

Investment strategy/risk aversion (alpha)	Less than high school degree	High school and/or some college	College and/or postgraduate
alpha = 0			
100% riskless bonds	172.7	230.4	248.2
50% bonds, 50% stocks	345.9	456.8	475.8
100% stocks	730.6	960.9	973.1
50% bonds, 50% equity return reduced 300bp	250.4	331.9	350.9
100% stocks, equity return reduced 300bp	369.6	487.8	506.7
alpha = 1			
100% riskless bonds	172.7	230.4	248.2
50% bonds, 50% stocks	331.7	440.8	464.2
100% stocks	580.5	779.6	831.2
50% bonds, 50% equity return reduced 300bp	241.9	322.6	344.2
100% stocks, equity return reduced 300bp	311.7	420.3	455.6
alpha = 2			
100% riskless bonds	172.7	230.4	248.2
50% bonds, 50% stocks	319.0	426.2	453.5
100% stocks	483.2	660.9	734.1
50% bonds, 50% equity return reduced 300bp	234.3	314.0	337.9
100% stocks, equity return reduced 300bp	272.3	373.5	418.3
alpha = 4			
100% riskless bonds	172.7	230.4	248.2
50% bonds, 50% stocks	297.0	400.7	434.4
100% stocks	368.5	517.6	609.8
50% bonds, 50% equity return reduced 300bp	220.9	298.8	326.7
100% stocks, equity return reduced 300bp	222.4	312.3	366.6

This is only 10 percent higher than the certainty equivalent of the all-index-bond strategy, $230,400. However, the certainty equivalent of the all-stock strategy rises to $443,300 in table 1.9 and $517,600 in table 1.10. These values are 1.9 times and 2.2 times the values with the all index bond portfolio.

1.7   Conclusions and Directions for Further Work

This paper presents new evidence on the valuation of risky retirement saving assets when investors have a choice between investing in corporate stocks and index bonds. We find that the historical return distribution for equities leads investors to earn higher expected utility, in most cases, if they invest primarily in stocks rather than in index bonds. We have explored the robustness of this finding to reducing the expected return on corporate stocks by 300 basis points per year. While this shifts the distribution of re-

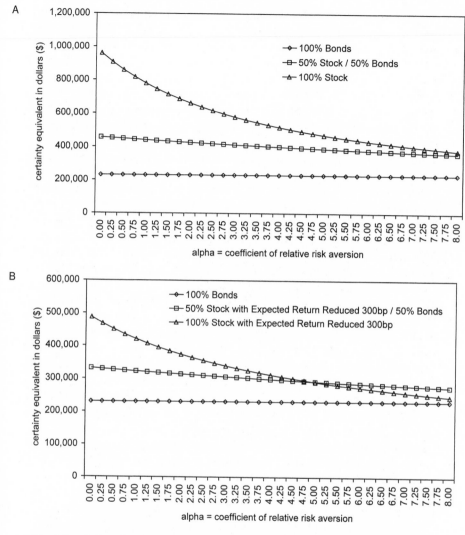

Fig. 1.8   *A,* Certainty equivalents and risk aversion for households with high school or some college education, baseline equity returns, and all non-401(k) wealth; *B,* certainty equivalents and risk aversion for households with high school or some college education, reduced equity premiums, and all non-401(k) wealth

tirement balances to lower values and reduces the expected utility of holding stocks, we still find that only highly risk-averse investors would choose not to hold corporate stocks.

Data on asset allocation in retirement accounts are broadly consistent with the expected utility results that emerge from our simulations. Bergstresser and Poterba (2004) report that of the 51.1 million households in the 2001 Survey of Consumer Finances with some assets in a tax-deferred account, just over 20 percent (10.4 million) hold only bonds. The overall allocation between stocks and bonds in tax-deferred accounts is similar to that in DB plans, which are managed by professional investment managers. One important difference is that there is a higher concentration of company stock in DC plan accounts.

One of our goals is to compare two alternative approaches to evaluating the riskiness of portfolio strategies for retirement wealth accumulation. First, we presented pictures of the distribution of wealth outcomes for different investment allocation rules. This approach is closely related to the techniques used by many financial planners, who show clients the set of outcomes that they might achieve under a given set of assumptions about future returns and investment strategy. It is also the approach that we, and others, have used in past studies that considered the returns to different investment strategies. Feldstein and Ranguelova (2001) use a related approach to summarize the potential returns associated with different investment strategies in a partially privatized Social Security system. Second, we tried to synthesize the information in the distribution of wealth outcomes by computing an expected utility measure corresponding to each distribution. This approach allows for the possibility that the marginal utility of wealth declines with wealth, so that a given increment to wealth is more valuable when wealth is at a low level than when it is high.

Both the picture and the parametric utility function approaches are useful. The picture provides the information that any household that is considering retirement saving needs to evaluate the various investment strategies. It could be used, and sometimes is used, by financial planners who are trying to elicit a household's preferences with respect to risk. The planner can show the household several distributions of potential wealth outcomes and then ask which of these outcome distributions is preferred. In such a setting, different households would be expected to reach different conclusions about which strategy to pursue. This would reflect heterogeneity in their risk preferences.

The parametric utility function approach starts from the premise that a household's relative risk aversion can be characterized by a single parameter. Conditional on this parameter, it is straightforward to characterize the optimal portfolio strategy for the household. This approach assumes away the problems associated with eliciting a household's preferences with regard to risk, and it requires strong parametric assumptions about the form of the household's utility function. When it is reasonable to maintain these assumptions, however, the parametric utility function approach delivers simple rankings of different portfolio strategies.

The parametric utility function approach can potentially provide some guidance on the extent to which observed portfolio choices can be reconciled with the optimizing choices of households that are trying to maximize their expected utility. Any analysis of such choices requires data on assets held outside retirement accounts as well as inside these accounts, since there are important asset location issues that combine tax planning with investment choices in both taxable and tax-deferred accounts. If we are prepared to assume that past returns will characterize future returns on various asset classes, we can make estimates of how risk averse a household would have to be to forego any investment in corporate stock, or to hold only one quarter of its overall portfolio in stock. From these calculations, one could implicitly evaluate the fraction of households in the overall population that would need to have risk aversion above a given level in order to rationalize observed portfolio holdings.

The findings in this paper suggest a number of promising directions for future work. One is to develop a richer stochastic structure for the determination of 401(k) balances as well as the other components of the household balance sheet. The states of nature in which DC plan balances are low are likely to be states of nature in which other wealth balances are also low—for example, because aggregate stock market returns have been low. To the extent that fluctuations in real interest rates affect 401(k) values, and that such movements also affect the present discounted value of Social Security benefits and DB pension benefits, virtually all of the balance sheet components may exhibit some covariance.

It should also be possible to extend our framework to consider other assets that could be held in the retirement account. There is particular interest in the role of employer stock in 401(k) plans, as indicated in Mitchell and Utkus (2003), Munnell and Sunden (2002), and Poterba (2003). While we have focused on index bonds as a low-risk investment strategy for 401(k) investors, we could also consider investments in corporate bonds, which expose investors to inflation risk. Our earlier work on portfolio holdings in 401(k) plans, Poterba, Venti, and Wise (2001), considered the risk of investment portfolios with nominal bonds and corporate stock.

A second natural direction for further work concerns the comparison between the risks associated with DB and DC pension arrangements. Samwick and Skinner (2004) use data from the Survey of Consumer Finances (SCF) to compare the risks of the two types of retirement schemes from the standpoint of retirement income security. The SCF includes detailed information on the structure of pension arrangements for survey respondents, through the Pension Provider Survey, but it does not include data on the earnings history for survey participants. Yet the risks associated with DB plans depend significantly on the pattern of job changes, job loss, and retirement decisions for individual workers, as documented in a series of papers by Kotlikoff and Wise and reviewed in Kotlikoff and Wise (1989). The HRS data, linked with SSA earnings records, make it possible to assess these risk sources in DB plans. We are currently developing an algorithm to evaluate DB plan risk.

Finally, further work can explore the extent to which simple utility functions, such as power functions of wealth, provide an adequate description of the criterion that individuals use to evaluate their choices in the face of asset price risk. There is a long tradition, illustrated by many studies that are cited in surveys by Rabin (1998) and Starmer (2000), of finding inconsistencies with standard expected utility analysis. Kahneman and Tversky (1979) is a seminal example. Even within the framework of parametric CRRA utility functions, there is little consensus on the "correct" value of the relative risk aversion coefficient. We are concerned more generally that choices predicted by the CRRA function may be a poor guide to actual behavior when the distribution of wealth outcomes includes values near zero. We hope to gain a better understanding of individual preferences over uncertain levels of future retirement assets by developing a set of survey questions designed to elicit respondent preferences over alternative wealth outcomes. We hope to include these questions on household surveys like the HRS. Kapteyn and Teppa (2002) have had some success in using a similar approach to explain household portfolio choices as a function of risk preference, as revealed by a set of survey questions. Ultimately, we aim to improve our ability to judge how individuals rank the distributions associated with different asset allocation and saving strategies.

Appendix

Table 1A.1   Household sample counts

	HRS 2000[a]	SS earnings only	Final earnings only	Couples with final earnings	Couples with final earnings and male aged 63–67
	Unweighted observations				
Total	6,195	4,233	3,749	2,275	759
Couples	3,838	2,446	2,275	0	0
Singles	2,357	1,787	1,474	0	0
At least one person working	3,269	2,194	2,096	1,413	459
Couples, two people working	899	592	581	581	166
Receives DB pension	2,293	1,609	1,430	1,027	373
Expects DB pension	478	370	364	270	72
Receives Social Security	3,681	2,550	2,203	1,411	575
Has IRA	2,531	1,737	1,618	1,192	417
Has DC	1,333	884	862	629	216
	Weighted observations (millions of households)				
Total	16.7	11.6	10.4	6.4	2.1
Couples	10.4	6.8	6.4	6.4	2.1
Singles	6.4	4.8	4.0	0.0	0.0
At least one person working	9.0	6.2	5.9	4.0	1.3
Couples, two people working	2.6	1.8	1.7	1.7	0.5
Receives DB pension	6.3	4.5	4.0	2.8	1.0
Expects DB pension	1.4	1.1	1.0	0.8	0.2
Receives Social Security	9.7	6.9	6.0	3.9	1.6
Has IRA	7.5	5.2	4.9	3.6	1.2
Has DC	3.8	2.6	2.5	1.9	0.6

[a]Accounting for household splits and excluding households with missing birthdays. Each HRS household is defined uniquely by its household identifier (HHID) and wave 5 subhousehold identifier (GSUBHH).

References

Bell, Felicitie, and M. Miller. 2002. *Life tables for the United States Social Security area 1900–2100.* Social Security Administration Actuarial Study 116. Washington, DC: Social Security Administration.

Bergstresser, Daniel, and James Poterba. 2004. Asset allocation and asset location: Household evidence from the Survey of Consumer Finances. *Journal of Public Economics* 88 (August): 1916–33.

Feldstein, Martin, and Elena Ranguelova. 2001. Individual risk in an investment-based social security system. NBER Working Paper no. 8074. Cambridge, MA: National Bureau of Economic Research.

Ibbotson Associates. 2003. *Stocks, bonds, bills, and inflation: 2003 yearbook: Market results for 1926–2002.* Chicago: Ibbotson Associates.

Kahneman, Daniel, and Amos Tversky. 1979. Prospect theory: An analysis of decisions under risk. *Econometrica* 47:313–27.

Kapteyn, Arie, and Federica Teppa. 2002. Subjective measures of risk aversion and portfolio choice. RAND Report no. DRU-2902. RAND Corporation, February.

Kotlikoff, Laurence J., and David A. Wise. 1989. *The wage carrot and the pension stick.* Kalamazoo, MI: W. E. Upjohn Institute for Employment Research.

Mehra, Rajneesh, and Edward Prescott. 2003. The equity premium puzzle in retrospect. In *Handbook of economics of finance,* ed. G. Constantinides, M. Harris, and R. Stulz. Amsterdam: North Holland.

Mitchell, Olivia, and Stephen P. Utkus. 2003. The role of company stock in defined contribution plans. In *The Pension Challenge: Risk Transfers and Retirement Income Security,* ed. Olivia Mitchell and Kent Smetters. Philadelphia: University of Pennsylvania Press.

Munnell, Alicia, and Annika Sunden. 2002. 401(k) and company stock: How can we encourage diversification? Issue Brief no. 9. Boston College, Center for Retirement Research, July.

Poterba, James. 2003. Employer stock and 401(k) plans. *American Economic Review* 93 (May): 398–404.

———. 2004. Valuing assets in retirement saving accounts. *National Tax Journal* 57 (June): 489–512.

Poterba, James, Steven Venti, and David Wise. 1998. Implications of rising personal retirement saving. In *Frontiers in the economics of aging,* ed. D. Wise, 125–67. Chicago: University of Chicago Press.

———. 2001. Pre-retirement cashouts and forgone retirement saving: Implications for 401(k) asset accumulation. In *Themes in the economics of aging,* ed. D. Wise, 23–56. Chicago: University of Chicago Press.

———. 2004. The transition to personal accounts and increasing retirement wealth: Macro and micro evidence. In *Perspectives on the economics of aging,* ed. D. Wise, 17–71. Chicago: University of Chicago Press.

Rabin, Matthew. 1998. Psychology and economics. *Journal of Economic Literature* 36 (March): 11–46.

Samwick, Andrew, and Jonathan Skinner. 2004. How will 401(k) pension plans affect retirement income? *American Economic Review* 94 (March): 329–43.

Starmer, Chris. 2000. Developments in non-expected utility theory: The hunt for a descriptive theory of choice under risk. *Journal of Economic Literature* 38 (2): 332–82.

Venti, Steven F., and David A. Wise. 2001a. Aging and housing equity. In *Innovations for financing retirement,* ed. Zvi Bodie, Brett Hammond, and Olivia S. Mitchell, 254–81. Philadelphia: Pension Research Council and the University of Pennsylvania.

———. 2001b. Choice, chance, and wealth dispersion at retirement. In *Aging issues in the United States and Japan,* ed. S. Ogura, T. Tachibanaki, and D. Wise, 25–64. Chicago: University of Chicago Press.

———. 2004. Aging and housing equity: Another look. In *Perspectives on the economics of aging,* ed. David A. Wise, 127–75. Chicago: University of Chicago Press.

Comment   Robert J. Willis

The extent to which individuals are willing to trade off the risk of low retirement wealth against the expectation of higher wealth is a critical question both for individual retirement planning and for public policies toward
401(k) plans or for Social Security reforms that endeavor to raise expected
returns through the creation of individual accounts that may be invested in
equities. The high historical returns of stocks relative to alternative instruments, at least in the United States during the past century, have given rise
to a large literature on the "equity premium puzzle" (Mehra and Prescott
2003), so named because the excess returns on risky assets appear to be
larger than would be demanded by investors with plausible degrees of risk
aversion. An early study of the implications of high equity returns for retirement saving and pension wealth by MaCurdy and Shoven (1992) found
that an all-stock portfolio would have dominated an all-bond portfolio for
every career that ended in retirement over the period 1926–89. This striking result implies that a portfolio held all in stocks would dominate alternative portfolios no matter how risk averse the household. Putting their
money where their mouth is, MaCurdy and Shoven reported that their own
pension contributions were 100 percent in stocks—a great place to have
been in the early 1990s! The puzzle, of course, is why anyone holds bonds
in their retirement portfolio.

I shall refer to this aspect of the equity premium puzzle as the "retirement portfolio puzzle" and organize much of my discussion of the Poterba,
Rauh, Venti, and Wise (PRVW) paper around the question of whether their
work helps resolve the puzzle. In fairness, I should point out that this is not
an explicit goal of their paper. Indeed, the paper is really not so much an
exercise in positive economics as it is an exploration of the normative or
prescriptive implications of alternative portfolio strategies that may be relevant for private policies of firms and their workers who participate in
401(k) plans and for public policies concerning the regulation of these savings vehicles. Still, it seems to me that one's confidence in basing advice on
a model that is contradicted by behavior is undermined if one cannot understand why actual behavior diverges from the optimal behavior implied
by the model.

PRVW present new evidence on the riskiness of retirement portfolios by
simulating the probability distribution of 401(k) balances generated by alternative contribution strategies for hypothetical households over their
working life cycles. They compare the performance of making 401(k) contributions all in stocks, all in riskless index bonds, or in a fifty-fifty mix of
stocks and bonds. Their methodology allows for a much richer set of pos-

Robert J. Willis is a professor of economics at the University of Michigan.

sible sample paths of returns implied by the historical data than in Ma-
Curdy and Shoven's analysis. Specifically, PRVW treat the observed distribution of historical returns, illustrated by the histogram in figure 1.2 of
their paper, as an estimate of the probability distribution of future returns.
Each simulated life-cycle portfolio containing stocks is based on a vector
of thirty-five independent draws from this distribution and estimates of the
distribution of retirement wealth are based on 300,000 replications. In general, like MaCurdy and Shoven, they find that expected wealth is a sharply
increasing function of the fraction of the portfolio held in stocks. For example, their table 1.6 shows that a high school graduate household contributing 9 percent of earnings to a 401(k) for thirty-five years would have
expected 401(k) wealth at retirement of $234,000 under the all-bond strat-
egy, $465,000 under the fifty-fifty strategy, and $936,000 under the all-
stock strategy. There is, however, about a 5 percent chance that the 100 percent stock portfolio will be worth less at retirement than a portfolio
containing bonds. Thus, unlike MaCurdy and Shoven, PRVW find that retirement wealth generated by a stock-only strategy does not dominate a
bond portfolio, implying that a sufficiently risk-averse household would
prefer a less risky strategy.

This finding motivates PRVW to calculate the certainty equivalent value
of terminal wealth for households with varying degrees of risk aversion,
under the assumption that households have constant relative risk aversion
(CRRA) utility functions. They find that households with risk aversion coefficients over 4.5 would prefer an all-bond to an all-stock portfolio and
that those with a coefficient over 2.75 would prefer a fifty-fifty portfolio to
an all-stock portfolio. Survey evidence on the distribution of risk tolerance
(the reciprocal of the coefficient of relative risk aversion) among fifty-one-
to sixty-one-year-olds in the HRS by Barsky and others (1997, note 18) indicates that about three-quarters of the sample have a risk tolerance less
than 0.25 and about 90 percent less than 0.5. This distribution, in combination with the PRVW results, suggests that only 10 percent of households
would be better off with a 401(k) plan containing 100 percent stocks and
only a quarter would optimally choose a contribution strategy with at least
50 percent stocks. These figures can be compared with the portfolio
choices of TIAA-CREF participants reported by MaCurdy and Shoven
(1992): only about 3 percent chose 100 percent stocks, about half chose a
fifty-fifty contribution rate, and most of the rest chose a still more conservative strategy. During the bull market of the 1990s, however, there was a
sharp increase in the fraction of contributions going to stocks by TIAA-
CREF participants with, for example, a rise in those choosing 100 percent
stocks from 3 percent in 1989 to 25 percent in 1998 (Ameriks and Zeldes
2001).

Does the PRVW analysis help resolve the retirement portfolio puzzle?
The evidence just discussed suggests that it might. According to their find-

ings, it appears that there is a small chance that a 401(k) portfolio containing significant amounts of stock will do worse than a safe portfolio and that this risk is sufficient to cause a large fraction of households with empirically plausible levels of risk aversion to be better off with a conservative investment strategy even at considerable sacrifice to the expected value of their portfolios. However, PRVW extend their analysis in two directions, one weakening this conclusion and the other potentially strengthening it.

The retirement portfolio puzzle reappears when PRVW consider the safety net created by retirement resources outside the 401(k) plan. Giving a representative household the present value of median Social Security and DB pension plan annuities dramatically increases the threshold of risk aversion below which a household would maximize expected utility by holding a 100 percent stock portfolio. Another factor working in this direction that PRVW do not consider is variable labor supply. If a household's 401(k) portfolio turns out badly near the planned time of retirement, the option to continue working cushions this event. Looking forward, households with flexible work options should be willing to bear greater risk in their 401(k) plans. This effect would be smaller, the less likely such options are to be available because of employer inflexibility, chance of disabling illness, and so on.

A major attraction of the 100 percent stock strategy is, of course, the (puzzlingly) high historical returns on stocks relative to safe assets. A key question for a long-term investor is whether these historical returns will hold far into the future. PRVW examine the sensitivity of their results to the possibility that future returns will average 300 basis points less than the historical average, by simulating portfolios with an average rate of return reduced from 9.7 percent to 6.7 percent. They report that a reduction of this magnitude in the expected rate of return has a substantial effect, especially for households with high levels of risk aversion. While lower expected returns on stocks would help rationalize why people do not hold all stock 401(k) portfolios, clearly they cannot explain the failure of large numbers of households to hold such portfolios in the past unless we assume that ex ante expectations were systematically much lower than the historical average.

Another way to interpret uncertainty about future returns is to suggest that stock returns are riskier than implied by the historical data used by PRVW. Their procedure treats these returns, as depicted in the histogram in figure 1.2, as if it is an exact estimate of the distribution of returns. An alternative view is that the expected return calculated from historical data is estimated with error and that the investors should take this error into account when choosing their investment strategy. For example, Brennan (1998, p. 300) finds that the variance of an investor's prior distribution of the mean market return is $(0.0243)^2$ if he forms his estimate based on sixty-nine years of data and $(0.0452)^2$ if only the past twenty years are used.

Intuitively, it would seem that increased uncertainty about the mean rate of return on stocks would increase the riskiness of stocks, leading risk-averse investors to choose a smaller fraction of stocks in their portfolio. This conclusion is correct for investors with CRRA utility with $\alpha > 1$ who decide on fixed contribution rates and hold their wealth until retirement, as is assumed in the PRVW model. However, if investors are able to trade continuously and returns follow a diffusion process (i.e., a continuous time random walk), finance researchers have established "an important and surprising result: the variance of the instantaneous rate of return on the risky asset that is used to determine the optimal portfolio is unaffected by the uncertainty about the mean of the process" (Brennan 1998, p. 297). The intuition for this counterintuitive result is that the optimal balance at any given time depends only on the instantaneous expected return since the loss due to uncertainty about this parameter is second order and disappears as the trading horizon goes to zero. Uncertainty does have an effect on portfolio decisions, as Brennan (1998) shows, if the investor revises his estimate of the expected rate of return in light of the observed pattern of returns. For risk-averse investors with $\alpha > 1$, the potential for learning creates a negative hedging demand for stock that may even be strong enough to reduce the demand for stocks to zero (Kézdi and Willis 2003). On the other hand, Brennan's model suggests that the run-up of the stock market during the 1990s would lead investors to revise their subjective expected rate of return upward, causing them to increase the fraction of stocks in their monthly allocations. This is consistent with trends in behavior, noted earlier, of TIAA-CREF participants reported by Ameriks and Zeldes (2001).

This discussion suggests that a useful extension of the PRVW analysis might be to consider alternatives to the assumption that households follow a fixed contribution rule for thirty-five years in order to assess the riskiness of 401(k) portfolios that allow for dynamic optimization and learning. For example, it would be possible to use the distribution of historical returns to simulate how Bayesian updating of expectations would influence optimal portfolio choice and the implied distribution of 401(k) wealth. Another avenue for future research is to explore how households' subjective expectations of stock returns, their degree of subjective uncertainty about these returns, and changes in expectations over time are related to the distribution of expected returns that a rational agent derives from examination of historical returns. Beginning with its 2002 wave, the HRS has added questions on subjective probabilities of stock market gains that will facilitate research on this topic. For instance, Kézdi and Willis (2003) find very substantial heterogeneity in expectations that is significantly related to actual stock holdings. They also find that households who generally appear to have imprecise views about probabilities tend to be less likely to hold stocks.

An increase in our ability to resolve puzzles about the actual functioning of equity markets and behavior of individual households is, in my view, an important component in developing sound public policies to help increase the well being of older Americans. The line of research presented by PRVW is a significant step toward this goal, but more remains to be done.

References

Ameriks, John, and Stephen P. Zeldes. 2001. How do household portfolio shares vary with age? Columbia University. Working Paper, December 3.

Barsky, R., M. S. Kimball, F. T. Juster, and M. D. Shapiro. 1997. Preference parameters and behavioral heterogeneity: An experimental approach. *HRS Quarterly Journal of Economics* 112:S537–S579.

Brennan, M. J. 1998. The role of learning in dynamic portfolio decisions. *European Finance Review* 1:295–306.

Kézdi, Gábor, and Robert J. Willis. 2003. Who becomes a stockholder? Expectations, subjective uncertainty, and asset allocation. Paper presented at the Fifth Annual Joint Conference for the Retirement Research Consortium. 15–16 May, Washington, DC.

MaCurdy, Thomas E., and John B. Shoven. 1992. Stocks, bonds and pension wealth. In *Topics in the economics of aging,* ed. David A. Wise, 61–75. Chicago: University of Chicago Press.

Mehra, Rajneesh, and Edward Prescott. 2003. The equity premium puzzle in retrospect. In *Handbook of economics of finance,* ed. M. Harris Constantinides and R. Stulz, Amsterdam: North Holland.

2

Passive Decisions and Potent Defaults

James J. Choi, David Laibson, Brigitte C. Madrian, and Andrew Metrick

Default options have an enormous impact on household choices. Such effects have now been extensively documented in the literature on 401(k) plans (Madrian and Shea 2001; Choi et al. 2002b, 2004). Defaults have been shown to affect participation, savings rates, rollovers, and asset allocation. For example, Choi et al. (2004) study three firms that use automatic enrollment. When employees at these firms are automatically enrolled in their 401(k) plan, only a tiny fraction opt out, producing participation rates exceeding 85 percent regardless of tenure. But when employees at these firms were not automatically enrolled, participation rates were significantly lower, ranging from 26 percent to 43 percent after six months of tenure, and from 57 percent to 69 percent after three years of tenure.

James J. Choi is a Ph.D. candidate in economics at Harvard University. David Laibson is a professor of economics at Harvard University and a research associate of the National Bureau of Economic Research. Brigitte C. Madrian is the Boettner Associate Professor in Financial Gerontology and an associate professor of business and public policy at the Wharton School, University of Pennsylvania, and a research associate of the National Bureau of Economic Research. Andrew Metrick is an associate professor of finance at the Wharton School, University of Pennsylvania, and a faculty research fellow of the National Bureau of Economic Research.

This paper is a longer version of a paper titled "Optimal Defaults" (Choi et al. 2003). We thank Hewitt Associates for their help in providing the data. We are particularly grateful to Lori Lucas, Jim McGhee, and Scott Peterson, three of our many contacts at Hewitt. We are grateful for the comments of Robert Barro, Robert Hall, Mark Iwry, Antonio Rangel, Richard Thaler, and seminar participants at Harvard, Massachusetts Institute of Technology, the National Bureau of Economic Research, the University of Chicago, the University of Minnesota, the University of Southern California, and Wharton. Numerous research assistants have contributed to this work. We are particularly indebted to Nelson Uhan. We acknowledge financial support from the National Institute of Aging (grant R01AG021650). Choi acknowledges support from a National Science Foundation graduate research fellowship. Laibson acknowledges financial support from the National Science Foundation (grant 0099025).

Defaults matter for three key reasons that we model in this paper. First, acts of commission—for example, opting out of a default—are costly. Second, these costs change randomly over time and therefore generate an option value of waiting to change a default. Decision makers would like to wait for a low-cost period (e.g., a free weekend) to make a change. Third, people have a tendency to procrastinate. Even if they want to make a change, they have a tendency to delay that change longer than they should.

Because of these effects, the choice of a particular default can have a significant effect on consumer welfare. However, it is not always obvious how to select a socially optimal default.

If *all* employees would like to be saving at a rate of exactly 5 percent in their 401(k) plan, then the employees' welfare will be maximized if the employer sets a 5 percent default. But the calculation of an optimal default is not as straightforward if different employees have different optimal savings rates. For example, what is the optimal default savings rate if employees have optimal savings rates that are distributed uniformly with a mean of 5 percent?

In this paper, we develop a theory of optimal defaults that implies that the obvious answer to the previous question—5 percent—is not necessarily the right answer. In a world of heterogeneous agents, it may sometimes be optimal to set *extreme* defaults that are far away from the mean optimal savings rate. This effect arises for two reasons. First, a default that is far away from a consumer's optimal savings rate may make that consumer *better off* than a default that is closer to the consumer's optimal savings rate. Intuitively, if an agent suffers from a procrastination problem, then a "bad" default— that is, one that is far from the consumer's optimal savings rate—will be more motivating than a better default. Hence, sometimes bad defaults make people better off than better but imperfect defaults. Second, our theory implies that optimal defaults are highly sensitive to the actual distribution of optimal savings rates. In particular, optimal defaults are often associated with the modal optimal savings rate and not the mean optimal savings rate. Since these modes are sometimes extreme (e.g., minimum or maximum contribution rates), optimal defaults will sometimes be extreme as well.

At the end of our paper we calibrate our model and use it to calculate optimal defaults for employees at four different companies. For two of our companies, the optimal default is close to the mean optimal savings rate, whereas for the other two companies the optimal defaults are extreme: 0 percent and 15 percent, respectively. Our work suggests that optimal defaults are likely to be at one of three savings rates: the minimum savings rate (0 percent), the employer match threshold (typically 5 percent or 6 percent), or the maximal savings rate (around 15 percent in our sample of companies from the late 1990s).[1]

1. More recently, regulatory changes under the Economic Growth and Tax Relief Reconciliation Act of 2001 (EGTRRA) have led many companies to raise their maximum savings rates well above the historical norm of 15 percent.

2.1   A Model of Savings Choices

We adapt the model of Choi et al. (2002a) to describe the 401(k) enrollment decisions of employees that have been newly hired at a firm. However, the model is general enough to describe any problem in which an actor decides when to move from a default state s_D to an optimal state s^*.

We assume that each employee at a firm has a fixed optimal savings rate (i.e., optimal state) s^*, with density function f characterizing the distribution of these optimal savings rates for the population of employees in the firm. When new employees join the firm, the employees are automatically enrolled at a default savings rate of s_D, which is a choice variable for the firm. In this paper, we consider the case in which this default can only take values in the support of f.[2] We assume that the firm uses a single default savings rate for all of its employees either because the firm does not observe an employee's true type, s^*, or because of legal or practical costs of implementing employee-specific defaults.[3]

Employees remain at the default election s_D unless they opt out of the default by incurring a cost c. This opt-out cost is drawn each period and takes the value 1 with probability $\mu > 1$ and value 0 with probability $1 - \mu$. The value of the cost is known when the agent decides on her action. We suppress individual and time subscripts to simplify notation.

When the agent opts out, she sets her savings rate equal to her optimal savings rate s^*, which we assume the agent knows with certainty.[4] Until that action takes place, the agent suffers a flow loss of $L = L(s_D, s^*) \geq 0$, where the first argument of L is the current savings rate and the second argument of L is the optimal savings rate. After the action occurs, the agent suffers a flow loss of $0 = L(s^*, s^*)$.

Finally, we assume that agents are *naive* hyperbolic discounters, with discount function 1, $\beta\delta$, $\beta\delta^2$, ...[5] Such naive agents believe that their future selves will make choices that are consistent with their current preferences. We adopt such naive beliefs because they increase the force of procrastination, but our qualitative results would be unchanged if we instead assumed that agents are sophisticated in their beliefs. For sim-

---

2. See Choi et al. (2002a) for a generalization.

3. Such employee-specific defaults are a natural extension of our current framework and merit theoretical and practical evaluation.

4. Another natural generalization is to consider the case in which agents have imperfect information about their personal value of s^*. If agents learn more about this value over time, they have another motive for delaying the costly action of opting out of the default.

5. See Laibson (1997) for a discussion of hyperbolic discount functions and Akerlof (1991) and O'Donoghue and Rabin (1999) for a discussion of naifs and procrastination. Note that the term "hyperbolic" is overly restrictive, since the important property of these preferences is simply that they are characterized by more discounting in the short run than in the long run.

plicity and analytical tractability, we set $\delta = 1$ (no long-run discounting).[6] We also adopt the standard hyperbolic assumption of $\beta < 1$.

We use the following timing convention. If the employee has not previously opted out of the default, the period begins with a flow loss of L. The employee then draws a current opt-out cost c and decides whether to delay opting out or to instead pay the cost, thereby ending the game. If the employee delays, she will pay a flow cost of L next period and also face an anticipated continuation value function, which we denote $v(c')$, where c' represents next period's draw from the cost distribution. Hence, the employee chooses to pay c and end the game if the cost today is less than the discounted cost of delay, or

$$c < \beta [L + Ev(c')].$$

When this inequality is not satisfied, the employee chooses to delay. Ignoring mixed strategies, which only arise on a zero measure region of the parameter space, the employee's strategy is thus

(1)   "Opt out only when $c = 0$"   if $\beta [L + Ev(c')] < 1$

"Opt out only when $c = 0$ or $c = 1$"   if $\beta [L + Ev(c')] \geq 1$

2.1.1   Naive Expectations and the Continuation Value Function $v(c)$

Since the employee is assumed to be a naive hyperbolic agent, the continuation value function is constructed under the (mistaken) belief that all future selves will exhibit no time discounting, since this is what today's self wants those future selves to do. Recall that $\delta = 1$.

The strategy of opting out whatever the draw from the cost distribution means that the employee's expected loss is $\mu = E(c)$. Waiting until $c = 0$ to opt out implies that the employee's expected loss would be

$$Ev(c \mid \text{wait until } c = 0) = \mu[L + Ev(c \mid \text{wait until } c = 0)]$$

$$= \frac{\mu L}{1 - \mu}.$$

This formula has a natural interpretation: the expected costs are equal to the expected per-period loss, μL, multiplied by the expected duration of the losses, $1/(1 - \mu)$.

If $L < 1 - \mu$, then $\mu L/(1 - \mu) < \mu$, implying that the expected losses generated by waiting to opt out until $c = 0$ are less than the losses from opting out immediately at cost $c = 1$. So if $L < 1 - \mu$, the employee will plan to wait until $c = 0$ to opt out. If $L \geq 1 - \mu$, the employee anticipates that next period she will act with certainty. In summary,

---

6. We will calibrate our model at the frequency of a pay cycle. So if the annual long-run discount rate is 0.05, then the discount rate per pay cycle is approximately $0.05/26 = 0.002$ or $0.05/12 = 0.004$, implying respective δ values of 0.998 and 0.996. Relative to these values, setting $\delta = 1$ has little impact on our results.

(2)
$$Ev(c) = \begin{cases} \dfrac{\mu L}{1 - \mu} & \text{if } L < 1 - \mu \\ \mu & \text{if } L \geq 1 - \mu \end{cases}$$

We reiterate that $Ev(c)$ is based on naive beliefs, so this expectation reflects the actor's incorrect model of her future behavior.

2.1.2 Actual Actions and Welfare

Using equations (1) and (2), the probability of opting out in any period will be

$$p = \begin{cases} 1 - \mu & \text{if } L < \dfrac{1}{\beta} - \mu \\ 1 & \text{if } \dfrac{1}{\beta} - \mu \leq L \end{cases}$$

So the expected cost of opting out, conditional on opting out, will be

$$E(c \mid \text{opt out}) = \begin{cases} 0 & \text{if } L < \dfrac{1}{\beta} - \mu \\ \mu & \text{if } \dfrac{1}{\beta} - \mu \leq L \end{cases}$$

Let $w(c)$ represent the employee's expected total costs, discounted with the agent's long-run discount factor. A recursive representation for $w(c)$ is given by

$$Ew(c) = pE(c \mid \text{opt out}) + (1 - p)\delta[L + Ew(c')]$$
$$= pE(c \mid \text{opt out}) + (1 - p)[L + Ew(c')].$$

We evaluate social welfare using the long-run discount factor δ and omitting the short-run discount factor β. These preferences represent the actor's preferences at economic birth, which we assume occurs before she starts working at the firm. The last equation contains *no discounting,* since it reflects the fact that $\delta = 1$ in our calibration. Note however that our results would not change qualitatively if we had instead assumed $\delta < 1$ throughout our analysis.

Because $Ew(c) = Ew(c')$, we can show that

$$Ew(c) = \begin{cases} \dfrac{\mu L}{1 - \mu} & \text{if } L < \dfrac{1}{\beta} - \mu \\ \mu & \text{if } \dfrac{1}{\beta} - \mu \leq L \end{cases}$$

We are now in a position to characterize the relationship between defaults and welfare. To do this, we consider the relationship between expected (dis)utility and L, the per-period flow losses of not being at an optimum. To focus on the role of L, we stop suppressing L in our notation and consider

$$W(L) = Ew(c)_{|L}.$$

$W(L)$ is the expected losses for an agent with initial flow losses per period of L.

In a standard model with exponential discounting (i.e., $\beta = 1$), $W(L)$ would increase as flow costs L increase. But for hyperbolics (i.e., $\beta < 1$), it will always be the case that W is nonmonotonic in L. To see this, note that $W(L) = \mu$ when $L = 1 - \mu$. This is the level of L at which an exponential (i.e., dynamically consistent) agent should opt out of the default whatever the cost realization. But when $c = 1$, a hyperbolic agent will only opt out of the default if $L \geq (1/\beta) - \mu$, which is greater than $1 - \mu$. Hence, when $1 - \mu < L < (1/\beta) - \mu$, the hyperbolic agent is insufficiently motivated to act, and this motivational gap produces self-defeating procrastination. In this region of L values, the expected loss function lies above μ, the value that $W(L)$ would take if the agent were not procrastinating and were willing to act at the high cost realization. But once L is high enough—specifically, above $(1/\beta) - \mu$—the procrastination effect vanishes and expected costs fall back to μ, since the hyperbolic agent is now willing to act whatever the cost realization. Figure 2.1 plots the expected cost function against the flow costs L, revealing the nonmonotonicity that arises whenever $\beta < 1$.

In a world with procrastination, moving the agent further from the optimum (i.e., increasing flow costs L) can make an agent *better* off, since it decreases the agent's tendency to procrastinate. This effect is not everywhere offset by the direct effect of reduced welfare arising from the increase in the delay cost, L.

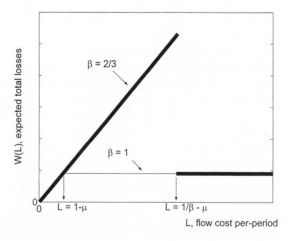

Fig. 2.1   Expected total losses as a function of flow cost per period

2.1.3 The Firm's Optimization Problem

We now analyze the employer's choice of a default savings rate under the assumption that the employer is interested in maximizing the welfare of the firm's employees. We recognize, however, that employer and employee incentives need not generally be aligned. This is particularly likely in the case presented here, since naive hyperbolic agents will not anticipate their own tendency to procrastinate and hence will not pick an employer based on the employer's ability to mitigate the harms of such procrastination. Therefore, this normative exercise is also relevant for regulators or unions that can influence the defaults that firms pick. Identifying and incorporating the other motivations and constraints that firms face in designing their benefit plans (e.g., nondiscrimination testing, good corporate citizenship, reputational value in the labor market, or personal altruism, to name a few) is beyond the scope of the current paper.

We derive the optimal default, s_D^*, that minimizes the social welfare function,

$$(3) \qquad \int_{\underline{s}}^{\bar{s}} W(L(s_D, s^*)) f(s^*) ds^*.$$

We adopt the cost function

$$L(s_D, s^*) = \kappa(s_D - s^*)^2.$$

This quadratic cost function is convex in deviations from the optimal savings rate, s^*, and has the advantage of analytic tractability. However, it does not reflect the particular institutional features of many 401(k) plans (e.g., an employer match that ends at a threshold, implying a discontinuity in the cost function). We believe that the quadratic cost function represents a good compromise between tractability and realism.

We will minimize equation (3) numerically, using the actual estimated distribution of optimal savings rates. However, for the purposes of exposition, it is useful to consider the case in which $f(s^*)$ is uniform over support $[\underline{s}, \bar{s}]$. In this case, one can prove the following result when $\beta < 1$:

$$s_D^* = \begin{cases} \dfrac{\bar{s} + \underline{s}}{2} & \text{if } \bar{s} - \underline{s} \text{ is small} \\[2ex] \underline{s} + \sqrt{\dfrac{1}{\kappa}(1 - \mu)} \text{ or } \bar{s} - \sqrt{\dfrac{1}{\kappa}(1 - \mu)} & \text{if } \bar{s} - \underline{s} \text{ is large} \end{cases}.$$

Intuitively, when there is little variation in optimal savings rates, it is best to design a default that is in the middle of the range of optimal savings rates, since all employees will then be very close to their optimal savings rate and delays in opting out of the default will not be very costly. By contrast, when there is a great deal of variation in optimal savings rates, it is better to design a default that is close to one of the two boundaries of the support. This "boundary" strategy reduces the proportion of employees who engage in costly procrastination, since the boundary strategy reduces the fraction of employees who fall in the "procrastination" interval $1 - \mu < L < (1/\beta) - \mu$.

Finally, note that if $\beta = 1$ and f is uniform, then $s_D^* = (\bar{s} + \underline{s})/2$ will always be an optimum[7] because the procrastination effect does not apply and there is no gain in welfare from moving agents away from their optima.

It is also useful to emphasize a trivial property of these models, which is important in the empirical analysis that follows. This additional effect is easiest to understand if we assume that f is a discrete density on the domain of feasible savings rates: $\{0.00, 0.01, 0.02, \ldots\}$. Then it is easy to show that

$$\lim_{\kappa \to \infty} s_D^* \in \arg \max_{s^*} f(s^*).$$

In other words, as the cost of deviations rises ($\kappa \to \infty$), the optimal default converges to the mode of the distribution of s^*. This effect is driven by the fact that for large costs of deviating from s^*, all employees will immediately adjust to their s^* except those who are already at their optima. Hence, the optimal social policy minimizes adjustment costs by setting the default equal to the most common value of s^*. We refer to this as the mode effect.

2.1.4   Calibration

Our model has very few free parameters: the density of optimal savings rates, $f(s^*)$; the short-term discount factor, β; the scaling variable, κ; and the probability of a high-cost draw, μ. We further restrict this list by using individual employee data to pin down the density f (see next section). We set $\beta = 2/3$ reflecting a large body of experimental evidence and a growing body of field evidence. For example, Laibson, Repetto, and Tobacman (2003) use the method of simulated moments to estimate β using household financial data. Their benchmark estimate is 0.70 with a standard error of 0.11.

Only κ and μ remain to be calibrated. Before doing this we need to pick units for the variables in our model. We assume that time units are periods of a pay cycle (about two weeks). We assume that utility units can be interpreted in terms of a money metric in which one unit of utility is equal in value to one-tenth of a pay cycle of income. So when the cost realization is high ($c = 1$), opting out of the default generates a time cost that is equal in value to one-tenth of the agent's income during that pay cycle. We assume that such busyness is the norm and set $\mu = 0.9$. It then follows that the cost realization will be zero $0.1 = (1 - \mu)$ of the time.

---

7. However, it will not generally be the unique optimum.

To set κ, we use the following thought experiment. Suppose that a consumer is 10 percentage points away from her optimal savings rate: $| s_D - s^* |$ = 0.1. What is the money-metric cost of this deviation? Let x represent the loss in units of one-tenth of one pay cycle of income. Then, $\kappa(0.1)^2 = x$. We will consider a range of values for x: 0.1, 1, 10. This translates into the following range of values for κ: 10, 100, 1000. We consider this wide range for two reasons. First, we are agnostic about the appropriate calibration value. Second, we wish to explore the sensitivity of our results to the choice of κ. However, if forced to choose, we would set κ = 100, implying that a 10 percentage point deviation in one's savings rate is as bad as losing one-tenth of one's income during that pay cycle. For companies with an employer match, one could motivate losses of this magnitude by considering the missed match payments induced by undersaving.

2.2   Empirical Analysis

Table 2.1 shows the variation in both 401(k) plan design and employee characteristics of the four companies for which we compute the optimal default 401(k) savings rate. We denote these four companies by their industry: Health, Office, Food, and Finance. All are large employers with well-established 401(k) plans.

There are two key differences in the 401(k) plan environment that vary across the companies. First, two of the companies (Health and Office) match employee contributions up to 6 percent of pay, while the other two have no match at all. These latter companies are of interest because the distribution of employee contribution rates will not be affected by the pres-

Table 2.1   **Characteristics of employees and their 401(k) plans**

	Health company (1)	Office company (2)	Food company (3)	Financial company (4)
Employer match	$0.50/$1 to 6%	$0.67/$1 to 6%	None	None
Contribution rate range (%)	0 to 15	0 to 16	0 to 15	0 to 15
Company DB plan	No	Yes	Yes	No
401(k) participation rate (%)	61.9	74.2	32.8	63.4
Avg. 401(k) contribution rate (%)	4.3	4.5	2.0	6.0
Median salary ($)	31,034	27,629	25,355	41,109
Median age (years)	37.9	36.7	38.5	28.9
Median tenure (years)	4.8	5.4	5.6	2.0
Fraction female (%)	77.8	30.1	54.0	50.0
Year	1997	1998	1998	1998

Source: Company summary plan descriptions and calculations of the authors.

Notes: The sample in column (1) is all employees with 1+ year of tenure. The sample in column (2) is all employees with 2+ years of tenure. The sample in columns (3) and (4) is all employees.

ence of a match threshold. Having an employer match may either raise or lower the desired 401(k) contribution rate. Because the match subsidizes saving in the 401(k) plan, employees with a match may desire to contribute more, at least up to the match threshold. However, the match also increases the total amount of savings that is being done, and the employees may use the match as a means to offset their own contributions.

The second key difference in plan environment is that two of the companies (Office and Food) have an employer-sponsored defined benefit pension plan, while the other two do not. Other things being equal, we would expect a lower desired savings rate for employees in companies with a defined benefit pension.

The workforce demographics of our four companies also vary quite considerably. The median pay ranges from $25,000 per year in Food to $41,000 per year in Finance. Because Social Security replaces a higher fraction of income for low-income employees, we would expect a higher desired savings rate for high-income employees. There is also significant variation in the fraction of employees that are female (from 30 percent in Office to 78 percent in Health) and the median age of the workforce (from twenty-nine years in Finance to thirty-nine years in Food).

To estimate the distribution of optimal savings rates (i.e., the density f in the model), we use two approaches. First, we report densities over 401(k) savings rates for "medium-tenure" employees. We informally reason that such medium-tenure employees have been at a firm long enough to select their optimal savings rate (i.e., the option value of waiting and procrastination hurdles have been surmounted) but not so long that tenure-driven selection effects dominate the data. These savings densities are reported in table 2.2 for employees with three to five years of tenure (density f_1) and five to seven years of tenure (density f_2).

Second, we use a regression framework to control for demographic variables. We run an ordered logit regression in which the explanatory variable is the actual 401(k) contribution rate chosen by each individual employee. We include nonparticipation, which implies a 0 percent contribution rate, as one of the categories. The control variables in the regressions are ln(pay), ln(age), ln(tenure), and a gender dummy variable ($D = 1$ if the employee is female). We then predict the distribution of contribution rates that would obtain if each employee had thirty years of tenure, holding other demographic characteristics constant. The underlying presumption behind this exercise is that thirty years is enough time to overcome any delays due to procrastination or the option value of waiting. The projected density from this procedure is reported as density f_3 in table 2.2.

With these densities in hand, we are now in a position to estimate the optimal savings rate by minimizing equation (3), the social welfare function. We undertake this minimization for $3 \times 3 \times 4$ cases of interest: three different values for κ, three different ways of calculating the density f, and four

Table 2.2   Savings rate distributions

s^* (%)	Health company $f_1(s^*)$	$f_2(s^*)$	$f_3(s^*)$	Office company $f_1(s^*)$	$f_2(s^*)$	$f_3(s^*)$	Food company $f_1(s^*)$	$f_2(s^*)$	$f_3(s^*)$	Financial company $f_1(s^*)$	$f_2(s^*)$	$f_3(s^*)$
0	0.35	0.26	0.20	0.32	0.23	0.12	0.72	0.59	0.51	0.22	0.19	0.19
1	0.01	0.01	0.01	0.01	0.01	0.01	0.02	0.04	0.04	0.02	0.02	0.01
2	0.06	0.06	0.03	0.15	0.14	0.09	0.04	0.06	0.06	0.02	0.02	0.02
3	0.06	0.07	0.05	0.05	0.05	0.04	0.04	0.05	0.05	0.04	0.02	0.02
4	0.04	0.05	0.03	0.04	0.05	0.04	0.02	0.03	0.03	0.03	0.03	0.02
5	0.04	0.05	0.04	0.04	0.04	0.04	0.06	0.09	0.12	0.09	0.09	0.07
6	0.26	0.28	0.30	0.24	0.31	0.36	0.01	0.02	0.02	0.04	0.05	0.04
7	0.02	0.02	0.02	0.01	0.01	0.02	0.01	0.01	0.01	0.04	0.04	0.03
8	0.02	0.03	0.03	0.02	0.02	0.03	0.01	0.01	0.01	0.05	0.04	0.04
9	0.01	0.01	0.01	0.00	0.00	0.01	0.00	0.00	0.00	0.02	0.02	0.02
10	0.05	0.06	0.09	0.06	0.06	0.10	0.03	0.04	0.06	0.13	0.13	0.13
11	0.01	0.00	0.01	0.00	0.00	0.00	0.00	0.00	0.00	0.02	0.02	0.02
12	0.01	0.01	0.02	0.01	0.01	0.02	0.00	0.00	0.00	0.03	0.03	0.03
13	0.00	0.00	0.01	0.00	0.00	0.00	0.00	0.00	0.00	0.01	0.01	0.01
14	0.00	0.00	0.00	0.00	0.00	0.00	0.00	0.00	0.00	0.06	0.08	0.06
15	0.07	0.09	0.15	0.01	0.01	0.01	0.04	0.05	0.08	0.20	0.20	0.30
16	n.a.	n.a.	n.a.	0.04	0.05	0.11	n.a.	n.a.	n.a.	n.a.	n.a.	n.a.
Mean (%)	4.29	5.00	6.40	4.02	4.65	6.43	1.77	2.40	3.19	7.50	7.97	8.82

Notes: This table reports distributions of savings rates. $f_1(s^*)$ is the savings rate distribution of eligible employees at December 31, 1997, whose tenure is between three and five years. $f_2(s^*)$ is the savings rate distribution of eligible employees at December 31, 1997, whose tenure is between five and seven years. $f_3(s^*)$ is the distribution of optimal savings rates based on predicted values from an ordered logit regression of savings rate on age, gender, pay, and tenure. Predicted values are calculated using thirty years of tenure instead of actual tenure. n.a. = not applicable.

different test companies. The results of these minimizations are reported in table 2.3.

Table 2.3 documents six findings. First, the analysis reveals a high degree of heterogeneity in policy recommendations. The optimal default ranges from 0 percent to 15 percent. Moreover, even within a single firm there exists a large degree of variation in optimal defaults (e.g., Finance). Second, the range of variation in optimal defaults is twice as large as the range of average optimal savings rates. Third, the optimal default calculation is extremely sensitive to distributional assumptions on s^*. To see this, fix $\kappa = 100$ and read across the columns. The defaults show substantial variation arising from very small (within-company) differences in $f_1, f_2,$ and f_3 (see table 2.2). Fourth, as κ gets large, much of the variation in optimal defaults is driven by the mode effect. For $\kappa = 1,000$, five out of twelve of the optimal defaults are equal to the modal optimal savings rate. Fifth, the optimal defaults vary in a sensible way with the underlying firm-specific attributes. Firms whose employees have a high motive to save turn out to have higher optimal defaults than firms whose employees have a low motive to save. For example, the employees in Food have a defined benefit plan and a low average salary (i.e., a high average Social Security income replacement rate) and hence very low optimal defaults (0 percent to 3 percent). By contrast, the employees in Finance have no defined benefit plan, a high average salary, and a median optimal default of 14 percent. Sixth, and finally, the optimal defaults tend to cluster in one of three regions: close to 0 percent, close to the match threshold (6 percent for Health and Office), or close to the maximum contribution rate allowed under the plan.

2.3   Discussion and Conclusion

This paper has presented a model of 401(k) enrollment. The model includes four components: costs of opting out of a default, an option value of waiting to incur those costs, procrastination in opting out of a default, and heterogeneity in optimal savings rates.

One should also consider other important psychological and economic issues when picking socially optimal defaults. First, some employees may interpret defaults as implicit advice, an issue that does not arise in the current model since each employee is assumed to know her true optimal savings rate.[8] Second, defaults may be particularly sticky because of loss aversion.[9] If the default is perceived to be a reference point, then deviations from that reference point may be psychologically aversive, since the resulting "gains" from the deviation (e.g., higher current consumption) are only

8. Employees may treat a zero default as weaker implicit advice than a nonzero default.
9. See Kahneman and Tversky (1979), Thaler (1980), and Samuelson and Zeckhauser (1988) for a discussion of loss aversion and status quo bias.

Table 2.3   **Optimal default savings rates**

κ(%)	Health company			Office company			Food company			Financial company		
	$f_1(s^*)$	$f_2(s^*)$	$f_3(s^*)$	$f_1(s^*)$	$f_2(s^*)$	$f_3(s^*)$	$f_1(s^*)$	$f_2(s^*)$	$f_3(s^*)$	$f_1(s^*)$	$f_2(s^*)$	$f_3(s^*)$
10	4	5	6	4	5	6	2	2	3	7	8	9
100	2	2	14	2	2	5	1	1	2	2	14	14
1,000	0	0	15	6	6	6	0	0	0	15	15	15
Mean (%)	4.29	5.00	6.40	4.02	4.65	6.43	1.77	2.40	3.19	7.50	7.97	8.82
Mode (%)	0.00	6.00	6.00	0.00	6.00	6.00	0.00	0.00	0.00	0.00	15.00	15.00

Notes: This table shows the optimal savings rate for four different firms. Food company and Financial company have no employer match in their plans. See table 2.2 notes for explanations of variables. Predicted values are calculated using thirty years of tenure instead of actual tenure.

weighted half as much as the resulting "losses" (e.g., lower saving). Third, if households do not know how to think about the future or are overoptimistic about future income, they may undervalue savings. In such a world, it may be optimal to pick a high default savings rate, even if households eventually move away from it. Fourth, households may know the optimal savings rate but not appreciate how important it is to implement it, increasing action delays. Fifth, choosing a long-run savings rate that is 1 percentage point too low is more costly than choosing a long-run savings rate that is 1 percentage point too high (since retirement is short relative to working life and the utility function generates a precautionary savings motive[10]), suggesting a desirable upward shading of optimal defaults. Sixth, optimal savings rates are not constant over time (as we assume) but instead are likely to trend up slowly with working age. Seventh, the firm may wish to pick an optimal default that weights some employees more heavily than others. For example, it may be sensible to calculate optimal defaults that overweight the interests of employees that are likely to have a long duration of employment at the firm and underweight employees that are likely to separate relatively quickly. Future work should extend our theoretical framework by incorporating many of these additional considerations.

Future work should also explore the empirical implications of our model. The model makes quantitative predictions about the timing of savings rate changes. Employees who change their savings rate soon after they are hired should select larger changes than employees who change their savings rate long after they are hired. This is because employees who are willing to wait a long time for a low-cost opportunity to opt out of the default are likely to have little to gain from doing so. The model also predicts that average savings rates will not necessarily increase monotonically with the default savings rate. As the default savings rate rises, procrastination effects can strengthen, leading more agents to delay selecting an even higher savings rate. Such perverse effects have already been observed in the data (Madrian and Shea 2001; Choi et al. 2004).

Finally, the model suggests one important generalization that we are currently exploring (Choi et al. 2002a). If it is occasionally optimal to select "bad" defaults—that is, defaults that are not close to one's optimum saving rate—then it may be optimal to pick defaults that are so bad that all consumers feel compelled to immediately opt out of them. Such a setup is equivalent in practice to something that we call "active decision," a regime that forces new employees to pick their own savings rate early in their tenure at the company without the benefit of a fallback default. In a world with significant procrastination, such active decision regimes are sometimes the best "defaults" of all.

---

10. Precautionary savings effects arise when $u''' > 0$, a common assumption in applied economic models.

References

Akerlof, George A. 1991. Procrastination and obedience. *American Economic Review Papers and Proceedings* 81 (2): 1–19.

Choi, James J., David Laibson, Brigitte Madrian, and Andrew Metrick. 2002a. Active decisions: A natural experiment in saving. Harvard University, Department of Economics. Mimeograph.

———. 2002b. Defined contribution pensions: Plan rules, participant decisions, and the path of least resistance. In *Tax policy and the economy,* ed. James M. Poterba, 67–113. Cambridge, MA: MIT Press.

———. 2003. Optimal defaults. *American Economic Review Papers and Proceedings* 93 (2): 180–85.

———. 2004. For better or for worse: Default effects and 401(k) savings behavior. In *Perspectives in the economics of aging,* ed. David Wise, 81–121. Chicago: University of Chicago Press.

Kahneman, Daniel, and Amos Tversky. 1979. Prospect theory: An analysis of decision under risk. *Econometrica* 47 (2): 263–92.

Laibson, David. 1997. Golden eggs and hyperbolic discounting. *Quarterly Journal of Economics* 112 (2): 443–77.

Laibson, David, Andrea Repetto, and Jeremy Tobacman. 2003. Instant gratification over the lifecycle. Harvard University, Department of Economics. Mimeograph.

Madrian, Brigitte C., and Dennis Shea. 2001. The power of suggestion: Inertia in 401(k) participation and savings behavior. *Quarterly Journal of Economics* 116 (4): 1149–87.

O'Donoghue, Ted, and Matthew Rabin. 1999. Doing it now or later. *American Economic Review* 89 (1): 103–24.

Samuelson, William, and Richard Zeckhauser. 1988. Status quo bias in decision making. *Journal of Risk and Uncertainty* 1 (1): 7–59.

Thaler, Richard H. 1980. Toward a positive theory of consumer choice. *Journal of Economic Behavior and Organization* 1 (1): 39–60.

Comment   Antonio Rangel

The Question

A large number of companies and governments have introduced savings plans into the workplace. In a typical plan, individuals are allowed to contribute a percentage of their wages in exchange for a financial benefit such as a subsidized rate of return or a tax deduction. Since most plans offer significant financial advantages, one would expect participation rates to be high. Surprisingly, this is not the case. A series of recent papers have shown that a large fraction of employees either take too long to sign up for the plan (if they sign up at all) or fail to reoptimize their choices as their finan-

Antonio Rangel is an assistant professor of economics at Stanford University and a faculty research fellow of the National Bureau of Economic Research.

cial circumstances change. Subsequent research has shown that features of the savings plans that *have no effect on budget constraints,* such as the choice of defaults (Madrian and Shea 2001) or the timing and framing of questions (Benartzi and Thaler 2004), can have a sizable impact on the number and size of contributions.

These findings provide the motivation for the behavioral public economics question studied in this paper: How should a benevolent planner (e.g., the firm's benefit office) select defaults to minimize the mistakes made by individual workers?

Background

In order to understand the contribution and scope of this paper it is useful to start with a brief review of some of the psychological mechanisms have been proposed to explain the puzzling behaviors just described.

Transaction or decision-making costs (TCs). Deciding how much to contribute takes time and effort. Since the opportunity cost of these resources fluctuates with time, individuals are likely to wait for a period when TCs are low and to favor investment strategies that require little reoptimizing.

Procrastination. A sizable literature has shown (see, for example, Loewenstein, Read, and Baumeister 2003) that individuals tend to suboptimally postpone decisions that look like investments in the sense that they are costly in the present and generate benefits only in the future. This mechanism introduces an additional reason why employees may delay signing up for a savings plan, but only in cases where the financial costs of procrastination are not too large.

Imperfect attention. Individuals face a large number of decisions and routinely ignore most of them. In particular, unsophisticated decision makers may not think about savings unless appropriately cued to do so (Bernheim and Rangel 2003). Under this mechanism, workers postpone any choices related to the savings plan until they are exposed to a cue (such as an advertisement, a benefits fair, or a conversation with a family member) that helps them to focus their attention.

Fear of making mistakes and loss aversion. The psychological literature has shown that individuals postpone decisions when they are not sure about the right course of action. Some researchers have suggested that these fears are particularly paralyzing when poor choices can lead to financial losses.

Undersaving. All of the previous mechanisms provide reasons why workers may waste time in signing for the savings plan, but they cannot explain the low contribution rates. The mechanisms that have been proposed to explain that part of the puzzle include imperfections in internalizing the future benefits of savings, mistakes in calculating the amount of resources that are needed in retirement, and overoptimistic beliefs about investment returns.

It is important to emphasize that, with the exception of TCs, all of the mechanisms described in this section lead to systematic mistakes in decision making. A key assumption in this paper is that we can model the underlying psychological mechanisms at work and thus predict how mistakes change with behavioral features of the savings plan such as defaults.

A Sketch of the Model

The paper studies the role of default in a simple, elegant, and stationary model. Individuals are infinitely lived and need to choose how much they want to contribute to the savings plan every period. Once the choice is made, the contribution rate is fixed forever. Individuals differ on their optimal per-period savings rate s^*. Workers are required to contribute the default amount s^D unless they have explicitly signed up for a different rate. They incur a per-period quadratic *loss* in periods where their savings rate differs from s^* and do not discount future losses. Making decisions is costly. Transaction costs fluctuate stochastically: with probability μ the cost equals 1, with probability $1 - \mu$ the cost is zero.

Decision makers have a very special form of naive hyperbolic discounting. They always choose their optimal savings rate s^* when they show up to sign up for the plan. However, they may procrastinate in making that decision. More formally, the authors assume that individuals mistakenly over-discount all future utility flows by $\beta \in (0,1)$ when deciding when to sign for the plan. Their naïveté also leads them to incorrectly believe that they will not make similar mistakes in the future.

We can now provide a more precise description of the question studied in the paper: How should a benevolent planner set up defaults when (a) there are time-varying TCs and (b) people procrastinate in making saving choices (but then act optimally)? Psychological mechanisms such as imperfect attention or loss aversion are not taken into account.

Contribution and Intuition

The paper develops the following three nice insights.

Insight 1: In the presence of decision-making costs, the choice of default matters even without procrastination. The intuition is straightforward. Let $L = (s^D - s^*)^2$ denote the per-period losses incurred by an individual who has yet to sign up for the plan. Straightforward computations show that individuals with $L > 1 - \mu$ sign immediately, whereas the rest do so in the first time TCs are zero. Figure 2C.1 plots the expected lifetime total losses (including decision-making costs) for individuals with different s^*. An individual with $s^* = s^D$ never signs up for the plan and thus never experiences losses or pays TCs. Individuals with an optimal contribution rate that is sufficiently different from the default sign up immediately. This group experiences a lifetime loss equal to the expected TCs in period 1. Finally, individuals with optimal contribution rates between s^L and s^H wait to sign up

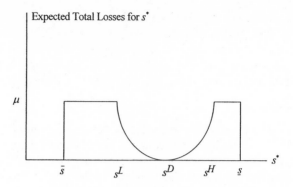

Fig. 2C.1   **Losses without procrastination**

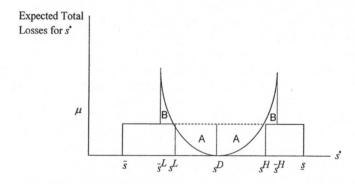

Fig. 2C.2   **Losses with procrastination**

for the plan until TCs are zero, and thus they experience an expected loss that increases with the square of $\left| s^* - s^D \right|$.

As can easily be seen in this picture, the optimal default depends on the distribution of individual preferences. If optimal saving rates are uniformly distributed between $\underline{s}$ and $\bar{s}$, then any default that is sufficiently far away from the corners is optimal. By contrast, if the distribution is a truncated normal centered around $(\underline{s} + \bar{s})/2$, the optimal default lies in the middle.

Insight 2: If there are TCs, procrastination, and sufficient heterogeneity, extreme defaults can be desirable. The intuition for this result is also simple. Straightforward computations show that the introduction of naive hyperbolic discounting induces a mistake for individuals with $L \in (1 - \mu, [1/\beta] - \mu)$: they should sign up immediately for the plan, but instead they procrastinate and wait until TCs are zero. The rest of the workforce behaves as before. This leads to the pattern of losses depicted in figure 2C.2. A comparison with figure 2C.1 illustrates the role that procrastination plays in the results. Individuals with optimal savings rates between $(\bar{s}^L, s^L)$ and $(s^H, \bar{s}^H)$

wait too long to sign up and thus experience additional losses. The number of individuals making mistakes and the size of their losses increase with the strength of the procrastination.

The potential attractiveness of extreme defaults follows immediately. Suppose that individuals are homogeneously distributed. If area B is larger than area A, then the optimal default is to set a default that is extremely high or low, which induces everyone to sign up in the first period. This increases social TCs by A but reduces the size of mistakes by an even larger amount.

Insight 3: In a large class of environments the optimal default is better than forcing all employees to make a choice. The intuition for this point follows immediately from the previous discussion since forcing everyone to make a choice is equivalent to picking a default that is sufficiently unattractive for everyone.

Other Issues to be Considered when Choosing Defaults

I conclude this discussion by developing some conjectures about what happens to the optimal default policy when additional psychological forces are at work.

Undersaving. Suppose that individuals choose suboptimally low contribution rates when they sign up for the plan. This would be predicted, among others, by a model where individuals exhibit hyperbolic discounting in all dimensions. Conjecture: When the undersaving mistakes are large enough, the optimal default looks like a mandatory contribution rate: TCs are increased to the point where all individuals stay with the default, and the default targets the average worker.

Imperfect attention. Suppose that there are no TCs but that individuals only think about savings in any given period with some probability p that is increasing in the size of the loss L. Conjecture: In this case the optimal default is close to average optimal savings rate and favors groups which, perhaps due to a lack of sophistication or education, exhibit lower probabilities of thinking about savings.

Inertia and Ignorance. Suppose that the presence of a default leads individuals to make a mistake when choosing their contribution rate. For example, they might mistakenly assume that the default is the right contribution rate for them. In that case forcing individuals to make a choice at time 1 might dominate the class of default policies studied in this paper (see Choi, Madrian, and Metrick 2002 for a related discussion).

References

Benartzi, Shlomo, and Richard Thaler. 2004. Save more tomorrow: Using behavioral economics to increase employee savings. *Journal of Political Economy* 112 (1): 164–87.

Bernheim, Douglas, and Antonio Rangel. 2003. Emotions, cognition, and savings: Theory and policy. Stanford University, Department of Economics. Manuscript.

Choi, James J., Brigitte C. Madrian, and Andrew Metrick. 2002. Defined contribution pensions: Plan rules, participant decisions, and the path of least resistance. In *Tax policy and the economy,* ed. James M. Poterba, 67–113. Cambridge: MIT Press.

Loewenstein, George, Daniel Read, and Roy F. Baumeister. 2003. *Time and decision: Economic and psychological perspectives on intertemporal choice.* Russell Sage Foundation.

Madrian, Brigitte, and Dennis Shea. 2001. The power of suggestion: Inertia in 401(k) participation and savings behavior. *Quarterly Journal of Economics* 116 (4): 1149–87.

3

Characterizing the Experiences of High-Cost Users in Medicare

Thomas MaCurdy and Jeff Geppert

3.1 Introduction

Public expenditures on health care for the elderly are rising at a relentless rate, with government unable to maintain the current per capita level of services in the next decade without either substantial increases in taxes or radical reductions in other domestic spending. Medicare and Medicaid expenses for the elderly reached over 4 percent of gross domestic product (GDP) in 2000, having grown at more than a 4 percent real rate during the past decade. The majority of this growth has been concentrated among a small segment of Medicare beneficiaries. Those ranked in the top 5 percent of the expenditure distribution alone accounted for nearly half of the growth in total Medicare expenditures; those in the top 20 percent accounted for more than 80 percent of this growth. Clearly, any policy offering hope of success in mitigating the unsustainable rise in Medicare/Medicaid expenses must focus its impacts on these highest-cost groups.

A key source of knowledge required for policy design concerns identification of the high-cost users of health care and characterizing the patterns of their use. Discovering high-intensity users is not as easy a task as one might first surmise, for this alone provides few insights unless one can also

Thomas MaCurdy is a professor of economics and senior fellow of the Hoover Institution, Stanford University, and a research associate of the National Bureau of Economic Research. Jeff Geppert is a senior research associate of SPHERE Institute and member at Acumen, L.L.C.

The authors gratefully acknowledge research support from NIA grant AG05842 from the National Institute on Aging. We are grateful for substantive research contributions and comments from our colleague Grecia Marrufo and for sophisticated research assistance from Hugh Roghmann and West Addison. Opinions expressed in this paper are those of the authors and do not represent the official position or policy of any agency funding this research.

develop profiles linking attributes of these groups to their intense utilization. Characterizing such attributes reveals what behaviors policies must alter to be successful in curtailing program costs. For example, studies indicating that the majority of high-cost users are in their last year of life suggest that a large fraction of expenditures go to postponing inevitable mortality, implying that society must value short extensions in life at high values to justify the expenditures. Further, it suggests that capping expenses per person over a year will have only a minor impact on mortality, for such a policy primarily brings about an inevitable death earlier. Alternatively, programs proposed in Medicare to manage diseases or chronic conditions maintain that these afflictions identify high-cost uses and improved treatment will lower overall expenditures by preventing worsening circumstances leading to utilization of expensive services.

Upon identifying high-cost users, a vital characteristic for policy design concerns the concentration and persistence of their utilization. Do the bulk of expenses for these users occur in a short period, such as a year, or are they spread out over time? If costs are concentrated over short periods, annual limits on spending will be effective in containing overall costs and programs such as medical savings accounts will have poor prospects in lowering costs. On the other hand, if persistence exists in costs per person over time, then lifetime limits on expenses must be in force to control total expenditures.

The following analysis explores patterns of expenses for high-cost users of Medicare, with the aim of creating a transparent approach for identifying those beneficiaries responsible for the bulk of expenditures and for discovering the concentration of their health care utilization. In undertaking this analysis, the study exploits a rich longitudinal sample that we have constructed from detailed Medicare claims data for the years 1989 to 1999 for 5 percent of all beneficiaries. This data set supplies comprehensive monthly information for each beneficiary, tracking expenditures, treatments, and diagnoses associated with each month. The analysis considers a variety of time frames and approaches for selecting groups of intense users of medical services and for summarizing their monthly experiences.

An important first step required in undertaking such a study involves understanding how secular growth in overall Medicare expenditures influences the incidence of high-cost users over time. Indeed, given the substantial and sustained growth in Medicare seen throughout most of the 1990s, highest-cost users would mostly consist of those beneficiaries who live in the later part of the period if one naively considers only the real levels of expenditures to define intensity of use. If, on the other hand, one defines intense use by indexing expenses in a way to capture the quantity of services consumed, then the consequences of secular growth depend on whether growth occurs differentially across the amounts of medical services acquired by Medicare beneficiaries. In particular, if secular growth disproportionately induces larger increases for the most intense users, then their share of total expenditure rises; and it falls if the lowest-intensity users consume the services experiencing the larger growth in expenses.

To develop knowledge of how Medicare expenditures have grown during the 1990s, and the degree to which growth has occurred disproportionately across intensity of medical usage, we update a cohort-time empirical framework that we have implemented extensively in previous work. The analysis naturally accommodates such issues as the changing composition of the population of Medicare enrollees. Some hypotheses about the sources of expenditure growth can also be investigated well by this approach. For example, there have been proposals in the United States and elsewhere to limit the use of expensive procedures among the very old, based at least in part on the belief that expenditure growth has been concentrated among the very old. Alternatively, if expenditure growth is equally distributed across all ages and cohorts, then the most promising approaches to cost containment will not be limited to a particular demographic group. Although this descriptive work does not seek to identify the specific sources of expenditure growth, it provides important information needed for more detailed analyses.

Using our cohort framework and annual expenditure thresholds to define various classifications for high-cost users, we characterize the monthly experiences of these beneficiaries by describing properties of the intertemporal distribution of their expenditures. This includes not only the number of high-cost months experienced by these intense users of medical services, but also the number and length of spells associated with high-cost months. Knowledge of these properties informs one about not only the level of lifetime expenditures allotted to persons but also the degree of concentration in this spending within and across years. Moreover, it promises to offer a valuable approach for identifying high-cost users based on monthly experiences rather than annual measures, which might miss some of the more intense users whose experiences are spread out over longer periods of accumulated expenses. The work report provided here is not designed to assess the effectiveness of specific policies but instead is designed to provide insight into the potential usefulness of a variety of broad strategies toward cost containment.

The remainder of this paper consists of four sections. Section 3.2 describes our monthly longitudinal Medicare data, and section 3.3 summarizes methods for characterizing the growth in annual Medicare expenditures using our cohort approach that identifies separate trends among low- and high-cost users of Medicare services by beneficiary age. Section 3.3 ends with a discussion of our findings on the growth in expenditures. Section 3.4 presents an array of results revealing properties of the monthly experiences of high-cost users over their lifetimes. Finally, section 3.5 offers a summary of our findings and concluding remarks.

3.2   Overview of Our Longitudinal Medicare Data

Developing a comprehensive picture of the concentration and persistence of health care expenditures across people and over time requires detailed longitudinal data summarizing the experiences of individuals during extended portions of their lifetimes while recognizing that profiles may be changing across years or cohorts. Our data consist of a 5 percent sample of all Medicare beneficiaries, starting with a random cross section of participants in 1989 supplemented by random samples of new entrants in each year covered by our data. For each sample member, our data provide information by month describing the expenses paid by Medicare for the person's medical services—both part A and B—along with the treatments and diagnoses assigned to the expenditure. No individual leaves our sample unless they die.

After describing the derivation and structure of our longitudinal Medicare data, the following discussion summarizes results from a comprehensive analysis undertaken to validate our variable constructions through comparison of statistics on the levels and trends in aggregate enrollment, program payments, and participation rates computed from our data to a variety of published statistics reported by the Centers for Medicare and Medicaid Services (CMS). The section goes on to present summary statistics characterizing the evolution of participation rates and averages for program payments and expenditures, distinguishing beneficiaries according to whether they received part A or part B services.

3.2.1   Description of the Data

The source of our longitudinal Medicare data is annual enrollment and claims data collected by the CMS. These are administrative data used by CMS to verify eligibility and to process hospital and physician claims for payment on behalf of Medicare beneficiaries. Enrollment data capture eligibility and demographic information at a point in time (typically July 1 of each calendar year). Claims data are requests for payment for a particular service provided during a given period of time, and they include information on the ICD-9-CM diagnosis and procedure codes, CPT-4/HCPCS codes, revenue center codes, provider type or specialty, Medicare reimbursement, third-party payments, beneficiary copayments, and deductibles. Claim formats vary depending on the type of provider and whether the claims were processed by a fiscal intermediary (hospital insurance under part A) or a carrier (supplemental medical insurance under part B). Only those beneficiaries enrolled in Medicare fee-for-service generate claims data. Medicare collects some encounter data on beneficiaries en-

Table 3.1   **Summary of Medicare enrollment and claims data**

File name	Description	Number of claims[a]
	Enrollment	
Denominator	Beneficiary eligibility, demographic and geographic data	38,000,000
Group health plan	Medicare managed care enrollment data	5,700,000
	Hospital insurance (part A)	
Inpatient	Claims for inpatient hospital services, including rehabilitation and psychiatric hospitals	618,159
Skilled nursing facility	Claims for skilled nursing facility services	166,782
Home health agency	Claims for home health agency	614,019
Hospice	Hospice enrollment and claims	57,078
	Supplement Medicare insurance (part B)	
Outpatient	Hospital outpatient claims	5,255,402
Physician/Supplier	Physician claims (including clinical laboratory)	30,101,027
Durable medical equipment	Durable Medicare equipment claims	1,978,433

[a]5 percent random sample of Medicare beneficiaries.

rolled in Medicare managed care, but the data are not complete.[1] Table 3.1 summarizes the enrollment and claim files and the number of claims per service type in a random 5 percent sample of Medicare beneficiaries.

Claims data in raw format are not useful for analyses of beneficiary utilization and expenditures over time because such an analysis requires aggregating enrollment, service use, program payments, and beneficiary payments across claims, service types, and dates of service. Information on diagnoses and procedures need to be summarized for analyses of beneficiaries with particular conditions and treatments. Enrollment data capturing point-in-time status must be validated and made consistent to reflect continuous enrollment status in Medicare fee-for-service and managed care.

To convert these data into a format useful for conducting analyses of beneficiary utilization and expenditures over time, we created longitudinal enrollment, utilization, and expenditure files that summarize data on approximately two million Medicare beneficiaries over an eleven-year time period

1. The absence of Medicare expenditures for the elderly enrolled in managed care plans is the one shortcoming of this data set, and it is difficult to predict how this limitation affects our results. Conventional wisdom suggests that managed care enrollees are likely to be healthier than fee-for-service Medicare recipients, meaning that their expenditures are likely to be lower. However, the growth in expenditures for Medicare managed care is likely to mirror that observed in fee-for-service claims, and it is the trends (rather than levels) in expenses in which we are primarily interested. Over time, the fraction of the Medicare population electing managed care has fallen, with the peak occurring in the early 1990s, followed by a steady decline.

from 1989 to 1999. These data contain the beneficiaries' monthly enrollment status, including part A and part B enrollment, managed care enrollment, and mortality using date of death information from linked Social Security records. These data also contain monthly utilization and expenditure data by service type, including inpatient hospital, skilled nursing facility (SNF), home health agency, hospice, outpatient hospital, physician (including clinical lab), and durable medical equipment. Inpatient hospital utilization and expenditure data are separated into two categories: inpatient stays paid under the prospective payment system (PPS) and non-PPS stays, which include rehabilitation and psychiatric stays, in addition to some non-PPS hospitals. Utilization data include monthly counts of the number of inpatient hospital and skilled nursing admissions by diagnosis-related group (DRG) and number of home health, outpatient hospital, and physician visits by principal diagnosis. Physician visits are further separated by physician specialty. Expenditure data include monthly Medicare program payments, third-party payments, and beneficiary payments (copayments and deductibles), with indicators supplied signaling assigned DRG (for inpatient hospital and SNF) or principal diagnosis (home health, outpatient hospital, and physician). ICD-9-CM diagnosis and procedure codes are summarized into monthly arrays by service type and separately by principal and secondary codes. Likewise, CPT-4/HCPCS codes and revenue center codes are summarized into monthly arrays by service type.

Our longitudinal Medicare data greatly facilitate analysis of beneficiary utilization and expenditures over the life of a beneficiary by allowing aggregation of service use and program payments over time (e.g., identifying high-cost monthly or annual expenditures), across services types (e.g., summarizing into total hospital insurance [HI] or supplemental medical insurance [SMI]), across beneficiary demographic characteristics (e.g., age or enrollment status), and across various conditions and treatments. These data permit a much richer set of analyses of the sources of Medicare expenditure growth than is possible with aggregate statistics on Medicare spending by broad demographic groups, such as those used by actuaries to forecast future Medicare trust fund balances.

3.2.2   Validation with CMS Published Statistics

To ensure, however, that our longitudinal Medicare data accurately reflect aggregate Medicare spending, we conducted a series of analyses to validate Medicare enrollment and spending calculated from claims against published statistics reported by the CMS in the annual statistical supplement of the *Health Care Financing Review*. Although the statistics published by the CMS are also derived from claims data, our claims data may potentially yield different results due to errors in data processing during the copying and conversion process from the CMS mainframe files or due to a lag in the claims reconciliation process when the claims data that we use were extracted. There are also methodological issues to replicate, such as the determination of the appropriate denominator for calculation of participation rates and average spending. Here we present our results replicating CMS published statistics on enrollment and total spending.

The Balanced Budget Act of 1997 (BBA97) had a significant impact on aggregate Medicare spending and therefore on the trends in average Medicare spending that we report later in this paper. The major provisions of BBA97 included direct reductions to the PPS inpatient hospital annual operating update, PPS inpatient capital payments, indirect medical education (IME) payments, disproportionate share (DSH) payments, direct medical education (DME) payments, and expansion of the transfer policy (which reduces payments for transfers of short-term acute patients in ten DRGs who were discharged to an SNF, PPS-exempt facilities, or a home health agency). Other provisions included the implementation of prospective payment systems for outpatient hospital, skilled nursing facilities, and home health agencies, and the creation of Medicare+Choice managed care plans and more equitable payments for such plans across geographic areas. As the following results demonstrate, however, these changes appear to have caused a large one-time reduction in aggregate Medicare spending, but growth rates and trends appear largely to have reverted to pre-BBA97 levels.

Enrollment

Figure 3.1 compares Medicare enrollment as reported by the CMS in the statistical supplement through 2003 to the same statistic calculated by us

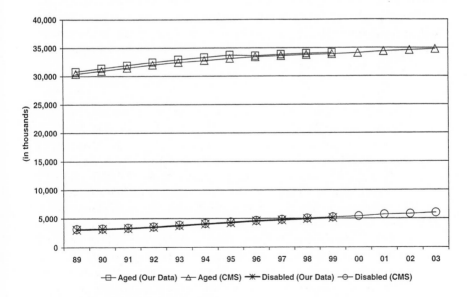

Fig. 3.1   **Total Medicare enrollment**

using Medicare enrollment files for calendar years 1989 to 1999. Enrollment is reported in units of one thousand. The CMS reports enrollment as a count of beneficiaries at a point in time, namely July 1 of the calendar year, rather than as a count of any beneficiary enrolled at any time during the calendar year. We follow the CMS methodology and report enrollment separately by entitlement (i.e., aged or disabled). In general, enrollment from claims and from the CMS is very close, differing by about 1–2 percent on average for aged beneficiaries, with the difference less than 1 percent for more recent years (since 1996). That amounts to a difference of about 300,000 per year out of 32 to 34 million aged beneficiaries. Our enrollment is slightly higher than the CMS's, which may reflect an imputation on our part of enrollment for beneficiaries that are Medicare eligible due to reaching age sixty-five but that do not appear in Medicare enrollment files until they use Medicare services at an age greater than sixty-five. For disabled beneficiaries, our enrollment counts are slightly lower than CMS's, differing by about 2–3 percent on average. The absolute magnitude of the difference is only about 100,000 beneficiaries out of three to five million.

The results show that Medicare enrollment for aged beneficiaries has grown by about 1 percent per year from 1989 to 1999, from slightly over 30 million to slightly over 34 million. The growth rate was nearly 2 percent in the early years of the decade and declined to less than 1 percent in more recent years. Medicare enrollment for disabled beneficiaries has grown much more rapidly, averaging more than 5 percent per year over the eleven-year time period. As a consequence, the share of beneficiaries entitled due to disability has grown from 9 percent to 13 percent over the decade. Current CMS estimates show that the share reached nearly 15 percent by 2003. Because disabled beneficiaries use more services on average than aged beneficiaries, the growing share of disabled beneficiaries has potential implications for growth in Medicare spending.

Program Payments

Figure 3.2 shows total Medicare program payments from claims data for calendar years 1989 to 1999 and from the CMS through 2003. Medicare reports program payments, which only include monies dispensed from the Medicare trust funds and do not include third-party or beneficiary payments. They also do not include payments made to health plans for Medicare managed care enrollees. We report spending separately for part A (HI) and part B (SMI). For part A, total spending from claims differs from total spending reported by CMS by about 2 percent each year, with spending from claims slightly lower than spending reported by the CMS. In part, this might be due to a lag in claims for larger expenses that take more time to adjudicate. However, the trend in part A spending from claims tracks very closely with the trend in part A spending reported by

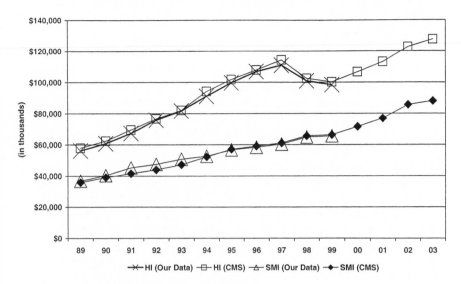

Fig. 3.2   Total Medicare program payments

CMS. Part A spending grew by more than 6 percent per year, with growth exceeding 9 percent per year until the BBA97, when total part A spending actually dropped by 3 percent per year on average. Part A spending grew from $56 billion in 1989 to a peak of $111 billion in 1996, before falling to $98 billion by 1999. More recent statistics reported by the CMS suggest that part A spending has returned to pre-BBA97 levels and growth rates. Part A spending reached $128 billion in 2003, growing at an annual rate of 6 percent since 1999.

Total part B spending from claims differs from part B spending reported by the CMS by 2.5 percent per year on average, although in more recent years the difference is only around 1 percent. The difference is greatest from 1991 to 1994, when CMS was converting to a different claims process for durable medical equipment. The trend in part B spending from claims tracks very closely to the trend in part B spending reported by CMS. Part B spending grew by more than 6 percent per year, and the rate of growth was not affected by the BBA97 as dramatically as part A spending. Part B spending grew from $36 billion in 1989 to $66 billion in 1999. In recent years, part B spending has continued to grow at 6–7 percent per year, reaching $88 billion in 2003. Before the BBA97, part B spending as a share of total Medicare spending had fallen from 40 percent to 35 percent, primarily because of rapid growth in nonacute part A spending in home health agency and skilled nursing facility services. After the BBA97, part B spending reverted to its earlier 40 percent share of total spending, and this share remained constant through 2003.

Participation Rates

Figure 3.3 shows participation rates under part A and part B for calendar years 1989 to 1999. The participation rate is defined as the number of Medicare beneficiaries receiving services paid for with program funds during the calendar year divided by the number of Medicare beneficiaries enrolled during the calendar year. For both part A and part B, participation rates calculated from claims and reported by CMS in published statistics are very close. Validation of participation rates (in addition to aggregate spending and enrollment) is important for accurately reflecting trends in average beneficiary spending. Part A participation rates rose slightly from 1989 to 1994, from 201 to 219 per 1,000 beneficiaries. Starting in 1995, CMS began excluding managed care enrollees from the denominator of participation rates, so the participation rates increased slightly to 230 per 1,000 beneficiaries, where it has remained relatively constant in recent years. Part B participation rates also rose slightly from 1989 to 1994, from 755 to 815 per 1,000 beneficiaries. After managed care enrollees were excluded from the denominator, the part B participation rate rose to 833 per 1,000 in 1996 and has continued to increase slightly, reaching 842 per 1,000 beneficiaries in 1999, an increase of around 1 percent per year from 1995 to 1999. Figure 3.3 also shows managed care enrollment, which increased from 5 percent in 1989 to 18 percent in 1999, an increase of 12 percent per year, with most of the increase occurring after 1994. The BBA97, which included provisions to encourage managed care enrollment, seems to have

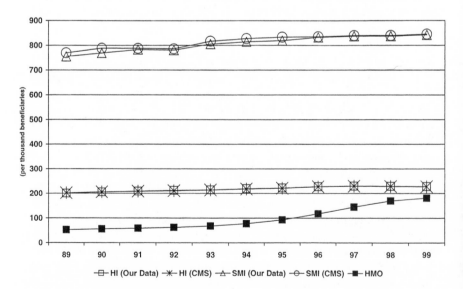

Fig. 3.3   Medicare participation rates

reduced or reversed the rate of growth. The most recent estimates from CMS place managed care enrollment at 5.3 million of 40.8 million beneficiaries (13 percent).

3.2.3   Simple Summaries of Trends in Aggregate Spending

Using the validated longitudinal Medicare data, we calculated summary statistics and trends on the average Medicare program payments and expenditures for the period 1989 to 1999. As mentioned earlier, program payments are funds paid by the Medicare program on behalf of the beneficiary. Expenditures include third-party payments, in addition to beneficiary copayments and deductibles. All results are reported in constant (2000) dollars.

Table 3.2 shows participation rates and average program payments and expenditures for beneficiaries with some part A service use and with some part A or B service use. In other words, the denominator of the averages excludes beneficiaries with no part A or no part A or B service use. For part A, participation rates have risen steadily over the time period, as mentioned earlier, at an average annual increase of 1 percent per year. In addition, for those receiving part A services, the average program payment has risen from $11,168 to $13,259 in constant dollars, an average annual increase of 1.7 percent per year. Prior to BBA97, the average annual increase was nearly 3 percent per year. Expenditures are approximately 8 percent higher than program payments due to third-party payments and beneficiary copayments and deductibles. For those receiving part A services, expenditures have grown slightly faster than program payments from $11,938 to $14,443, an average annual increase of 1.9 percent per year (3.1 percent per year prior to BBA97). Taken together, these results suggest

Table 3.2   Average Medicare program payments, expenditures, and participation rates (2000 $)

	Part A only			Parts A and B		
Year	Participation rate (%)	Program payments ($)	Expenditures ($)	Participation rate (%)	Program payments ($)	Expenditures ($)
1989	20.6	11,168	11,938	81.1	4,542	5,299
1990	21.1	11,020	12,125	82.3	4,552	5,434
1991	21.5	11,304	12,452	84.5	4,668	5,599
1992	21.8	11,971	13,134	84.4	4,896	5,862
1993	22.0	12,234	13,365	85.6	4,960	5,914
1994	22.6	12,847	14,030	85.9	5,188	6,170
1995	22.9	13,441	14,623	86.1	5,466	6,484
1996	23.6	13,868	15,037	87.4	5,640	6,675
1997	23.9	14,099	15,292	87.8	5,775	6,843
1998	23.8	13,542	14,738	87.6	5,632	6,734
1999	23.1	13,259	14,443	87.4	5,495	6,599

that the total increase in part A program payments from 1989 to 1999 can be approximately attributed to the following factors: the increase in beneficiaries (3.5 percent), the increase in the part A participate rate (37.8 percent), the increase in the average program payment per part A service recipient (53.7 percent), and residual (8 percent). Therefore, over one-half of the increase in part A program payments is attributable to an increase in program payments per part A recipient, even after the direct reductions in part A payments implemented by the BBA97.

For part A or B, participation rates have also risen steadily over the time period from 81 percent to 87 percent, an average annual increase of nearly 1 percent per year. In addition, for those receiving part A or B services, the average program payment has risen from $4,542 to $5,495 in constant dollars, an average annual increase of 1.9 percent per year. Prior to BBA97, the average annual increase was nearly 3 percent per year. Expenditures are approximately 17 percent higher than program payments due to third-party payments and beneficiary copayments and deductibles. For those receiving part A or part B services, expenditures have grown slightly faster than program payments, from $5,299 to $6,599, an average annual increase of 2.2 percent per year (3.2 percent per year prior to BBA97). Taken together, these results suggest that the total increase in part A or B program payments from 1989 to 1999 can be approximately attributed to the following factors: the increase in beneficiaries (3.8 percent), the increase in the part A or B participant rate (24.3 percent), the increase in the average program payment per part A or B service recipient (65.7 percent), and residual (6 percent). Therefore, almost two-thirds of the increase in part A or B program payments is attributable to an increase in program payments per part A or B recipient. An even larger share of the increase in part B program payments is attributable to an increase in program payments per part B recipient.

Table 3.3 shows average Medicare program payments and expenditures per Medicare beneficiary, including those with and without services. In other words, the change in the averages over time reflects both changes in the participation rate and changes in program payments or expenditures per service recipient. The top panel shows averages for both aged and disabled beneficiaries. The bottom panel shows averages for aged beneficiaries only. For all beneficiaries, the average part A program payment increased from $2,301 to $3,066, an average annual increase of 2.9 percent. The average part B program payment increased from $1,385 to $1,737, an average annual increase of 2.3 percent. The average total program payment increased from $3,686 to $4,803, an average annual increase of 2.6 percent. Expenditures were higher than program payments by 8 percent for part A, 31 percent for part B, and 17 percent overall, and they grew about 0.5 percent faster than program payments.

Table 3.3   **Average Medicare program payments and expenditures, by year and type of beneficiary (2000 $)**

	Part A		Part B		Total	
	Program payments ($)	Expenditures ($)	Program payments ($)	Expenditures ($)	Program payments ($)	Expenditures ($)
All beneficiaries						
1989	2,301	2,460	1,385	1,840	3,686	4,300
1990	2,324	2,557	1,422	1,915	3,746	4,472
1991	2,430	2,677	1,517	2,057	3,947	4,734
1992	2,611	2,865	1,520	2,081	4,131	4,945
1993	2,691	2,940	1,553	2,120	4,244	5,060
1994	2,901	3,168	1,557	2,134	4,458	5,302
1995	3,076	3,347	1,627	2,234	4,703	5,580
1996	3,271	3,547	1,658	2,286	4,929	5,833
1997	3,375	3,660	1,696	2,348	5,070	6,007
1998	3,218	3,502	1,713	2,394	4,931	5,896
1999	3,066	3,339	1,737	2,429	4,803	5,768
Aged						
1989	2,253	2,407	1,370	1,822	3,623	4,230
1990	2,273	2,500	1,406	1,896	3,680	4,396
1991	2,389	2,629	1,509	2,047	3,898	4,675
1992	2,570	2,816	1,507	2,065	4,077	4,881
1993	2,665	2,908	1,534	2,096	4,200	5,003
1994	2,898	3,161	1,544	2,115	4,442	5,276
1995	3,091	3,360	1,614	2,214	4,705	5,574
1996	3,299	3,573	1,643	2,265	4,942	5,838
1997	3,423	3,706	1,682	2,327	5,105	6,033
1998	3,254	3,537	1,709	2,383	4,963	5,921
1999	3,109	3,387	1,739	2,429	4,848	5,816

For aged beneficiaries, the average part A program payment increased from $2,253 to $3,109, an average annual increase of 3.2 percent. The average part B program payment increased from $1,370 to $1,739, an average annual increase of 2.4 percent. The average total program payment increased from $3,623 to $4,848, an average annual increase of 2.9 percent. Expenditures are higher than program payments in the same proportions as above, and grew slightly faster. Average part A program payments and expenditures for the aged are lower than program payments and expenditures overall until around 1995, when part A program payments and expenditures for the aged become greater than the equivalent amounts overall. Average part B program payments and expenditures for the aged are consistently lower than the equivalent amounts overall throughout the time period because average program payments and expenditures for disabled beneficiaries are greater, and disabled beneficiaries are becoming a higher share of the total population. Despite the increase in the share, however, part A program payments and expenditures for the disabled population declined relative to the aged population since 1996.

3.3   Characterizing Growth in Annual Expenditures

The subsequent discussion presents a concise characterization of the growth in annual Medicare spending during the 1990s, characterizing the experiences of cohorts and describing how cross-section distributions have changed over time. Descriptive tables provide the foundation for more formal models summarizing the secular growth in expenditures, along with the disproportionate impact of this growth on various segments of Medicare beneficiaries distinguished by their age and intensity of medical-care use. Our cohort analysis offers a rich framework for describing the rate of growth of expenditures by percentile groups by age, along with the cross-sectional relationship between expenditures and age. In addition, our analysis summarizes growth in participation rates in part A and part B services.

3.3.1   Shifts in the Distribution of Medicare Expenditures

We characterize the growth in annual Medicare expenditures by identifying separate trends among low- and high-cost users of Medicare services by beneficiary age.

Annual Expenditure Percentiles

Table 3.4 shows the level of annual expenditures by beneficiary percentile by year from 1989 to 1999. Percentiles shown are the 10th, 25th, 50th, 80th, 90th, 95th, and 98th. Expenditures are highly concentrated. In

Table 3.4   Percentiles for annual expenditures for Medicare participants

Year	Levels of annual cost percentiles (2000 $)						
	10	25	50	80	90	95	98
1989	117	316	960	6,892	14,779	24,753	40,578
1990	124	334	1,020	7,090	15,221	25,313	41,261
1991	136	362	1,088	7,301	15,707	26,075	42,351
1992	151	384	1,142	7,576	16,479	27,418	43,841
1993	145	379	1,142	7,464	16,618	27,968	44,879
1994	153	394	1,202	7,754	17,677	29,702	46,879
1995	161	415	1,279	8,114	18,655	31,430	49,323
1996	161	415	1,308	8,337	19,317	32,539	51,384
1997	167	433	1,372	8,520	19,940	33,647	53,011
1998	179	459	1,436	8,265	19,256	32,592	51,849
1999	196	495	1,501	8,134	18,678	31,551	49,928

1989, annual expenditures for the 90th percentile were 125 times greater than the annual expenditures for the 10th percentile. The levels ranged from $117 to $14,779. Annual expenditures for the 98th percentile were 2.7 times greater than the annual expenditures for the 90th percentile, with the level of the 98th percentile reaching $40,578. The median annual expenditure was $960. In any given year there are a few Medicare beneficiaries with extremely high expenditures, while most beneficiaries spend less than $1,000 annually.

In general, the growth rates have been greater for the lower percentiles than for the higher percentiles over the decade. For example, average annual expenditures for the 10th percentile increased from $117 to $196, an average annual growth rate of 5.1 percent. The average annual expenditure for the 50th percentile increased from $960 to $1,501, an average annual growth rate of 4.5 percent. The average annual expenditure for the 98th percentile increased from $40,578 to $49,928, an average annual growth rate of 2.1 percent. Post-BBA97 growth rates for the 80th, 90th, 95th, and 98th percentiles were actually negative, at –2.3 percent, –3.3 percent, –3.2 percent, and –3.0 percent, respectively. The BBA97 had the greatest impact on the high end of the annual expenditure distribution.

Share of Total Expenditures by Percentile

Table 3.5 shows the share of total Medicare expenditures accounted for by beneficiaries in the 0–50, 50–80, 80–90, 90–95, 95–98, and 98+ average annual expenditure percentile categories. In 1989, beneficiaries below the median average annual expenditure accounted for only 3.5 percent of total Medicare expenditures; beneficiaries in the 50–80 percentile category accounted for 16.7 percent; beneficiaries in the 80–90 percentile category

Table 3.5   **Share of annual Medicare expenditures accounted for by annual percentile groups (%)**

	Annual percentile categories						
Year	0–50	50–80	80–90	90–95	95–98	98+	Total
1989	3.5	16.7	19.3	18.3	18.0	24.2	100.0
1990	3.6	17.0	19.4	18.3	17.9	23.8	100.0
1991	3.8	17.1	19.4	18.3	17.9	23.6	100.0
1992	3.8	17.1	19.5	18.4	17.9	23.4	100.0
1993	3.8	16.6	19.2	18.5	18.1	23.9	100.0
1994	3.7	16.5	19.3	18.7	18.2	23.6	100.0
1995	3.8	16.5	19.4	18.8	18.1	23.4	100.0
1996	3.7	16.3	19.4	18.8	18.2	23.6	100.0
1997	3.7	16.3	19.3	18.9	18.2	23.6	100.0
1998	4.0	16.5	19.0	18.6	18.1	23.9	100.0
1999	4.4	16.9	19.0	18.4	17.8	23.6	100.0

accounted for 19.3 percent; beneficiaries in the 90–95 percentile category accounted for 18.3 percent; beneficiaries in the 95–98 percentile category accounted for 18.0 percent; and beneficiaries in the 98+ percentile category accounted for 24.2 percent. Because average annual expenditures grew more slowly for the higher percentiles, the share of total expenditures accounted for by the higher percentiles fell slightly. In 1999, the share of total Medicare expenditures accounted for by the 98th percentile fell from 24.2 percent to 23.6 percent. Overall, however, the share of total Medicare expenditures accounted for the various percentile categories has been quite stable over time.

3.3.2   A Cohort Framework for Describing Differential Growth in Medicare Expenditures

These descriptive tables provide the foundation for more formal models describing the sources of Medicare expenditure growth, therefore illuminating growth forecasts and more effective simulations of policy reforms. We have already developed and applied such models (Garber, MaCurdy, and McClellan 1997). This section summarizes our cohort analysis methods, which model expenditure growth for groups of Medicare beneficiaries as a function of various characteristics, including birth year, time, and rankings in the expenditure distribution. This approach is particularly useful for assessing whether and how expenditure growth has differed between high-cost and low-cost enrollees, as our descriptive analyses suggested.

Specifications for Characterizing Trends

Considering the types of statistical formulations found in the empirical literature for describing the growth of variables—such as expenditures—in a population where differential rates operate across ages and time, two basic frameworks are well suited for our purposes: (a) one that describes the evolution of the cross-sectional relationships between age and a variable y over a sequence of years, and (b) one that models the movements of the life-cycle profiles of y associated with successive cohorts. Without arbitrary identifying assumptions, these two frameworks are statistically indistinguishable. Whereas existing studies of Medicare expenditures invariably apply some variant of the first framework as a basis for projecting growth, our research exploits frameworks falling into the second category for capturing the underlying features of Medicare growth.

To describe the trends of an aggregate quantity y over time—where y may represent a measure of Medicare expenditures, participation rates, and so on—one can model movements in the quantities $y(c, \alpha)$ measuring the values of y associated with cohort c at age α in the year $c + \alpha - 65$. The most popular approach for describing the evolution of y is to specify the relationship

(1) $$y(t - \alpha + 65, \alpha) = f(t, \alpha) + u.$$

The deterministic function f measures the systematic variation in y, and the errors u capture the contribution of period effects reflecting either cyclical or transitory phenomena. For fixed t, estimating f via equation (1) with observations on different values of y and α yields an estimate of the mapping between age and y at a point in time of the sort obtained in conventional cross-section analyses. Knowledge of how f behaves as a function of t determines how cross-section profiles shift from one year to the next.

The second approach for describing variation in y focuses on modeling the life-cycle profiles of cohorts by specifying the relationship

(2) $$y(c, \alpha) = g(c, \alpha) + u.$$

The deterministic function g measures trends, and the errors u reflect the deviations from these trends. For fixed c, estimating g via equation (2) with observations on different values of y and α yields an estimate of the life-cycle profile followed by y for cohort c. Knowledge of how g shifts as a function of c determines how the age-y relationships differ across cohorts.

The two approaches for characterizing profiles of y are linked by the equalities

(3) $$f(t, \alpha) = g(t - \alpha + 65, \alpha).$$

Thus, there is no statistical advantage to using either f or g to model the growth of y because both functions convey the same information. This observation reflects nothing more than the inherent identification problem, which is well known in the literature (e.g., Heckman and Robb, 1985), that prevents one from being able to distinguish among age, period, and cohort effects. Using equation (3), it is straightforward to translate cross-section estimates into cohort estimates and vice versa. Our research strategy focuses on estimating g, and we will construct f from these results.

Cohort Profiles and Expenditure Growth

In the empirical analysis, we develop parameterizations of the cohort profiles $g(c, \alpha)$ to model the growth of two categories of quantities: (a) the fraction of the population using services under part A or part A or B, $R(c, \alpha)$ (i.e., the participation rate); and (b) statistics describing the distributional characteristics of the expenditure variables m_{it} (the value of real Medicare expenditures in year t incurred for individual i who is a member of cohort c and is age α in year t). These quantities jointly determine how distributions of Medicare outlays evolve across ages and over time. Use of the cohort profile $g(c, \alpha)$ to examine the trends followed by the various determinants of Medicare expenses offers a simple framework for understanding the process underlying the growth of health expenses.

To illustrate the concept of a cohort profile, consider the use of such a formulation to characterize the evolution of an expenditure statistic, $\mu_{c\alpha}$, measuring, for example, average annual expenditures per individual in cohort c at age α. Members of the cohort who are sixty-five years old in year 0 experience a life-cycle profile of Medicare expenditures designated by $g(c_2, \alpha)$. Members of an older cohort who turn sixty-five in year c_1 (< 0) have expenditures following the path given by $g(c_1, \alpha)$. Finally, members of a younger cohort who turn sixty-five in year c_3 (> 0) have lifetime expenditures tracking the profile $g(c_3, \alpha)$. The growth of health expenditures experienced by cohort c in year t corresponds to the derivative

$$\left. \frac{\partial g}{\partial t} \right|_c = \left. \frac{\partial g}{\partial \alpha} \right|_c \equiv g_\alpha(c, \alpha) = g_\alpha,$$

evaluated at the point $\alpha = t - c$. Letting α^* denote any particular age, the function $g(t - \alpha^*, \alpha^*)$ specifies the level of expenditure in year t. The growth of this level is

$$\left. \frac{\partial g}{\partial t} \right|_\alpha = \left. \frac{\partial g}{\partial c} \right|_\alpha \equiv g_c(c, \alpha) = g_c(t - \alpha, \alpha).$$

Plotting $g(t - \alpha^*, \alpha^*)$ against t shows how the level of Medicare outlays were expended at age α^* or how participation at this age shifted over time. In the figure this plot is designated as "entry expenditure" when α^* is set equal to age sixty-five. In the figure the cross-section profile of expenditures in year t^* is given by the values of g intersecting the vertical line drawn at t^*.

Describing the Evolution of the Distribution of Expenditures

Using this framework, we describe many attributes of the distributions of Medicare expenses by choosing the dependent variables $y(c, \alpha, x)$ as various statistics computed using the individual observations on y making up cell (c, α, x). Choosing $y(c, \alpha, x)$ as the fraction of persons with Medicare service use ($R[c, \alpha]$) implies that the function g describes the life-cycle profile of Medicare participation rates of a cohort at different ages. Finally, choosing $y(c, \alpha, x)$ as percentiles of the Medicare expenditure distribution describes the profile of different points in the distribution of utilization by a cohort.

To estimate how the distribution of Medicare outlays evolve, we model the behavior of several percentiles by interpreting the quantity $y(c, \alpha)$ in equation (2) as a particular percentile of the distributions of the variables m_{it} corresponding to a specified cohort for a given age or year. In particular, we interpret $y(c, \alpha) = P\#\#_{c\alpha}(m_{kt})$, which represents the ##th percentile of the distribution of Medicare expenditures in year t per patients who are members of cohort c at age α. With $y(c, \alpha)$ calculated as a specified percentile, g depicts its life-cycle profile. By combining information on several such formulations of g, we can infer how the distributions of Medicare expenditures vary across cohorts, within cohorts, across ages, and over time during our five-year horizon. We consider three percentile formulations for $y(c, \alpha)$: the 10th, 50th, and 90th. Knowledge of these three percentiles provides a useful tool with which to examine changes in the shape of the distribution of Medicare utilization since it allows us to describe the entire conditional distribution, including the life-cycle and time-series patterns of the spreads of the distributions.

Parameterization and Estimation of Cohort Specifications

To outline our approach for estimating parameterizations of g, denote y_{it} as the observation on the ith individual in year t. Let the quantities $y(c, \alpha, x)$ correspond to the statistics computed using the values of y_{it} associated with the appropriate cohort c, age α, and set of demographic characteristics x. After forming the variables $y(c, \alpha, x)$, an observation on equation (2) may be written as

(4)
$$y(c, \alpha, x) = g(c, \alpha, x) + u_{c\alpha x}.$$

We assume that the disturbances follow the error components model

(5)
$$u_{c\alpha x} = \bar{u}_t + \bar{u}_{t\alpha x},$$

where the subscripts (c, α) map into the subscripts (t, α) via the relation $c = t - \alpha$, the errors $\bar{u}_t$ are common time effects, and the errors $\bar{u}_{t\alpha x}$ are the idiosyncratic deviations from trends for cohort c at age α after the removal of common year components. The time effects $\bar{u}_t$ are estimated as parameters subject to the restrictions that they are orthogonal to $g(c, \alpha, x)$ for any c. Thus, the $\bar{u}_t$s represent deviations from trends; they can be interpreted as (macroeconomic) cyclical variations in Medicare utilization.

We estimate a formulation of g that is a variant of the parameterization

(6)
$$g(c, \alpha) = \sum_j \beta_j(c)\, \phi_j(\alpha).$$

The quantities $\phi_j(\alpha)$ determine the shape of a cohort's lifetime profile with respect to age, and the functions $\beta_j(c)$ capture cross-cohort variation in life-cycle profiles. One can readily consider transformations of expenditures other than logarithms as a dependent variable when using equation (6) as a specification of g; and one can incorporate individual characteristics in the functions β_j and ϕ_j to allow profiles to vary across demographic groups.

The particular parameterization of equation (6) estimated in this analysis is

(7)
$$g(c, \alpha) = \beta_0(c) + \beta_1(c)\alpha + \beta_2(c)\alpha^2$$
$$\beta_j(c) = \beta_{0j} + \beta_{1j}c + \beta_{2j}c^2, \quad j = 1, 2, 3.$$

According to this parameterization, each cohort's expenditure function is a quadratic in age, and the coefficients of these cohort profiles vary according to a quadratic polynomial in cohort year.

The analysis estimates the coefficients β_{kj} and the time effects $\bar{u}_t$ by applying ordinary least squares (OLS) to equation (6) with g specified by equation (7). The sample includes all available annual observations, with regressions run separately for demographic groups under consideration. As mentioned, the time effects are constrained to be orthogonal to $g(c, \alpha)$ for all c, thus requiring $\bar{u}_k$ to satisfy the restrictions

$$\sum_{k=86}^{90} \bar{u}_k k^j = 0 \text{ for } j = 0, 1, 2$$

Our empirical work indicates that specification (7) is sufficiently rich to capture the shifts in Medicare expenditures that occurred during the 1990s. Increasing the degree of either the polynomial in age or the polynomial in cohort year fails either to improve the goodness of fit of the statistical model at conventional significance levels or to change the main empirical findings.

3.3.3   Underlying Trends in Medicare Expenditures

We estimate the previous specifications for annual Medicare participation rates and expenditure percentiles—the 10th, 50th, 90th, 95th, and 98th—using all years covering the 1989 to 1999 period.

Growth in Participation

Figure 3.4 shows the rate of growth in participation rates for part A and part A or B. The cross-sectional curves (marked with Xs) show the 1995 participation rates by age. For both part A and part A or B, participation rates increase with age until around age ninety, when participation rates begin to decrease. Part A participation rates increase with age more rapidly than participation rates for part A and B combined until more than 40 percent of beneficiaries in their late eighties or early nineties receive some part A service (i.e., inpatient hospitalization, skilled nursing facility, home health agency, or hospice). The figure also shows three cohort profiles for beneficiaries that turned sixty-five in 1991 (marked with squares), 1981 (marked with diamonds), or 1971 (marked with triangles), respectively. Each cohort profile intersects the cross-sectional curve in 1995 (that is, at age sixty-nine, seventy-nine, and eighty-nine, respectively). The fact that the cohort profiles are steeper than the cross-sectional curve indicates that Medicare participation rates for each cohort increase more rapidly than can be attributed to pure aging. For the 1991 cohort, the percentage change in the part A participation rate was 44 percent (of the 1995 level) and the percentage change in the part A or B participation rate was 27 percent. For the 1981 cohort, the percentage change in the part A participation rate was

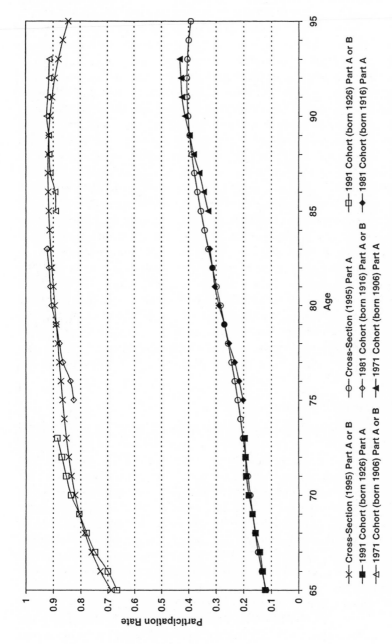

Fig. 3.4 **Predicted annual reimbursement participation rates, including time effects, cross section (1995), and cohort profiles for part A and part A or B**

44 percent, and the percentage change in the part A or B participation rate was 11 percent. For the 1971 cohort, the percentage change in the part A participation rate was 26 percent, and the percentage change in the part A or B participation rate was only 2 percent. Service use was increasing more rapidly for the younger cohorts, at least until the later years of the decade.

The rapid increase in the part A participation rate was due primarily to an increase in service use for skilled nursing facilities, home health agencies, and hospices, although inpatient hospital service use increased as well. Our estimates indicate that the participation rate for skilled nursing facility services increased from 1.9 percent to 4.3 percent from 1989 to 1997; the participation rate for home health agency services increased from 4.9 percent to 9.8 percent; and the participation rate for inpatient hospital services increased from 18.7 percent to 19.5 percent. After BBA97, part A and part A or B participation rates actually decreased, as shown in table 3.2. The participation rate for home health agency services decreased from 9.8 percent to 7.1 percent from 1997 to 1998. Participation rates for inpatient hospital and skilled nursing facility services remained constant. In figure 3.4, the part A participation rate cohort profiles increase until 1997, and then either flatten or decrease slightly, especially in the youngest (1991) cohort. The fact that the cohort profiles are less steep than the cross-sectional curve after 1997 indicates that part A participation rates for the 1991 and 1981 cohorts decreased more rapidly during this time period than can be attributed to pure age effects. Part A participation rates for the oldest cohort (1971) continued to increase despite the policy changes, but at a much lower rate.

Growth across Different Intensities of Use

Figure 3.5 shows the rate of growth across the distribution of annual Medicare expenditures. The cross-sectional curves show a snapshot of average annual Medicare expenditures in 1995 for the 10th, 50th, and 90th percentiles by age. Intensity of service use increases with age for all three percentile categories, at least until the late eighties or early nineties, when intensity of service use declines. Intensity of service use by age actually increases the most for the median percentile, as can be seen more clearly in figure 3.6, which shows only the 10th and median percentile categories. From age sixty-five to age ninety, the percent change in average annual expenditures is 162 percent for the 10th percentile, 266 percent for the median, and 133 percent for the 90th percentile.

Three cohort profiles are shown for the same percentiles for beneficiaries that turned sixty-five in 1991, 1981, or 1971. The cohort profiles show the actual life cycle growth in Medicare expenditures for the specified percentiles of each cohort. The cohort profiles intersect the cross-section profile at the ages of the cohorts in 1995 (that is, at age sixty-nine, seventy-nine, and eighty-nine). The fact that the cohort profiles are steeper than the

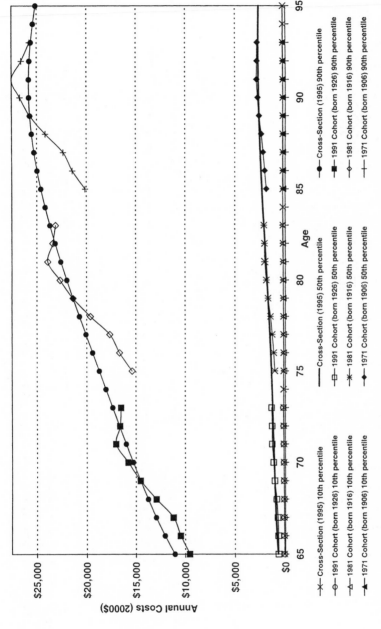

Fig. 3.5 Predicted annual total costs per patient, including time effects, cross section (1995), and cohort profiles for 10th, 50th, and 90th percentiles

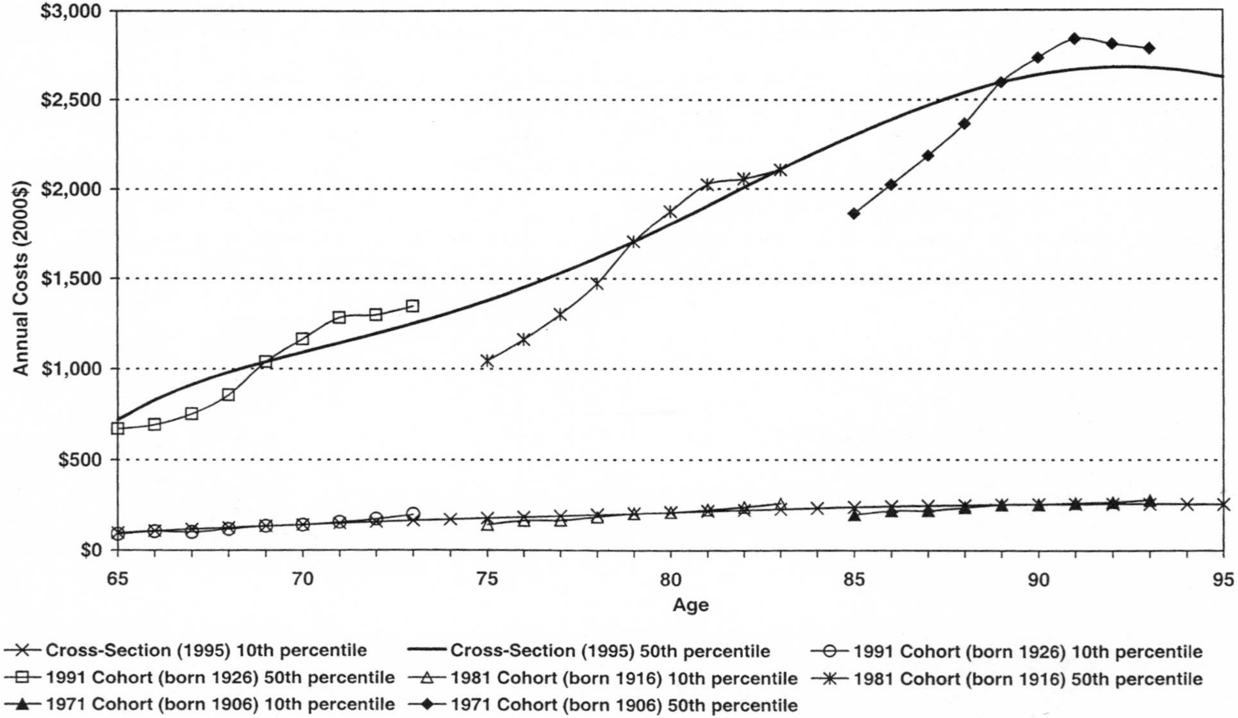
$3,000
$2,500
$2,000
$1,500
$1,000
$500
$0
Annual Costs (2000$)
65
70
75
80
85
90
95
Age
Cross-Section (1995) 10th percentile
Cross-Section (1995) 50th percentile
1991 Cohort (born 1926) 10th percentile
1991 Cohort (born 1926) 50th percentile
1981 Cohort (born 1916) 10th percentile
1981 Cohort (born 1916) 50th percentile
1971 Cohort (born 1906) 10th percentile
1971 Cohort (born 1906) 50th percentile

Fig. 3.6 Predicted annual total costs per patient, including time effects, cross section (1995), and cohort profiles for 10th and 50th percentiles

cross-sectional curve indicates that average annual Medicare expenditures grew much more rapidly for each cohort than can be attributed to pure aging, especially for the 90th percentile. However, the cohort profiles also show that annual Medicare expenditures after 1997 declined rapidly in the 90th percentile, remained constant in the median percentile (except for the oldest cohort, where there was a decline; see figure 3.6), and increased for the 10th percentile. The fact that the cohort profiles for the 10th percentile are steeper than those for the 50th or 90th percentiles indicates that Medicare expenditures grew more rapidly at the lower end of the expenditure distribution. The growth at the higher end was mitigated by the impact of BBA97, as indicated by the downward slope of the curves after 1997.

For the youngest (1991) cohort, the percentage change in total expenditures for the period from 1991 to 1999 was 48 percent (of the 1995 level) for the 90th percentile, 65 percent for the 50th percentile, and 80 percent for the 10th percentile. The pre-BBA97 percentage changes were 58 percent, 71 percent, and 57 percent, respectively. For the 1981 cohort, which was seventy-five years old in 1991, the rates of growth were 36 percent, 62 percent, and 57 percent, respectively. The pre-BBA97 percentage changes were 43 percent, 66 percent, and 44 percent, respectively. For the 1971 cohort, which was eighty-five years old in 1991, the rates of growth were 22 percent, 35 percent, and 32 percent, respectively. The pre-BBA97 percentage changes were 30 percent, 41 percent, and 27 percent, respectively. Collectively, our results indicate that expenditures grew more rapidly in the 10th and median percentile expenditure categories than for the 90th percentile category. Expenditures also grew more rapidly in the youngest cohort and less rapidly in the oldest cohort, with the middle cohort in between. Finally, the BBA97 reduced the rate of growth across all cohorts for the median and 90th percentile categories, but especially for the oldest cohort. The BBA97 actually increased the rate of growth for the 10th percentile, especially for the younger cohorts.

Figure 3.7 shows the rate of growth of average annual Medicare expenditures in 1995 for "high-cost" beneficiaries in the 90th, 95th, and 98th percentiles by age. Intensity of service use increases with age for all three percentile categories, at least until the late eighties or early nineties, when the intensity of service use declines. For the 98th percentile, the intensity of service use begins to decline around age eighty. Intensity of service use by age increases the most for the 90th percentile. From age sixty-five to age ninety, the percent change in average annual expenditures is 133 percent for the 90th percentile, 67 percent for the 95th percentile, and 29 percent for the 98th percentile.

Three cohort profiles are shown for the same percentiles for beneficiaries that turned sixty-five in 1991, 1981, or 1971. Similar to the results in figure 3.5, the cohort profiles are much steeper than the cross-sectional curve, indicating that average annual Medicare expenditures grew much more

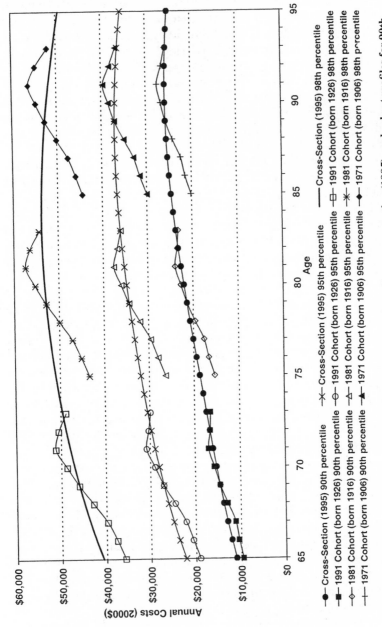

Fig. 3.7 Predicted annual total costs per patient, including time effects, cross section (1995), and cohort profiles for 90th, 95th, and 98th percentiles

rapidly for each cohort that can be attributed to pure aging, especially in the 98th percentile. The cohort profiles show that average annual Medicare expenditures for high-cost beneficiaries declined rapidly after 1997 in the 90th, 95th, and 98th percentiles. The fact that the cohort profiles for the 90th percentile are steeper than for the 95th or 98th percentiles indicates that Medicare expenditures grew less rapidly for the highest-cost users of Medicare services.

For example, for the youngest (1991) cohort, the percentage change in total expenditures for the period from 1991 to 1999 was 28 percent (of the 1995 level) for the 98th percentile, 40 percent for the 95th percentile, and 48 percent for the 90th percentile. The pre-BBA97 percentage changes were 36 percent, 48 percent, and 58 percent for the 98th, 95th, and 90th percentiles, respectively. For the 1981 cohort, seventy-five years of age in 1991, the rates of growth were 21 percent, 28 percent, and 36 percent, respectively. The pre-BBA97 percentage changes were 28 percent, 35 percent, and 43 percent, respectively. For the 1971 cohort, those eighty-five years of age in 1991, the rates of growth were 14 percent, 18 percent, and 22 percent, respectively. The pre-BBA97 percentage changes were 24 percent, 27 percent, and 30 percent, respectively. Collectively, our results indicate that expenditures grew more rapidly in the 90th percentile category, less rapidly in the 95th percentile category, and the least rapidly in the 98th percentile category. Expenditures also grew the most rapidly in the youngest cohort across each percentile category and less rapidly in the oldest cohort, with the middle cohort in between. Finally, the BBA97 reduced the rate of growth across all cohorts and all percentile categories, but especially for the oldest cohort and the 98th percentile category.

Trends Have Changed

Figures 3.8, 3.9, and 3.10 show the growth rate of expenditures for an earlier time period than the previous figures. Figures 3.8 and 3.9 show the cross-sectional curves and the cohort profiles using the 1991 cross section as reference for the 10th, median, and 90th percentiles by age. The cohort profiles intersect the cross-section profile at the ages of the 1967, 1977, and 1987 cohorts in 1991 (that is, at age sixty-nine, seventy-nine, and eighty-nine, respectively). Comparison of figures 3.8 and 3.5 demonstrates that the trends forecasted by previous studies were not realized. Using the earlier cohort suggests growth rates of 49 percent, 62 percent, and 58 percent for the 90th, median, and 10th percentiles, respectively. For the 1977 cohort, the growth rates were 41 percent, 67 percent, and 50 percent. For the 1967 cohort, the growth rates were 36 percent, 43 percent, and 30 percent. The policy changes of the late 1990s mitigated these growth rates, especially for the older cohorts and the higher percentiles.

Similarly, figure 3.10 shows the cross-sectional curves and the cohort profiles using the 1991 cross section as reference for the 90th, 95th, and

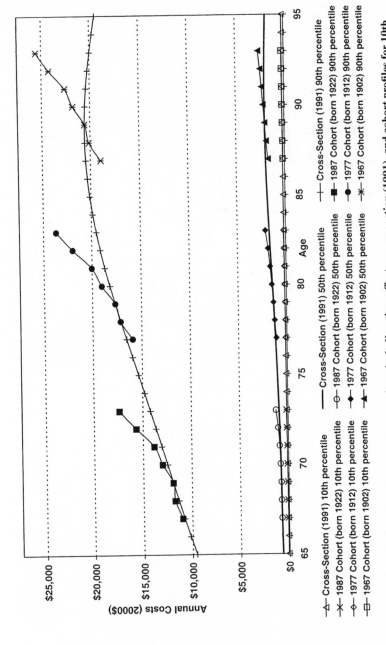

Fig. 3.8 Predicted annual total costs per patient, including time effects, cross section (1991), and cohort profiles for 10th, 50th, and 90th percentiles

- Cross-Section (1991) 10th percentile
- 1987 Cohort (born 1922) 10th percentile
- 1977 Cohort (born 1912) 10th percentile
- 1967 Cohort (born 1902) 10th percentile
- Cross-Section (1991) 50th percentile
- 1987 Cohort (born 1922) 50th percentile
- 1977 Cohort (born 1912) 50th percentile
- 1967 Cohort (born 1902) 50th percentile
- Cross-Section (1991) 90th percentile
- 1987 Cohort (born 1922) 90th percentile
- 1977 Cohort (born 1912) 90th percentile
- 1967 Cohort (born 1902) 90th percentile

Annual Costs (2000$)

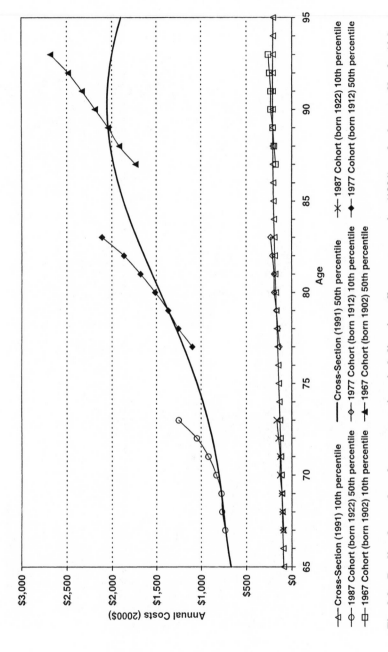

Fig. 3.9 Predicted annual total costs per patient, including time effects, cross section (1991), and cohort profiles for 10th and 50th percentiles

Legend:
- —△— Cross-Section (1991) 10th percentile
- —⊖— 1987 Cohort (born 1922) 50th percentile
- —□— 1967 Cohort (born 1902) 10th percentile
- ——— Cross-Section (1991) 50th percentile
- —◇— 1977 Cohort (born 1912) 10th percentile
- —◆— 1967 Cohort (born 1902) 50th percentile
- —✕— 1987 Cohort (born 1922) 10th percentile
- —◆— 1977 Cohort (born 1912) 50th percentile

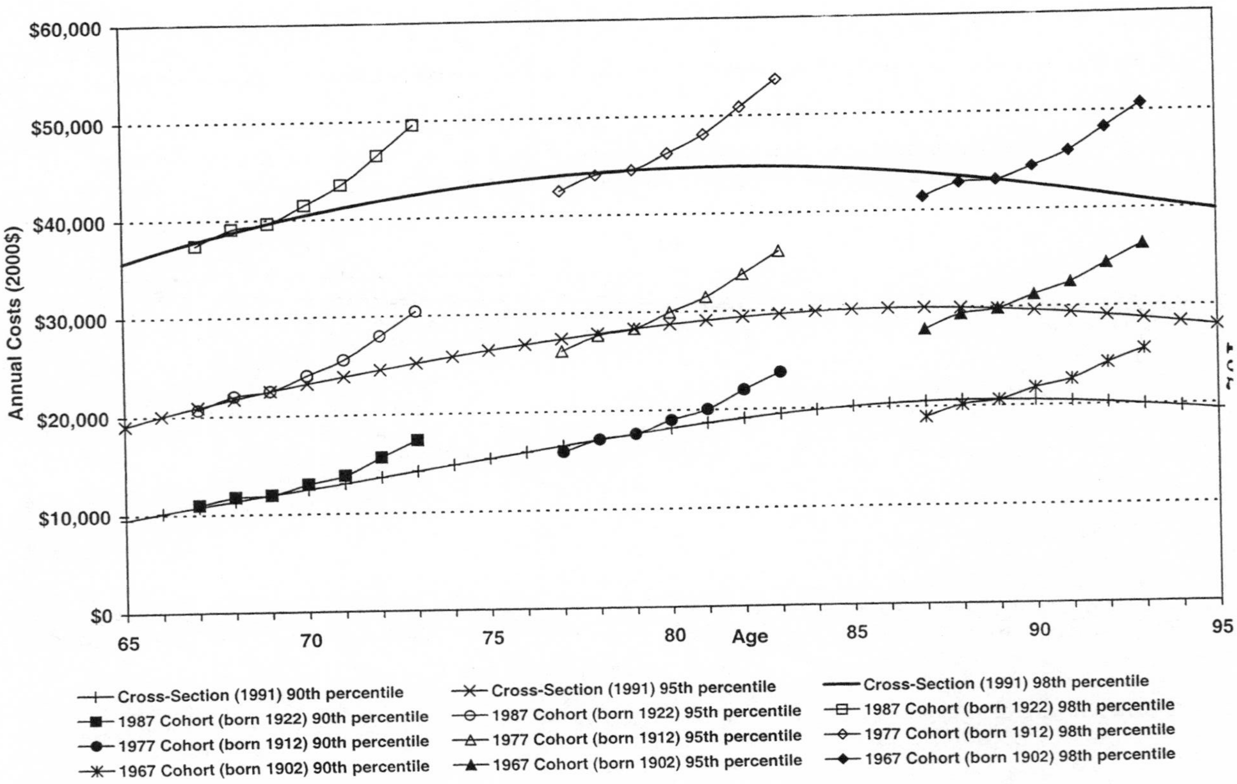

Annual Costs (2000$)
$60,000
$50,000
$40,000
$30,000
$20,000
$10,000
$0
65
70
75
80
Age
85
90
95
Cross-Section (1991) 90th percentile
1987 Cohort (born 1922) 90th percentile
1977 Cohort (born 1912) 90th percentile
1967 Cohort (born 1902) 90th percentile
Cross-Section (1991) 95th percentile
1987 Cohort (born 1922) 95th percentile
1977 Cohort (born 1912) 95th percentile
1967 Cohort (born 1902) 95th percentile
Cross-Section (1991) 98th percentile
1987 Cohort (born 1922) 98th percentile
1977 Cohort (born 1912) 98th percentile
1967 Cohort (born 1902) 98th percentile

Fig. 3.10 Predicted annual total costs per patient, including time effects, cross section (1991), and cohort profiles for 90th, 95th, and 98th percentiles

98th percentiles by age. Using the earlier cohort suggested growth rates of 29 percent, 41 percent, and 49 percent for the 98th, 95th, and 90th percentiles, respectively. For the 1977 cohort, the growth rates were 24 percent, 33 percent, and 41 percent. For the 1967 cohort, the growth rates were 21 percent, 27 percent, and 30 percent. Again, the policy changes of the late 1990s mitigated these growth rates, especially for the older cohorts and the higher percentiles. However, the results from section 3.2 suggest that this reduction in the growth rate represents only a temporary change as the result of policy changes implemented concurrently with BBA97. Administrative data from recent years through 2003 indicate that Medicare expenditures have reverted back to the trends suggested by the 1991 cross section. Therefore, the growth profiles suggested by figures 3.5 and 3.7 are unlikely to be realized as well. The trends in administrative data presented in section 3.2 indicate that the growth in Medicare expenditures has reverted to previous rates and may have even accelerated.

3.4   Concentration of Expenditures among High-Cost Users

Characterizing Medicare beneficiaries by their annual expenditures severely limits both the identification of high-cost users of health care and the intensity of utilization over short periods. It is possible that a beneficiary who has high expenses over two adjacent years may not register as being in a high-cost category in either of the years, even though total costs expended on treating this person's health affliction exceed the annual thresholds in the years when treatment occurs. Further, assessing the extent of concentration in expenditures becomes fuzzy because expenses overlapping two calendar years suggest persistence, whereas none would be inferred if these expenses were merely shifted slightly in time to fit more expenditure months into a single calendar year.

The following analysis explores several options for overcoming these shortcomings by developing profiles of Medicare costs from our monthly longitudinal expenditure data. Although the discussion relies on calendar years as a reference time frame to integrate the analysis with previous results, it also considers a variety of other time frames with the aim of creating a transparent approach for identifying the high-cost users and for discovering patterns of their use. This section initially considers alternative definitions of high-cost months, paralleling the analysis done characterizing high-cost years. Using several candidate definitions, the analysis then summarizes experiences across various populations of Medicare beneficiaries. The discussion next takes up the problem of using monthly experiences to explore simple ways of identifying beneficiaries responsible for the bulk of Medicare expenditures. Finally, this section ends with a summary of the monthly experiences of the high-cost users.

3.4.1 Allocation of Expenditures across High-Cost Months

After considering several time frames for computing the percentiles associated with monthly expenditures, we selected the following procedure: (a) index all expenditures to be in 2000$, (b) compute percentiles for the sample consisting of all months having positive expenditures in a given calendar year, and (c) assign months based on whether they lie above the 80 percent, 90 percent, 95 percent, and 98 percent portion of the distribution of months for the year in which they fall. This procedure produces a classification for all months, with the 80 percent months referring to the 20 percent of months with the highest expenditures during the year, the 90 percent months designating the 10 percent of months with the highest expenditures during the year, and so on.

We examined the implications of using time frames both shorter and longer than a year when computing percentiles for months. For time frames shorter than a year, substantial influences of seasonality occur. This results in many lower-cost months being classified in high-cost categories due to their occurrence in periods of the year when patients disproportionately elect less intensive health treatments. For time frames longer than a year, the secular growth in health expenses over time means that a disproportionate number of months are selected in the latest year, when costs are higher overall.

Table 3.6 presents the percentiles of monthly expenditures by year, measured in 2000$ including only months with positive expenses. Generally, the 98th percentile is about 350 times greater than the 10th percentile, nearly 100 times larger than the 50th percentile, almost five times the size of the 90th percentile, and about twice as large as the 95th percentile. Not surprisingly, the distribution of monthly expenditures exhibits extreme

Table 3.6   **Percentiles for monthly expenditures for Medicare participants**

Year	Levels of monthly cost percentiles (2000 $)					
	10	50	80	90	95	98
1989	28	101	452	1,588	5,063	9,884
1990	28	104	475	1,628	4,983	9,806
1991	29	107	501	1,636	4,845	9,667
1992	30	113	539	1,762	4,933	9,846
1993	29	111	554	1,773	4,755	9,737
1994	31	111	577	1,937	4,961	10,295
1995	33	117	622	2,075	5,087	10,712
1996	32	115	634	2,106	5,160	11,023
1997	32	115	644	2,127	5,178	11,233
1998	32	114	583	1,959	5,028	11,075
1999	33	117	558	1,863	4,863	10,631

Table 3.7   **Share of annual Medicare expenditures accounted for by monthly percentile groups (%)**

Year	Monthly percentile categories						
	0–50	50–80	80–90	90–95	95–98	98+	Total
1989	2.6	6.9	9.1	17.1	22.9	41.4	100.0
1990	2.7	7.2	9.5	17.0	22.7	40.9	100.0
1991	2.8	7.6	9.9	16.6	22.5	40.7	100.0
1992	2.9	7.8	10.3	16.6	22.3	40.1	100.0
1993	2.8	7.9	10.6	16.2	21.9	40.5	100.0
1994	2.8	7.6	10.9	16.4	22.0	40.4	100.0
1995	2.8	7.8	11.2	16.3	21.8	40.1	100.0
1996	2.7	7.7	11.3	16.1	21.9	40.3	100.0
1997	2.7	7.5	11.4	15.9	21.7	40.7	100.0
1998	2.8	7.3	10.7	15.6	21.9	41.8	100.0
1999	3.0	7.5	10.4	15.6	21.8	41.7	100.0

skewness, as found for annual expenditures. Also, the trends followed by the various percentiles over time mirror the trends discussed previously for the annual percentiles.

Table 3.7 reports the shares of total Medicare expenditures accounted for by the various monthly percentile ranges by year. Similar to the findings for annual ranges, the shares for the monthly ranges remain remarkably stable over the 1989 to 1999 period. This phenomenon has occurred even though the growth rates in overall Medicare expenditures have varied considerably over the period. According to the table, the 2 percent of months making up the 98+ percentile account for about 41 percent of total annual expenditures, the 5 percent of months making up the 95+ percentile cover nearly 63 percent of yearly Medicare expenditures, the 10 percent of months in the 90+ group include 79 percent of total expenses, and the top 20 percent of months in the 80+ group account for almost 90 percent of expenditures. Thus, describing the occurrence of months with expenditures above the 80th percentile captures essentially all of Medicare expenditure, and these months make up far less than 20 percent of all months since many months have zero expenditures.

3.4.2   Patterns for Monthly Medicare Expenditures across Participants

Tables 3.8 through 3.11 present an array of statistics summarizing the incidence of high-cost months for various populations of Medicare beneficiaries. Each table describes the distributions of experiences for months classified as high cost by the table, with definitions of "high cost" different across tables. In addition to months of experience, these tables report shares indicating the size of the beneficiary population and the fraction of total Medicare expenditures accounted for by each group identified in rows of the tables.

Table 3.8 Summary of incidence of 80%-high-cost months among Medicare patients with experience: Elderly (1989–99)

Patient characteristics	Share of Medicare patients (%)		Total no. of high-cost months				No. of high-cost month spells				Length of high-cost spells				Share of Medicare expenditures (%)	
	All	High-cost month group	Mean	20	50	80	Mean	20	50	80	Mean	20	50	80	All months	High-cost months
				Percentiles				Percentiles				Percentiles				
Patients w/ experience	86.8	100.0	9.1	2	6	14	4.9	2	4	8	2	1	1.4	2	99.6	89.7
Gender																
Male	36.2	41.7	8.8	2	6	13	4.8	1	4	8	1.9	1	1.4	2	41.9	38.2
Female	50.6	58.3	9.4	2	6	14	5	2	4	8	2	1	1.4	2	57.7	51.4
Age																
65–69	26.5	30.5	4.7	1	3	7	2.8	1	2	4	1.7	1	1	2	15.7	14.0
70–74	28.3	32.7	5.4	1	3	8	3.1	1	2	5	1.8	1	1.2	2	19.4	17.4
75–79	25.0	28.8	5.9	2	4	9	3.2	1	3	5	2	1	1.3	2	18.8	17.0
80–84	18.8	21.7	6.3	2	4	9	3.2	1	3	5	2.1	1	1.4	2.3	14.9	13.6
85–89	11.8	13.6	6.4	2	4	9	3.1	1	2	5	2.3	1	1.5	2.5	9.4	8.6
90+	5.5	6.4	6.8	2	4	10	3.1	1	2	5	2.4	1	1.5	2.7	4.7	4.3
Cost percentile any year																
GE 80th percentile	58.5	67.4	12.1	4	9	17	6	2	5	9	2.3	1.2	1.6	2.5	93.1	85.6
GE 90th percentile	38.1	43.9	14.7	6	11	21	6.6	3	6	10	2.8	1.3	1.8	3	79.4	74.3
GE 95th percentile	22.4	25.8	17.3	7	14	25	7	3	6	11	3.3	1.5	2	3.6	59.9	56.9
GE 98th percentile	10.1	11.6	20.5	9	16	30	7.2	3	6	11	4	1.7	2.4	4.5	36.2	34.8
Cost percentile any 2 years																
GE 80th percentile	32.0	36.9	17.2	8	14	24	7.8	4	7	11	2.8	1.3	1.8	3	72.1	67.1
GE 90th percentile	14.6	16.8	22.8	12	19	31	8.6	4	8	12	3.7	1.6	2.2	4	47.1	44.8
GE 95th percentile	5.9	6.8	28.7	15	24	40	8.8	4	8	13	5.1	1.9	2.8	5.7	26.1	25.2
GE 98th percentile	1.7	2.0	35.6	20	31	49	8.5	4	8	13	7.5	2.3	3.7	9	11.0	10.7

Table 3.9 Summary of incidence of 90%-high-cost months among Medicare patients with experience: Elderly (1989–99)

Patient characteristics	Share of Medicare patients (%)		Total no. of high-cost months				No. of high-cost month spells				Length of high-cost spells				Share of Medicare expenditures (%)	
	All	High-cost month group	Mean	Percentiles			Mean	Percentiles			Mean	Percentiles			All months	High-cost months
				20	50	80		20	50	80		20	50	80		
Patients w/ experience	75.3	100.0	5.3	1	3	8	3.3	1	3	5	1.6	1	1.2	1.9	98.1	79.1
Gender																
Male	31.6	41.9	5.2	1	3	8	3.3	1	3	5	1.6	1	1.2	2	41.3	34.1
Female	43.8	58.1	5.3	1	3	8	3.4	1	3	5	1.6	1	1.1	1.8	56.8	45.0
Age																
65–69	18.9	25.1	3.2	1	2	4	2.1	1	1	3	1.5	1	1	1.7	14.9	12.3
70–74	21.6	28.7	3.5	1	2	5	2.2	1	2	3	1.6	1	1	2	18.6	15.3
75–79	20.1	26.7	3.7	1	2	5	2.3	1	2	3	1.6	1	1	2	18.2	15.0
80–84	15.8	21.0	3.8	1	3	5	2.4	1	2	3	1.6	1	1	2	14.6	12.0
85–89	10.2	13.5	3.8	1	3	5	2.4	1	2	3	1.6	1	1	2	9.2	7.6
90+	4.9	6.5	4	1	3	6	2.5	1	2	4	1.7	1	1.2	2	4.6	3.8
Cost percentile any year																
GE 80th percentile	58.4	77.6	6.3	2	5	9	3.9	2	3	6	1.7	1	1.3	2	93.1	76.6
GE 90th percentile	38.1	50.6	8	3	6	11	4.5	2	4	7	2	1.1	1.5	2.1	79.4	67.4
GE 95th percentile	22.4	29.7	10	4	8	14	5	2	4	7	2.3	1.3	1.7	2.5	59.9	52.4
GE 98th percentile	10.1	13.4	12.6	5	10	17	5.4	2	5	8	2.9	1.4	2	3	36.2	32.6
Cost percentile any 2 years																
GE 80th percentile	32.0	42.4	9.1	4	7	12	5.3	3	5	7	1.9	1.1	1.4	2	72.1	60.1
GE 90th percentile	14.6	19.4	12.9	7	10	17	6.4	4	6	9	2.5	1.3	1.7	2.5	47.1	40.8
GE 95th percentile	5.9	7.8	18	9	14	24	7.2	4	7	10	3.5	1.5	2	3.5	26.1	23.4
GE 98th percentile	1.7	2.3	25	13	20	35	7.5	4	7	11	5.5	1.8	2.6	6	11.0	10.2

Table 3.10   Summary of incidence of 95%-high-cost months among Medicare patients with experience: Elderly (1989–99)

Patient characteristics	Share of Medicare patients (%)		Total no. of high-cost months				No. of high-cost month spells				Length of high-cost spells				Share of Medicare expenditures (%)	
	All	High-cost month group	Mean	Percentiles 20	50	80	Mean	Percentiles 20	50	80	Mean	Percentiles 20	50	80	All months	High-cost months
Patients w/ experience	60.7	100.0	3.3	1	2	5	2.6	1	2	4	1.2	1	1	1.5	93.3	62.9
Gender																
Male	26.0	42.8	3.2	1	2	5	2.5	1	2	4	1.3	1	1	1.5	39.6	27.6
Female	34.8	57.2	3.3	1	2	5	2.6	1	2	4	1.2	1	1	1.5	53.7	35.3
Age																
65–69	12.7	21.0	2.3	1	1	3	1.8	1	1	2	1.2	1	1	1.3	13.5	9.8
70–74	15.1	24.9	2.4	1	2	3	1.9	1	1	3	1.3	1	1	1.5	17.0	12.2
75–79	14.6	24.0	2.5	1	2	4	1.9	1	1	3	1.3	1	1	1.5	16.8	11.9
80–84	12.0	19.7	2.5	1	2	4	2	1	1	3	1.3	1	1	1.5	13.5	9.5
85–89	8.1	13.4	2.5	1	2	4	2	1	2	3	1.3	1	1	1.5	8.6	6.1
90+	4.1	6.8	2.6	1	2	4	2	1	2	3	1.3	1	1	1.5	4.4	3.1
Cost percentile any year																
GE 80th percentile	56.2	92.6	3.4	1	2	5	2.7	1	2	4	1.3	1	1	1.5	91.7	62.1
GE 90th percentile	38.0	62.5	4.3	2	3	6	3.2	1	3	5	1.4	1	1.2	1.7	79.2	55.8
GE 95th percentile	22.4	36.9	5.4	3	4	8	3.8	2	3	5	1.5	1	1.3	1.9	59.9	44.1
GE 98th percentile	10.1	16.6	7	3	6	10	4.5	2	4	6	1.7	1.1	1.5	2	36.2	28.0
Cost percentile any 2 years																
GE 80th percentile	31.6	52.1	4.8	2	4	7	3.7	2	3	5	1.3	1	1.1	1.5	71.7	48.7
GE 90th percentile	14.6	24.0	6.8	4	6	9	4.9	3	4	7	1.4	1	1.3	1.7	47.1	33.5
GE 95th percentile	5.90	9.70	9.3	5	8	12	6.1	4	6	8	1.6	1.2	1.4	1.8	26.1	19.3
GE 98th percentile	1.70	2.90	13	8	11	17	7.4	4	7	10	1.9	1.3	1.6	2.2	11.0	8.5

Table 3.11 Summary of incidence of 98%-high-cost months among Medicare patients with experience: Elderly (1989–99)

Patient characteristics	Share of Medicare patients (%)		Total no. of high-cost months				No. of high-cost month spells				Length of high-cost spells				Share of Medicare expenditures (%)	
	All	High-cost month group	Mean	20	50	80	Mean	20	50	80	Mean	20	50	80	All months	High-cost months
Patients w/ experience	39.7	100.0	2	1	1	3	1.8	1	1	2	1.1	1	1	1	78.6	40.8
Gender																
Male	17.5	44.0	2	1	1	3	1.7	1	1	2	1.1	1	1	1	34.0	18.5
Female	22.2	56.0	2	1	1	3	1.8	1	1	2	1.1	1	1	1	44.6	22.3
Age																
65–69	7.3	18.5	1.7	1	1	2	1.5	1	1	2	1.1	1	1	1	10.8	6.6
70–74	9.0	22.7	1.7	1	1	2	1.5	1	1	2	1.1	1	1	1	13.8	8.2
75–79	8.8	22.1	1.7	1	1	2	1.5	1	1	2	1.1	1	1	1	13.5	7.9
80–84	7.0	17.8	1.7	1	1	2	1.5	1	1	2	1.1	1	1	1	10.6	6.0
85–89	4.6	11.6	1.7	1	1	2	1.5	1	1	2	1.1	1	1	1	6.6	3.7
90+	2.3	5.8	1.7	1	1	2	1.5	1	1	2	1.1	1	1	1	3.3	1.8
Cost percentile any year																
GE 80th percentile	39.7	100.0	2	1	1	3	1.8	1	1	2	1.1	1	1	1	78.6	40.8
GE 90th percentile	34.1	86.0	2.1	1	2	3	1.9	1	1	3	1.1	1	1	1	74.3	38.8
GE 95th percentile	21.7	54.6	2.6	1	2	4	2.2	1	2	3	1.2	1	1	1.5	58.5	31.9
GE 98th percentile	10.0	25.2	3.4	2	3	5	2.7	1	2	4	1.3	1	1	1.5	36.0	21.2
Cost percentile any 2 years																
GE 80th percentile	25.8	65.0	2.4	1	2	3	2.1	1	2	3	1.1	1	1	1.2	64.5	31.7
GE 90th percentile	13.9	35.1	3.2	2	3	4	2.7	2	2	4	1.2	1	1	1.3	45.6	23.1
GE 95th percentile	5.80	14.60	4.3	2	4	6	3.5	2	3	5	1.2	1	1	1.5	25.8	13.7
GE 98th percentile	1.70	4.40	6.2	4	6	8	4.7	3	4	6	1.4	1	1.3	1.6	10.9	6.2

Characteristics of High-Cost Users and Structure of Tables

The first column of tables 3.8 through 3.11 lists the groups of Medicare beneficiaries whose experiences are summarized in the remaining columns. The rows designated in the first column specify the classifications of beneficiaries considered in the analysis. The table groups rows into five categories:

- *Patients w/experience:* This row describes population shares and attributes of the distributions of high-cost months for all beneficiaries who experience at least one month classified as high cost by the table any time during the 1989–99 period. All of the remaining rows report results for segments of this population.
- *Gender:* The top set of rows reports experiences for males and females separately.
- *Age:* The next set of rows presents distributions of high-cost months by age groups. Groups consist of beneficiaries who were the age indicated at the start of the bracket, with observations included for years covered by the bracket, or until the person died if this event occurred before reaching the age at the end of the age bracket. Beneficiaries can, of course, be members of more than one age group if they experience multiple high-cost episodes that occur at different ages.
- *Cost percentile, any year:* This set of rows summarizes the incidence of high-cost months for groups of beneficiaries classified by whether their calendar-year expenditures reach particular thresholds. The "GE 80th percentile" refers to all beneficiaries who had expenditures above the 80th calendar-year percentile in any year during the 1989–99 period, the "GE 90th percentile" group includes all beneficiaries with expenditures above the 90th annual percentile in any year of the period, and so on through the 98 percent level of annual expenditures.
- *Cost percentile, any 2 year:* The final set of rows categorizes beneficiaries according to whether their calendar-year expenditures attain the "GE 80th percentile," "GE 90th percentile," "GE 95th percentile," and "GE 98th percentile" categories in two or more years.

The second through the last columns of tables 3.8 through 3.11 present five categories of statistics for each of the Medicare beneficiary groups:

- *Share of Medicare patients:* These columns report the share of Medicare patients in the group (defined by the row) for two different Medicare populations. The first column ("All") shows the share of all patients, where "patients" refers to all beneficiaries who received any Medicare services during the 1989–99 period. The second column ("High-cost month group") gives the percentage of the group of patients with at least one month classified as high cost by the table.

For example, table 3.8 shows that female patients who experienced at least one of month falling into the 80th expenditure percentile category comprise 50.6 percent of all the beneficiaries who received at least one Medicare service between 1989 and 1999. Further, females account for 58.3 percent of all the patients who make up the 80th percentile group.

Referring to the rows designating age brackets, table 3.8 shows that 26.5 percent of elderly receiving at least one Medicare service between 1989 and 1999 were ages sixty-five to sixty-nine when they experienced a high-cost month falling into the 80th expenditure percentile category, and 30.5 percent of those in the 80th expenditure percentile category were sixty-five to sixty-nine years old when they experienced at least one high-cost month. The corresponding figures for the seventy to seventy-four age group are 28.3 percent and 32.7 percent, implying that more of the 1989–99 Medicare beneficiary population experienced a high-cost month during ages seventy to seventy-four. Because members of the 1989–99 Medicare beneficiary population are typically represented in several age groups and may experience multiple high-cost episodes at different ages, percentages in these rows do not add up to 100 percent or to the overall population.

- *Total no. of high-cost months:* This group of columns summarizes properties of the distribution of the total number of high-cost months experienced during the 1989–99 period. The column labeled "Mean" presents the average number of months experienced by beneficiaries in the specified row, and the next three columns show the percentiles of the distribution of the number of high-cost months.

   Referring again to female patients, this group of columns in table 3.8 shows that women with at least one high-cost month (i.e., in top 20 percent of months) had an average of 9.4 high-cost months during the 1989–99 decade. Twenty percent had two or fewer high-cost months during this period, half had six or fewer such months, and 80 percent experienced up to fourteen high-cost months.

- *No. of high-cost spells:* The next set of columns reports statistics describing the number of high-cost month spells experienced by the prescribed population during the 1989–99 period, with a spell defined as a continuous series of high-cost months. These columns show the average number of spells, along with percentiles associated with the distribution.

   Continuing the above example for table 3.8, women with at least one high-cost month (i.e., in top 20 percent of months) had an average of five high-cost spells during the 1989–99 decade. The median such woman had four high-cost spells. Twenty percent had two or fewer high-cost spells, and 80 percent had eight or fewer of these spells.

- *Length of high-cost spells:* This set of columns presents statistics characterizing the lengths of all high-cost spells experienced by beneficiaries in the specified group of beneficiaries, giving the average and percentiles describing the lengths (in months) of completed spells.

According to table 3.8, the average length of high-cost spells for women with at least one high-cost month (i.e., in top 20 percent of months) was two months. The 20th, 50th, and 80th percentiles were 1, 1.4, and 2 months, respectively.

- *Share of Medicare expenditures:* The last set of columns reports two shares of total Medicare expenditures spent during the 1989–99 period attributable to the group of beneficiaries in a given row, with all quantities measured in nondiscounted 2000$. The left column in this set ("All months") shows the share of total expenditures accounted for by the sum of expenditures for all months for the population of beneficiaries specified in the row. The right column ("High-cost months") lists the share of total expenditures due to the sum of expenditures in only over those months classified as high cost by the table.

Inspection of table 3.8 reveals that female patients who experienced at least one of month classified in the 80th expenditure percentile category account for 57.7 percent of total Medicare expenditures during the 1989–99 period. Counting expenditures for this group that occur only in their high-cost months accounts for 51.4 percent of total Medicare expenditures.

Portrait of High-Cost Month Experiences

Tables 3.8 through 3.11 present results considering only the elderly segment of the Medicare population—beneficiaries 65 years and older. Results differ only marginally considering Medicare beneficiaries of all ages (which also includes the younger disabled population). Table 3.8 reports the distributions of experiences for months classified as having expenditures above the 80th percentile. Table 3.9 gives findings for months with expenditures above the 90th percentile. Table 3.10 lists distributions for the 95th percentile of monthly expenditures. Finally, table 3.11 presents findings for months in the 98th percentile of expenditures.

Inspecting the first row of table 3.8, we see in the first set of columns that 86.8 percent of elderly Medicare beneficiaries experience at least one month during the 1989–99 decade in which they receive medical services costing above the 80th percentile for months during the year of expenditures. So practically everyone can be considered a high-cost user at some time in their lifetime over a short enough period.

Moving to the farthest left set of columns, we see that this group of beneficiaries accounts for 99.6 percent of all Medicare expenditures totaled over the 1989–99 decade. Counting only expenses incurred during their high-cost months covers 89.7 percent of total expenditures. Thus, knowledge of the expenses incurred during only high-cost months for this group essentially accounts for all but a minor portion of Medicare spending.

According to the other columns in table 3.8 for the "Patients w/ experience" row, the average number of high-cost months experienced was 9.1, with 20 percent of the group having two or fewer months, 50 percent having six or fewer months, and 20 percent having fourteen or more months classified as high cost. This group experienced an average of 4.9 spells, with 20 percent having eight or more. Spells are short, lasting two months on average, with less than 20 percent of beneficiaries experiencing spells lasting longer. On average, women had slightly more high-cost months than men (9.4 versus 8.8).

Examining table 3.9 for the group of elderly beneficiaries who received health services during a month costing above the 90th percentile level for months during the year, we see that 75.3 percent of all beneficiaries make up this group. Total spending on this group accounts for 98.1 percent of all Medicare expenditures for the 1989–99 decade, and expenses incurred during high-cost months for this group cover 79.1 percent of total expenditures. Thus, considering only this classification of high-cost months covers all but about 20 percent of the decade's expenditure on Medicare. The average number of months defined as high cost by this definition equals 5.3, occurring in an average of 3.3 spells per recipient. Only 20 percent of the group had eight or more months classified as high cost, and 20 percent had five or more spells. Once again, spells tend to be short. Further, women had slightly more high-cost months than men (5.3 versus 5.2 months).

Turning to tables 3.10 and 3.11, which classify high-cost months as achieving expenses reaching the 95th and 98th percentiles for monthly expenditures, reference to the top row indicates that the fraction of beneficiaries experiencing these high levels of spending still involves a substantial segment of the elderly population: 60.7 percent have at least one 95th percentile month, and 39.7 percent have one or more 98th percentile months. Spending on the 98th percentile group consumes 78.6 percent of all Medicare expenditures accumulated over the 1989–99 decade, and the sum of those expenses incurred during only high-cost months covers 40.8 percent of total expenditures. The spending on the 95th percentile group accounts for 62.9 percent of total expenditures for the decade according to the last column of table 3.10. Thus, knowledge of the incidence of 95th percentile months alone explains nearly two-thirds of Medicare spending over the decade.

Inspecting the rows in tables 3.8 through 3.11 describing experiences by age groups reveals that average high-cost months are nondecreasing in age, consistent with the view that costs rise with age given the onset of chronic illness. A notable increase in averages can be seen for the 80th percentile months; however, the difference decreases at higher percentiles. In particular, for 98th percentile months, averages and distributions remain constant across age groups. The shares of total Medicare expenditures accounted for by high-cost-month beneficiaries and by high-cost months do not exhibit a monotonic relationship with age. This reflects the fact that although average Medicare experiences generally rise with age, the overall size of age groups declines the older the group. Consequently, the contribution of age groups to the high-cost month population depends on how mortality rates balance against the occurrence of illnesses leading to the incidence of intense use of medical services.

Across all demographic groups considered in tables 3.8 through 3.11, spells of high-cost months are short. Higher months of experience come about due to the occurrence of more spells rather than the length of spells.

3.4.3   Experiences for High-Cost Users of Medicare

The lower rows of tables 3.8 through 3.11 summarize the monthly experiences of the highest-cost users of Medicare defined by their expenses accumulated over calendar years. The group in the top row of the "Cost percentile, any year" portion of the tables refer to beneficiaries who had expenditures above the 80th calendar-year percentile in any year during the 1989–99 period, and the top row of the "Cost percentile, any 2 years" portion selects beneficiaries who had annual costs exceeding the 80th calendar-year percentile in two or more years. The other rows designate equivalent groups for the 90th, 95th, and 98th annual percentiles.

Calculations based on the first columns of these tables imply that all of the high-cost groups experienced at least one 80th percentile month, a hardly surprising result given their large annual expenses. All but a trivial number of the "GE 80th percentile" group also incurred one or more 90th percentile months, and all but a very small proportion of the "GE 80th percentile" and "GE 90th percentile" groups also experienced 95th percentile months. The vast majority of these users further realized at least one 98th percentile month of expenses, with only 10 percent of the "GE 90th percentile in any year" group being excluded from this experience.

Regarding the statistics summarizing the distributions of high-cost months, patterns correspond fully with intuition. We see that more intense users classified by annual measures experience more high-cost months considering both the total number of months over the decade and the number of spells; this pattern holds irrespective of the level of percentile considered. Also, the number of high-cost months experienced is notably large. For example, the "GE 90th percentile in any year" group averaged eight of the 90th percentile months, 4.3 of the 95th percentile months, and 2.1 of the 98th percentile months. The "GE 98th percentile in any year" group averaged seven of the 95th percentile months and 3.4 of the 98th percentile months, with 20 percent of this group experiencing seventeen or more 90th percentile months. As for variation in spell length, we see once again that all spells of high-cost months are short, and more months of experience come about due to the incidence of more spells.

To assist in understanding the circumstances of these high-cost groups, table 3.12 extracts selected statistics from tables 3.8 through 3.11 and supplements the information for these groups. Moreover, table 3.12 introduces

Table 3.12 Annual high-cost users of Medicare and their share of expenditures: Elderly (1989–99)

					Intensity and duration of utilization					
Data: HCFA (1989–1999)	Top 5% in at least 1 year	Top 5% in at least 2 years	Top 10% in at least 1 year	Top 10% in at least 2 years	Top 10% in at least 3 years	Top 20% in at least 1 year	Top 20% in at least 2 years	Top 20% in at least 3 years
Percent of all beneficiaries	22.4	5.9	38.1	14.6	5.7	58.5	32.0	17.0
Percent in age categories								
65–69	21.7	24.9	22.9	24.3	26.6	27.0	26.5	26.9
70–74	23.2	24.9	22.7	23.9	25.0	22.9	23.4	24.2
75–79	22.0	22.4	21.2	22.0	22.3	20.1	21.2	22.0
80–84	16.9	15.7	16.6	16.4	15.3	15.2	15.8	15.7
85–89	10.6	8.4	10.6	9.3	7.8	9.5	9.0	8.2
90–100	5.7	3.6	6.0	4.1	2.9	5.3	4.1	3.1
Percentiles for "decade" costs (2000 $)								
10th percentile	43,379	91,669	29,443	61,078	95,066	16,644	34,626	52,922
25th percentile	58,682	114,791	41,749	77,995	116,394	26,100	47,167	68,457
50th percentile	84,731	150,159	62,971	104,832	149,304	44,339	68,980	94,092
75th percentile	124,439	201,244	97,343	146,138	199,046	76,304	104,518	134,762
90th percentile	179,510	270,712	147,175	205,106	269,359	123,081	156,203	192,722
Mean "decade" costs (2000 $)	102,151	169,945	79,491	123,134	170,057	60,785	86,063	112,606
Percent of total costs accounted for by group	59.9	26.1	79.4	47.1	25.5	93.1	72.1	50.2

additional groups specifying beneficiaries whose Medicare expenditures place them in the upper percentiles for multiple years as persistently high-cost users. In addition to showing the shares of beneficiaries and expenses encompassed by these high-cost groups, the second set of rows in table 3.12 gives the age composition of the groups. The third and fourth set of rows list the percentiles and means of the distribution of expenditures for the individuals comprising these groups accumulated over the 1989–99 decade.

According to table 3.12, 22.4 percent of the elderly Medicare beneficiaries experience at least one year with expenses placing them in the 95th percentile in calendar-year expenditures, and this group accounts for 59.9 percent of all Medicare expenditures totaled over the 1989–99 decade. Half of this group has expenses over $84,731 during the decade, and 10 percent has expenditures exceeding $179,510. About 6 percent of the beneficiaries are in the top 5 percent of expenditures for two or more years, and they consume slightly more than a quarter of Medicare spending.

Table 3.12 suggests the importance of persistence in expenditures over long periods of time. More than a quarter of beneficiaries in the top 5 percent of expenditures in one year end up in this category in at least one other year as well. Nearly 6 percent of beneficiaries have expenditures placing them in the top 10 percent of expenditures in three or more years, and 17 percent receive services costing amounts falling into the upper two deciles in three or more years. Such evidence clearly reveals that the spells of high-cost months experienced by many users are spread out over several years. This knowledge, combined with our evidence of short spells, implies that sophisticated specifications will be required to build duration models that effectively capture monthly expenditure patterns.

3.5   Summary and Concluding Remarks

Our findings reveal several valuable insights into the growth of Medicare expenditures in recent years, both in projecting aggregate trends and in discovering the extent to which the concentration of spending on high-cost users contributes to overall expenditures.

In the analysis validating our monthly longitudinal Medicare data set, summary statistics reveal that 20–30 percent of the total growth in Medicare program payments from 1989 to 1999 arises from an increase in the participation rate, and 50–60 percent results from an increase in average program payments per service recipient. Comparing spending on the elderly segment of the Medicare population to all beneficiaries (including qualified individuals below age sixty-five), average payments and costs for part A services are lower for the elderly until around 1995, when the relationship reverses. Averages for part B spending for the aged remain consistently lower than comparable quantities for overall population, reflecting the facts that the disabled have higher average expenditures and also become a steadily increasing share of the total Medicare population. Despite the increase in this share, however, part A program payments and expenditures for the disabled population declined relative to the aged population continually after 1996.

Examining the extent to which the growth in Medicare expenditures differs across various segments of the beneficiary population, receipt of part A services increased more rapidly for the younger cohorts, at least until later years of the decade. This rise in the part A participation rate primarily reflected greater utilization of skilled nursing facilities, home health agencies, and hospices, although use of inpatient hospital services rose as well. Further, our results indicate that expenditures grew more rapidly in the lower percentile categories and for the youngest cohort. The BBA97 appears to have reduced the rate of growth across all cohorts, especially in the upper half of the expenditure distribution, with the greatest reductions occurring for the oldest cohorts. Indeed, after BBA97, expenditures actually fell for the highest-cost users of Medicare services. However, the results in section 3.2 relying on administrative data extending beyond our sample period suggest that policy impacts achieved in the late 1990s are only temporary; starting in 2000, the overall growth in Medicare expenditures reverted to its previous rate and may have even accelerated.

Annual Medicare spending is highly concentrated among a small segment of the beneficiary population, and shares of spending attributable to high-cost users have been remarkably stable over the 1989–99 decade, even though growth rates have varied considerably during the period and across intensity of use. Those beneficiaries classified in the top 2 percent of the annual expenditure distribution alone account for about one-quarter of total expenditures; those in the top 5 percent cover almost half of annual expenditures; and the beneficiaries in the highest 10 percent of annual expenditures account for nearly two-thirds of total Medicare spending in a year. Considering spending by months only reinforces this picture of concentration. The 2 percent of months making up the 98 + percentile account for around two-fifths of total annual expenditures; the top 5 percent of months cover nearly two-thirds of yearly Medicare expenditures; and around four-fifths of annual spending occurs in the top 10 percent of months.

Viewed over a decade, the majority of beneficiaries experience high-cost episodes at some point in their lifetime, implying far less concentration in expenditures. Three-quarters of the elderly receive medical services during a month costing above the 90th percentile level for months during a year, and total spending for this group covers virtually all expenditures during the 1989–99 decade. Three-fifths of the beneficiaries experienced at least one 95th percentile month in the decade, and two-fifths realize one or more 98th percentile months. Knowledge of the incidence and expenditures of 95th percentile months alone explains nearly two-thirds of Medicare spending over the decade. Spending accumulated for those in the 98th percentile months comprises almost four-fifths of total decade expenditures. Concentration of Medicare expenditures will dissipate even further if one were to extrapolate our findings to lifetime experiences rather than over just a decade. In particular, this decade-based study ignores the consequences of both left and right censoring in the data, which unambiguously result in lower estimates of the incidences of high-cost events.

A major challenge faced by researchers involves identifying intense users of health care services along with the factors leading to the incidence and duration of their utilization. Such a task requires a detailed understanding of the patterns of medical care for periods much shorter than a year to adequately capture the onset of health events and the relationships linking the persistence of costs in the short and long runs. Many surmise that restricting attention to those individuals in their last year of life identifies most of the high-cost users, but existing work shows that the majority of the most-intense users (measured by accumulating expenses annually) live beyond a year after incurring their high expenses. Further, previous work has met with limited success in associating large fractions of the highest-cost users with particular diagnoses or chronic conditions. The availability of our monthly longitudinal Medicare data greatly enhances options for improving our understanding of the sources of high-cost utilization.

References

Garber, A. M., T. MaCurdy, and M. McClellan. 1998. Persistence of Medicare expenditures among elderly beneficiaries. In *Frontiers in health policy research I*, ed. A. Garber, 153–80. Cambridge: MIT Press.
———. 1999. Medical care at the end of life: Diseases, treatment patterns, and costs persistence of Medicare expenditures among elderly beneficiaries. In *Frontiers in health policy research*, Vol. 2, ed. A. Garber, 77–98. Cambridge: MIT Press.
Heckman, J. J., and R. Robb. 1985. Alternative methods for evaluating the impact of interventions. In *Longitudinal analysis of labor market data*, ed. J. Heckman and B. Singer, 156–245. Cambridge: Cambridge University Press.
Medicare and Medicaid statistical supplement. *Health care financing review*. Baltimore, MD: Centers for Medicare and Medicaid Services.
Wolf, J., B. Starfield, and G. Anderson. 2002. Prevalence, expenditures, and complications of multiple chronic conditions in the elderly. *Archives of internal medicine* 162:2269–76.

Comment   Jonathan Skinner

In this paper, the authors have created a first-order data set to address first-order research questions. The data are a longitudinal sample of Medicare claims data for more than two million enrollees between 1989 and 1999. This allows MaCurdy and Geppert to capture the longitudinal life-cycle patterns of utilization, as well as measuring secular change in Medicare expenditures during the 1990s. The research questions they address—to identify, measure, and (one hopes) ultimately to affect utilization of the high-cost users—are critical for the financial stability of the Medicare program.

We need all the help we can get to put Medicare on a firm financial basis. Unlike Social Security, where potential policy levers include shifting back monthly benefits or changing the degree of progressivity in monthly benefits, the options available for reducing Medicare costs are few and far between. As an insurance program, the Medicare program can reduce reimbursement rates, but this is neither an equitable nor a particularly effective way to effect long-term reductions in expenditures. In the fee-for-service program, health care providers (and their patients) still control quantities of services, so it is entirely possible—and indeed, policymakers in Washington came to expect that—reductions in reimbursement rates will be offset in part by increases in quantities of service. While the Balanced Budget Act of 1997 (BBA97) made it clear that the government *could* cut back on expenditures by restricting payments, those cuts were short-lived; within a few years, as MaCurdy and Geppert show, the previous trend had reasserted itself. Furthermore, cutting reimbursement rates across the board tends to harm the more conservative hospitals and physicians, given that providers are paid more only when they perform more services. As well, even with current reimbursement rates, some physicians no longer accept new Medicare patients, and cutting back further will simply exacerbate the problem of access.

The Medicare+Choice program attempted to save money using a different approach, to attract elderly patients into risk-bearing managed care. Unfortunately, this program was no more successful at saving money; either healthier low-cost patients enrolled (thus earning profits for the health maintenance organization [HMO]), or insurance companies didn't want to offer policies under the prevailing reimbursements when they didn't keep pace with the fee-for-service costs. In recent years, as a consequence, there has been a sharp decline in Medicare+Choice enrollment (Thorpe and

Jonathan Skinner is the John French Professor of Economics and professor of community and Family Medicine at Dartmouth College, and a research associate of the National Bureau of Economic Research.

Atherly 2002). Thus, neither adjusting reimbursement rates, nor trying to attract managed care coverage, seems likely to solve the looming imbalance in funding for the Medicare program.

MaCurdy and Geppert have followed a different strategy, which is to identify those who are likely to be the high-cost patients who account for the majority of Medicare spending. As the authors have shown, there is typically a great deal of concentration in Medicare spending, with a small fraction of elderly people accounting for most of the overall spending. The authors pursue this approach along two dimensions. The first is to test whether some groups over time have accounted for a disproportionate share of the increases in Medicare spending during the 1990s. For example, if the top 2 percent of people accounted for an ever larger share of expenditures over time, it would suggest that the Medicare program has focused increasingly on health care for the very sickest of the Medicare population.

The surprising answer to this question was that expenditures seemed to rise reasonably consistently across different groups of patients, with the share of spending accounted for by the top 5 percent or 10 percent of patients remarkably stable over time. As well, there was somewhat higher growth in Medicare expenditures among younger Medicare enrollees compared to older enrollees during the 1990s, but that pattern may reflect a reversion to the mean following an earlier relative growth in spending among older Medicare enrollees (Cutler and Meara 1999). Nearly all of the variation observed over time reflects a common aggregate year effect that appears to cause expenditures among all groups at the national level to rise. In short, the demographic composition of the population does not provide much information regarding future expenditures. Instead, there is some aggregate shock to spending (typically positive), and this common factor, reflecting both health provider behavior, and changes in Medicare reimbursement rates and rules, largely determines future aggregate spending.

MaCurdy and Geppert's second approach to modeling expenditures is to examine properties of life-cycle Medicare expenditures at the monthly level. As they show, identifying the small number of months with high expenditures essentially captures nearly all Medicare spending. Furthermore, a large fraction of Medicare enrollees end up in at least one or two of the high-expenditure months. This latter fact, however, is probably less surprising than one might think. In 1999, the 80th percentile Medicare expenditure was $558, and the 90th percentile $1,863. It does not take much in the way of utilization to spend more than $558 in a month (e.g., an angiogram or a sigmoidoscopy), and one visit to an emergency room can easily result in several thousand dollars in spending. Thus I am not entirely convinced that monthly data provide a clearly superior perspective compared with annual data.

A major component of this paper is simply to create a data set that is accurate and matches official Center for Medicare and Medicaid Services

(CMS) aggregate statistics on annual expenditures (as in their figure 3.2). As one who has encountered the raw Medicare claims data, I know that getting it into usable format and one that is consistent over time is a tremendous task. Given this enormous fixed cost, the question now is—what's next on the research agenda? In other words, what are some additional hypotheses that might be tested using these data?

Given that their primary objective is to identify high-cost users, a first step would be to begin using the rich diagnostic data contained in the Medicare claims data. Knowing that an individual has been diagnosed with congestive heart failure (CHF) or with chronic obstructive pulmonary disease (COPD) is a very strong predictor of a long-term and expensive interaction with the health care system. Similarly, metastatic lung cancer would also predict high expenditures, but with a much shorter time horizon, as there is less variability with regard to impending death. In recent studies, Lunney, Lynn, and Hogan (2002) and Lunney et al. (2003) have characterized the different patterns of health declines prior to death depending on the type of disease. For patients experiencing sudden death, functioning does not decline prior to the date of death; these are presumably otherwise healthy (and low-cost) elderly people who experience a sudden cardiac arrest or other catastrophic illness. By contrast, those with cancer experienced the sharpest dropoff in functioning during the five months prior to death, while those with organ failure (e.g., chronic illnesses) were subject to sharp declines in functioning, followed by recovery, followed by decline, recovery, and finally death. Because these patients often survive for many years, albeit years punctuated with hospital admissions and adverse events, they are likely to account for a large fraction of health care costs. In sum, using the detailed clinical data on diagnosis can provide one of the most straightforward ways of identifying high-cost patients.

Even when high-cost patients can be identified, there is another, more difficult question—are we spending too much on these patients, or too little? It's not a shock that spending should be greatest on the sickest patients, but the real question is, what's the right amount of spending? One strategy is to identify regions in the United States where health care expenditures or utilization appears to be consistently higher than in others and focus on those regions as potential sources of saving to the Medicare program. The *Dartmouth Atlas of Health Care* has documented the wide ranges in health care utilization in the last six months of life (Wennberg and Cooper 1999). Physician visits per decedent in the last six months, for example, range from an average of eleven in Salem, Oregon, to forty-eight visits in Miami, Florida (see Skinner, Fisher, and Wennberg, chap. 4 in this volume). Expenditures for the top 5 percent of the population exhibit a similar degree of variation. As Anderson and others demonstrate (2003), average expenditures for the top 5 percent of Medicare enrollees averaged $50,809 during 1995–99. However, across hospital referral regions, the standard deviation in expenditures was $9,122. Assuming a normal distribution, the 10th percentile region in terms of spending for this expensive group of patients would be $39,132 in contrast to the 90th percentile region, where spending would be $62,485. Some of the difference may be attributed to differences in burdens of disease. However, identifying regions or even hospitals that cost much more to treat patients with similar clinical diagnoses would certainly be a first step in identifying "excess" Medicare spending.

Finally, these data could be used as a valuable proving ground for testing economic or epidemiological models of health and health care. For example, one could estimate a simultaneous equations model of health care expenditures and health care outcomes, and attempt to test for links between the two, again using the very detailed clinical data to provide covariates or to stratify the data. Similarly, one could test the impact of the BBA97 on health outcomes, particularly among patients where the cutbacks were the greatest in magnitude. For example, one of the major changes in Medicare reimbursement policies following BBA97 was to sharply restrict the use of home health care payments, in part by limiting the number of visits to 100 annually. In some regions of the country—particularly in Texas—this was a major change in overall reimbursements. Did the patients suffering from the sudden cutbacks experience any change in health outcomes, as measured by mortality, emergency room use, or hospital admissions? To sum up, it is difficult to imagine a better data set to address the important issues facing Medicare in the future, and I look forward to the next installment in the authors' research agenda.

References

Anderson, Todd, Dan Crippen, Julie Lee, and Steve Lieberman. 2003. Lowering Medicare costs: Regions or beneficiaries? Washington, DC: Congressional Budget Office. Mimeograph.

Cutler, David, and Ellen Meara. 1999. The concentration of medical spending: An update. NBER Working Paper no. 7279. Cambridge, MA: National Bureau of Economic Research, August.

Lunney, June R., Joanne Lynn, and C. Hogan. 2002. Profiles of older Medicare decedents. *Journal of the American Geriatric Society* 50:1108–12.

Lunney, June R., Joanne Lynn, Daniel J. Foley, Steven Lipson, and Jack M. Guralnik. 2003. Patterns of functional decline at the end of life. *Journal of the American Medical Association* 289 (18): 2387–92.

Thorpe, Kenneth E., and Adam Atherly. 2002. Medicare+choice: Current role and near-term prospects. *Health Affairs* (Web Exclusives, July 2002):W242–W252. Available at http://www.healthaffairs.org/WebExclusives/Thorpe_Web_Excl _071702.htm.

Wennberg, John E., and Megan M. Cooper. 1999. The quality of medical care in the United States: A report on the Medicare program. In *The Dartmouth atlas of health care in the United States,* ed. John E. Wennberg and Megan M. Cooper. Chicago: American Health Association Press.

4

The Efficiency of Medicare

Jonathan Skinner, Elliott S. Fisher,
and John E. Wennberg

4.1 Introduction

The United States spends more on health care in per capita terms and as a percentage of gross domestic product (GDP) than any other developed country (Reinhardt, Hussey, and Anderson 2004). This can be interpreted in two ways. One is that the elevated spending is symptomatic of failure in the health care system. Money is wasted through administrative overhead, the overuse of fully insured health care, or the provision of expensive tertiary but only marginally useful technology.[1] A different view is that U.S. citizens demand, and get, a higher quality level of health care than anywhere else in the world. It may be expensive, but the technological advances provided in the United States have led to dramatic improvements in functioning and life expectancy.[2]

Jonathan Skinner is the John French Professor of Economics and professor of community and family medicine at Dartmouth College, and a research associate of the National Bureau of Economic Research (NBER). Elliott S. Fisher is a professor of medicine and of community and family medicine at Dartmouth Medical School. John E. Wennberg is the Peggy Y. Thomson Professor for the Evaluative Clinical Sciences and a professor of community and family medicine (epidemiology) and of medicine at Dartmouth Medical School.

Support by the Robert Wood Johnson Foundation and the National Institute on Aging (PO1 AGI9783) is gratefully acknowledged. The views expressed here are those of the authors alone and not of the Department of Veterans' Affairs. We are grateful for very helpful comments from Esther Duflo, Alan Garber, David Laibson, Douglas Staiger, Duncan Thomas, Frank Vella, and seminar participants at the NBER Conference on Aging, Boulder, Arizona; at the University of California, Los Angeles; Rand; Georgia State University; and the Universities of Virginia, Maryland, and North Carolina. Dan Gottlieb provided excellent data analysis.

1. For a good presentation of this view, see Evans and Stoddart (1994).
2. For a general exposition of the view that current high spending levels for medical technology will yield benefits that could even lower costs in the future, see Pardes and others (1999). For specific measures of improvements in outcomes following the use of more intensive technology, see Cutler and others (1998) and Cutler and Meara (1999).

Knowing which story holds true is crucial for any kind of health care reform, and particularly for Medicare reform. Unfortunately, the answer is elusive. While the evidence strongly suggests substantial technological gains in the treatment of specific diseases such as heart attacks or specific groups such as low-birth-weight infants (e.g., Cutler et al. 1998; Cutler and Meara 1999), it is not clear how well these specific paradigms generalize to the entire health care system where medical progress has not been nearly so robust. More importantly, the secular improvements in mortality are "average" effects of technology rather than the marginal impact of greater health care intensity on health outcomes (see Cutler 2000).

Researchers have attempted to exploit "natural randomization" in outcomes data to estimate the marginal effectiveness of specific medical technologies on outcomes such as mortality for people with heart attacks (McClellan, McNeil, and Newhouse 1994) or for infants (Currie and Gruber 1996). For example, in McClellan, McNeil, and Newhouse the "treatment" group was people experiencing heart attacks who lived relatively near a hospital equipped with diagnostic laboratory facilities that helped physicians decide whether to proceed with surgery. The "control" group was those living relatively far away. They found minimal benefits among the population treated most intensively for heart attacks. It is not known how well this finding for heart attack patients, where the quality of the scientific evidence is high, generalizes to daily decisions about treatment for chronically ill patients, where the scientific evidence is quite modest.

In this paper, we use the idea of natural randomization to evaluate the efficiency of the Medicare program more generally. The macro-level equivalent of living near a hospital with advanced diagnostic laboratories for heart attack patients is whether the health care *system* provides a higher-than-average intensity of health care, ranging from flu shots in the outpatient setting, to hospitalization instead of outpatient care, surgery instead of watchful waiting, and three-month waiting periods for physician appointments instead of six-month waiting periods for appointments.

Simply comparing outcomes between regions with higher-than-average and lower-than-average Medicare expenditures risks the reverse causality problem; the sickest regions tend to experience more spending on health care.[3] A deeper issue is the difficulty in comparing multidimensional health care systems across regions. One region may spend more to provide "effective" care of proven clinical value (such as flu shots, mammograms among women over age fifty, and eye examinations for diabetics), another region

---

3. In an earlier study, Hadley (1988) used as instruments for Medicare expenditures factors such as nursing home residence rates; he found a positive impact of Medicare spending on survival. However, nursing home residence rates are probably correlated with unmeasured regional health status.

may spend more because it provides surgery where nonsurgical alternatives often exist (such as back surgery or knee replacements), while physicians in a third region could be more likely to admit chronically ill patients to a hospital or refer them to a specialist.

In the empirical section, we focus on several "markers" for the different dimensions of intensity. With regard to effective care, we need not instrument for reverse causality, since there is no reason why annual eye examinations for diabetics (for example) should be lower or higher in regions with greater incidence of disease. In every region, the "right rate" among the relevant population is nearly 100 percent, and so we can use this marker for quality without adjusting for potential reverse causality. However, finding a marker for intensity of care among chronically ill patients is more difficult, since patients in regions with greater prevalence of disease might be expected to account for more Medicare spending. We use two types of instruments that we believe on clinical grounds should not be biased by differences across regions in underlying health status. The first focuses on utilization (physician visits and intensive care unit [ICU] days) in the last six months of life. By definition, these patients are similar with regard to health status across regions for one important dimension of health: their six-month survival rate. Obviously, one cannot use treatment patterns in the last six months to make inferences about Medicare efficiency in this group, since they are all dead by the end of the period. Instead, the intensity of care in the last six months is used as an instrument to measure whether Medicare enrollees who are alive at the beginning of the year gain survival benefits from higher levels of Medicare spending for the type of care typically provided to those with chronic illnesses.

The second instrument takes a prospective approach for a disease with "high-tech" treatments: regional price-adjusted averages of one-year Medicare part A (hospital) expenditures for a cohort of patients following acute myocardial infarction (AMI), or heart attacks. Again, expenditures for AMI are likely to be good measures of the intensity of health care in the region, although in this case the dimension of intensity may differ since regions with more aggressive surgical treatment of AMI will tend to experience higher costs for the treatment of AMI patients. Like end-of-life Medicare enrollees, patients who have experienced an AMI tend to be similar across regions with regard to their initial health status.

Using data from the *Dartmouth Atlas of Health Care* as well as supplemental information from the U.S. Census and the Centers for Disease Control, we estimate the incremental effects of these different types of spending, both in a linear model and, where appropriate, in a nonlinear framework (Newey, Powell, and Vella 1999). We find that higher measures of "efficient" care are associated with better survival for the general population but are not associated with higher costs. However, we also find that higher levels of spending associated with more intensive end-of-life physician visits, and with more intensive treatment of AMI patients, are not associated with greater overall rates of survival in the Medicare population; in other words, we estimate a "flat of the curve" segment in which regions spend more but gain no benefit in higher survival.

These results are consistent with two recent studies focusing on outcomes for cohorts of AMI, colon cancer, and hip fracture patients (Fisher et al. 2003a,b), rather than the entire Medicare population, as we do here. They found evidence of worse outcomes—that is, higher mortality rates—associated with higher levels of health care intensity. In short, our estimates imply that physicians and hospitals participating in the Medicare program provide too little in the way of inexpensive and effective care, while at the same time spending $26 billion annually, or nearly 20 percent of the Medicare program's budget for health care that appears to be of questionable value with regard to survival benefits.

4.2 The Nature of the Problem: Per Capita Medicare Expenditures in the United States

We first consider the magnitude and extent of regional differences in Medicare expenditures in the United States. Primary data sources are samples of either 20 percent (outpatient) or 100 percent (inpatient) of the Medicare claims data during 1995 and 1996. The basic unit of analysis is the hospital referral region (HRR), of which there are 306 in the United States. The HRR was constructed in the *Dartmouth Atlas of Health Care* as a unit of analysis that reflected the actual hospital migration patterns of Medicare patients for tertiary care. An HRR must include at least one hospital that performs cardiac surgery and neurosurgery. Each zip code in the United States is assigned to an HRR depending on what hospital the majority (or, in some cases, the plurality) of Medicare enrollees seek their hospital care; see Wennberg and Cooper (1999) for details. Thus, the HRR may cross county or state boundaries or, in some cases, follow interstate highways.

The important thing to note about HRRs for this study is that all rates are based upon the zip code of residence and not where the person actually sought care. Thus, if an individual lives in Lebanon, New Hampshire, and is admitted to a hospital in Boston, all utilization is assigned to the Lebanon HRR. Most care is delivered locally; 80 percent of the U.S. population lives in HRRs in which over 85 percent of care is delivered by providers within the HRR. In the analysis that follows, utilization rates have been adjusted for differences across HRRs in the age, sex, and racial composition of the population, and (where necessary) differences in the price level. We restrict our attention to the fee-for-service Medicare population

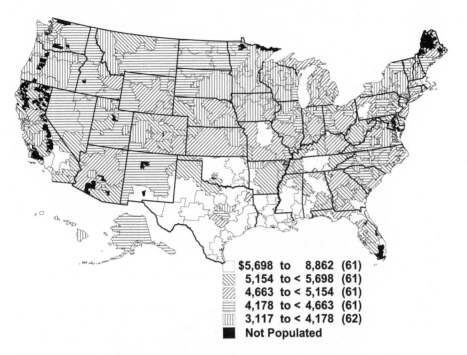

$5,698 to   8,862 (61)
5,154 to < 5,698 (61)
4,663 to < 5,154 (61)
4,178 to < 4,663 (61)
3,117 to < 4,178 (62)
Not Populated

Fig. 4.1   Noncapitated Medicare expenditures per enrollee, 1996

that during the study period accounted for more than 85 percent of the total Medicare population.[4]

Figure 4.1 uses these data from Wennberg and Cooper (1999) to construct a map showing the distribution of per capita Medicare expenditures across the United States in 1996; these are adjusted for differences across regions in age, sex, and race (black and nonblack). There are clearly wide variations in the extent of spending, with per capita expenditures ranging from $3,341 in Minneapolis, for example, to $8,414 in Miami. There are clusters of high-expenditure regions largely concentrated in Florida, the deep South, and urban areas on the East and West coasts. There are exceptions as well: inexpensive regions in Florida and low-cost cities on the West Coast (e.g., Portland, Oregon) and the East Coast (Richmond, Virginia).

This figure raises some immediate policy issues. If the higher expendi-

---

4. One concern with using the fee-for-service population is the selection problem; healthier patients tend to enroll in health maintenance organizations (HMOs). We control for this in part by measuring health status (discussed presently) for the same fee-for-service population. Thus, if a healthy region experiences a high rate of HMO enrollment, leaving an unhealthy fee-for-service population, this will be reflected in both health status measures and in per capita spending. In practice, either including the percentage of the HMO population in the HRR, or excluding regions with more than 10 percent HMO enrollment, has little impact on the results.

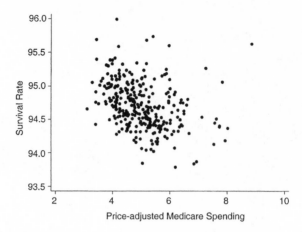

Fig. 4.2   Per capita Medicare expenditures and mortality rates in the Medicare population, 1996

Note: Medicare expenditures and mortality rates are age, sex, and race adjusted; both apply to the fee-for-service population.

tures in some regions actually lead to better health, then the Medicare program may be inequitable to the extent that taxpayers in the low-expenditure regions are paying for the better health of those in the high-expenditure regions (Feenberg and Skinner 2000). Conversely, if the higher expenditures yield nothing in health benefits, then there is tremendous waste in the program; reducing spending in the high-expenditure areas can save enough money to preserve the solvency of the Medicare trust fund by a decade (Skinner and Wennberg 2000). It could also be the case that people in the high-expenditure areas simply prefer more intensive care. One might then ask why other regions should be subsidizing their preferences.

To consider the efficiency of Medicare, we provide a simple graph in figure 4.2 that shows per capita Medicare expenditures (age, sex, race, and price-adjusted) on the horizontal axis and survival, which we define as the $(1 - \text{age-sex-race-adjusted mortality}) \times 100$, on the vertical axis. There is a clear negative correlation between expenditures and survival. This in itself is not too surprising; spending should be higher in regions with poorer levels of health, so we might expect to observe Mobile, Alabama, spending more than Grand Junction, Colorado. In the next section, we consider a simple model that formalizes how to evaluate the efficiency of Medicare given that Medicare spending is likely to be higher in regions with poor health.

4.3   Medicare Expenditures and Outcomes: Theoretical and Measurement Issues

In this section, we first develop a theoretical model of Medicare expenditures and outcomes and show that the observed negative correlation between Medicare expenditures and survival in figure 4.2 is at least consistent with the Medicare program meeting stringent efficiency conditions. We then develop criteria for determining what one *should* expect in terms of better survival.

4.3.1 A Theoretical Model of Regional Differences in Medicare Expenditures

We next turn to evaluating the efficiency of the Medicare program with regard to differences across regions in health care spending. It is important to emphasize at the outset that there are many inputs into the production of health care, some of which may yield substantial health benefits at little costs, and others of which may provide little in benefits but exert a larger impact on costs. In this study, it is impossible to characterize all of these inputs, but we can try to provide a rough categorization of regional differences in the intensity of three dimensions of inputs to health care.[5]

The first is "effective" care, treatments where there is strong clinical evidence as to their efficacy and where, among the relevant population of patients, nearly 100 percent should be receiving the treatment. Examples include eye examinations for diabetics, flu shots for the elderly, mammograms for women over age fifty, and the use of beta blockers and aspirin among appropriate heart attack candidates. The second categorization is "preference-sensitive" care, or treatments where there are valid options for how to treat the specific disease, and choices often involve trade-offs between risks and benefits of treatment. For example, knee replacement surgery can provide long-term benefits in functioning, but there is a nontrivial risk of surgical complications and a lengthy period of recovery. Similarly, angioplasty for the treatment of ischemic heart disease carries with it the risk of stroke or operative death, but it can provide relief of symptoms.[6] These treatment options typically do not have a large impact on long-term survival but can potentially affect functioning and quality of life. Unfortunately, we cannot measure quality of life, only quantity in terms of survival rates. Thus, there is unlikely to be any influence on mortality of greater intensity of preference-sensitive care.

Finally, the third category is "supply-sensitive" care, where the quality of scientific evidence regarding use of care is poor and the quantity of care tends to be associated with the supply of resources such as specialists and hospital beds. Measures of the prevalence of supply-sensitive care include the frequency of physician visits and the use of ICU days among chronically ill patients. Note that we do not presume causality from supply to the

5. This categorization is developed in Wennberg, Fisher, and Skinner (2002).
6. Angioplasty is proven to be effective for reperfusion within twenty-four hours of the onset of an AMI, and for this use it is less likely considered preference sensitive. However, the vast majority of angioplasties (more than 85 percent) are performed on *non-AMI* patients.

use of supply-sensitive care, simply a correlation between factors of supply and the quantity of supply-sensitive care.

There are separate efficiency conditions for each of these inputs and in each region. Suppose that the value function of the "social planner" is written in terms of

(1) $V = V[S(R, H), Q(R, H), Y(1 - \tau) - (1 - \theta)M^*, P]$,

where V is a concave value function, the bold-faced S denotes the vector of (regional) per capita survival measures for regions $i = 1, \ldots N$, Q the vector measuring quality of life (conditional on survival), and R is the $K \times N$ vector of inputs (for example, inputs that are efficient, preference sensitive, and supply sensitive) for each of the N regions. With regard to the third argument, after-tax income (assumed to be equal to consumption), M^* is the level of real per capita total health care expenditures, and within each region total expenditures are a function of the intensity of inputs conditional on health status and the health of the population H so that $M^* = H(R, H)$.

Nonmedical consumption is given by $Y(1 - \tau) - (1 - \theta)M^*$: gross income Y after the Medicare tax τ has been paid and Medicare's share of (out-of-pocket) medical expenses θ has been paid. Note that total Medicare expenditures are therefore $M = \theta M^*$. Medicare taxes are assumed to be proportional to income.[7] Finally, the population of each region is given by P; this is to allow for larger regions to receive a larger weight in the social welfare function. While the Medicare program is a complex intergenerational transfer mechanism in which younger workers pay most of the taxes ultimately consumed by the elderly, we assume for analytic simplicity that the people paying the taxes in region i are the same ones experiencing the benefits in region i.[8]

Increasing Medicare spending in just one region i is assumed to result in an increase in the overall Medicare tax rate τ: $\Delta M_i \cong \Delta \tau \Sigma_j [(P_j Y_j)/P_i]$. Thus, the balanced budget change in the tax rate necessary to fund an extra (per capita) Medicare dollar spent in region i is

(2) $$\frac{d\tau}{dM_i} = \left[\sum_{j=1}^{k} \frac{P_j}{P_i} Y_j \right]^{-1},$$

and the first-order condition for Medicare expenditures across regions is, for each i,

(3) $$\frac{dV}{dR_{ki}} = V_{1i} \frac{dS_i}{dR_{ki}} + V_{2i} \frac{dQ_i}{dR_{ki}} - \sum_{j=1}^{k} V_{3j} Y_j \frac{d\tau}{dM_i} \frac{dM_i}{dR_{ki}},$$

---

7. The Medicare payroll tax that funds part A, or the hospital component, is proportional to earnings. While the part B (physician) premium is regressive, the larger proportion funded by general tax revenue is progressive; overall, the tax is not far from proportional. See McClellan and Skinner (1999).

8. See, for example, Feenberg and Skinner (2000).

where V_{1i} is the contribution of an incremental increase of survival in region i to the social welfare function, V_{2i} the contribution of quality of life (conditional on survival), and V_{3i} the impact of after-tax nonmedical income on social welfare of the entire country. (Note that the constant fraction $\theta = dM_i/dM_i^*$ drops out of equation [3].)

The first-order condition can be written

$$
(4) \qquad \frac{dS_i}{dR_{ki}} + \frac{V_{2i}}{V_{1i}} \frac{dQ_i}{dR_{ki}} - \left(\frac{\displaystyle\sum_{j=1}^{k} V_{3j} Y_j \frac{d\tau}{dM_i} \frac{dM_i}{dR_{ki}}}{V_{1i}} \right) = 0
$$

The first term on the left-hand side measures the marginal value of Medicare expenditures on survival in region i, while the second term is the improvement in functioning and quality of life, expressed in terms relative to the incremental social value of increasing survival (V_2/V_1). Unfortunately, we do not have good data on Q_i, the level of functioning in a region, and so we will not be able to estimate dQ_i/dR_{ik} directly, although evidence on this question is discussed presently.

Suppose that the value function V is linear, so there is a uniform social trade-off between increasing survival by one unit and reducing after-tax income by β. Thus, β is the conventional cost-effectiveness "hurdle," or how much is society willing to spend to increase survival rates by a given amount under the assumption that the health inputs have no impact on quality of life, hence $dQ_i/dR_{ik} = 0$. In this special case, $\beta = V_3/V_1$, $\forall\, i, j$, which allows us to simplify equation (4) to

$$
(5) \qquad \frac{dS_i^k}{dM_i^k} = \frac{\dfrac{dS_i}{dR_{ki}}}{\dfrac{dM_i}{dR_{ki}}} = \beta^{-1}.
$$

In other words, all regions should devote expenditures up to the point where the marginal gains are equal, both across types of care, and across regions. In the case of a specific factor that raises spending, we can consider this scenario in figure 4.3, with the same dimensions as those shown in figure 4.2: expenditures (or intensity) on the horizontal axis and survival on the vertical axis. Combinations of expenditures and survival rates are shown for three regions, A, B, and C, as well as each of their concave health "production functions." The slopes of each of the straight tangential lines are equal to β so that $dS_i/dM_i = \beta$ across regions. Furthermore, this graph replicates the general pattern of spending and survival shown in the empirical data in figure 4.2. Accounting for the concavity of the value function V would imply efficiency conditions that would move region A further along its production function to A', and would move C to C', resulting in a reduction in health disparities across regions.

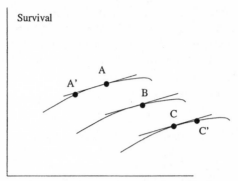

Fig. 4.3   Efficiency in health care
Note: A, B, and C represent regions. At each point, the slope of the health care productivity curve is equal (and shown by the straight line passing through points A, B, and C).

To capture the implicit function dS_i/dM_i as "traced out" by the markers (or instruments) for the intensity of care, we specify a model where survival S_i is a general nonlinear function of Medicare expenditures in that region, $S(M_i)$, that is,

(6) $$S_i = S(M_i, \mathbf{Z}_i) + u_i,$$

where $\mathbf{Z}_i$ is a vector of underlying observable health characteristics. A simplified version of this equation is

(6') $$S_i = S(M_i) + \varphi \mathbf{Z}_i + u_i,$$

where φ is the corresponding vector of coefficients; thus, $\varphi \mathbf{Z}_i$ shifts the productivity curves vertically with respect to observable differences in health status. To the extent that *unobservable* health status is reflected in the error term u_i, it will be correlated with Medicare spending, leading to inconsistent estimates in a single-equation model. We therefore model Medicare expenditures as a nonlinear function of the (uncontaminated) measures of intensity R_{ik} so that as regions increase R_{ik}, spending on this input (and associated treatments) also would tend to increase in a potentially nonlinear way:

(7) $$M_i = M(R_{ik}) + \mathbf{Z}_i \prod + e_i,$$

where $\prod$ is a vector of coefficients and e_i the error term. This block-diagonal structure is well suited to estimation using the methods developed in Newey, Powell, and Vella (1999); we return to estimation issues in section 4.4.

4.3.2   How much should survival rates differ across regions?

The theoretical model suggested that it is important in assessing efficiency to measure the impact of the marginal dollar of Medicare spending (for each dimension) on health outcomes. As a first step, we would like to know how much difference in survival rates we would expect to see under the null hypothesis that incremental Medicare expenditures yield first-order health benefits. In the short term, we would expect to see a jump in survival. If we viewed the social β to be $100,000 per additional year of life, then spending an extra $1,000 per capita in Medicare spending should, in the short term, yield a drop in mortality rates (or increase in survival rates) of 1.0 percentage points. Over the long term, the mortality rate would climb back up as those patients saved early on ultimately die.

To quantify the change in survival and mortality rates at the level of the population that is consistent with the micro-level cost-effectiveness benchmarks, we develop a simple model using the life tables for 1991 from Wilmoth (2001). Figure 4.4 shows the benchmark survival pattern for the U.S. population in 1991 (the leftmost curve); the average mortality rate is 5.2 percent in this population, which is consistent with mortality in the Medicare population. Next, suppose an innovation is introduced that reduces annual mortality rates by 25 percent, for example, leading to the

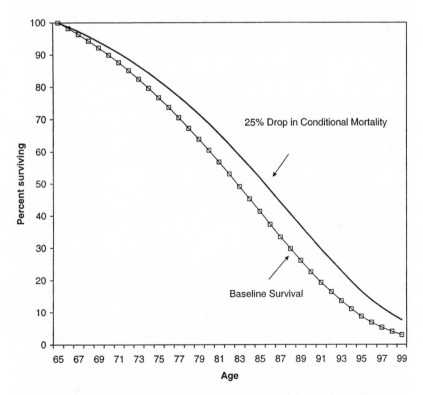

Fig. 4.4   Baseline survival curve and counterfactual survival curve after 25 percent decline in mortality rate

rightward shift in the survival curve (figure 4.4). The population-weighted decline in the mortality rates is 1.3 percentage points, down to 3.9 percent. In the steady state (assuming no population growth), the population is larger by 11 percent, the area between the two curves. In other words, the implicit numerical derivative of the percentage change in steady-state life years per 1 percentage point change in the mortality rate is equal to $11/(5.2 - 3.9)$ or 9.0.[9] Conversely, a "hurdle" rate of $100,000 per life year implies that every increase of $1,000 in per capita Medicare expenditures should increase survival rates by 1/9, or 0.11 percentage points.

This hurdle rate may be too low. As noted previously, short-run effects are larger than long-run effects, and to the extent that Medicare spending has risen dramatically in the last decade, we might expect to observe a larger impact on survival. Second, Medicare does not cover all expenditures for the care measured in the claims data, so we are underestimating the true cost of the medical care, which will tend to bias our results toward finding that Medicare spending at the margin is efficient. Finally, the $100,000 hurdle is often given for a year of life in perfect health, and one is rarely extending life years in perfect health; indeed, the increased survival may be at the expense of quite poor health functioning. On the other hand, if functioning is improved as well as survival, one may require less improvement in survival to justify the incremental Medicare expenditures, an issue to which we return presently.

4.4   Measuring Health Care Intensity

First, with regard to the intensity of "efficient" care, Wennberg and Cooper (1999) measured the frequency of use where appropriate for eleven treatments or screening methods that are generally agreed upon to be effective in medical care; this includes the fraction of women in the Medicare population who were screened for breast cancer (mammography), the percentage of diabetics administered blood tests and eye exams, and the percentage receiving a pneumonia vaccination. Averaged in with these measures are quality measures for the treatment of heart attacks; the percentage of appropriate patients in each HRR who received effective drug treatment such as aspirin, beta blockers, and angiotensin-converting enzyme (ACE) inhibitors, for example.[10] One would not expect 100 percent compliance for a variety of reasons, but in general the quality indexes were quite low, with a (weighted) mean of 48 percent and a range from 32 to 57 percent (see table 4.1), with a higher index indicating better quality care.

9. We chose the 25 percent mortality decline to make the differences apparent in figure 4.4. Smaller changes in mortality yield the same numerical derivatives, however.
10. These latter indicators are drawn from the Cooperative Cardiovascular Project, or CCP, a detailed study of more than 200,000 heart attacks in the United States. See Jencks, Huff, and Cuerdon (2003) for a more comprehensive measure of quality by state.

Table 4.1   **Summary statistics**

Dependent variable	Mean	Standard deviation	Minimum	Maximum
Medicare expenditures (in $1,000)	5.08	0.86	3.12	8.86
Heart attack (AMI) rate (per 1,000)	19.45	2.91	11.44	29.44
Stroke (CVA) rate (per 1,000)	22.95	2.84	15.24	32.47
Gastrointestinal bleeding rate (per 1,000)	15.16	1.64	10.54	20.43
Colon cancer rate (per 1,000)	4.74	0.54	2.83	6.34
Lung cancer rate (per 1,000)	1.42	0.28	0.50	2.28
Hip fracture rate (per 1,000)	15.55	1.53	9.20	19.62
Physician visits in the last 6 months (per decedent)	24.20	7.12	8.5	47.9
Decedents admitted to ICU in last 6 months (%)	31.26	5.71	14.2	49.3
Avg. AMI Medicare Part A expenditures (in $1,000)	15.63	1.69	11.66	21.92
Fraction living in poverty	13.10	5.59	4.66	32.73
Avg. Social Security income (in $1,000)	7.760	0.61	6.056	9.532
Elderly living alone (%)	35.02	3.62	20.8	41.9
Cigarette smokers (%)	23.47	2.47	13.7	30.8
Obese (%)	17.09	1.84	11.9	22.0
Seat belt users (%)	28.39	8.23	12.8	59.6
Binge drinkers (%)	13.41	3.61	6.3	23.2
High school graduates (%)	49.37	4.68	31.91	58.89
College graduates (%)	25.55	6.23	11.49	52.24
Effectiveness index	47.08	4.06	32.21	56.74
Survival rate (%)	94.70	0.34	93.78	95.99

We also include a measure for preference-sensitive care that averages age-sex-race-adjusted rates of ten surgical procedures by HRR that include back surgery, angioplasty, bypass surgery, prostatectomy, knee replacements, and hip replacements. We note, however, that because our outcomes measures do not reflect functioning and quality of life—the factors most likely to be affected by these procedures—we would *not* expect that survival should be affected strongly by the intensity of surgical rates. There may even be trade-offs where more intensive surgical rates lead to greater operative mortality, but better functioning, for those who survive. Thus, while we do not consider whether preference-sensitive care is associated with better survival, we can ask whether regions that are more aggressive with regard to surgery also experience higher Medicare costs.

We also consider instruments for supply-sensitive care where there are few guidelines for the appropriate treatment of chronically ill patients. As noted earlier, we consider two approaches to providing a marker for this type of care. The first is physician visits per decedent in the last six months of life. We focus on this group because by looking at those near death, we are at least comparing health care utilization across a group of largely very

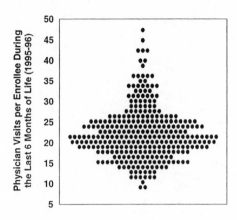

Fig. 4.5   Average number of physician visits per decedent during the last six months of life (1995–96)
Source: www.dartmouthatlas.org, Wennberg and Cooper (1999).

sick patients. Figure 4.5 shows a turnip graph of the distribution of physician visits in the last six months of life; each dot represents average rates for a hospital referral region (HRR).[11] The rates vary widely, from 8.5 in Grand Junction, Colorado, to 43 in Ridgewood, New Jersey, and nearly 48 in Miami. As well, we also consider the percentage of Medicare enrollees who in their last six months are admitted to an ICU. This value again varies widely, from 14 percent in Sun City, Arizona, to 49 percent in Miami, Florida, and Munster, Indiana.

In addition to end-of-life care, which might be expected to reflect that fraction of health care spending devoted toward ineffective care, we also take a prospective approach and consider twelve-month part A Medicare expenditures for a 100 percent sample of fee-for-service Medicare patients aged sixty-five and over who were admitted during 1993–94 for AMI. (Different years are used to ensure that AMI expenditures are not themselves components of overall Medicare expenditures in 1995–96.) Costs have been adjusted for the underlying demographics (age, sex, race) and comorbidities of each patient (at the individual level); as well, price differences across regions have been adjusted using the *Dartmouth Atlas* price index, which is in turn based on Zuckerman, Welch, and Pope (1990). This measure of intensity reflects both the propensity of hospitals to treat heart attacks using high-tech revascularization and the likelihood of follow-up hospitalization and other inpatient treatments during the subsequent year, and thus reflects a broader dimension of care than just treatments for chronically ill patients. The mean level of expenditures is $15,632, with a range from $11,664 to $21,917.

11. Think of this as a vertical histogram with the rows centered.

4.5   Estimating the Efficiency of Medicare Expenditures

The basic set of covariates Z includes age-sex-race-adjusted population-based measures at the HRR level of hospital admissions (per 1,000 elderly population) for AMI, stroke (CVA), gastrointestinal bleeding, hip fractures, colon cancer, and lung cancer (Wennberg and Cooper 1999). Hospital admission rates for these diseases are accurate measures of the population incidence since nearly every person with these diseases is admitted to the hospital. In addition, we include rates of poverty in the elderly population and average Social Security income among households receiving this source of income, measured using the CensusCD data (based on primary census data) at the zip code level in 1990. Since Social Security benefits are based on lifetime earnings, these provide a good (albeit nonlinear) index of lifetime earnings. We also use the census data to measure the fraction of elderly people living alone, since such patients may have fewer potential caretakers and thus would be more likely to spend their last six months receiving inpatient care.[12] We consider measures of behavioral health status from the general population such as obesity, binge drinking, cigarette smoking, and seat belt use; these are derived from Centers for Disease Control data (Bolen et al. 2000) at the state level and assigned to the HRR level according to the relative state population weights in each HRR. These variables are summarized in table 4.1.

Table 4.2 demonstrates that these variables combined are strongly associated with survival rates, with an R^2 of 0.56 for the full model. Interestingly, the poverty rate enters with a positive coefficient (that is, a higher poverty rate implies a higher survival rate, holding constant income). In part, this is the consequence of including comorbidities such as heart attacks and hip fractures; poverty works primarily through its impact on disease categories.[13]

We first consider factors that can affect Medicare expenditures in the context of a first-stage regression. Here we use expenditures that have been adjusted for age, sex, race, and differences in cost-of-living reimbursement rates for Medicare services (Wennberg and Cooper 1999). To show the extent to which variations in Medicare expenditures across regions are correlated with covariates Z, we first consider a parsimonious model that includes just the six measures of health status (heart attack rates, stroke rates, etc.), with results in column (C) of table 4.2. The set of underlying health measures explain 27 percent of the total variation in Medicare spending. Column (D) of table 4.2 includes additional socioeconomic and behavioral

12. This is defined as the ratio of people over age sixty-five living alone divided by the total number of people over sixty-five not in institutions or living with unrelated people.

13. Holding income constant, a larger poverty rate is consistent with a widening of the income distribution—for example, more income inequality. However, the hypothesis that income inequality is bad for health (e.g., Wilkinson 1997) would predict a negative coefficient on poverty rates, not a positive coefficient. See also Deaton and Paxson (1999).

Table 4.2 **Regression models of survival and Medicare expenditures**

	Survival		Medicare expenditure ($1,000)		
Dependent variable	(A)	(B)	(C)	(D)	(E)
AMI rate (per 1,000)	−0.010	−.007	−0.061	−0.004	0.028
	(1.2)	(0.8)	(2.3)	(0.2)	(1.3)
Stroke rate (per 1,000)	−0.038	−0.043	0.048	−0.022	−0.030
	(4.5)	(4.4)	(1.8)	(0.7)	(1.1)
Gastrointestinal bleeding rate (per 1,000)	−0.051	−0.054	0.190	0.168	0.050
	(2.6)	(3.4)	(3.6)	(3.8)	(1.2)
Colon cancer rate (per 1,000)	−0.011	−0.006	−0.062	0.152	−0.172
	(0.4)	(0.2)	(0.6)	(1.4)	(1.7)
Lung cancer rate (per 1,000)	0.133	0.140	0.467	0.590	0.360
	(1.4)	(1.9)	(2.3)	(3.2)	(2.3)
Hip fracture rate (per 1,000)	−0.047	−0.031	0.056	0.123	0.172
	(3.8)	(2.0)	(1.4)	(3.1)	(5.8)
Fraction living in poverty		.026		0.068	0.058
		(3.0)		(2.8)	(3.4)
Avg. Social Security income (in $1,000)		0.205		0.440	0.040
		(2.8)		(2.4)	(0.3)
High school graduate (%)		−0.008		−0.045	0.018
		(1.6)		(2.5)	(1.3)
College graduate (%)		−0.003		−0.016	−0.005
		(0.6)		(1.3)	(0.5)
Binge drinking (%)		0.003		0.060	0.064
		(0.6)		(3.7)	(4.8)
Cigarette smokers (%)		−0.027		−0.073	−0.067
		(2.8)		(3.0)	(3.1)
Obesity (%)		−0.002		0.003	0.021
		(0.1)		(0.1)	(0.8)
Seat belt use (%)		0.011		−0.003	−0.000
		(4.6)		(0.3)	(0.1)
Elderly living alone (%)		−0.017		−0.051	−0.033
		(.2)		(2.3)	(2.3)
Index of effective care				−0.037	−0.023
				(2.3)	(1.8)
Index of preference-sensitive care				−0.001	0.010
				(0.0)	(1.0)
Physician visits in the last 6 months (avg.)					0.063
					(6.5)
One-year expenditures for AMI					0.112
					(3.8)
Constant	97.124	96.372	1.052	2.474	−0.792
R^2	0.46	0.56	0.27	0.46	0.64

Notes: $N = 306$. Robust standard errors; absolute value of t-statistics in parentheses. All sample sizes weighted by Medicare population. Low variation conditions (e.g., AMI, stroke) and effectiveness index are from 1995–96, Medicare expenditures data are for 1996, poverty and Social Security data from 1990 Census, and CDC behavioral data from 1997.

explanatory variables, as well as measures of effective and preference-sensitive care; these combined raise the R^2 to 0.46. The counterintuitive signs of some coefficients (such as for smokers and elderly living alone), as well as the robust correlation between income and Medicare spending, suggest that the coefficients may reflect factors other than health status (McClellan and Skinner 1999). As well, note that the quality index is *negatively* associated with Medicare expenditures; in other words, Medicare spending does not appear to buy better quality of care. Finally, the preference-sensitive index is not correlated with overall spending. While certain components of surgery may be correlated (for example, cardiac bypass surgery is positively associated with per capita Medicare expenditures), on the whole, high-tech surgery does not appear to be the primary (or even secondary) cause of geographical variations in spending (see Wennberg, Fisher, and Skinner 2002).

Finally, physician visits in the last six months and expenditures for AMI patients are highly significant (table 4.2, column [E]) and raise the R^2 to 0.64. To give some sense of how expenditures differ by physician visits in the last six months, we also report predicted Medicare spending (controlling for Z) from a regression with dummy variables reflecting the regional decile ranking for physician visits in the last six months. These coefficient estimates are shown visually in figure 4.6, where decile 1 (the lowest decile) is anchored at the average Medicare spending in that decile. We can use these estimates to calculate overall Medicare expenditures that are explained by end-of-life physician visits; noting that each decile contains 2.77 million elderly people in 1996, we find net spending relative to the bottom decile is $26 billion larger. Since overall expenditures during the same year were about $138 billion, the variation in expenditures attributable to end-of-life care accounts for nearly 20 percent of overall spending.

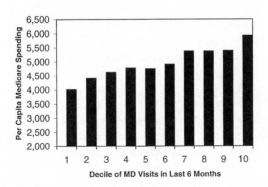

Fig. 4.6   Average per capita Medicare spending 1995–96, by decile of physician visits in the last six months

4.5.1   The Association between Health Care Intensity Measures and Regional Health Status

To what extent are the markers for intensity associated with the measures of health Z? Presumably the instruments or measures of intensity are chosen because on a theoretical basis they are deemed exogenous. Further findings that the health care intensity measures are uncorrelated with measured health status Z would be supportive of the exogeneity presumption for the following reason. If the health intensity measures R are uncorrelated with Zs, which are themselves randomly measured from among the wide variety of health status measures, it would be difficult to argue that the health intensity measures are in addition correlated with unmeasured health status (see Altonji, Elder, and Taber 2005). To examine this correlation, we create terciles of HRRs based on three measures of intensity: the efficiency index, physician visits in the last six months, and AMI expenditures, with results in table 4.3. To summarize the correlation of the health care intensity measure with regard to underlying health status in the region, we create a predicted survival measure based on coefficient estimates in column (C) of table 4.2. As noted above, this predicted measure explains 56 percent of the variation in mortality.[14]

For the index of effective care, there is a positive and significant correlation with predicted survival, suggesting that regions with better initial health status (as measured by the incidence of heart attacks, stroke, colon cancer, obesity, binge drinking, poverty, and other factors) also have higher quality physicians as well. Here we do have a strong theoretical presumption that there is no reverse causation; both sick and healthy patients should be receiving effective care. As noted previously, effective care is negatively correlated with Medicare expenditures ($p < 0.01$). By contrast, for physician visits in the last six months of life, and one-year expenditures for AMI, predicted survival is nearly identical across the terciles. For example, the correlation coefficient between end-of-life physician visits and predicted survival is just 0.01 with a p-value of 0.88, suggesting that they are unlikely to be associated with unmeasured health status. As expected, these latter two factors are positively associated with overall Medicare per capita expenditures.[15]

4.5.2   Linear Two-Stage Regressions

We next consider the linear two-stage regression, presented in table 4.4. The first two columns present regression results for the limited set of covariates (the six health conditions, Social Security income, and poverty

14. Note that this predicted measure of mortality is a linear function only of Z, not of S or u.
15. The final measure of intensity, ICU days in the last six months, is negatively associated with survival, with a correlation coefficient of -0.27 ($p < 0.01$).

Table 4.3   **Terciles of Medicare expenditures and predicted survival by effective care, average physician visits in the last six months, and one-year inpatient expenditures for a cohort of AMI patients**

Dependent variable	1st (lowest) tercile: Effective care	2nd (middle) tercile: Effective care	3rd (highest) tercile: Effective care	Correlation coeff. (*p*-value) (effective care)
Effective care (%)	43.76	47.93	51.48	1.00
Medicare expenditures (in $1,000)	5.375	4.983	4.906	−0.263 (<0.01)
Predicted survival (from table 4.2, column [B])	94.58	94.67	94.83	0.39 (<0.01)

	1st tercile: Physician visits	2nd tercile: Physician visits	3rd tercile: Physician visits	Correlation coeff. (*p*-value) (Physician visits)
Avg. physician visits in last 6 months	17.49	22.90	32.15	1.00
Medicare expenditures (in $1,000)	4.486	5.187	5.576	0.53 (<0.01)
Predicted survival (from table 4.2, column [B])	94.74	94.60	94.74	0.01 (0.88)

	1st tercile: AMI expenditures	2nd tercile: AMI expenditures	3rd tercile: AMI expenditures	Correlation coeff. (*p*-value) (AMI expenditures)
Avg. 1 year Part A AMI expenditures (in $1,000)	14.06	15.40	17.42	1.00
Medicare expenditures (in $1,000)	4.82	4.98	5.46	0.36 (<0.01)
Predicted survival (from table 4.2, column [B])	94.70	94.68	94.71	0.01 (0.89)

rates), with column (A) weighted by the Medicare population and column (B) unweighted and where the model is just identified using physician visits in the last six months as an instrument. The coefficient estimates are stable with regard to whether they are weighted or not. The estimated linear coefficient estimates in columns (A) and (B) of table 4.4 of Medicare expenditures on survival are 0.009 and −0.047, respectively. Neither is significantly different from zero. In other words, these results imply that the roughly $26 billion in Medicare expenditures explained by the instrument generate no clinically important (or economically important) influence on survival. Using the Altonji, Elder, and Taber (2005) approach, we also compare the regression coefficient when all covariates Z are excluded. The

Table 4.4   Instrumental variable regression estimates of factors affecting survival (dependent variable is the one-year survival rate)

	Physician visits, last 6 months		Medicare spending, AMI 1993–94		All instruments[a]
	(A)	(B)	(C)	(D)	(E)
Medicare expenditures (in $1,000)	0.009	−0.047	−0.011	−0.002	0.003
	(0.2)	(0.9)	(0.2)	(0.0)	(0.1)
AMI rate (per 1,000)	−.014	−.015	−.014	−.010	−.014
	(1.7)	(2.2)	(1.7)	(1.3)	(1.7)
Stroke rate (per 1,000)	−0.039	−0.037	−0.035	−0.028	−0.035
	(4.3)	(5.0)	(3.8)	(3.6)	(3.7)
Gastrointestinal bleed rate (per 1,000)	−0.048	−0.044	−0.047	−0.057	−0.049
	(2.5)	(2.7)	(2.5)	(3.1)	(2.7)
Colon cancer rate (per 1,000)	0.002	0.003	−0.011	−0.019	−0.013
	(0.1)	(0.1)	(0.3)	(0.6)	(0.3)
Lung cancer rate (per 1,000)	0.051	0.019	0.100	0.051	0.089
	(0.7)	(0.4)	(1.3)	(1.0)	(1.3)
Hip fracture rate (per 1,000)	−0.052	−0.056	−0.032	−0.040	−0.034
	(3.8)	(4.9)	(2.0)	(2.9)	(2.3)
Fraction living in poverty	0.030	0.037	0.030	0.032	0.029
	(3.8)	(5.2)	(3.5)	(4.0)	(3.4)
Avg. Social Security income (in $1,000)	0.205	0.215	0.205	0.200	0.199
	(2.9)	(3.3)	(3.0)	(4.0)	(2.9)
Effectiveness index	0.019	0.013	0.020	0.018	0.021
	(3.4)	(2.7)	(4.0)	(3.9)	(4.1)
Constant	94.51	94.83	95.38	95.14	95.38
Regression weighted by Medicare population?	Yes	No	Yes	No	Yes
R^2	0.52	0.52	0.58	0.58	0.58

Notes: $N = 306$. Additional health measures include percent high school graduates, percent college graduates, percent of elderly population living alone, and percentage of population who are binge drinkers, cigarette smokers, obese, and seat belt users. Robust standard errors; absolute value of t-statistics in parentheses. All sample sizes weighted by Medicare population. Low variation conditions (e.g., AMI, stroke) and effectiveness index are from 1995–96, Medicare expenditures data are for 1996, poverty and Social Security data from 1990 Census, and CDC behavioral data from 1997.

[a]Instruments are physician visits in the last six months, percentage of decedents admitted to the ICU in their last six months, and Medicare expenditures for a cohort of AMI patients in 1993–94.

results are similar (the coefficient for Medicare expenditures is −0.015, with a t-statistic of 0.25), providing further support for the view that the results are not systematically biased by unobservable health status.

Recall from our earlier discussion that one should expect to find in the steady state an improvement in survival rates of 0.11 from an incremental $1,000 in Medicare expenditures per capita. However, we can reject the null hypothesis that the coefficient is 0.11 at the 0.05 significance level for both columns (A) and (B). Similar results obtain when AMI expenditures are used as the instrument, as shown in columns (C) and (D); once again the coefficients on Medicare expenditures are not significantly different from zero, and we can reject the null hypothesis of 0.11 at the 0.05 level, while ruling out statistically the hypothesis that regional variations in Medicare spending satisfy conditions for efficiency.[16]

Note also that in these four columns of table 4.4 the coefficient on the index of effective care is positive and significant; a 10 percent increase in the index is associated with survival rates roughly 0.2 percentage points higher. This is large in both a clinical sense and in an economic sense; it implies that increasing the index by 4 percentage points, or 1 standard deviation (table 4.1), would increase survival rates by 0.8 percentage points and, using the benchmark of $100,000 per life-year, yield benefits equivalent to about $7,000 per person. This estimate should be interpreted cautiously, since it may be the case that the effectiveness index is associated with a variety of other characteristics of the health care system that we have not controlled for in the regression analysis.

We include all instruments (percent with ICU days in the last six months, as well as physician visits in the last six months, and AMI expenditures) in column (E) of table 4.4. Once again, the coefficient on Medicare expenditures is not significant and is near zero in magnitude. Furthermore, the model does not reject an overidentification test for the additional two instruments ($p = 0.92$).

4.5.3 Semiparametric Instrumental Variable Estimates

To this point, we have not allowed for nonlinearities in either $S(M, Z)$ or in $M(R)$ as in equations (6) and (7). We adopt the general model developed in Newey, Powell, and Vella (1999; hereafter NPV), but because of the limitations on the size of the data set, we adopt a simple splined function $S(M)$ and $M(X)$ where the five intervals of the spline are evenly distributed along the ranges of M and X. The NPV method estimates the first-stage regression as in equation (7). Rather than using the fitted value of M in the second stage (as one would normally do in two-stage least squares), one uses the nonlinear transformations of M and the fitted value of the error term from the first-stage regression.

We estimated the simplified $S(M)$ function with results shown in panels A (weighted) and B (unweighted) of figure 4.7 using physician visits in the last six months as the instrument, with the incremental gain in survival set

16. We also experimented with a variety of other variables, such as the percentage in HMOs and the percentage urban population. These variables tended to have similar effects on the coefficient estimates (since they were quite closely correlated) and tended to increase the coefficient estimate to between 0.04 and 0.06, but not significantly different from zero, or 0.11. (Using the urban variable resulted in the loss of one HRR; Ocala, Florida, revamped its zip codes substantially between the 1990 census and the 1996 HRR crosswalk.) Excluding HRRs with more than 10 percentage point HMO enrollment resulted in a *negative* estimated effect of expenditures on survival (–0.147, significant at the 10 percent level).

a. Weighted Data

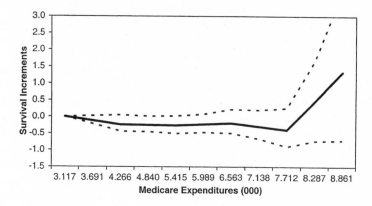

b. Unweighted Data

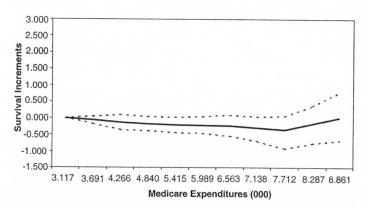

Fig. 4.7   Semiparametric estimates of the marginal effectiveness of Medicare expenditures: *A*, weighted data; *B*, unweighted data

at zero for the minimum level of Medicare expenditures. The 95 percent confidence intervals are also shown in figure 4.7; these are estimated by bootstrapping the combined first- and second-stage regressions.[17] Rather than having a concave shape, as is suggested by diminishing returns (as in figure 4.3), the predicted function is convex in panel A and nearly flat in panel B. The jump up in survival in the weighted regression can be explained almost entirely by the presence of Miami, which, conditional on other factors, is a surprisingly healthy region (e.g., Fuchs, McClellan, and

17. This is done by predicting the entire $S(M)$ curve for each of the bootstrapped iterations, and then graphing the 2.5th and 97.5th percentiles of the bootstrapped values for $S(M)$ along the entire range of M. For computational convenience, the true distribution is evaluated for ten evenly spaced values of M, and interpolated linearly.

Skinner 2004). However, neither estimated model, nor the models estimated using AMI expenditures as the instrument, rejects the hypothesis
that Medicare expenditures have zero incremental marginal effectiveness.

4.5.4   Does supply-sensitive care improve functioning and health status rather than survival?

One might object to the statistical models because the higher rates of
health care spending may improve patient functioning rather than just survival. We have already shown that higher surgery rates in a region do not
appear correlated with higher Medicare spending, suggesting that higher-
cost regions are not simply the result of elderly patients' demanding (and
getting) more invasive high-tech surgery. But perhaps the end-of-life
spending also provides benefits with regard to a better process of care for
chronically ill patients. We provide a heuristic impression of differences in
health care intensity by considering utilization rates for two groups of regions in the United States. The first sample for the top decile of regions as
ranked by physician visits in the last six months of life (weighted by the size
of the Medicare population) during 1995–96. These regions include much
of the New York and New Jersey metropolitan areas; Takoma Park, Maryland; Philadelphia; and McAllen, Texas; average visits per decedent range
from thirty-six to forty-eight. The second sample is for HRRs that are classified in the lowest decile of regions (decile 1); these are all regions with
fewer than sixteen visits per decedent. These include Lynchburg, Virginia;
Minneapolis, Minnesota; Portland, Oregon; and Salt Lake City, Utah.

In table 4.5, we consider rates of physician procedures (from part B
Medicare claims data), using a sample of about 32,000 decedents who died
during 1995–96 between the ages of seventy and ninety. The two groupings
of HRRs were nearly identical with regard to the age distribution of death
and broadly similar with regard to (state-level) causes of death.[18] Rates are
expressed as average counts per person in the sample; thus a higher number may reflect more people receiving the treatment or a larger number of
treatments per person.

It is perhaps not surprising that physician visits per decedent are higher
in decile 10 than decile 1, since that is how the categories were chosen.
However, the types of visits show quite different patterns. Outpatient office
visits were 46 percent higher in decile 10 regions, relative to our benchmark
of the lowest (decile 1) regions, and 79 percent higher for the initial visit by

---

18. Cause-of-death data are from the Centers for Disease Control web site (www.cdc.gov).
Rates are adjusted for age and sex for the population over age sixty-five and are drawn from
state measures and merged (by zip code) to the relevant hospital referral regions (HRRs). The
age-adjusted mortality rates were roughly identical in the two deciles, 4.97 percent in decile
1 and 4.96 in decile 10. While the percentage of deaths due to cancer in the two groups was
similar (22.7 percent in decile 10, 22.1 percent in decile 1), as was diabetes (2.6 and 2.7 percent), cardiovascular diseases were higher in decile 10 (49.1 percent versus 44.1 percent), and
chronic obstructive pulmonary diseases were lower (4.9 versus 5.8 percent).

Table 4.5   **Rates of specific procedures per 1,000 decedents, by regional frequency of physician visits in last six months**

Physician service code	Highest decile of physician visits during last six months	Lowest decile of physician visits during last six months	Ratio
Physician visits			
Physician office outpatient visits	4,453	3,051	1.46
Physician visit for initial hospital care	1,442	804	1.79
Specialist initial inpatient consult	3,087	628	4.92
Diagnostic testing			
Upper gastrointestinal endoscopy	132	64	2.06
Cat scan of head/skull/brain	492	236	2.08
Chest x-ray	6,631	2,700	2.46
Doppler/echocardiagram of heart	799	268	2.98
Electrocardiogram and report	3,888	1,161	3.35
Treatments for serious chronic illnesses			
Insertion of emergency airway	140	42	3.33
Hemodialysis (related to kidney failure)	384	87	4.41
Gastrostomy tube placement/change (feeding tube)	136	25	5.44
Continuous ventilator management (mechanical breathing apparatus)	387	50	7.74

Notes: Age 75–90; $N = 15,097$ (Decile 1); $N = 17,225$ (Decile 10).

the physician when the patient was admitted to the hospital. The real differences occur for the initial visit by a specialist newly brought on to the case (392 percent more in decile 10 regions). In other words, there is greater *scope intensity*—more specialists treating separate organs or systems—in regions with a large number of physician visits in the last six months of life.

Regions in the top decile are also characterized by their greater use of diagnostic techniques such as endoscopies, X-rays, Doppler echocardiograms, and electrocardiograms; their use is between 106 and 235 percent greater in decile 10 regions. Finally, the greatest divergence in specific medical procedures comes in those that are used to maintain survival among seriously and chronically ill patients: insertions of emergency airways, dialysis for failing kidneys (hemodyalisis), feeding tubes inserted into the stomach (gastrostomy tube placement), and mechanical breathing assistance (continuous ventilator management). These rates are consistently higher, with rates in decile 10 ranging from 233 percent to 674 percent above those in decile 1. Note that these procedures are not designed to improve quality of life but instead are directed toward maintaining short-term survival. In short, it seems unlikely that this supply-sensitive care could be justified on the basis of improving quality of life for Medicare patients.

4.6   Discussion and Conclusion

In this paper, we have attempted to test whether the Medicare program is broadly consistent with the efficiency criterion commonly used in public economics where the marginal social value of the last dollar spent on specific types of health care (in each region) is equal to the marginal social benefits of the dollar that could have been spent for other worthy causes. We used data on survival rates, Medicare expenditures, and health status measures across 306 hospital referral regions in the United States to test these hypotheses. Our best estimates of the incremental value of Medicare spending with regard to *effective* care suggests that spending for these types of services is too low, especially considering how this type of care is associated with overall Medicare expenditures. On the other hand, the *supply-sensitive* dimension of care is a major factor in explaining overall Medicare expenditures—roughly 20 percent annually—but does not show any impact in terms of improving survival rates across regions. These results suggest that the inefficiency inherent in the Medicare program is as much as 20 percent of total Medicare expenditures.[19]

One explanation for these results is that while survival may not be improved, patients either enjoy better health functioning or they may simply prefer preference-sensitive care. However, neither the results presented here nor other studies provide much support for this view (see, e.g., Guadagnoli et al. 1995). In the SUPPORT study, seriously ill patients were asked about their preferences regarding dying in the hospital and intensive life-saving care, and efforts were made to ensure that they got what they wanted (Lynn et al. 2000). However, there was no correlation between expressed preferences and what they actually got; Pritchard and others (1998) found the only predictor of whether patients died in the hospital was the supply of hospital beds in the area. And when asked directly, patients in high-intensity regions (based on overall expenditures in the last six months of life) did not respond that they enjoyed better access to care, nor were they more satisfied with their care (Fisher et al. 2003a,b).

One potential shortcoming with this study is the difficulty in interpreting "the" effect of an instrumental variable on health care across regions. The problem is the highly multidimensional nature of a health care system. For example, when we observe that regions with higher values of physician visits in the last six months of life also experience higher Medicare expenditures, we cannot specify exactly along what dimensions the quality and quantity of care differ. Physician visits for chronically ill patients (many of whom are in their last six months), or AMI inpatient care, could be a pro-

---

19. Fisher and others (2003a,b) suggest an even larger percentage based on their cohort analysis.

ductive use of Medicare funds, but the other unobserved treatment characteristics with which these are correlated may not be. Or it could be the case that incremental physician visits in the last six months of life are not particularly efficacious, and by choosing a marker most likely associated with inefficient care, we are predisposed toward finding that Medicare expenditures don't have a large impact on outcomes. In this latter case, the surprising result is therefore not that these factors have an indifferent impact on outcomes but that these factors are so highly correlated with overall Medicare expenditures, even after controlling for obvious covariates.

There are three other potential objections to the methodology of the study. The first is that using end-of-life measures of treatment can bias results, given that the effectiveness of the regional health care system will tend to affect the denominator of who is in the end-of-life sample. However, in this case the bias will tend to go toward finding that Medicare expenditures improve survival. Suppose that region A is more aggressive and more effective in treating patients than region B. As a consequence, some of the patients receiving the most aggressive (and expensive) care in region A survive, and hence they do not appear in the end-of-life sample. Hence, region A's end-of-life spending would be biased downward, making it appear relatively more cost effective.

A second objection is that if regions are already optimizing with regard to their Medicare expenditures (i.e., they are at points A, B, and C in figure 4.3), one would not expect to find any difference in outcomes conditional on expenditures. Any variation in Medicare expenditures (and in outcomes) observed in the data is for other factors not adequately captured by the regression model—for example, because of unobservable health needs. However, it seems difficult to reconcile how these unmeasured factors would be so highly correlated with the measures of health care intensity, given that our health care intensity measures for supply-sensitive care are not themselves correlated with observable health needs.

A final concern with the paper is that we are not learning about the efficiency of Medicare per se, because Medicare is an insurance program that is designed to protect the financial health of enrollees, rather than a direct provider of health care such as the Veterans Affairs hospital system. Strictly speaking, to evaluate the efficiency of the Medicare program, one would need to compare the current system to the counterfactual structure of health and health care that would have occurred had Barry Goldwater won the election in 1964 and chosen not to push forward universal health care for the elderly. Absent such an exercise, however, we can ask whether the Medicare program, in its developing role as health regulator rather than passive insurance agency, is getting its money's worth by allowing providers in some states to provide a much higher level of health care intensity (or allowing consumers to receive a much higher level of health care intensity) than in other states.

This macro-level study does not provide an easy prescription for how to fix the Medicare program or how to encourage the greater use of effective care. The Medicare program is federal, with roughly uniform prices paid for procedures (apart from cost-of-living adjustments), so that one cannot appeal to differences in relative nominal prices to explain why Miami spends so much more than other regions in the United States. Nor can reimbursement rates be lowered in high-cost regions without risking a response by physicians of increasing the number of procedures. (As well, lower reimbursement rates in high-cost regions punish those physicians who do practice conservative care.) Still, the potential benefits of reducing regional variation—a saving of nearly 20 percent of current Medicare expenditures—suggests that a central focus of Medicare research should be to better understand why and how some regions are able to provide effective care at relatively low cost.

References

Altonji, Joseph G., Todd E. Elder, and Christopher R. Taber. 2005. Selection on observed and unobserved variables: Assessing the effectiveness of Catholic schools, *Journal of Political Economy,* forthcoming. Northwestern University, Department of Mimeograph.

Angrist, Joshua D. 1990. Lifetime earnings and the Vietnam era draft lottery: Evidence from Social Security administrative records. *American Economic Review* 80 (3): 313–36.

Bolen, Julie C., Luann Rhodes, Eve E. Powell-Griner, Shayne D. Bland, and Deborah Holtzman. 2000. State-specific prevalence of selected health behaviors, by race and ethnicity—behavioral risk factor surveillance system, 1997. *MMWR* 49 (SS02): 1–60.

Cutler, David M. 1995. The incidence of adverse medical outcomes under prospective payments. *Econometrica* 63 (1): 29–50.

Cutler, David M. 2000. Walking the tightrope on Medicare reform. *Journal of Economic Perspectives* 14 (2): 45–56.

Cutler, David, Mark McClellan, Joseph Newhouse, and Dahlia Remler. 1998. Pricing heart attack treatments. *Quarterly Journal of Economics* 113 (4): 991–1024.

Cutler, David, and Ellen Meara. 1999. The technology of birth: Is it worth it? NBER Working Paper no. 7390. Cambridge, MA: National Bureau of Economic Research, October.

Currie, Janet, and Jonathan Gruber. 1996. Saving babies: The efficacy and cost of recent changes in the Medicaid eligibility of pregnant women. *Journal of Political Economy* 104 (6): 1263–96.

Deaton, Angus, and Christina Paxson. 1999. Mortality, education, income, and inequality among American cohorts. NBER Working Paper no. 7140. Cambridge, MA: National Bureau of Economic Research, May.

Evans, Robert G., and G. S. Stoddart. 1994. Producing health, consuming health care. In *Why are some people healthy and others not?* ed. Robert G. Evans, Morris L. Barer, and Theodore R. Marmor, 27–64. Hawthorne, NY: Aldine de Gruyter.

Feenberg, Daniel, and Jonathan Skinner. 2000. Medicare transfers across states: Winners and losers. *National Tax Journal* 53 (September): 713–32.

Fisher, Elliott S., David Wennberg, Therese Stukel, Daniel Gottlieb, F. L. Lucas, and Etoile L. Pinder. 2003a. The implications of regional variations in Medicare spending. Part 1: The content, quality, and accessibility of care. *Annals of Internal Medicine* 138 (4): 283–87.

Fisher, Elliott S., David Wennberg, Therese Stukel, Daniel Gottlieb, F. L. Lucas, and Etoile L. Pinder. 2003b. The implications of regional variations in Medicare spending. Part 2: Health outcomes and satisfaction with care. *Annals of Internal Medicine* 138 (4): 288–99.

Fuchs, Victor, Mark McClellan, and Jonathan Skinner. 2004. Area differences in utilization of medical care and mortality among U.S. elderly. In *Perspectives on the economics of aging,* ed. D. Wise, 367–406. Chicago: University of Chicago Press.

Guadagnoli, Edward, Paul J. Hauptman, John Z. Ayanian, Chris L. Pashos, Barbara J. McNeil, and Paul D. Cleary. 1995. Variation in the use of cardiac procedures after acute myocardial infarction. *New England Journal of Medicine* 333: 573–78.

Hadley, Jack. 1988. Medicare spending and mortality rates of the elderly. *Inquiry* 25:485–93.

Hearst, Norman, Thomas B. Newman, and Stephen B. Hulley. 1986. Delayed effects of the military draft on mortality. *New England Journal of Medicine* 314 (10): 620–24.

Jencks, Stephen F., Edwin D. Huff, and Timothy Cuerdon. 2003. Change in the quality of care delivered to Medicare beneficiaries, 1998–1999 to 2000–2001. *Journal of the American Medical Association* 289 (3): 305–12.

Lynn, Joanne, Hal R. Arkes, Marguerite Stevens, Felicia Cohn, Barbara Koenig, Ellen Fox, Neal V. Dawson, Russell S. Phillips, Mary Beth Hamel, and Joel Tsevat. 2000. Rethinking fundamental assumptions: SUPPORT's implications for future reform. *Journal of the American Geriatric Society* 48:S214–S221.

McClellan, Mark, Barbara J. McNeil, and Joseph P. Newhouse. 1994. Does more intensive treatment of acute myocardial infarction in the elderly reduce mortality? Analysis using instrumental variables. *Journal of the American Medical Association* 272 (September): 859–66.

McClellan, Mark, and Jonathan Skinner. 1997. The incidence of Medicare. NBER Working Paper no. W6013. Cambridge, MA: National Bureau of Economic Research, April.

McClellan, Mark, and Jonathan Skinner. 1999. Medicare reform: Who pays and who benefits? *Health Affairs* 18 (1): 48–62.

Newey, Whitney K., James L. Powell, and Francis Vella. 1999. Nonparametric estimation of triangular simultaneous equations models. *Econometrica* 67 (3): 565–603.

Pardes, Herbert, Kenneth Manton, Eric Lander, Dennis Tolley, Arthur Ullian, and Hans Palmer. 1999. Effects of Medicare research on health care and economy. *Science* 283:36–37.

Pritchard, R. S., E. S. Fisher, J. M. Teno, S. M. Sharp, D. J. Reding, W. A. Knaus, J. E. Wennberg, J. Lynne, and SUPPORT investigators. 1998. Influence of patient preferences and local health system characteristics on the place of death: SUPPORT investigators study to understand prognoses and preferences for risks and outcomes of treatment. *Journal of the American Geriatric Society* 46: 1242–50.

Reinhardt, Uwe E., Peter S. Hussey, and Gerard F. Anderson. 2004. U.S. Health care spending in an international context. *Health Affairs* 23 (3): 10–25.

Skinner, Jonathan, and John E. Wennberg. 2000. Regional inequality in Medicare spending: The key to Medicare reform? In *Frontiers of health economics 3,* ed. A. Garber, 69–90. Cambridge: MIT Press.

Wennberg, John E., and Megan M. Cooper. 1999. *The Dartmouth atlas of health care in the United States: The quality of medical care in the United States; A report on the Medicare program.* Chicago: American Health Association Press.

Wennberg, John E., Elliott Fisher, and Jonathan Skinner. 2002. Geography and the debate over Medicare reform. *Health Affairs* 21:W96–W114.

Wilkinson, Richard. 1997. *Unhealthy societies: The affliction of inequality.* London: Routledge.

Wilmoth, John R. 2001. Human mortality database. http://www.mortality.org.

Zuckerman, Stephen, W. P. Welch, and Gregory C. Pope. 1990. A geographic index of physician practice costs. *Journal of Health Economics* 9 (1): 39–69.

Comment   Alan M. Garber

This paper is part of a rich tradition of research exploring geographic variation in the utilization of medical services. John Wennberg, one of the coauthors, is a pioneer in this field of research, which has demonstrated the pervasiveness of variation (Wennberg and Gittelsohn 1973). Variation has been documented in multiple settings and at different periods of time, and it is not fully explained by differences in the prevalence of disease or in other observed health characteristics of the populations (Phelps and Mooney 1993). The literature suggests that supply factors, though they are incompletely measured, may play an important role (Wennberg, Barnes, and Zubkoff 1982). This literature also documents that variation tends to be greater when there is greater uncertainty about the effectiveness of care. Thus, the propensity to hospitalize patients with heart attacks, for example, is much less variable than the use of surgery as a treatment for back pain, for which high-quality evidence of effectiveness is scant.

If variation in utilization is not attributable to unmeasured health characteristics, there is at least a presumption that someone, somewhere, is not providing care efficiently. Then it might be possible to reallocate health resources to improve health without increasing resource consumption. This is the issue that Skinner and colleagues explore, looking specifically at the Medicare program.

The Medicare population might appear at first to be an odd choice for a study of practice variation. One would expect to see extensive variation in utilization among the nonelderly population, if only because many lack in-

Alan M. Garber is a staff physician with the Veterans Affairs Palo Alto Health Care System; Henry J. Kaiser, Jr., Professor and professor of medicine at Stanford University; and a research associate and director of the Health Care Program at the National Bureau of Economic Research.

surance and cost-sharing provisions of commercial health insurance policies vary greatly. Among the elderly, hospital insurance coverage under Medicare part A is effectively universal, and the overwhelming majority of elderly have Medicare part B coverage. A large majority also have supplemental (Medigap) private insurance. Thus, health insurance coverage among the elderly would seem to be far more uniform than among Americans younger than sixty-five years of age. Nevertheless, as Skinner and colleagues show, the elderly in different parts of the country receive different amounts and forms of care.

What does "efficiency" mean? According to Skinner and colleagues, efficiency requires that benefits from Medicare expenditures be equated at the margin across different geographic units. One can readily imagine that if beneficiaries in Miami are treated more intensively than similar patients in Chicago, and there are diminishing marginal benefits to treatment, a reallocation of resources from Miami to Chicago would result in an improvement of health outcomes among Medicare beneficiaries overall.

To test efficiency empirically, they develop an econometric specification in which survival is a function of expenditures, which is a proxy for intensity. The problem with expenditures (or intensity) is that they are undoubtedly endogenous and influenced by unmeasured health characteristics. As instruments for intensity, they use a few measures, most prominently physician visits per decedent in the last six years of life within the unit area. A secondary set of instruments consists of expenditures for patients admitted for hip fracture.

The interpretation of the empirical results depends in large part upon one's view of the validity of the instruments. There are few examples of good instruments in studies of health care and health outcomes. One important exception is myocardial infarction, in which location of residence strongly influences the choice of treating hospital. Myocardial infarction, or heart attack, is considered a true medical emergency, so there is little opportunity for selection effects. Patients with symptoms of heart attacks are usually admitted to the nearest hospital, whether it is a small community hospital or a major referral center. Thus, proximity to an advanced hospital (capable of performing cardiac catheterization and heart surgery) can serve as a measure of intensity of care that is plausibly independent of patient characteristics (McClellan, McNeil, and Newhouse 1994).

One can argue that area-wide intensity measures, such as treatment within the last six months of life, are independent of individual patient characteristics and are therefore valid instruments, though it is also easy to posit circumstances in which such an instrument is not valid. The interpretation of the instrument depends upon the sources of variation in treatment intensity at the end of life and one's views about the difference between the intensity of end-of-life care and the intensity of care overall.

If the correlation between physician visits at the end of life and the general intensity of care is perfect, we need not worry about which measure is used. But if the two measures are not highly correlated, physicians in regions with high intensity at the end of life might be allocating (relative to other areas) more intensive treatment to people who won't benefit. In itself, this would be an interesting finding, but its interpretation is different from the interpretation that one would attach to a relationship between general intensity and outcomes. Intensive care in general might have a positive marginal effect on survival and other health outcomes, while intensive care (or physician visits) at the end of life might have no effect on outcomes. That is, there is no contradiction between the statement that Medicare beneficiaries who live in regions that treat dying patients intensively do not have better health outcomes, and the statement that regions that generally treat Medicare beneficiaries more intensively have better outcomes. Consequently, policies that reduced overall intensity might lead to worsened health outcomes, even if there was no relationship between end-of-life intensity and health.

The definition of efficiency is a crucial consideration for this work. By asking whether treatment intensity is equated at the margin across regions, Skinner and colleagues are implicitly addressing movement along a production possibility frontier. But they note that there is substantial variation in "process quality" of care, or in compliance with generally accepted guidelines for care. Although such variation may in part reflect intensity and represent different points on a production possibility frontier, variation in process quality can be a manifestation of x-inefficiency. That is, poor performance on process quality measures may mean that the care in some areas is interior to the production possibility frontier.

Movement along a production possibility frontier and elimination of x-inefficiency can both lead to better health outcomes for given expenditures. However, they are not likely to be equally acceptable, nor do they have the same economic implications. Elimination of x-inefficiency means that no Medicare beneficiary need be made worse off—that is, an actual Pareto improvement is possible. Movement along a production possibility frontier may satisfy the Kaldor-Hicks criterion, meaning that it will generate a *potential* Pareto improvement, but that does not mean that an actual Pareto improvement will occur. Residents of areas that use care more intensively will have to receive less care to equate treatment intensity at the margin across areas. If they do not receive compensation, they will be made worse off. Any policy that led to this shift of resources would meet with strong political resistance. Elimination of x-inefficiency would be an important contribution to health and health care, while movement along the production possibility frontier may be more feasible in the lecture hall than in the real world of medical practice.

This paper asks the right questions and analyzes a rich data set to provide some tentative yet provocative answers. It establishes the importance of learning more about the causes of variation in intensity and about the consequences of intensity variation for health. Until such information is forthcoming, though, the work by Skinner and colleagues casts doubt on the belief that more care inevitably leads to better health outcomes.

References

McClellan, M. B., B. J. McNeil, and J. P. Newhouse. 1994. Does more intensive treatment of acute myocardial infarction reduce mortality? *Journal of the American Medical Association* 272 (11): 859–66.

Phelps, C. E., and C. Mooney. 1993. Variations in medical practice use: Causes and consequences. In *Competitive approaches to health care reform,* ed. R. J. Arnould, R. F. Rich, and W. D. White, 139–78. Washington, DC: Urban Institute.

Wennberg, J. E., B. A. Barnes, and M. Zubkoff. 1982. Professional uncertainty and the problem of supplier-induced demand. *Social Sciences and Medicine* 16: 1811–24.

Wennberg, J. E., and A. Gittelsohn. 1973. Small area variations in health care delivery. *Science* 182:1102.

5

Intensive Medical Technology and the Reduction in Disability

David M. Cutler

Substantial recent evidence shows a reduction in disability among the elderly in the United States. Manton and Gu (2001), for example, document a 25 percent decline in disability among the elderly population between 1982 and 1999—a reduction of over 1 percent per year. Cutler (2001) shows similar measures of disability decline in a variety of different surveys. The consensus among researchers has moved toward the conclusion that the elderly are getting healthier, even as they are living longer (Freedman, Martin, and Schoeni 2002).

The major issue raised by these findings is why disability has declined. There is, of course, a scholarly interest in knowing why disability has fallen. But there are public policy reasons to care as well. Understanding disability trends is essential in making forecasts about the medical needs of the elderly population. The disabled spend seven times what the nondisabled do on medical care. Reductions in disability, if they continue, could thus have large effects on the medical burden of an aging society (Pardes et al. 1999). Feedback the other way is possible as well. To the extent that lower disability is driven by increased medical spending, changes in the medical system could influence the future health of the elderly population. Reductions in Medicare payments that reduce the growth of intensive procedure use, for example, might adversely affect the health of the aged population.

Very little is known about what factors have influenced disability trends, although there are many possibilities. Medical advance is clearly one fac-

David M. Cutler is the academic dean of the faculty of arts and sciences and a professor of economics in the Department of Economics and Kennedy School of Government at Harvard University, and a research associate of the National Bureau of Economic Research.
I am grateful to Danielle Ferry for excellent research assistance, to Alan Garber for comments, and to the National Institute on Aging grant R01 AG19805 for research support.

tor. People who are sick receive more intensive medical care than they used to, often with the goal of reducing disability (in addition to extending life). For the purposes of this paper, I divide medical advances into major procedures such as surgery for hip problems or heart disease, and less intensive forms of therapy such as prescription medications. This is largely for data reasons; the data that I use have information on intensive procedures but not medication usage.

Beyond medical advance, some have attributed reduced disability to an increasingly educated elderly population (Freedman and Martin 2002), environmental changes such as fewer buildings with only stairs (Institute of Medicine 1997), less strenuous work when younger (Case and Deaton, chap. 6 in this volume), and increased use of technological aids to overcome potential impairment (Manton, Corder, and Stallard 1993).

In this paper, I present preliminary evidence on the role of one of these factors in explaining reductions in disability: increased medical procedure use in response to acute episodes of disease. Procedures consist largely of major surgical operations—open-heart surgery for people with cardiovascular disease and hip replacements for people with fractures or severe arthritis, for example. Use of these procedures has diffused widely, in many cases doubling or tripling over a decade, suggesting they could play a large role in improved health.

I document two facts about procedure receipt and disability change. First, I show that most of the reduction in disability is not from people having fewer disabling conditions. The share of people with a stroke, fracture, or other serious condition has increased over time. Rather, reduced disability is because fewer people who have these conditions become disabled. Since intensive medical care is most important after a person has an acute event, this suggests the potential role of increased utilization of medical services in reducing disability.

Examining specific technologies shows that receipt of intensive procedures is associated with some reduction in disability, but not an enormous amount. People with musculoskeletal problems and circulatory disease are much more likely to get surgery now than in the past, and disability for people with these conditions has fallen. But this is not a large share of the total decline. Other medical and nonmedical interventions are more important in aggregate. I speculate about what other factors might be relevant, but I do not provide conclusive evidence.

This paper is structured as follows. The first section explains the measure of disability and presents trends in disability over time. The second section divides declining disability into reduced incidence of major conditions and reduced disability for people who experience those conditions. The third section examines the role of medical technology in explaining why serious diseases are not as disabling as they used to be. The last section concludes.

5.1 Trends in Disability

Disability has both a medical and a social component.[1] In the broadest definition, a person is disabled if he or she cannot perform the activities usually associated with a person of that age and position in life. The expectation about what one can do clearly involves a number of different factors. A twenty-five-year-old who cannot lift a twenty-pound box would probably be classified as disabled; a seventy-year-old with the same inability, in contrast, would not.

The definition of physical needs then becomes important. What is a person supposed to be able to do? In practice, most researchers focus on basic activities associated with independent living: people are classed as disabled if they cannot perform the necessary activities needed to live on their own. These necessary activities are of two types: physical activities of daily living (ADLs) and social or cultural instrumental activities of daily living (IADLs). Activities categorized as ADLs include eating, getting into and out of bed, getting around inside, dressing, bathing, and using the toilet. Activities categorized as IADLs consist of shopping, doing laundry, doing light housework, demonstrating outdoor mobility, managing medications, managing money, getting to places out of walking distance, and preparing meals.

The definition of disability here is very strict. Disability is the very low end of the spectrum of independent living. A person who cannot climb a flight of stairs but has no difficulty getting places without stairs, for example, would not be disabled. In analyzing medical interventions, this distinction is important. Many medical interventions are designed to improve health through better higher-end functioning. The impact of these interventions may be missed with such a measure of disability. Still, the majority of research in the area examines the severe disability measure, so it is a useful starting point.

The bulk of research on disability uses data from the National Long-Term Care Survey (NLTCS).[2] The NLTCS began in 1982 with a sample of the community-dwelling population. It was conducted again in 1984, 1989, 1994, and 1999. In each case, people in one wave are followed in subsequent waves, and a new sample is drawn to keep the survey nationally representative. The nearly twenty years of comparable data make the NLTCS unique in health surveys.

The NLTCS has been linked to Medicare claims records. This is important because claims records are the most reliable source of information on

---

1. See Pope and Tarlov (1991) and Verbrugge and Jett (1994) for discussion.
2. Information on the NLTCS can be found on the Duke University web site, www.cds.duke.edu.

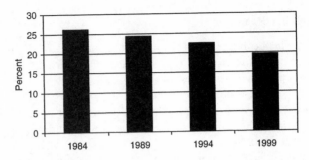

Fig. 5.1 Disability among the elderly
Source: Manton and Gu (2001).

intensive medical care receipt. These claims records figure prominently in the analysis reported here. Medicare covers hospital, physician, and laboratory services. Prescription drugs are not paid for by Medicare; hence, there is no record of them. Nor does the NLTCS ask about prescription medications. Thus, I cannot examine the role of pharmaceutical innovation.

Reliable hospital data are available from 1982 on. Physician data are generally not reliable until the early 1990s. To measure disability trends over the longest possible time period, I use data from 1989 and 1999, restricting myself to the hospital records.[3] In practice, the most reliable information on hospital records is the major procedures that were performed. Surgical admissions are reimbursed at a higher rate than are medical admissions. Thus, hospitals take particular care in recording any surgical procedures that were performed. The procedures that I examine are all surgical.

Figure 5.1 shows basic information on trends in disability in 1984 and every five years thereafter (see Manton and Gu 2001). The data are age adjusted to the 1999 population; thus, the increasingly aged population does not mechanically lead to increased disability. In 1984, 26 percent of the elderly population was disabled. That declined steadily in the subsequent fifteen years. By 1999, less than 20 percent of the population was disabled. The overall decline in disability is 25 percent, or 1.8 percent per year. It is this major decline in disability that I seek to explain.

5.2 Disabling Conditions and the Extent of Disability

One way to begin the understanding of disability decline is to decompose disability changes into the incidence of different conditions and the extent

---

3. Analysis that I have done from the 1994 and 1999 surveys using physician data as well are generally similar.

to which those conditions produce disability. Denote medical conditions by $j = 1, \ldots, J$. Assuming that each person has only one condition, the probability that a person is disabled in any year is given by

(1) $$\mathrm{Pr(Disability)} = \sum_{j} \mathrm{Pr}(C_j) \cdot \mathrm{Pr}(D \mid C_j),$$

where C_j is an indicator for whether a person has condition j and D indicates whether the person is disabled.

To operationalize this disaggregation, we need to define a set of conditions. The choices here are limited by the nature of the data. Whether the person is disabled can be determined from surveys conducted in 1989 and 1999. The only information on the incidence of disability conditions, however, comes from claims records. We thus need to find conditions that will be reliably coded in claims data.

In determining whether a person had a condition, we need to decide on a time period for measurement. The medical record data permit a measure of disease incidence over many years. Conditions that occurred many years in the past are unlikely to be a cause of current disability, however. To balance these concerns, I choose a time interval of two years before the survey date.

After some exploration, I settled on the thirty-three conditions listed in table 5.1.[4] The conditions are divided by major diagnostic category. The major categories with the most entries include musculoskeletal disorders (for example, hip fractures and arthritis); respiratory disease (chronic obstructive pulmonary disease and similar diseases); circulatory disorders (stroke and heart disease); cancer (colorectal, lung, breast, and prostate); mental disorders (especially depression); nervous system disorders (dementia, Parkinson's); and endocrine disorders (especially diabetes). There are thirty-one specific diseases. The last row is the composite of other conditions. Some people who are disabled have no hospital admissions beforehand; these are included in the penultimate "no condition" row.

The last column of table 5.1 shows the share of people with that condition who were disabled in the individual survey. Admissions for dementia and other brain diseases have the highest disability rate. Three-quarters of people with such an admission are disabled. Other conditions with very high disability rates are hip and pelvic fractures (74 percent), paralysis and Parkinson's disease (73 percent), and acute renal failure (63 percent). At the bottom end, most cancers have only a 20 percent disability rate, and genitourinary diseases are similarly nondisabling. Somewhat surprisingly, 15 percent of people never admitted to a hospital in a two-year period are disabled at the end of that period.

These relative disability rates are important in considering equation (1).

---

4. McClellan and Yan (2000) use a similar list.

Table 5.1   **List of conditions and disability probability**

Condition	ICD-9-CM codes	Disability probability (%)
Musculoskeletal		
Arthritis and arthropathy	274.*, 390.*, 710.*–716.*	38
Back/Neck pain	720.*–724.*, 839.0–839.5, 846.*, 847.*	31
Hip and pelvic fracture	808.*, 820.*	74
Musculoskeletal disorders	717.*–739.* (~#29), 800.*–999.* (~#29, #30)	34
Digestive		
Gastrointestinal disease	530.*–579.*, 789.0, 787.0, 787.7	30
Respiratory		
Chronic obstructive pulmonary diseases and related diseases	466.*, 490.*–496.*, 518.12	36
Respiratory failure and insufficiency	518.*, 799.1	46
Respiratory diseases	460.*–519.* (~#22, #23), 786.0, 786.1, 786.52, 793.1	37
Circulatory		
Stroke	362.34, 430.*, 431.*, 432.9, 433.*–436.*	50
Hypertension	401.*–405.* (~#16), 437.0, 437.9	32
Ischemic heart disease	410.*–414.* (~414.11, 414.19), 429.5–429.7	30
Heart failure and arrhythmia	425.*, 427.1, 427.3–427.5, 428.*, 429.1, 429.3	46
Peripheral vascular disease	440.*, 442.*, 443.* (~443.2), 444.*, 446.*, 447.* (~447.6), 451.*, 453.1	41
Circulatory diseases	391.*–459.* (~#13, #14, #16, #17, #18, #19, #20), 786.5, V717.*	32
Infectious disease		
Infectious diseases	001.*–139.*, 320.*–323.*, V09.*	40
Cancer		
Colorectal and lung cancer	153.*, 154.*, 162.*	30
Breast and prostate cancer	174.*–175.*, 185.*	20
Other cancers	140.*–239.* (~#2, #3), 611.72, V10	23
Genitourinary diseases		
Chronic renal failure	403.01, 403.11, 403.91, 404.02, 404.12, 404.92, 585.*–586.*, V45.1, V56.*	54
Acute renal failure and insufficiency	584.*, 587.*, 588.*	63
Genitourinary diseases	580.*–629.* (~#4, #16, #25, #26), 788.* (~788.3, 788.4), 793.8, V44.5–V44.6, V55.5–V55.6	28
Mental disorders		
Depression	296.* (~296.9), 298.0, 300.4, 311.*	44
Other mental disorders	290.*–319.* (~#10, #11), 797.*	49
Nervous system and sensory		
Dementia and organic brain diseases	290.*, 294.*, 310.*, 330.*, 331.*	78
Paralysis, Parkinson's, etc.	332.*, 340.*–344.*, 438.*	73
Glaucoma and cataract	365.*–366.*, 743.2–743.3	28

Table 5.1   (continued)

Condition	ICD-9-CM codes	Disability probability (%)
Blood		
Anemia	280.*–285.*	43
Other blood diseases	285.*–289.*	37
Endocrine, nutritional, metabolic		
Diabetes	250.*, 251.3	40
Thyroid disorders	240.*–259.* (~#5)	30
Other metabolic and immunity disorders	270.*–273.*, 275.*–279.*	28
Other		
No condition		15
Composite category	All other codes	29

Equation (1) is only correct if each person has only one condition. In practice, some people have more than one condition. There is a generalization of equation (1) that allows for multiple conditions.[5] The cross-correlations between conditions are generally fairly low, however, meaning that there are a lot of cross-conditions with few people in them.

To avoid dealing with many comorbidities with small numbers, I assign each person to only one condition—the one with the highest disability probability. For example, a person admitted with respiratory failure and insufficiency (46 percent disability rate) and diabetes (40 percent disability rate) is classified as having respiratory failure and insufficiency.

With this assignment system, table 5.2 shows how these conditions contribute to lower disability. The first two columns show the probability of having each condition and the disability associated with that condition in 1989; the next two columns report the same figures for 1999. The fifth and sixth columns show disability through each of these paths (the product of the two columns for that year), and the seventh column shows the change in disability from that path.

Overall, disability rates fell by 5.7 percentage points, as shown in the last row of the table.[6] The biggest decline in disability comes from musculoskeletal disorders. Reduced disability through that channel accounts for one-quarter of the total decline. Digestive and respiratory disorders together account for that amount as well. There is also a large decline in disability for people with no hospitalizations. This path accounts for 40 percent of the total reduction in disability.

5. Multiple conditions can conceptually be treated as conditions of their own. In practice, following this strategy does not change the conclusions.
6. These numbers differ from those in figure 5.1 because of different years of age adjustment.

Table 5.2   **Medical conditions associated with reduced disability (%)**

Condition	1989		1999		Disability probability			
	Pr[C]	Pr[D|C]	Pr[C]	Pr[D|C]	1989	1999	Change	Total
Musculoskeletal								
1 Arthritis and arthropathy	2.6	37.4	3.6	25.0	1.0	0.9	−0.1	−1.3
2 Back/Neck pain	1.2	20.3	1.8	15.8	0.3	0.3	0.0	
3 Hip and pelvic fracture	1.8	77.1	1.4	67.8	1.4	0.9	−0.5	
4 Musculoskeletal disorders	8.6	27.6	9.0	17.9	2.4	1.6	−0.8	
Digestive								
5 Gastrointestinal disease	4.9	21.0	3.1	12.2	1.0	0.4	−0.6	−0.6
Respiratory								
6 Chronic obstructive pulmonary diseases and related diseases	1.9	31.6	2.1	17.2	0.6	0.4	−0.2	−0.6
7 Respiratory failure and insufficiency	0.6	55.3	0.9	39.1	0.3	0.3	0.0	
8 Respiratory diseases	3.4	32.5	3.6	21.2	1.1	0.8	−0.3	
Circulatory system								
9 Stroke	3.8	51.2	4.7	39.1	1.9	1.8	−0.1	−0.3
10 Hypertension	1.5	22.0	2.5	16.0	0.3	0.4	0.1	
11 Ischemic heart disease	1.8	25.7	1.4	17.1	0.5	0.2	−0.2	
12 Heart failure and arrhythmia	3.6	43.3	5.3	37.0	1.6	2.0	0.4	
13 Peripheral vascular disease	1.3	35.7	1.5	24.2	0.5	0.4	−0.1	
14 Circulatory diseases	3.3	22.5	2.8	12.3	0.8	0.3	−0.4	
Infectious disease								
15 Infectious diseases	1.4	39.8	1.4	25.9	0.5	0.4	−0.2	−0.2
Cancer								
16 Colorectal and lung cancer	0.3	23.4	0.1	31.0	0.1	0.0	0.0	−0.1
17 Breast and prostate cancer	0.2	13.5	0.2	14.9	0.0	0.0	0.0	
18 Other cancers	1.1	12.8	0.6	7.5	0.1	0.0	−0.1	
Genitourinary diseases								
19 Chronic renal failure	0.3	59.0	0.5	52.5	0.2	0.3	0.1	−0.1
20 Acute renal failure and insufficiency	0.1	74.5	0.2	54.8	0.1	0.1	0.0	
21 Genitourinary diseases	2.2	17.2	1.1	14.6	0.4	0.2	−0.2	
Mental disorders								
22 Depression	0.3	23.7	0.5	33.0	0.1	0.2	0.1	0.0
23 Other mental disorders	1.4	41.5	1.3	36.9	0.6	0.5	−0.1	
Nervous system and sense organs								
24 Dementia and organic brain diseases	1.1	82.2	1.5	77.5	0.9	1.2	0.3	0.1
25 Paralysis, Parkinson's, etc.	1.0	70.0	1.1	67.0	0.7	0.7	0.0	
26 Glaucoma and cataract	1.4	25.0	0.7	13.8	0.3	0.1	−0.2	

Table 5.2   (continued)

	1989		1999		Disability probability			
Condition	Pr[C]	Pr[D | C]	Pr[C]	Pr[D | C]	1989	1999	Change	Total
Blood								
27 Anemia	1.4	37.4	2.1	30.7	0.5	0.6	0.1	0.1
28 Other blood diseases	0.4	11.5	0.4	14.3	0.0	0.1	0.0	
Endocrine, nutritional, metabolic								
29 Diabetes	2.2	31.3	3.9	24.9	0.7	1.0	0.3	0.2
30 Thyroid disorders	0.3	14.6	0.5	4.8	0.0	0.0	0.0	
31 Other metabolic and immunity disorders	0.4	30.8	0.3	8.2	0.1	0.0	−0.1	
Other								
32 No condition	37.1	17.2	31.7	12.8	6.4	4.1	−2.3	−2.8
33 Composite category	7.3	22.0	8.3	13.2	1.6	1.1	−0.5	
Total		26.9		21.2			−5.7	

Notes: These are weighted (using CDS screener cross-sectional weights) observed rates in 1989 and 1999. Weights are age and sex standardized to 1999.

Table 5.2 suggests a mixed conclusion about the potential importance of intensive interventions in explaining the decline in disability. Musculoskeletal disorders are certainly responsive to medical intervention; hip replacements and back or neck procedures are among the most rapidly expanding medical procedures. On the other hand, there is little surgical therapy for infectious disease and respiratory disease, each of which have had reductions in disability. And clearly, no surgical therapy was performed on people without a hospital record. Increased use of intensive therapies can thus explain some, but certainly not all, of the reduction in disability.

5.2.1 Incidence of Conditions and Disability Rate

More information on the nature of reduced disability comes from decomposing disability declines into changes in the probability of having a disease and the extent to which diseases lead to disability. Following equation (1), we can approximate[7] the change in disability between two time periods as

$$(2) \quad \Delta\mathrm{Pr}(\mathrm{Disability}) = \sum_j \Delta\mathrm{Pr}(C_j) \cdot \mathrm{Pr}(D \mid C_j) + \sum_j \mathrm{Pr}(C_j) \cdot \Delta\mathrm{Pr}(D \mid C_j).$$

The first term on the right-hand side is the effect of changes in event probabilities on disability; the second is the effect of changes in the conditional disability rate. Performing this decomposition will tell us whether

7. The equation is approximate because there is an omitted covariance term between changes in incidence and conditional disability rates.

disability is falling because fewer people are at risk for disability or because the same events are less disabling over time. Intensive medical care will be more likely to reduce disability among people with a disease than to prevent the disease in the first place.

Table 5.3 shows the decomposition. In total, more people have conditions in 1999 than did in 1989. As the penultimate row shows, 5.4 percent fewer people had no condition in 1999 than did in 1989. As a result of this increase in the probability of having disabling conditions, changes in the event probability rate alone would suggest an increase in disability over time. The amount, shown in the last row of the table, is 1.8 percent.

The overwhelming reason why disability has declined is because the conditions that people have are less disabling than they used to be. This finding is true for the vast bulk of conditions. For the typical condition, the disability rate for people who have the condition was about 10 percent lower in 1999 than it was a decade earlier.

The findings that more people have each condition and that fewer people with each condition are disabled suggests a possible selection story—more people survive severe episodes now than in the past and thus report hospitalizations for them. That would not be a particular problem for the analysis; we want to capture increasing disability resulting from more "marginal survivors."

Two other possibilities are more problematic, however. One possibility is that diagnosis of marginal cases has increased, and the new people with each condition are not as seriously affected as those who were diagnosed previously. This would lead to a mechanical finding that the incidence of disabling conditions was rising but that disability for people with those conditions was falling. Since the conditions chosen are generally severe and relatively clear to diagnose, however, this is somewhat less likely. A hip fracture is not a very ambiguous diagnosis, for example.

Alternatively, it may be that people have these diagnoses because they are obtaining particular therapies that were not previously provided. For example, a person with severe arthritis who now receives a hip replacement will be admitted to a hospital for the operation and receive an arthritis drug, where previously there was no admission for that condition. In these data, we have no way to test for this. It is thus necessary to interpret the decomposition with some caution.

5.3   Intensive Medical Care and Disability

The question I address is how much of the reduction in disability can be explained by increased use of intensive procedures. To assemble a list of important interventions, I looked at the procedures that are common for these diseases. Table 5.4 shows the resulting list, and table 5.5 shows a concordance between diseases and procedures. Relevant procedures differ

Table 5.3　　　　**Decomposition of changes in disability**

	Effect of change in:					
	Probability of condition			Conditional disability rate		
Condition	$d\Pr[C]$	$\Pr[D\,|\,C]$	Total	$d(\Pr[D\,|\,C])$	$\Pr[C]$	Total
Musculoskeletal						
1　Arthritis and arthropathy	1.0	37.4	0.4	−12.4	2.6	−0.3
2　Back/Neck pain	0.5	20.3	0.1	−4.5	1.2	−0.1
3　Hip and pelvic fracture	−0.4	77.1	−0.3	−9.3	1.8	−0.2
4　Musculoskeletal disorders	0.4	27.6	0.1	−9.8	8.6	−0.8
Digestive						
5　Gastrointestinal disease	−1.8	21.0	−0.4	−8.8	4.9	−0.4
Respiratory						
6　Chronic obstructive pulmonary diseases and related diseases	0.2	31.6	0.1	−14.4	1.9	−0.3
7　Respiratory failure and insufficiency	0.3	55.3	0.1	−16.3	0.6	−0.1
8　Respiratory diseases	0.2	32.5	0.1	−11.3	3.4	−0.4
Circulatory system						
9　Stroke	0.9	51.2	0.5	−12.1	3.8	−0.5
10　Hypertension	1.0	22.0	0.2	−6.0	1.5	−0.1
11　Ischemic heart disease	−0.4	25.7	−0.1	−8.6	1.8	−0.2
12　Heart failure and arrhythmia	1.7	43.3	0.7	−6.3	3.6	−0.2
13　Peripheral vascular disease	0.2	35.7	0.1	−11.5	1.3	−0.1
14　Circulatory diseases	−0.6	22.5	−0.1	−10.2	3.3	−0.3
Infectious disease						
15　Infectious diseases	0.0	39.8	0.0	−13.9	1.4	−0.2
Cancer						
16　Colorectal and lung cancer	−0.2	23.4	0.0	7.5	0.3	0.0
17　Breast and prostate cancer	0.0	13.5	0.0	1.5	0.2	0.0
18　Other cancers	−0.5	12.8	−0.1	−5.2	1.1	−0.1
Genitourinary diseases						
19　Chronic renal failure	0.2	59.0	0.1	−6.5	0.3	0.0
20　Acute renal failure and insufficiency	0.1	74.5	0.1	−19.7	0.1	0.0
21　Genitourinary diseases	−1.1	17.2	−0.2	−2.7	2.2	−0.1
Mental disorders						
22　Depression	0.2	23.7	0.0	9.3	0.3	0.0
23　Other mental disorders	−0.1	41.5	0.0	−4.6	1.4	−0.1
Nervous system and sense organs						
24　Dementia and organic brain diseases	0.5	82.2	0.4	−4.7	1.1	0.0
25　Paralysis, Parkinson's, etc.	0.1	70.0	0.1	−2.9	1.0	0.0
26　Glaucoma and cataract	−0.7	25.0	−0.2	−11.3	1.4	−0.2
Blood						
27　Anemia	0.7	37.4	0.3	−6.7	1.4	−0.1
28　Other blood diseases	0.0	11.5	0.0	2.9	0.4	0.0

(*continued*)

Table 5.3   (continued)

	Effect of change in:					
	Probability of condition			Conditional disability rate		
Condition	dPr[C]	Pr[D|C]	Total	d(Pr[D|C])	Pr[C]	Total
Endocrine, nutritional, metabolic						
29 Diabetes	1.7	31.3	0.5	−6.4	2.2	−0.1
30 Thyroid disorders	0.1	14.6	0.0	−9.7	0.3	0.0
31 Other metabolic and immunity disorders	−0.1	30.8	0.0	−22.6	0.4	−0.1
Other						
32 No condition	−5.4	17.2	−0.9	−4.4	37.1	−1.6
33 Composite category	1.0	22.0	0.2	−8.8	7.3	−0.6
Total			1.8			−7.2

Note: See table 5.2 notes.

Table 5.4   **List of common procedures**

No./Procedure	ICD-9-CM codes
3 Ops on spinal cord and spinal canal structures	03.* (~03.3)
13 Ops on lens	13.*
14 Ops on retina, choroid, vitreous, and posterior chamber	14.* (~14.1)
34 Ops on chest wall, pleura, mediastinum, and diaphragm	34.* (~34.2)
35 Ops on valves and septa of heart	35.*
36 Ops on vessels of heart	36.*
37 Other ops on heart and pericardium	37.* (~37.2)
38 Incision, excision, and occlusion of vessels	38.* (~38.2)
39 Other ops on vessels	39.*
45 Incision, excision, and anastomosis of intestine	45.0 (~45.1, 45.2)
51 Ops on gallbladder and biliary tract	51.* (~51.1)
53 Repair of hernia	53.*
54 Other ops on abdominal region	54.* (~52.2)
57 Ops on urinary bladder	57.* (~57.3)
60 Ops on prostate and seminal vesicles	60.* (~60.1)
79 Reduction of fracture and dislocation	79.*
80 Incision and excision of joint structures	80.*
81 Repair and plastic ops on joint structures	81.*
84 Other procedures on musculoskeletal system	84.*
85 Ops on the breast	85.*
99 Conversion of cardiac rhythm	99.6

greatly across diseases. People with musculoskeletal diagnoses receive joint replacement and other surgeries, for example, and people with cardiovascular disease receive various heart procedures. For some conditions—respiratory problems, mental illness, and nervous system disorders—no surgical therapy is common.

Table 5.5 Matching of conditions and major procedures

Condition	Major procedure codes

Condition	03	13	14	34	35	36	37*	38	39	45*	51	53	54	57*	60*	79	80	81	84	85	99*
Musculoskeletal																					
1 Arthritis and arthropathy	X																				
2 Back/Neck pain																		X			
3 Hip and pelvic fracture																X	X	X			
4 Musculoskeletal disorders																X	X	X			
Gastrointestinal																					
5 Gastrointestinal disease											X	X									
Respiratory																					
6 Chronic obstructive pulmonary diseases and related diseases																					
7 Respiratory failure and insufficiency																					
8 Respiratory diseases				X																	
Circulatory																					
9 Stroke								X													
10 Hypertension																					
11 Ischemic heart disease						X	X														
12 Heart failure and arrhythmia							X														
13 Peripheral vascular disease							X	X	X										X		
14 Circulatory diseases					X		X	X													
Infectious disease																					
15 Infectious diseases																					X

(*continued*)

Table 5.5   (continued)

Condition	Major procedure codes																				
	03	13	14	34	35	36	37*	38	39	45*	51	53	54	57*	60*	79	80	81	84	85	99*
Cancer																					
16 Colorectal and lung cancer										X											
17 Breast and prostate cancer													X					X			
18 Other cancers										X											
Genitourinary disease																					
19 Chronic renal failure									X				X								
20 Acute renal failure and insufficiency																					
21 Genitourinary diseases														X	X					X	
Mental disorders																					
22 Depression																					
23 Other mental disorders																					
Nervous system and sense organs																					
24 Dementia and organic brain diseases																					
25 Paralysis, Parkinson's, etc.																					
26 Glaucoma and cataract		X																			
Blood																					
27 Anemia																					
28 Other blood diseases																					
Endocrine, nutritional, metabolic																					
29 Diabetes			X																X		
30 Thyroid disorders																					
31 Other metabolic and immunity disorders																					
Other																					
32 No condition																					
33 Composite category																					

Table 5.6 shows the share of people with each condition that received any of the indicated surgeries. There is a large increase in use of most procedures over time. Surgical increases are very common for patients with musculoskeletal disorders; the percent of patients receiving surgery rose by as much as 20 percent for many of these conditions. Surgery also increased substantially for patients with circulatory disorders (especially heart disease) and difficulty seeing. Surgical increases were much smaller, or declined, for patients with respiratory problems and cancer. The lower rate of use of surgery for cancer patients is somewhat troubling, since almost all such patients will receive some surgery. Most likely, the admissions for cancer here are palliative care patients, or patients who previously had surgery and are now admitted for other therapies. These types of problems point out the limitations of using claims data, but there is no alternative in this case.

Estimating the impact of medical therapies on disability is difficult. Consider a cross-sectional regression relating disability to an indicator for whether a person received an intensive procedure and a variety of other factors ($\mathbf{X}$):

(3) $\qquad \Pr(D \mid C_j) = \beta_0 + \beta_1 \cdot \text{Procedure Use}_j + \mathbf{X}_j\beta + \varepsilon_j.$

The difficulty with estimating this equation is the nonrandom decision about who receives which treatment. If the most severely ill patients receive surgical care and are also likely to wind up disabled, the regression will show that surgical procedure use is positively associated with disability, when that is not the case. Some measures of sickness can be controlled for in the $\mathbf{X}$ vector, but not all. Without an instrument for who receives different procedures that is independent of illness severity and general health status, there is no easy solution to this problem.

To make progress, I use time series rather than cross-section variation. The idea is the following: suppose that the underlying severity of disease for each condition is the same over time. Then, conditions where procedure use has expanded most should have the largest decline in disability. Formally, this can be expressed as

(4) $\qquad \Delta\Pr(D \mid C_j) = \beta_0 + \beta_1 \cdot \Delta\text{Procedure Use}_j + \varepsilon_j,$

where $\Delta\text{Procedure Use}_j$ is the average change in procedure use for people with each condition.

The identifying assumption here is that patient severity is the same over time (hence, equation [4] can be estimated without $\mathbf{X}$ variables). The increase in diagnosis of these conditions makes this somewhat problematic. More patients diagnosed may raise or lower average severity of the group with each condition. Future work could usefully address this by looking at changes in comorbidities or other factors that illustrate disease severity.

Another concern is that other factors might influence disability. Imagine

Table 5.6   **Use of surgery, by condition**

Condition	1989 % of surgery	N	1999 % of surgery	N	Change (%)
Musculoskeletal					
1 Arthritis and arthropathy	12.1	407	29.4	588	17.3
2 Back/Neck pain	6.2	177	16.1	279	9.9
3 Hip and pelvic fracture	52.8	291	73.7	264	20.9
4 Musculoskeletal disorders	6.9	1,292	8.0	1,440	1.1
Digestive					
5 Gastrointestinal disease	16.9	716	18.0	485	1.1
Respiratory					
6 Chronic obstructive pulmonary diseases and related diseases	—		—		
7 Respiratory failure and insufficiency	—		—		
8 Respiratory diseases	3.9	524	1.2	579	−2.7
Circulatory					
9 Stroke	9.5	579	12.0	805	2.5
10 Hypertension	—		—		
11 Ischemic heart disease	13.4	269	27.3	205	13.9
12 Heart failure and arrhythmia	4.5	549	10.2	954	5.7
13 Peripheral vascular disease	23.7	198	27.5	232	3.8
14 Circulatory diseases	7.1	495	7.5	418	0.4
Infectious disease					
15 Infectious diseases	—		—		
Cancer					
16 Colorectal and lung cancer	40.4	40	18.1	19	−22.3
17 Breast and prostate cancer	35.7	28	19.1	37	−16.6
18 Other cancers	5.7	166	22.2	98	16.5
Genitourinary diseases					
19 Chronic renal failure	48.3	40	43.1	80	−5.2
20 Acute renal failure and insufficiency	—		—		
21 Genitourinary diseases	22.3	315	13.4	172	−8.9
Mental disorders					
22 Depression	—		—		
23 Other mental disorders	—		—		
Nervous system and sensory					
24 Dementia and organic brain diseases	—		—		
25 Paralysis, Parkinson's, etc.	—		—		
26 Glaucoma and cataract	55.2	207	73.3	122	18.1
Blood					
27 Anemia	—		—		
28 Other blood diseases	—		—		
Endocrine, nutritional, metabolic					
29 Diabetes	5.1	328	1.4	595	−3.7
30 Thyroid disorders	—		—		
31 Other metabolic and immunity disorders	—		—		
Other					
32 No condition	—		—		
33 Composite category	—		—		

Notes: Surgeries are listed in table 5.5. Dashes indicate that no surgical procedures were identified.

that a new pharmaceutical is developed that substitutes for surgery in some cases. Surgery rates will fall, and concomitantly disability will decline. This will bias the findings against showing an impact of medical technology on health, although the opposite bias is possible as well. One task for the future will be to consider which of these conditions have had important non-surgical advances in treatments—pharmaceutical, environmental, or behavioral. For now, however, I do not address this.

Figure 5.2 shows the graphical relation between changes in intensive procedure use and disability rates for people who have been diagnosed with these conditions (the conditional disability rate). There is a clear negative relation between the two. The coefficient β_1 in the regression above is estimated to be $-.27$ (.13). The R^2 from the regression is not high (.13), but that is not particularly surprising: there are many factors other than surgical procedures that influence disability.

A comparison of the different disease categories indicates what is being picked up in the analysis. Intensive procedure use rose particularly rapidly for people with musculoskeletal problems. The increase in use was as high as 20 percent for some conditions. Those conditions also had very large declines in disability, placing them in the bottom right quadrant of the figure. Surgery rates for cancer fell or were relatively constant, however, and disability rates for cancer rose. Cancer diagnoses make up many of the conditions toward the top left of the figure.

Overall, increased use of surgical procedures does not explain a large part of the total reduction in disability. The constant term in the regression—the predicted change in disability with no change in surgery rates—is about 7 percent. That is near the overall decline in conditional disability rates shown in table 5.3. Further, the very strong declines in disability for conditions where surgery is not an option show the importance of other factors. Surgery seems to be important for some specific conditions, such

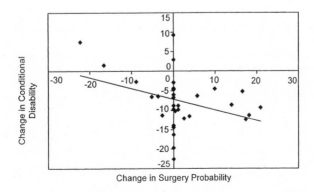

Fig. 5.2   Change in probability of surgery and conditional disability
Source: Author's calculations based on data from the National Long-Term Care Survey.

as musculoskeletal disease and circulatory disorders, but is not a major part of the decline for the vast bulk of patients.

5.4 Conclusions

This paper is a preliminary look at the factors leading to reduced disability among the elderly in the past two decades. Although the analysis is still at the beginning stages, there are several important results. The data show that lower disability is almost exclusively a result of reduced disability for people who experience serious diseases rather than a result of fewer people having serious diseases. The share of people who report having a serious condition is actually rising over this time period, and the overall disability rate among the elderly would have increased were the health of the disabled not improving. The substantial reduction in disability conditional on disease incidence strongly suggests the possibility that medical care is a factor in improved health.

Examining one important part of medical care—the use of intensive surgical therapy—yields mixed results. Rates of surgery increased for many disease categories. For conditions such as musculoskeletal problems and circulatory disorders, higher rates of surgery are plausibly related to reduced disability. But that is not true for all conditions. Many conditions are not treated by surgical intervention, and yet disability for those conditions fell as well. It is clear that other factors are also important in explaining the better health of the elderly. Determining what those other factors are is the subject of ongoing research. This paper presents a framework to examine such effects, and data that can shed light on the answers.

References

Cutler, David M. 2001. Declining disability among the elderly. *Health Affairs* 20 (6): 11–27.
Freedman, Vicki A., and Linda G. Martin. 2002. The role of education in explaining and forecasting trends in functional limitations among older Americans. *Demography* 36 (4): 461–73.
Freedman, Vicki A., Linda G. Martin, and Robert F. Schoeni. 2002. Recent trends in disability and functioning among older adults in the United States: A systematic review. *Journal of the American Medical Association* 288 (24): 3137–46.
Institute of Medicine. 1997. *Enabling America: Assessing the role of rehabilitation science and engineering.* Washington, DC: National Academy Press.
Manton, Kenneth G., Larry S. Corder, and Eric Stallard. 1993. Changes in the use of personal assistance and special equipment from 1982 to 1989: Results from the 1982 and 1989 NLTCS. *Gerontologist* 33 (2): 768–77.
Manton, Kenneth G., and Xiliang Gu. 2001. Changes in the prevalence of chronic

disability in the United States black and nonblack population above age 65 from 1982 to 1999. *Proceedings of the National Academy of Sciences* 98 (11): 6354–59.

McClellan, Mark, and Lijing Yan. 2000. Understanding disability trends in the US elderly population: The role of disease management and disease prevention. Stanford University, Department of Economics. Mimeograph.

Pardes, Herb, Kenneth G. Manton, Eric S. Lander, H. Dennis Tolley, Arthur D. Ullian, and Hans Palmer. 1999. Effects of medical research on health care and the economy. *Science* 283:36–37.

Pope, Andrew M., and Alvin Tarlov, eds. 1991. *Disability in America: Toward a national agenda for prevention.* Washington, DC: National Academy Press.

Verbrugge, Lois M., and Alan M. Jette. 1994. The disablement process. *Social Science and Medicine* 38 (1): 1–14.

Comment   Alan M. Garber

The Medicare Coverage Advisory Committee, appointed by the Health Care Financing Administration (now HCFA) to help the Medicare program make decisions about the coverage of specific medical procedures and products, met in March of 2003 to consider a promising new technology for the treatment of congestive heart failure. The technology, known as a left ventricular assist device (LVAD), was originally approved as a "bridge" to heart transplantation for patients with far advanced heart failure. Because the number of Americans with end-stage congestive heart failure greatly exceeds the number who could receive heart transplants, interest grew in the use of these devices as "destination therapy"—that is, as the primary treatment for people who could not receive transplants.

The LVAD is a portable device that acts as an external pump to assist in moving blood throughout the body, taking over part of the job of the irreversibly weakened heart of patients with very severe congestive heart failure. In a major clinical trial (REMATCH; Rose et al. 2001), patients who were near death from congestive heart failure were randomly assigned to treatment with LVAD placement or standard medical therapy. After twelve months of treatment, nearly 80 percent of the medically treated patients had died, while about half of the LVAD treated patients had died. Complementing the greater survival rate of the LVAD patients was evidence of improved quality of life. For example, the LVAD-treated group was less likely to be depressed at the end of one year, and the severity of congestive heart failure (New York Hospital Association score) was much lower in the LVAD group. The trial established that the LVAD improved survival and

Alan M. Garber is a staff physician with the Veterans Affairs Palo Alto Health Care System, the Henry J. Kaiser, Jr., Professor and professor of medicine at Stanford University, and a research associate and director of the Health Care Program at the National Bureau of Economic Research.

at least some dimensions of quality of life among patients with severe congestive heart failure. Thus, this technological innovation improved survival and, apparently, functional status. Because the prevalence of congestive heart failure rises with age and the syndrome is very common among Medicare beneficiaries, the LVAD has the potential to contribute to future decreases in disability among the elderly.

Recent findings that the prevalence of disability has been declining among older Americans have encouraged optimism about the health of future cohorts of elderly Americans. The potential ramifications of declining old age disability include longer working lives, diminishing needs for medical and long-term care, and general improvements in the quality of life. Particularly for aging baby boomers, these implications are momentous, since they determine how this outsized cohort will spend an increasingly large fraction of their lives. A better understanding of the causes of the disability decline might enable us to intervene to promote further declines in disability, while helping us to know which aspects of progress would be inadvertently threatened—or encouraged—by changes in health care financing and utilization. David Cutler's paper takes an important step toward addressing these issues by outlining an approach that relates changes in disability to changes in the use of major medical procedures. His approach, if it is successful, will elucidate the roles of devices like LVADs and other, less dramatic, procedures that may have contributed to the disability decline.

The Disability Decline and Its Causes

Findings of declining disability rates among the elderly shifted the balance of a long-standing debate about disability trends. Many prominent researchers hypothesized that medical advances were succeeding in keeping people alive whose health conditions would have led to an earlier death in years past (Verbrugge 1984). Though they could now survive longer with their chronic conditions, they suffered greater impairments than previous cohorts of survivors. This view of changes in health is based on the idea that medical progress affects survival more than functional status. The automated implantable defibrillator, which prevents sudden cardiac death by administering a shock to the heart when it goes into a deadly arrhythmia, is a recently introduced technology that reduces death rates but does little or nothing to alter the conditions that predispose patients to suffer sudden cardiac death, such as coronary artery disease and congestive heart failure.

My Stanford colleague James Fries argued more than two decades ago that trends pointed toward declining, not rising, old age disability (Fries 1980). Reductions in the incidence and severity of chronic diseases, he claimed, would lead to reductions in the disability caused by those diseases. Treatment of elevated blood pressure, for example, prevents death from stroke by preventing the strokes themselves. Prevention of this common complication of hypertension could result in declining age-adjusted functional limitations attributable to stroke survivors.

Trends in disability seemed to vary with the specific disease or health condition, and, until Kenneth Manton published his findings from the National Long-Term Care Survey, it was unclear whether overall disability among the elderly was increasing or decreasing. Manton showed that the prevalence of disability was declining in successive cohorts of elderly Medicare beneficiaries (Manton and Gu 2001). In the Manton study, as in many others, disability is defined by limitations in activities of daily living (ADLs) or the less severe limitations in instrumental activities of daily living (IADLs). The decline in the prevalence of IADL limitations was larger in both absolute and relative terms than the decline in the prevalence of ADL limitations.

These results, as David Cutler notes, have been confirmed by other investigators and soon became the conventional wisdom. The results have also changed the terms of debate in Washington, leading some legislators to argue that fears about the coming insolvency of the Medicare program are exaggerated.

There are at least two reasons to seek a better understanding of the causes of the disability decline. The first is that knowledge of the mechanisms would increase our confidence that the findings are valid and likely to continue. That is, if we knew why the apparent decline in disability has occurred, we would be in a better position to determine whether it is real and likely to continue. Despite the shift in conventional wisdom, not all the literature has confirmed declining disability. Furthermore, the disability decline reflects a disproportionate reduction in the prevalence of IADL impairments, whose causes may be different and impacts less significant than changes in the prevalence of limitations in basic ADLs. Instrumental activities of daily living are measures of higher-order functioning, such as the ability to balance a checkbook or shop without assistance. Simple technological aids, like availability of a calculator, might improve an IADL without causing any improvement in underlying health. By learning more about the mechanisms, we could obtain a more accurate impression of the magnitude and significance of the disability decline.

Second, a knowledge of mechanisms could point us toward interventions that are likely to continue or even accelerate the disability decline. A better understanding of the contributions of preventive care, medications, surgical procedures, and other interventions would suggest where we might see additional payoffs in the future. It is difficult to exaggerate the effects of such findings on the well-being of the elderly.

Decomposing the Disability Decline

Cutler approaches the disability decline by decomposing it into changes in the prevalence of disability-causing health conditions and changes in the probability of disability given the health condition. This is analogous to decomposing mortality rate changes into components due to changes in disease incidence and changes in case fatality rates, or mortality conditional on having the disease. This approach, if it can be applied successfully, will make it clear whether it is the avoidance of disabling diseases or their more effective treatment that deserves more credit for the disability decline.

Implementing this seemingly simple decomposition is empirically challenging. Strictly speaking, the conditions should form an exhaustive and mutually exclusive set, if they are to account for all of the changes in disability. Most people with severe disabilities have multiple chronic diseases, and without further simplifying assumptions, each combination of conditions (defined also by varying severities) should make up a single composite condition. Even with a fairly limited set of single conditions, it is infeasible to incorporate the vast number of possible combinations that people can have. Furthermore, Cutler reports that there is little clustering among combinations of conditions, so it is not possible to account for a large fraction of all combinations by limiting the analysis to a handful of the most common ones. Cutler addresses these problems by assigning each individual to the single most severe (i.e., highest probability of being associated with disability) of thirty-three conditions listed in his first table. His results show that, by and large, the incidence of health conditions rose with time, while the probability of disability, given the health conditions, declined with time. The decline in conditional disability was greater than the increase in the incidence of the health condition.

The approximation required to fit the conditions into a small number of categories can have nontrivial consequences. For example, if the mix of disease conditions aggregated into one of the thirty-three categories changed over time, it would falsely appear to be a change in conditional disability. Furthermore, changes in either the prevalence of a condition or in its conditional probability of disability may not be causal. For example, table 5.1 of Cutler's paper shows that hypertension—an asymptomatic condition—has a disability probability of 32 percent. Hypertension can eventually cause disability by causing a stroke or heart attack, but these are separate categories in the condition list, so it is hard to see why hypertension would have an effect on disability that is independent of these conditions. Genitourinary diseases, which by themselves are rarely disabling, by this method appear to have a disability probability of 28 percent. It is very likely that both of these conditions are associated with other health conditions that are disabling. Preventing hypertension and genitourinary diseases, without preventing associated conditions that cause the disabilities, would surely result in a much smaller decrease in disability than predicted by this framework.

Alternative approaches to the disability decomposition would give different, and possibly more accurate, results. One alternative would be to assign each individual to a primary condition (perhaps using fewer than thirty-three) and to use a count of additional conditions to assign them to an overall category.

Changes in diagnosis over time pose another problem for any attempt to parse the effects of changes in disease prevalence and changes in outcome given disease. Improvements in screening tests, and increases in their usage, are expected to introduce "lead-time bias." Earlier diagnosis—a longer lead time—means that survival conditional on disease will be longer even if there is no effective treatment. Improvements in diagnosis are unlikely for some conditions that Cutler studies, such as hip fracture, but for others—particularly some of the cancers—innovations in testing may have increased both the prevalence of diagnosed disease and the fraction of diagnosed disease that is in its early, and less symptomatic, stages.

The Relationship to Intensive Medical Care

As Cutler notes, "The important policy question is how much of the decline in conditional disability rates is a result of medical intervention." This crucial question provides an ambitious focus for the research that he has undertaken. He estimates the relationship between changes in conditional disability and changes in intensive procedure use, noting that the results may be confounded by a number of unmeasured characteristics. Among them, and likely to be very important, are changes in the health of the patients who undergo a procedure; if procedure use diffuses from the very sick to those who are less sick and at lower risk of disability, an increase in use of the procedure may be spuriously associated with decreased disability among those who receive it.

Despite the caveats that accompany any effort of this kind, it represents an important effort to address a timely set of problems. If it is possible to find data and apply methods that are capable of establishing causal relationships, the work can provide a number of important insights. Cutler's model and others like it offer basic building blocks toward projections of medical care utilization and expenditures. More important, they can help identify productivity opportunities at the margin, such as those that result from identifying a disease whose conditional disability has changed little despite changes in prevalence over time. Finally, his results can also shed light on the appropriateness of incentives embedded in the health care system. Many disabling conditions might have effective treatments that are not covered: assistive devices, like hearing aids and visual aids, often receive limited or no coverage under conventional health insurance contracts. Not all opportunities to limit disability will arise from prevention, pharmaceuticals, "medical" devices, or intensive procedures. A reevaluation of the incentives embedded in our current approaches to health care financing might well lead to more appropriate care and better outcomes.

References

Fries, J. F. 1980. Aging, natural death, and the compression of morbidity. *New England Journal of Medicine* 303:130–35.
Manton, K. G., and X. L. Gu. 2001. Changes in the prevalence of chronic disability in the United States black and nonblack population above age 65 from 1982 to 1999. *Proceedings of the National Academy of Sciences* 98:6354–59.
Rose, E. A., A. C. Gelijns, A. J. Moskowitz, D. F. Heitjan, L. W. Stevenson, W. Dembitsky, J. W. Long, D. D. Ascheim, A. R. Tierney, R. G. Levitan, et al. for the Randomized Evaluation of Mechanical Assistance for the Treatment of Congestive Heart Failure (REMATCH) study group. 2001. Long-term use of a left ventricular assist device for end-stage heart failure. *New England Journal of Medicine* 345:1435–43.
Verbrugge, L. 1984. Longer life but worsening health? Trends in health and mortality of middle-aged and older persons. *Milbank Memorial Fund Quarterly* 62: 475–519.

Broken Down by Work and Sex: How Our Health Declines

Anne Case and Angus Deaton

6.1 Introduction

The literature contains many examples of the relationship between health and various measures of socioeconomic status, including income, education, and employment. There are undoubtedly multiple causal links between these variables; income and education affect health, and health affects the ability to be educated and the ability to work. There are also third factors that affect both health and socioeconomic status, and that contribute to the correlation between them. Although mortality rates are the gold standard for measuring health status, they are of limited use for investigating the way that health changes over the life cycle, or the interactions between health, work, earnings, and age among the living. Instead, we can use measures of self-reported health status, admittedly imperfect, but certainly informative.

Figure 6.1 uses data from the National Health Interview Survey (NHIS) to plot self-reported health against age; a higher number means worse health, from 1 through 5, and the graph plots averages of these numbers by age. The age profiles of health for both men and women rise with age, although the rate at which health deteriorates with age diminishes sharply

Anne Case is professor of economics and public affairs and director of the Research Program in Development Studies at the Woodrow Wilson School of Public and International Affairs and the economics department, Princeton University, and a research associate of the National Bureau of Economic Research. Angus Deaton is the Dwight D. Eisenhower Professor of International Affairs and professor of economics and international affairs at the Woodrow Wilson School of Public and International Affairs and the economics department at Princeton University, and a research associate of the National Bureau of Economic Research.

We are grateful to Dan McFadden, Mike Rothschild, and members of the National Bureau of Economic Research (NBER) Aging Group, for comments on an earlier version. This work was funded by a grant from the National Institute of Aging to the NBER.

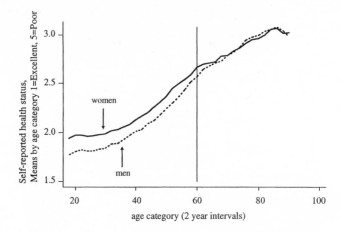

Fig. 6.1   Self-reported health status by age and sex, NHIS 1986–2001

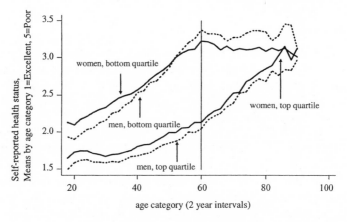

Fig. 6.2   Self-reported health status by age, sex, and income quartile, NHIS 1986–2001

after about age sixty to sixty-five. In spite of their lower mortality rates, women report worse health than men until about age sixty to sixty-five, after which there is convergence; women also make greater use of physicians' services, at least in the West, though most of this is associated with reproductive health (Waldron 1983). As far as we can tell, this pattern of self-reported health status (SRHS) by gender is close to universal around the world; it occurs in our own South African data, in India among the elderly, and in many other surveys around the world; see Sadana and others (2002).

This picture is substantially different if we stratify by income. Figure 6.2 shows age profiles for men and women in the top and bottom quartiles of family income. In the top quartile, the fraction reporting fair or poor health (which we will refer to here as "poor health") changes little with age until age forty-five, after which it rises steadily. For the same quartile, and at all ages, men are significantly less likely to report poor health than are women, although the differences are not large at any age (1 to 2 percentage points). In the bottom quartile, self-reported health is quite different. It is much worse than in the top quartile, and it deteriorates more rapidly with age. Indeed, at *age twenty,* men in the bottom quartile already report worse health than do men in the top quartile at *age fifty.* The gender pattern in the bottom quartile is also quite different; women report worse health at young ages, but there is a crossover around age fifty, with women reporting better health thereafter. Health in the bottom-income quartile wears out a good deal faster than does health in the top quartile, and, at the bottom, men's health deteriorates more rapidly than women's health.

Although there are clearly other factors at work, including mortality selection conditioned on both sex and self-reported health status, these figures suggest that work, especially low-paid or manual work, exacts a price in terms of health, as may the consumption patterns of poorer people, in terms of tobacco use, obesity, lack of exercise, and so on. If low-paid work is harder on health than is high-paid work, people at the bottom of the income distribution will have both lower health and more rapidly deteriorating health, at least while they are working. Women, who over this period had lower labor force participation than men, would suffer less from the ravages of work, and their health would deteriorate less rapidly. It is this suggestion and its implications that we investigate further in this paper.

6.2 A Theoretical Framework

As the epidemiological literature illustrates only too sharply, it is extremely difficult to untangle the links between work, earnings, health, and education, without some sort of guiding framework. Here we work with a simple intertemporal model of health based on Michael Grossman (1972), whose work is particularly useful in this context because it explicitly analyzes both the level and rate of change of health over the life cycle, something that, for the purposes of this paper, we take to be directly measured by SRHS. We also make use of some of the modifications to Grossman's model introduced by Jana Marja Muurinen (1982). Grossman's analysis has not been widely used for studying the gradient between income and health, perhaps because Grossman himself has emphasized education and not income or wealth, and perhaps because he sees education as making people more efficient at using medical care and other methods of health repair, an interpretation that is antithetical to the explanations favored in the literature on inequalities in health. Even so, Muurinen and Julian Le Grand (1985) have used the Grossman model to interpret the main findings of the Black report and have shown that the model is in fact well adapted to thinking about these issues.

Muurinen and Le Grand emphasize that people have three kinds of capital: health capital in the form of the health of their bodies, human capital in the form of education, and physical or financial capital in the form of assets. The first of these is more equally distributed across people than the other two; everyone has a body, and most people start life with a healthy body, which deteriorates over time. The rate at which health (body) capital declines with age is partly a biological process over which people have little control, but it is also affected by the extent to which health capital is used in consumption and in work. Manual work is harder on the body than non-manual work, and some kinds of consumption activity are harder on the body than others. Because the three types of capital are to some extent substitutable in generating earnings, as well as in generating utility from a given level of earnings, people who have less human and financial capital have little choice but to rely more heavily on their health capital. In consequence, through an optimal but heavily constrained choice, poorer and less-educated people will experience a more rapid deterioration of health as they age.

A simple model sharpens and modifies these results and generates explicit predictions about the level and evolution of health over the life cycle. Suppose that there is an instantaneous felicity function $v(c_t, H_t)$ where t indexes age, c_t is consumption, and H_t is the stock of health. Health is updated according to

$$(1) \qquad H_{t+1} = \theta m_t + (1 - \delta_t)H_t,$$

where m_t is the quantity purchased of medical care or other health-promoting activities, θ is the efficiency with which such purchases create health, and δ_t is the rate at which health deteriorates at age t. Equation (1), apparently an innocuous identity, has a number of serious implications, to which we return below.

Consumers maximize a life-cycle utility function

$$(2) \qquad U = \sum_{0}^{T} (1 + \rho)^t v(c_t, H_t),$$

where ρ is the rate of time preference, and T is the length of life, which is potentially a choice variable, though that is an issue that we do not explore here. The lifetime present-value budget constraint takes the form

$$(3) \qquad \sum_{0}^{T} \frac{c_t}{(1 + r)^t} + \sum_{0}^{T} \frac{p_m m_t}{(1 + r)^t} = A_0 + \sum_{0}^{T} \frac{y_t(H_t)}{(1 + r)^t},$$

where r is the market rate of interest, p_m is the price of health-repair goods, A_0 is initial assets, and $y_t(H_t)$ is earnings, which depends on health. For simplicity, we normalize the price of consumption to unity, and assume that the real interest rate and the price of medical care do not vary with age.

The basic equations of the model can most easily be seen by using the health evolution (equation [1]) to substitute for m_t in the budget constraint (equation [3]), which gives a single integrated constraint that respects both the financial and the health identities. After minor rearrangement, equations (1) and (3) yield

(4)
$$\sum_0^T \frac{c_t}{(1+r)^t} + \sum_0^T \frac{H_t}{(1+r)^t} \frac{p_m}{\theta} (r + \delta_t)$$
$$= A_0 + \sum_0^T \frac{y_t(H_t)}{(1+r)^t} - \frac{p_m}{\theta} (1+r) \left[\frac{H_{T+1}}{(1+r)^{T+1}} - H_0 \right].$$

In this version of the budget constraint, the elements of utility, consumption, and health are multiplied by their respective prices, which, in the case of the health stock in period t, is the discounted present value of its user cost. As usual, user cost is essentially a carrying charge, which is the sum of interest and physical deterioration, multiplied by the effective replacement price, p_m/θ. The right-hand side of equation (4), which represents the value of lifetime resources, includes the valuation of the health stock after death. In consequence, treating equation (4) as a standard intertemporal budget constraint implies that the value of the body is like any other asset, which can be accumulated but which can also be sold to finance consumption. The ability to turn one's body into cash, or allowing m_t to be negative, is clearly not realistic. Even so, the assumption is a convenient starting point, and we shall return later to the (important) consequences of abandoning it and requiring that $m_t \geq 0$, so that the rate of decline of health cannot exceed deterioration. As we shall see, it does not change our basic arguments.

From equation (4), the first-order conditions for consumption and health are

(5)
$$v_{ct} = \lambda \left(\frac{1+\rho}{1+r} \right)^t$$

(6)
$$v_{ht} = \lambda \left(\frac{1+\rho}{1+r} \right)^t \left[\frac{p_m}{\theta} (r + \delta_t) - y_{ht} \right],$$

where subscripts with respect to h and c denote partial derivatives. The Lagrange multiplier λ in equations (5) and (6) is the shadow price of lifetime wealth and is constant over the life cycle. The life-cycle evolution of consumption and health can therefore be conveniently analyzed by examining equations (5) and (6) with λ held constant, a device first used in this context by Adam Wagstaff (1986).

Equation (6) permits derivation of the standard comparative static results about the *level* of health. Provided that there is diminishing marginal utility of health as well as diminishing marginal productivity of health on earnings, the health stock throughout life will be higher (a) the lower is the price of health repair, p_m, (b) the higher is the efficiency of medical care or other purchases in repairing health, θ, (c) the lower is the *rate* of health *deterioration* $δ_t$, (d) the lower is the rate of time preference ρ, (e) the higher are initial assets, initial health, or lifetime earnings, and the lower are prices over the lifetime, all of which lower λ through lifetime income effects, and (f) the milder is the effect of diminishing returns to health in either consumption or production.

In Grossman's original model, of which this is a simplified form, the effect of education works to increase the parameter θ, so that health repair is more efficient with the same health inputs, the effective price of health repair is lower, and health is higher throughout the life cycle. This is true even in the "pure investment" version of the model, in which health has no direct effect on utility, so that v_{ht} is zero, and the health stock is determined through its effects on earnings, by setting the last term on the right-hand side of equation (6) equal to zero. In the pure consumption model, where y_{ht} is zero, or in mixed models with both consumption and earnings effects of health, education will also promote health by lowering λ through the lifetime income effects of higher earnings. Muurinen, in her version of Grossman's model, argues that education works so as to reduce the rate of health deterioration, which lowers the user cost of health and raises its optimal level. Provided that health affects consumption directly, there is also a direct income effect on the health stock through λ, so that both education and income, conditional on education, should promote health, albeit in different ways. Note finally that the correlation between health and the rate of time preference will also generate a correlation between health and education, if more patient people acquire more education. This is the classic "third factor" explanation of the correlation between health and education proposed by Victor Fuchs (1982).

Our main concern in this paper is the way that health declines over the life cycle, as well as with how that decline is affected by education, work, and income. The predictions of the theory come from differentiating equations (5) and (6) with respect to time. We make the assumptions that health and consumption are complementary (or additive) in utility, so that $v_{ch} \geq 0$, and that the instantaneous felicity functions are concave in health and consumption taken together. Then elementary but tedious algebra shows that, when the rate of interest is equal to the rate of time preference, health will decline over the life cycle if and only if the rate of health deterioration $δ_t$ increases with age. If the rate of interest is not equal to the rate of time preference, there is an additional factor that increases the rate of decline of health with age if the rate of time preference exceeds the rate of interest, and which moderates it if the rate of time preference is less than the rate of interest. A lower price of health repair, or a higher efficiency of health repair, through education (for example), boosts health throughout the life cycle but accelerates its rate of decline if y_{ht} is positive. At retirement, after which there are no earnings and therefore no effect of health on earnings, there will be a discrete increase in the user cost of health—see the right-hand side of equation (6), where y_{ht} reduces the net user cost—which will generate a corresponding drop in health. Subsequent to retirement, the effect of the increasing rate of deterioration on the user cost will be lower because of the absence of the effect of health on earnings, so that the rate of decline of health should be lower immediately after retirement than it was immediately prior to retirement.

When thinking about how health changes with age in this model, it is important to maintain a clear distinction between the rate of health *deterioration,* which is the quantity δ_t, and the rate at which the stock of health changes, ΔH_t. The two concepts, which sound very much alike, are quite different, but are linked by the identity (1), which can be written in the form

$$(7) \qquad \frac{\Delta H_{t+1}}{H_t} = \frac{\theta m_t}{H_t} - \delta_t,$$

so that expenditure on medical care and other health repair offsets, to a greater or lesser extent, the deterioration in health. There is an important question whether equation (7), or equation (1), can be an adequate description of health evolution. In particular, note that equation (7) implies that the technology allows perfect repair of the biological effects of aging, so that it is possible to put a halt to aging and to postpone death for ever. Grossman's model is different from ours, in that m_t is produced using market goods and time, but he assumes constant returns to scale in the technology so that, once again, death can be defeated by sufficiently large amounts of money and time. In a model where time is priced at the market wage, those who can afford to pay for it have the option of eternal life.

Eternal life is more than a hypothetical outcome that, while permitted by the technology, will never actually be chosen. If the rate of biological deterioration is constant, which is perhaps implausible but is hardly impossible (and if the rate of interest is at least as large as the rate of time preference), people will "choose" an infinite life. Otherwise, when the rate of deterioration is increasing with age, people "choose" a finite life, because at some point the cost of medical care is so high, or the unpleasantness of health repair (exercise?) so extreme, that even death is better. Death is not inevitable, but an optimal choice. That the technology exists to make this possible would not be claimed by even the most fanatical proponent of the effectiveness of medical care or of the latest programs of exercise and diet.

That the health technology permits complete repair is a problem for health capital models even apart from the possible choice of eternal life. According to equations (5) and (6), the rate at which health declines over time depends on the *rate of increase* of δ_t, not on its *level*. Given the identity (7), this implies that medical care or other repair is used fully to offset the level of δ_t; indeed, if δ_t is constant, the health stock is constant, and repair fully offsets deterioration. But deterioration is proportional to the stock of health, so that these models imply that, controlling for the rate of deterioration δ_t and its rate of change, health repair is *higher* for healthier people, because they have more stock to start with and deterioration is proportional to the stock. In Grossman's original work and in several papers since, authors have found a *negative* correlation between the stock of health and medical care, perhaps not surprisingly, given that people tend to seek medical care when they are sick, not when they are well. Of course, these findings may perhaps be attributed to problems with the empirical implementation of the model; as Wagstaff (1993) and Grossman (2000) himself have argued, neither the raw correlation nor the ordinary least squares (OLS) regression of medical care on health can be expected to give the right answer, because of simultaneity through the unobservable components of deterioration, and because health repair involves more than medical care. It is unclear whether there exist feasible methods for correcting these problems and whether an adequate test of the model is possible.

Instead, it is possible that the fundamental problem is not the assumption that people would offset health deterioration if they could, but the assumption that the technology exists that would allow them to do so. If perfect health repair is impossible, we have a very much simpler and more intuitive model of health in which it is the *level* of physical deterioration that determines the rate of decline of health, with only limited offset possible through behavior. In terms of the optimality conditions (5) and (6), the former will still hold, though the latter will not, because, in general, the medical or other technology does not exist to allow the marginal utility of health to be equated to its user cost. One of the issues that we shall examine in our empirical work is whether the rate of health decline in our data is better described by the *level* or by the *rate of change* of the rate of physical deterioration in health.

Even within the Grossman model, there is a source of health decline even when the rate of physical deterioration is constant. This comes from acknowledging something that we have ignored so far, which is that health cannot be sold, because purchases of health-enhancing goods m_t cannot be negative. Suppose that someone is approaching the end of life and in excellent health. According to the basic model (equation [4]), good physical health will be traded in for consumption prior to death, but if this is not possible, maintenance will stop, and health will be allowed to decline at the maximum rate possible, which is the rate of health deterioration δ_t. Hence, during this period at the end of life, and even within the standard Grossman model, the rate of health decline depends on the level of δ_t, not on its rate of change. However, this cannot be the explanation for health declines later in life, because it implies that during this period there would be no purchases of health-enhancing goods and $m_t = 0$. But this is contradicted by the obvious evidence that purchases of health care rise with age, not the opposite. And for all periods in which $m_t > 0$, we are back to the original analysis, in which the rate of health decline depends on the rate of change of the rate of deterioration, not its level.

A useful extension of the Grossman model, with or without the repair technology, comes from Muurinen and Le Grand's suggestion that people with low education are more likely to work in manual jobs, because non-manual occupations are not open to them. Further, in manual jobs, health deteriorates more rapidly, because the nature of the work makes direct demands on physical health through the amount of exertion required, and because many such jobs carry risks of injury (back problems associated with lifting, for example) or other environmental insults. Similarly, people with high wealth or high wages for their level of education will be better able to avoid such jobs. Those who are lucky enough to be born into wealth are rarely observed performing manual work, even when their intelligence and education equip them for little else. We can model such effects explicitly by extending the dependence of earnings on health to accommodate an additional choice variable that allows people to enhance their earnings at the expense of faster deterioration in health, effectively selling their health capital. If we write earnings as $y_t(H_t, z)$ with a positive partial derivative for z, and compensate by writing the rate of deterioration of the health stock as $\delta_t(z)$, also with a positive partial derivative, then equations (5) through (6) are unchanged (or equation [5] is unchanged if [6] does not hold), but we have the additional condition, directly from the budget constraint, that

$$(8) \qquad \frac{\partial y_t}{\partial z} = \frac{p_m}{\theta} \cdot \frac{\partial \delta_t}{\partial z} \cdot H_t,$$

so that the marginal addition to earnings from additional manual work is set equal to the marginal health costs, which is the product of the health stock multiplied by the marginal effect on the user cost. The effect of additional manual labor on earnings is lower at higher levels of education, because professors, unlike construction workers, delivery drivers, or professional boxers, get no increase in earnings by wearing out their bodies more rapidly, so that equation (10) implies that physical effort z and health deterioration are higher among those with lower education. If the health stock is optimally adapted to its user cost, the health stock will be higher among the better educated. If not, and the evolution of the health stock is primarily determined by its rate of physical deterioration, then health will decline more rapidly with age among those with less education. Those with education base their earnings on their human capital, which depreciates slowly if at all. Those without education sell their bodies, which depreciate more rapidly.

At a fixed level of education, equation (8) also implies that those with more health are less likely to undertake heavy labor to improve their earnings because, with more health, they have more to lose from an increase in its rate of depreciation.

We can also consider a formally identical effect that works through consumption. Suppose that the felicity function contains a second consumption good whose price is paid, not in money, but in the rate of health deterioration. This component includes activities such as smoking, the consumption of junk food, sloth, and cheap risk-taking activities such as unsafe sex, all of which are either low-cost or free, all of which are pleasurable, at least to some, but all of which are paid for out of a higher rate of health deterioration. If the second consumption item is w, say, the additional first-order condition is

$$(9) \qquad v_{wt} = \lambda \left(\frac{1 + \rho}{1 + r} \right)^t \frac{p_m}{\theta} \frac{\partial \delta_t}{\partial w} \cdot H_t,$$

which, once again, holds whether or not health is optimally adapted to its user cost. The difference between equations (8) and (9) is whether or not health is "sold" directly for utility, or indirectly through the labor market. Holding everything on the right-hand side constant, higher education that changes tastes away from (reduces the marginal utility of) w-goods will reduce their consumption and lower the rate of health deterioration. Of course, education is also likely to increase θ, which will increase the demand for w-goods, because it is now easier to repair their damage, and increase lifetime wealth, which increases demand through income effects. As in the production case, higher health status reduces the consumption of w-goods, because their effects are proportionately more costly for healthier people.

Note again that equations (8) and (9), with their implication for health deterioration, hold whether or not there is a technology that allows full health repair, although their implications for health and its evolution will differ. If the repair technology is less than perfect then, at least beyond some point, the level of health deterioration will show up as an actual decline in health. Manual workers, those with low education or low wealth, will have higher rates of health deterioration, and their physical health will deteriorate more rapidly with age. With full offset possible, there is no such implication. Unless manual work and unhealthy consumption increase the *rate* at which health deterioration *increases* with age, which although possible is far from obvious, they will affect the *level* of health, but not its rate of decline with age. In our empirical analysis we will examine both the level and rate of change of health across different occupations.

6.3   Empirical Evidence

Our data come from the sixteen successive waves of the NHIS from 1986 through 2001. This is a large nationally representative sample of households, whose members are either interviewed directly or, in the case of children, by proxy. There are 1,209,808 people in the sixteen-year sample, though for most of the calculations we work with the subsample of adults aged eighteen to sixty, of which there are 711,765. This provides us with a large enough sample to allow a good deal of disaggregation by age, sex, and occupation. The NHIS is a new cross section in each year so that, although we can track birth cohorts, for example, we cannot follow any particular individual over time.

The survey collects data on SRHS on a scale of 1 to 5, where 1 is "excellent," 2 is "very good," 3 is "good," 4 is "fair," and 5 is "poor," so that bigger numbers always indicate worse health. There is a very substantial literature on the advantages and disadvantages of this measure of nonfatal health; here we simply accept the measure, and our results are conditioned on that acceptance. In most cases we respect the ordinal nature of these data by using appropriate techniques, though we will often show averages based on the nominal 1 through 5 scale.

Family income is collected on a categorical basis, and we assign each person the midpoint of the income range to which they belong and then deflate by the Consumer Price Index (CPI) to bring income to 1982 prices. Education is the number of years of education completed. The survey collects information on whether people are in or out of the labor force, and for those who are working (around three-quarters of the sample) we have two-digit occupational codes. Summary data on education, income, race, and occupation are shown in table 6.1. All the means we present, as well as results from subsequent calculations, use the survey weights in order to describe the national population.

The distribution of men and women across occupations is shown down the columns; apart from the omitted category (new workers, military employees, and those whose status is unknown), the occupational columns would sum to one. A little less than 12 percent of the sample is black, and 51 percent are female. The nonmanual occupations are listed first, from executives to administrative support. Apart from the last, where workers are predominantly female, men and women are more or less equally represented in the nonmanual occupations. We also show ten manual occupations, where there is a great deal of variation in the percentage of workers who are female.

Our starting point is the information in figures 6.1 and 6.2, presented briefly in the introduction. Figure 6.1 shows that average health declines with age and is worse for women than for men but worsens somewhat more

Table 6.1   Sample means, men and women aged 18–60, NHIS 1986–2001

	All	Women	Men
Age	37.01	37.04	36.97
Education	13.04	12.98	13.10
Indicator: white	0.817	0.808	0.827
Indicator: black	0.117	0.128	0.106
Log(family income) in $1982	9.993	9.940	10.05
Indicator: Female	0.510	1.000	0.000
Occupation			
Executive	0.122	0.105	0.141
Professional/Specialty	0.121	0.129	0.112
Technician	0.033	0.031	0.034
Sales	0.098	0.096	0.100
Administrative support	0.127	0.198	0.054
Private household services	0.005	0.009	0.001
Protective services fire/police	0.015	0.005	0.025
Service (food, cleaning)	0.092	0.119	0.064
Farming/Fishing	0.021	0.007	0.036
Mechanic	0.031	0.003	0.061
Construction	0.025	0.001	0.050
Precision production	0.026	0.012	0.040
Machine operator	0.059	0.046	0.073
Transportation/Moving	0.037	0.007	0.067
Handler, equip. cleaner	0.033	0.013	0.053
Out of the labor force	0.146	0.211	0.078
No. of observations	711,765	374,700	337,065

Notes: Occupation columns add to less than one because new workers and military employees are omitted. All means are weighted, using individual level sample weights provided by the NHIS.

slowly with age for women than for men. Figure 6.2, which shows the same information for people in the top and bottom quartiles of family income, shows that rich and poor people have very different life-cycle patterns of health. The poor have worse health throughout life, and their health worsens more rapidly with age. Women "age" (in terms of worsening health) less rapidly than do men, but only in the bottom quartile of family income, not in the top quartile. Among the poor, average health stops worsening after age sixty. Although there is undoubtedly some role for health- and income-specific mortality in accounting for these results, the patterns of health change by age, by income groups, by sex, and by retirement age, are consistent with the hypothesis that manual work causes health to decline more rapidly than does professional work. As we saw in section 6.2, with a technology that allows complete health repair, there is no reason to expect such results, even if there are indeed differential rates of deterioration. Yet the existence of the technology is itself implausible, and figure 6.2 might be taken as evidence in that direction.

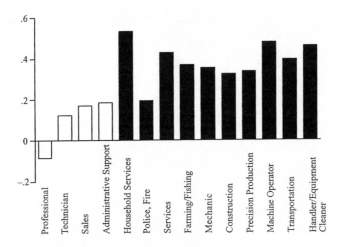

Fig. 6.3   Self-reported health status by occupation

Note: Coefficients on occupation from an ordered probit that includes controls for age, sex, and race. Omitted occupation = executive. The full occupation terms are listed in table 6.2.

A more comprehensive investigation requires that we examine occupational effects on health, on which summary evidence is presented in figure 6.3. Underlying this figure is an ordered probit for those in work in which SRHS is linked to a set of age, sex, race, and occupational dummies. The figure shows the estimated coefficients on the occupational dummies. Those to the right (dark bars) are manual occupations, those to the left (lighter bars) are nonmanual occupations. Consistent with all the theoretical predictions, those employed in manual occupations have worse health than those who work in professional occupations. Police and fire workers are an exception to the general pattern; they are in a manual occupation that carries significant risk of health deterioration, and yet their health status is more like professional than other manual workers. We do not have an explanation for these results, although it is possible that health-based selection into and out of police work and firefighting is sufficiently severe to offset the deterioration associated with the work itself. We can imagine that the same might be true of professional athletes, if we had such data. Selection is important for all of this analysis, and we shall investigate it further below.

Table 6.2 takes the results in figure 6.3 a step further, disaggregating by sex, and also including controls for income and education. The first column shows the results for men and women combined, while the second and third columns show the results by sex. These again come from ordered probits, now run separately for men and for women. The most notable finding here is how similar the results are for men and women. All nonmanual workers are less healthy than executive and administrative workers, with the smallest difference among those in professional and specialty occupa-

Table 6.2   **Self-reported health status and occupation, men and women aged 18–60, NHIS 1986–2001**

	All (1)	Women (2)	Men (3)
Log(household income)	−.192	−.179	−.203
	(.002)	(.003)	(.003)
Education	−.067	−.070	−.065
	(.001)	(.001)	(.001)
Occupation			
Professional/Specialty	.031	.056	.014
	(.006)	(.008)	(.009)
Technician	.085	.089	.080
	(.009)	(.013)	(.013)
Sales	.060	.089	.031
	(.006)	(.009)	(.009)
Administrative support	.069	.062	.386
	(.006)	(.008)	(.010)
Private household services	.145	.165	.141
	(.022)	(.022)	(.098)
Protective services fire/police	.071	.113	.066
	(.013)	(.028)	(.014)
Service (food, cleaning)	.160	.171	.167
	(.007)	(.009)	(.011)
Farming/Fishing	.020	.033	.019
	(.011)	(.024)	(.013)
Mechanic	.155	.139	.150
	(.009)	(.039)	(.010)
Construction	.074	.065	.067
	(.010)	(.061)	(.011)
Precision production	.123	.179	.103
	(.010)	(.019)	(.012)
Machine operator	.201	.253	.177
	(.008)	(.012)	(.010)
Transportation/Moving	.145	.185	.140
	(.009)	(.024)	(.010)
Handler, equip. cleaner	.147	.173	.159
	(.009)	(.019)	(.011)
No. of observations	502,374	243,079	259,295

Notes: Coefficients reported are estimates of the health status expected given this occupation, relative to the omitted category of "executive/administrative." Estimates are based on ordered probits that also include a full set of indicator variables for age, survey year, and indicators that race is white or black. The ordered probit in column (1) also includes an indicator for sex. All ordered probits have been weighted using the individual level sampling weights provided by the NHIS. Standard errors appear in parentheses.

tions. Male and female manual workers are typically less healthy on average, and the differences by sex are much smaller than differences across occupations. Compared with figure 6.3, the inclusion of controls for income and education markedly reduces the estimated occupational effects on health for construction workers, and for farmers who are among the least educated and worst-paid groups, and who, conditional on education and income, report no worse health than nonmanual workers. These effects are essentially the same for men and for women. The clearest exception to the similarity is for men who work in administrative support, an occupation in which there are four times as many women as men. While this case might well be attributed to differential selection, such an argument flies in the face of the evidence from other occupations where, in spite of substantial differences in the proportions of men and women, their reported health status is very similar. These results provide prima facie evidence for the existence of occupational specific health effects that operate, at least in part, independently of the personal characteristics of the workers. Note also that to the extent that occupational structure contributes to differences in men's and women's health, the effect comes from the allocation of men and women across occupations, not from differences by sex within them.

Table 6.2 also shows that there are protective effects of income and education on health even when we control for occupational status. Household income is substantially and significantly more protective for men than for women, a standard result in the literature. Years of education are more protective for women than men, and although the difference is significant given the sample size, it is not very large.

As we saw in section 6.2, the existence of *level* effects in health status across occupations is a less effective test of alternative theories than is the existence of differential *rates of change* of health. Figure 6.4 provides evidence on the way that health declines with age during the working life in manual compared with nonmanual occupations. Once again, underlying the results is an ordered probit in which SRHS is linked to a complete set of age, sex, and race indicators, and to education, the logarithm of family income, and an indicator for manual occupation. Education and income are interacted with age, and the manual occupation dummy is interacted with a complete set of age dummies. The figure shows the estimated coefficients on these interactions, so that each point shows the difference in health status between manual and nonmanual workers at that age. The graph shows a rising pattern from left to right, so that the health difference between manual and nonmanual workers is *increasing* with age. Table 6.3 shows the relevant results from separate ordered probit equations for males and females. The interaction coefficients are significantly positive for both, but not significantly different from one another. Older nonmanual workers, whether male or female, suffer a greater self-reported health disadvantage than younger nonmanual workers. It should be noted that these results are affected by

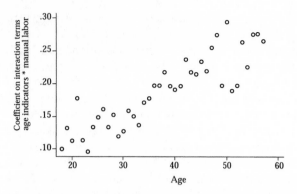

Fig. 6.4   Self-reported health status ordered probit results, manual labor–age indicator interactions, NHIS 1986–2001

Note: Ordered probit estimation included a complete set of age indicators, education, and education interacted with age, log(family income), and log(family income) interacted with age, and controls for sex, race, and manual labor.

Table 6.3   Self-reported health status by manual labor status, men and women aged 18–60, NHIS 1986–2001

	Women	Men
Manual labor	.0557	.0346
	(.0180)	(.0178)
Manual labor × age	.0017	.0013
	(.0005)	(.0005)
Log(household income)	−.0589	−.0902
	(.0093)	(.0101)
Log(household income) × age	−.0036	−.0034
	(.0003)	(.0003)
Education	−.0966	−.0848
	(.0038)	(.0035)
Education × age	.0007	.0005
	(.0001)	(.0001)
Year indicators?	Yes	Yes
Age indicators?	Yes	Yes
Race indicators?	Yes	Yes
No. of observations	243,079	259,295

Notes: Coefficients reported are estimates of the health status expected given this explanatory variable, relative to white-collar employment at age eighteen. Estimates are based on ordered probits that also include a full set of indicator variables for age and year, and indicators that race = white and race = black. All ordered probits weighted using individual sampling weights provided by the NHIS. Standard errors appear in parentheses.

health-specific selection, but because it is the less-healthy workers who are selected out—something on which we present evidence below—the increase in the health differential with age is biased *downward.* Selection cannot explain the upward slope that we see in figure 6.4.

As we argued in the theoretical section, it is hard to reconcile such effects with a story in which a full-repair technology allows people to adjust their health to its user cost. Although manual work causes greater deterioration in the health stock, this is supposed to be offset by repair, so that there is no reason for the health status of manual workers to decline more rapidly with age unless the rate of increase of deterioration with age is itself higher in manual occupations. There is no reason to suppose that this is the case, and indeed, Muurinen and Le Grand (1985) argue that the opposite is likely to be true. They point out that the biological component of health decline is very small among young workers, so that the difference between health deterioration rates of young manual and nonmanual workers is almost entirely attributable to differences in their work. Among older workers, by contrast, there is a large common biological component to health deterioration, so that differences due to the work environment generate a smaller proportional difference in overall health deterioration and thus in the user cost of health. In consequence, the health gradient between manual and nonmanual workers should diminish with age, which is exactly the opposite of what we see in figure 6.4.

As did table 6.2, table 6.3 shows that the effects of income and education on health status are not eliminated by controlling for whether people are manual or nonmanual workers. Income and education are separately protective, and when we allow for interactions with age, the log of family income has a substantially larger effect for men than for women. Although part of the effect of education works through the selection of occupation, there are other protective effects; according to the theory, there are several ways in which education can reduce the user cost of health. There are also effects of both income and education on the *rate* at which health declines with age. The protective effect of income *increases* over the working life, while that of education *decreases.* To account for these, the model with full-repair technology would require that the rate of increase of the depreciation rate be lower at high income and higher at high education. Without full repair, we would require that the *levels* of deterioration respond in the same way.

That health-based selection is indeed important is documented in figure 6.5. This is for men only, and it extends beyond the working years and up to age seventy-five. This is a version of figure 6.2 for men, but now separating those who are in the labor force from those who are not. The latter have much worse health, presumably because poor health is one of the reasons for being out of the labor force. It is the health of those out of the labor force that worsens rapidly with age until around age fifty, and then improves, presumably because more and more people with normal health for

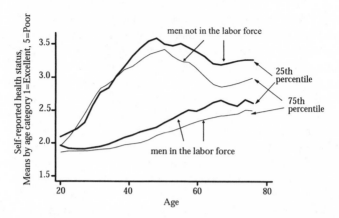

Fig. 6.5   Self-reported health status by age at the 25th and 75th percentile of the income distribution, by labor force status, men, NHIS 1986–2001

their age leave the labor force for normal, non-health-related retirement. Within these two classes, either in or out of the labor force, being at the first versus fourth quartile of income (here taken to be those whose income is within 5 percent of the 25th and 75th percentiles) still affects health in the usual direction, but the effect of income is swamped by the effect of being in or out of the labor force. Figures 6.2 and 6.5 are reconciled by noting that the group of those who are out of the labor force and in the top quartile of income is very small. As a result, we conclude that the gradient of health with respect to income in figure 6.2 is largely driven by causality running from health to income, through health-related participation in the labor force. As figure 6.5 shows, there is still a role for income in conditioning health within each group, and the earlier results of this section show that at least part of this relationship is attributable to the effects of different kinds of work on health, but the major features of figure 6.2 can be accounted for by health-based selection in and out of the labor force.

We turn finally to the issue of health selection at the occupational level and investigate whether the estimated rate of health decline with age is indeed biased downward by the fact that people who are less healthy drop out of occupations with high rates of wear and tear. Ideally, we would examine this question using panel data that follow people over time. We cannot do this with the NHIS, but we can match birth cohorts in specific occupations over time and track their size through the successive random population samples in the survey. In particular, we construct occupational birth cohorts by tracking, for example, how many fire and police workers born in 1956 show up in each of the surveys from 1986 through to 2001, and then test whether the number diminishes from one year to the next more rapidly the worse is the average health status of the occupational birth cohort in the first year. Clearly, this technique will only work well if recruitment starts early in the working life and the profession makes no new hires once its original intake is set. These assumptions are clearly restrictive, but they are the best that we can do given the data available.

Table 6.4 shows the results of the regressions, all of which control for a full set of age, year, and birth cohort dummies. Because of a change in weighting procedures, there is a seam in the series between 1996 and 1997, and this change is omitted from the regressions. The dependent variable is the proportionate change in the number of male workers in the occupation in a given birth cohort. There are 2,210 birth cohort per occupation per year cells for nonmanual workers, and 3,981 for manual workers. Column (1) shows the regression for nonmanual workers with different coefficients on health status for each occupation, and column (2) when the coefficients on

Table 6.4   Change in labor force participation in given occupations and self-reported health status, reported for men, NHIS 1986–2001

	White collar workers		Manual workers	
	(1)	(2)	(3)	(4)
Health status × Exec	.051			
	(.051)			
Health status × Prof	.065			
	(.053)			
Health status × Tech	.117			
	(.048)			
Health status × Sales	.055			
	(.049)			
Health status × Admin support	.070			
	(.045)			
Health status		.106		−.122
		(.041)		(.031)
Health status × Protective (fire, police)			−.082	
			(.037)	
Health status × Service (food, cleaning)			−.099	
			(.033)	
Health status × Farming/Fishing			−.101	
			(.034)	
Health status × Mechanic			−.131	
			(.035)	
Health status × Construction			−.079	
			(.036)	
Health status × Precision production			−.104	
			(.036)	
Health status × Machine operators			−.135	
			(.034)	
Health status × Transportation, moving			−.123	
			(.034)	
Health status × Handlers, equip. operators			−.099	
			(.032)	
No. of observations	2,210	2,210	3,981	3,981

Notes: All regressions include year indicators, age indicators, and birth cohort indicators.

health are constrained to be the same across occupations. All estimated coefficients are positive, and only one is significantly different from zero; collectively, the overall effect is positive and significant. While it is unclear why cohort size should rise with poor health, there is certainly no evidence that cohort size *falls* with worse (larger) health status for nonmanual workers. For manual workers, in columns (3) and (4), there is indeed such an effect. Over all the manual occupations, an increase in average health by 0.3, say, equivalent to the effect of about twenty years of normal aging from forty to sixty, would be to remove about 3.6 percent of the age cohort from the workforce. The size of this effect does not vary very much across occupations but is somewhat higher for machine operators and considerably lower for firemen and policemen. Health-based selection appears to be real among manual workers, but even those who remain in the occupation grow less healthy with age, and they do so at a rate that is larger than that for nonmanual workers, among whom there is no evidence of such health-based selection.

6.4 Conclusions

We started from the observation that SRHS worsens with age and that it does so much more rapidly among those at the bottom of the income distribution, who also start their working lives with lower health. Our original suspicion was that, because manual work involves more wear and tear on the body, the health of manual workers would decline more rapidly than that of nonmanual workers, thus offering an explanation for our starting facts. However, the standard health capital model of health, which assumes a technology by which health can be fully repaired, does not predict that health declines more rapidly among those whose work (or consumption) imposes greater demand on their bodies. Instead, people will use medical care or other health-repair mechanisms to offset the physical deterioration. Indeed, if the marginal utility of the health stock is set equal to its user cost, as intertemporal optimality requires, the rate of health decline is not affected by the rate of wear and tear but by the rate of increase with age of the rate of wear and tear. Standard arguments suggest that this rate of increase is likely to be lower, not higher, among manual workers. Yet the data from the NHIS show that the health of manual workers does in fact decline more rapidly during the working years than does the health of nonmanual workers, in spite of the existence of health-based selection out of manual work, which artificially inflates the health of those who remain. We do not find this result at all implausible. Instead, the implausibility lies in the health-repair technology that is routinely assumed in the health economics literature.

Although manual workers have worse health than do nonmanual workers, and although their health declines more rapidly, the major factor accounting for the differences in health and health decline in different parts of the income distribution is whether or not people are in the labor force, a mechanism where causality runs from health to income, not the reverse.

Even so, both income and education have independent protective effects on health for those who are in work, and these effects are reduced but not eliminated by controlling for occupation. With only a few exceptions, we find a marked similarity in all of these results between men and women.

References

Fuchs, Victor R. 1982. Time preference and health: An exploratory study. In *Economic aspects of health,* ed. V. R. Fuchs, 93–120. Chicago: University of Chicago Press.

Grossman, Michael. 1972. On the concept of health capital and the demand for health. *Journal of Political Economy* 80:223–55.

———. 2000. The human capital model. In *Handbook of health economics,* ed. A. J. Culyer and J. P. Newhouse, 1A:347–408. Amsterdam: Elsevier.

Muurinen, Jana Marja. 1982. Demand for health: A generalised Grossman model. *Journal of Health Economics* 1 (1): 5–28.

Muurinen, Jana Marja, and Julian Le Grand. 1985. The economic analysis of inequalities in health. *Social Science and Medicine* 20 (10): 1029–35.

Sadana, Ritu, Ajay Tandon, Christopher J. L. Murray, Irina Serdobova, Yang Cao, Wan Jun Xie, Somnath Chaterji, and Bedhiran L. Ustun. 2002. Describing population health in six domains: Comparable results from 66 household surveys. Global Programme on Evidence for Health Policy Discussion Paper Series no. 43. Geneva: WHO.

Wagstaff, Adam. 1986. The demand for health: Some new empirical evidence. *Journal of Health Economics* 5:195–233.

———. 1993. The demand for health: An empirical reformulation of the Grossman model. *Health Economics* 2 (2): 189–98.

Waldron, Ingrid. 1983. Sex differences in illness incidence, prognosis and mortality: Issues and evidence. *Social Science and Medicine* 17 (16): 1107–23.

Comment   Daniel McFadden

You might anticipate that a paper with a title as clever as this one will be fun to read, and you would be right. This is a paper about *health capital,* as opposed to physical or skill capital, and its dynamics over the life cycle. Just as the concept of skill or human capital informed the economic analysis of education as a life-cycle decision, the concepts of health capital and life-cycle decision making on health maintenance offer useful insights into the interactions of human biology, medical technology, and individual behavior. Case and Deaton start from a model of health capital introduced

Daniel McFadden is the E. Morris Cox Professor of Economics and director of the Econometrics Laboratory at the University of California at Berkeley, a 2000 Nobel Laureate in economics, and a research associate of the National Bureau of Economic Research.

by Michael Grossman in 1972. Let H denote the stock of health capital, m denote expenditure on health maintenance, θ denote the efficiency of investment, and σ denote a depreciation rate that may increase with age. The equation of motion for H is

(1) $$H_{t+1} = \theta m_t + (1 - \sigma_t)H_t.$$

In this model, health capital is like the stock of water impounded in a reservoir, with an evaporation rate σ that varies with temperature, or age in a health capital interpretation.

Is this an apt model for health capital? To begin a discussion of this issue, note first that equation (1) is an oversimplified model of the dynamics of a capital stock, even for water in a reservoir. The reservoir has finite capacity, and water added beyond capacity is spilled. There may be natural replenishment, seasonal in nature, in addition to budgeted water replacement. Because evaporation is proportional to surface area and stock is proportional to volume, the *rate* of depreciation depends on the geometry of the reservoir, and is often lower when stocks are high. Figure 6C.1 illustrates a cylindrical reservoir, where the amount of depreciation $D_t = \sigma_t H_t$ is independent of the stock, so the rate of depreciation is inversely proportional to the stock. Other cases in the figure are a reservoir with a triangular cross section, where D_t is proportional to the square root of H_t, and a flask-shaped reservoir, where D_t *rises* when H_t falls. Only when the reservoir is composed of a series of small vessels, so that storage and evaporation are both proportional to the number of vessels filled, is it correct to describe the dynamics of the capital stock using equation (1). This case corresponds to a capital stock that is an aggregate of many smaller units that have independent failure probabilities, such as light bulbs, or perhaps cells in the body. However, as the reservoir example illustrates, it may not describe well the evolution of a single system, such as a human body, where there may be a complex interaction between component failures and system failures.

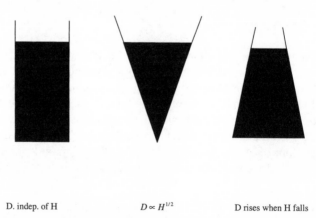

D. indep. of H $D \propto H^{1/2}$ D rises when H falls

Fig. 6C.1   Models of Depreciation

While the water reservoir analogy to health capital should not be stretched too far, it does suggest the possibilities that (a) early in life the body's self-repair and replenishment mechanisms are usually adequate to maintain the stock near capacity, (b) with age natural replenishment diminishes and more budgeted investment is needed to maintain the stock, and (c) the technology of depreciation may induce losses that are not proportional to stock and are relatively larger when the stock is small, old, and worn. This analogy provides a simple explanation as to why budgeted health investments can be low when we are young and health capital is high, and can rise sharply as we age and the remaining stock of health capital diminishes.

Other models of physical aging may be better analogs of biological aging. Automobiles are reputedly designed so the power train will usually operate for 70,000 miles, with sharply increasing hazard rates thereafter. Optional equipment is often less durable. Life can be prolonged by preventative maintenance and behavior (e.g., avoid wear and tear by driving only to church on Sundays), but repair frequency and costs rise with age, and it is sometimes easier to work around flaws than to fix them. When the power train fails, the machine is scrapped.

Is this a useful analogy for biological capital? Selection has designed us to stay healthy through our productive and reproductive years and is indifferent to our survival thereafter. Preventative maintenance is important, and hard use hurts, but hazard rates for various failures are largely beyond our control. We work around the failures of some body parts and repair others, until the power train fails and it's "goodbye, Charlie."

The automobile depreciation example suggests that it may be fruitful to look to failure-time models for description of the dynamics of health capital. There is ample precedent for this in both physical and biological applications, and in the epidemiology of aging. Multiple hazard models such as accelerated failure-time models with hazard rates influenced by exposure to various risk factors and by preventative and restorative investments may work to describe the evolution of health capital. If we are lucky in choosing our models, a one-dimensional index of health capital may suffice, perhaps a comprehensive analog of the activities of daily living (ADL) index we might call a "capacity for life-cycle living" (CLCL) index.

Life-cycle models readily accommodate exogenous mortality hazard. Do they remain tractable with the introduction of other health hazards, perhaps summarized in a single CLCL index, with hazard rates that are determined endogenously through preventative medical expenditures and behavior, with some failures requiring expensive repairs? If we are less lucky, health capital may be fundamentally multidimensional, requiring more work to identify and measure its components, but also inviting new analysis; for example, are mental, cardiovascular, and skeletal capital complements or substitutes, and can our portfolio of health capital stocks be rebalanced through the life cycle to minimize risk?

When considering life-cycle models with health capital, a few questions arise that parallel issues that appear in the dynamics of financial capital. To what extent do the precautionary motives to maintain "buffer stocks" of assets also operate on health capital? Is there any analog of the bequest motive in management of financial capital? We know that optimal life-cycle consumption jumps at retirement due to regime change in the consumption of leisure. Does this regime change also affect the productivity of health capital; for example, are leisure and health capital substitutes or complements? Can we as a result expect to see structural breaks in medical expenditures at the time of retirement?

Case and Deaton use SRHS as an indicator for health capital and show in a time series of cross sections that bad SRHS is associated with hard work, low income, and low education. Work and income associations strengthen with age; however, the reverse is true for education. There are sex differences, with females reporting somewhat worse health than males until old age, where the paths cross. They conclude that these patterns are inconsistent with the simple Grossman model for health capital and that the model of medical technology implicit in Grossman is wrong. I agree. The technologies implicit in survival models and some models of physical capital facing multiple hazards provide more plausible alternative starting points for life-cycle models with health capital.

How good is SRHS as an indicator of health capital? In analysis of AHEAD data, I find that an indicator for Poor/Fair SRHS (hereafter, P/F-SRHS) is predictive of future incidence of health conditions and of mortality; see Adams and others (2003). The Good/Very Good/Excellent gradient is not predictive. This may be a reporting effect, or if SRHS is a good indicator of health capital, may reflect sharply diminishing productivity of health capital above a threshold.

Baker, Stabile, and Deri (2001) find in Canada overreporting of health impairments among the unemployed, using medical records as a benchmark, a justification effect. Thus, SRHS may be susceptible to justification effects. In AHEAD, I find that P/F-SRHS is strongly associated with clinical depression and with a dwelling rated Poor/Fair, even with statistical control for overall socioeconomic status. This again suggests that reporting effects may influence SRHS.

Sex differences in SRHS may be largely due to plumbing differences and to the incidence and detection of problems that arise during the female reproductive years. In addition, my internist tells me that he sees sex-linked cultural differences, with females complaining more freely about health problems, males suppressing them. This may also be a factor in SRHS reports.

In Adams and others (2003a,b, 2003), probit models are estimated for prevalence and for incidence of P/F-SRHS, given objective health status indicators and a variety of measures of socioeconomic status. Tables 6C.1 and 6C.2 reproduce these models for the AHEAD panel. Consider first the explanation of prevalence in table 6C.1. For both females and males,

Table 6C.1   Prevalence of P/F-SRHS, AHEAD wave 1

Variable	Females Coefficient	Females t-statistic	Males Coefficient	Males t-statistic
One	−1.046	−4.18	−0.440	−1.21
Age since 70	0.002	1.85	0.004	3.62
Age since 80	−0.004	−3.31	−0.010	−5.20
Lowest quartile wealth	0.059	0.83	0.195	2.13
Highest quartile wealth	−0.215	−2.85	0.035	0.39
Lowest quartile income	0.036	0.51	−0.031	−0.33
Highest quartile income	−0.049	−0.67	−0.071	−0.80
High school	−0.149	−2.37	−0.127	−1.64
College	−0.308	−3.38	−0.239	−2.36
P/F neighborhood	0.121	1.44	0.233	2.06
P/F dwelling	0.368	4.51	0.460	4.33
Never married	−0.301	−1.81	0.216	1.06
Widow	−0.090	−1.47	−0.170	−1.77
Divorced/Separated	−0.046	−0.35	−0.129	−0.69
Mother death age	−0.001	−0.62	−0.002	−0.75
Father death age	−0.002	−1.12	−0.002	−0.69
Ever smoke	0.031	0.49	0.020	0.24
Cancer	0.207	2.74	0.295	3.34
Heart disease	0.0651	11.33	0.585	8.61
Stroke	0.347	3.47	0.405	3.55
Lung disease	0.609	7.19	0.747	8.32
Diabetes	0.547	6.32	0.253	2.58
High blood pressure	0.234	4.26	0.034	0.49
Arthritis	0.322	5.26	0.289	3.41
Incontinence	0.177	2.86	0.188	1.86
Fall	0.100	1.13	−0.064	−0.41
Hip fracture	0.144	1.35	−0.189	−0.96
Proxy respondent	0.257	2.19	0.306	2.77
Cognitive impairment	0.206	2.91	0.339	3.78
Psychiatric disease	0.016	0.20	−0.001	0.00
Depression	0.915	10.05	0.814	5.37
BMI	−0.005	−0.77	−0.032	−3.31
Smoker now	0.217	2.10	0.099	0.92
No. of ADL impairments	0.189	6.59	0.154	3.93
No. of IADL impairments	0.077	2.09	0.134	2.93
Likelihood	−1,449.1		−945.3	

	Count	Percent	Count	Percent
Observation				
Negative	2,079	66.06	1,351	66.65
Positive	1,068	33.94	676	33.35

Table 6C.2   Incidence of P/F-SRHS, AHEAD wave 1 to wave 3

Variable	Females Coefficient	Females t-statistic	Males Coefficient	Males t-statistic
One	−2.163	−1.71	−6.543	−3.78
Log months between waves	0.738	1.91	1.769	3.32
Age since 70	−0.001	−0.55	0.001	0.64
Age since 80	−0.001	−0.50	−0.005	−1.50
Lowest quartile wealth	0.066	0.72	−0.002	−0.02
Highest quartile wealth	−0.065	−0.61	0.123	0.88
Lowest quartile income	0.189	2.07	0.222	1.61
Highest quartile income	0.017	0.16	−0.018	−0.13
High school	−0.082	−0.99	−0.133	−1.14
College	−0.083	−0.61	0.096	0.57
P/F neighborhood	−0.022	−0.21	−0.088	−0.59
P/F dwelling	0.041	0.41	0.328	2.22
Never married	0.264	1.10	−0.170	−0.55
Widow	−0.173	−2.11	−0.375	−2.61
Divorced/Separated	−0.074	−0.42	−0.009	−0.03
Mother death age	−0.001	−0.61	0.000	0.05
Father death age	0.001	0.37	0.008	2.46
Ever smoke	0.076	0.90	0.102	0.82
Preexisting impairments				
Cancer	−0.015	−0.14	0.054	0.44
Heart disease	0.134	1.80	0.092	0.91
Stroke	−0.119	−1.08	0.116	0.77
Lung disease	0.259	2.49	0.496	3.90
Diabetes	0.018	0.19	−0.031	−0.23
High blood pressure	0.024	0.30	0.301	2.82
Arthritis	0.146	1.81	0.268	2.12
Incontinence	−0.032	−0.36	−0.156	−1.12
Fall	0.094	0.94	0.015	0.08
Hip fracture	0.384	2.73	0.042	0.15
Proxy respondent	−0.063	−0.38	0.028	0.14
Cognitive impairment	0.065	0.68	0.168	1.27
Psychiatric disease	0.196	1.90	−0.239	−1.53
Depression	0.266	2.67	0.042	0.21
Smoker now	0.001	0.01	0.155	0.90
High BMI	−0.010	−0.89	−0.036	−1.85
Low BMI	−0.158	−0.75	0.188	0.74
No. of ADL impairments	0.000	0.00	0.073	1.29
No. of IADL impairments	−0.053	−1.17	−0.078	−1.21
New impairments				
Cancer	0.260	1.27	0.566	2.49
Heart disease	0.247	2.42	0.511	3.58
Stroke	0.463	2.56	−0.070	−0.30
Lung disease	0.564	2.64	0.074	0.31
Diabetes	0.071	0.68	0.147	0.51
High blood pressure	0.143	0.82	0.309	1.27
Arthritis	0.210	1.82	0.062	0.38

Table 6C.2   (continued)

Variable	Females		Males	
	Coefficient	t-statistic	Coefficient	t-statistic
Incontinence	0.092	1.00	0.076	0.56
Fall	0.019	0.19	0.152	0.85
Hip fracture	−0.330	−1.60	0.216	0.43
Proxy respondent	−0.058	−0.40	0.035	0.18
Cognitive impairment	−0.040	−0.35	−0.033	−0.21
Psychiatric disease	0.103	0.69	0.272	0.92
Depression	0.300	1.94	0.089	0.37
BMI better	0.041	0.43	0.166	1.28
BMI worse	−0.120	−1.29	0.234	1.72
Smoke now	0.277	1.22	0.041	0.15
No. of ADL impairments	0.214	6.78	0.141	2.74
No. of IADL impairments	−0.049	−1.29	0.046	0.69
Likelihood	−822.73		−451.73	

	Count	Percent	Count	Percent
Observation				
Negative	420	25.81	244	26.24
Positive	1,207	74.19	686	73.76

prevalence of cancer, heart disease, stroke, lung disease, diabetes, arthritis, cognitive impairment, depression, ADL limitations, and IADL limitations are associated with P/F-SRHS. In addition, high blood pressure for females and low body mass index (BMI) for males are associated with P/F-SRHS. Thus, P/F-SRHS appears to correlate well with objective health impairments. The very strong association of depression and P/F-SRHS may reflect, in addition, a perception or reporting effect that could reduce the reliability of SRHS as an overall measure of health capital. Socioeconomic variables show some association with SRHS, with the prevalence of P/F-SRHS higher when socioeconomic status (SES) is lower for both females and males. The measurement problem is to disentangle true links between SES and health capital coming out of life-cycle planning and use of medical technology, and spurious associations arising from reporting effects.

Table 6C.2 is a model for incidence of new P/F-SRHS between waves 1 and 3 of the AHEAD panel, a period of about five years, as a function of preexisting SES and health status, and of incidence of new objective health impairments between the waves. In this model, at least some spurious reporting effects are controlled, and the model can be interpreted more plausibly as giving structural, causal effects of incidence of new objective health conditions or changes in SES. The pattern that emerges is that for both females and males some preexisting chronic conditions, such as lung disease, and some new acute conditions, such as cancer, heart disease, and ADL impairment, appear to induce a transition into P/F-SRHS. In addition, for females, preexisting hip fracture, depression, and new stroke, induce P/F-SRHS, while for males, preexisting high blood pressure and arthritis induce P/F-SRHS. The fact that all serious health impairments are not significantly related to incidence of P/F-SRHS is probably a consequence of the modest frequency with which various detailed impairments appear over a five-year period. There are weak impacts of SES on incidence of P/F-SRHS, notable primarily because these impacts are absent for incidence of most objective health impairments. The good news to be drawn from these models is that SRHS relates strongly to objective health conditions, meeting the one criterion for a measure of health capital that it be predictive for objectively measured health status. The bad news is that the strong dependence of P/F-SRHS on depression, and to a lesser extent on SES, may reflect reporting effects as well as the interdependence of health and financial status that life-cycle decisions on health investment would induce. Careful measurement and analysis will be needed to isolate reporting effects and construct health capital variables that capture the real health-wealth interactions embedded in the dynamics of life-cycle behavior.

References

Adams, P., M. Hurd, D. McFadden, A. Merrill, and T. Ribeiro. 2003a. Healthy, wealthy, and wise? Tests for direct causal paths between health and socioeconomic status. *Journal of Econometrics* 112:3–53.
———. 2003b. Healthy, wealthy, and wise? Addendum. University of California, Berkeley, Department of Economics. Working Paper.
Baker, M., M. Stabile, and C. Deri. 2001. What do self-reported objective measures of health measure? NBER Working Paper no. 8419. Cambridge, MA: National Bureau of Economic Research.

7

Consequences and Predictors
of New Health Events

James P. Smith

There is renewed interest in why people of lower socioeconomic status (SES) have worse health outcomes. No matter which measures of SES are used (income, wealth, or education), the evidence that this association is large is abundant (Marmot 1999; Smith 1999). The relation between SES and health appears also to be pervasive over time and across countries at quite different levels of economic development (Kitagawa and Hauser 1973; Townsend et al. 1988). Considerable debate remains about why the relation arises and what the principal directions of causation might be (Smith 1999; Adams et al. 2003; Deaton 2003). However, many analytical difficulties exist when one tries to understand its meaning. These difficulties include the complex dimensionality of health status that produces considerable heterogeneity in health outcomes, the two-way interaction between health and economic status, and the separation of anticipated from unanticipated health or economic shocks.

The emphasis in health research has been on understanding and disentangling the multiple ways in which socioeconomic status may influence a variety of health outcomes. Consequently, much less is currently known about the impact health may have on SES. But at least for working-aged individuals, health feedbacks to labor supply, household income, and wealth may be quantitatively quite important. Therefore, one aim of this paper will be to estimate the effect of new health events on a series of subsequent outcomes that are both directly and indirectly related to SES. These outcomes will include out-of-pocket (OOP) medical expenses, the intensive

James P. Smith is a senior economist at RAND. I would like to thank the expert programming assistance of David Rumpel and Iva Maclennan. Financial support was provided by the National Institute on Aging. The comments of Dana Goldman, David Cutler, and participants at the conference are gratefully acknowledged.

and extensive margins of labor supply, health insurance, and household income.

Finding evidence that there are significant feedbacks from new health events to these subsequent correlates of SES does not negate the real possibility that the probability of experiencing the onset of a minor or major new health event may not be uniform across several SES dimensions. This pathway is also explored here by examining whether the onset of new chronic conditions is related to household income, wealth, and education, once one conditions for a set of preexisting demographic and health conditions.

This research will use multiple waves of data on health status and transitions, medical expenses, labor supply, income, and wealth accumulation from the first five waves of the Health and Retirement Survey (HRS). HRS is a national sample of about 7,600 households (12,654 individuals) with at least one person in the household fifty-one to sixty-one years old, originally interviewed in the fall of 1992 and winter of 1993. The principal objective of HRS is to monitor economic transitions in work, income, and wealth, as well as changes in many dimensions of health status. The first follow-up of HRS respondents was fielded approximately two years after the baseline. HRS instruments span the spectrum of behaviors of interest: on the economic side, work, income, and wealth; on the functional side, health and functional status, disability, and medical expenditures.

The paper is divided into three sections. The first documents the considerable amount of new health activity that afflicts individuals during their fifties and early sixties. The second section analyses the impact of these new health events on a series of outcomes—medical expenses, work effort, income, and health insurance. In the third section, this perspective is reversed by examining which dimensions of SES—income, wealth, and education—are able to predict future health outcomes.

7.1   The Best of Times and the Worst of Times

Matters are pretty quiet for most people on the economic front when they are in their fifties. For better or worse, what one does for a living has long since been settled and salary adjustments stick pretty closely to Consumer Price Index (CPI) swings. But it is anything but quiet and settled on the health front. Table 7.1 documents the extent of this activity by listing in the first column prevalence rates of major and minor chronic conditions for respondents who were members of the original HRS cohort (those born between 1931 and 1941). Major conditions were defined as cancer, heart condition, stroke, and diseases of the lung. All other onsets are defined as minor. At baseline in 1992, 39 percent of HRS respondents claimed to have no chronic conditions at all while 43 percent reported that they had had

Table 7.1   **Preexisting and new health conditions—Original HRS cohort**

Preprevalence		Cond. Incidence	Incidence	Postprevalence
38.7	None		49.9	18.5
	None	47.8		
	Minor	36.4		
	Major	15.5		
42.6	Minor		28.9	45.5
	None	51.6		
	Minor	22.1		
	Major	26.5		
18.7	Major		21.4	36.0
	None	50.3		
	Minor	28.9		
	Major	21.9		

Source: Calculations by author from first five waves of HRS—sample born between 1931 and 1941. All data are weighted.

some minor onset sometime in the past. About one in five stated that they already had experienced a major condition onset.[1]

The extent of the new health problems reported during these eight years is impressive if not depressing. Independent of their baseline status, about half of all respondents experienced some type of onset during the first five HRS waves. Note that the conditional probability of a major onset is much higher if one had already reported some type of health problem at HRS baseline than if one was chronic condition free. To illustrate, the probability of experiencing a major onset sometime after HRS started is 53 percent higher if one had a minor condition at baseline instead of having no chronic condition at all. This no doubt reflects the progressive nature of disease, whereby having a relatively minor medical problem (such as hypertension), heightens the odds of experiencing another, much more severe one (such as a heart attack).

The final column in table 7.1 looks back and summarizes the consequences of all this activity by listing prevalence rates at the end of the 5th round of HRS. By this time, more than four out of every five HRS respondents had experienced an onset of some chronic condition, and for a third of them the onset was one that I label major. In less than a decade, the fraction of respondents without any health condition was cut in half while the proportion with a severe health problem doubled.

While certainly a real concern for the families involved, the sheer extent of this new and largely negative health activity raises several analytical questions and opportunities for research. The most direct question in-

1. In this and all other tables in this paper, major trumps minor. That is, an individual who reports both a minor and major onset is included in the major category.

volves what the financial consequences of this health deterioration might be, an issue I address in the next section. The analytical opportunities stem from the considerable variation in individual health status during these ages, especially compared to that observed in the standard mainstays of life-cycle models.

7.2 The Consequences of New Health Events

It is useful to first outline the essential issues in estimating effects of SES on health as well as the effects of health on SES. Current realizations of both economic status and health reflect a dynamic history in which both health (H_t) and SES (Y_t) are mutually affected by each other as well as by other relevant forces. Most of the relevant ideas can be summarized by the following two equations:

$$(1) \qquad H_t = \alpha_0 + \alpha_1 H_{t-1} + \alpha_2 Y_{t-1} + \alpha_3 \Delta \hat{Y}_t + \alpha_4 X_{t-1} + u_{1t}$$

$$(2) \qquad Y_t = \beta_0 + \beta_1 H_{t-1} + \beta_2 Y_{t-1} + \beta_3 \Delta \hat{H}_t + \beta_4 X_{t-1} + u_{2t}$$

where X_{t-1} represents a vector of other possibly nonoverlapping time and nontime varying factors influencing health and SES and u_{1t} and u_{2t} are possibly correlated stochastic shocks to health and SES. The key parameters α_3 and β_3 measure the effects of new innovations of SES on health, and health on SES, respectively. In this framework, we can also estimate whether past values of SES predict health ($\alpha_2 \neq 0$) or past values of health predict SES ($\beta_3 \neq 0$).[2]

To estimate the effect of either on the other (α_3 and β_3), we require exogenous variation in health (or SES) that is not induced by SES (health). In an earlier paper (Smith 1999), I proposed one research strategy for isolating new health events—the onset of new chronic conditions. While to some extent people may anticipate onset, much of the actual realization and especially its timing may be unanticipated. While new onsets may provide the best chance of isolating health shocks, not all new onset is a surprise. A set of behavioral risk factors and prior health or economic conditions may make some people more susceptible than others to this risk. Thus, predictors of new onsets should be included in models to increase one's confidence that the remaining statistical variation in new onsets is "news." Similarly, to estimate α_3 we require variation in SES not induced by health, and my approach to this issue will be outlined in the next section. In this section, I present my results for equation 2—the effect of health on SES—and in the section that follows I discuss my results relevant to equation 1.

---

2. For an insightful debate about the conditions under whether coefficients are zero or stationary also reveals something about causality, see the paper by Adams et al. (2003) and the comments on that paper in the same volume.

One thing that may happen when people become newly sick is that their medical expenses may rise, and the extent to which they rise may be influenced by the continued presence of health insurance. But medical expenses are by no means the only way health shocks can affect wealth accumulation. Most directly, healthier people may work longer hours in any given week and more weeks during a year, both of which may lead to higher earnings. To estimate the impact of the onset of new health conditions, a parallel set of models is estimated, predicting out-of-pocket medical expenses, the continued possession of health insurance, labor supply, household income, and wealth or savings.

A new health event in one year may affect medical expenditure, labor supply, and income, not only in the year in which the event occurred but in future years as well. For example, at one extreme, the onset of a new condition may induce only single-period changes in labor supply, after which labor supply may stabilize. But it is possible that spillover effects of a health shock may further depress work effort in future years; alternatively, some recovery to original levels may take place. One way of estimating such patterns is to estimate a series of four equations for each of HRS waves 2–5, summarizing changes in each outcome between adjacent waves, say

$$\Delta L_t = \alpha \mathbf{X} + \sum_{t=2}^{5} \beta_t \Delta H_t$$

where L_t is the between-wave change in labor supply and H_t the within-period health event from period t to $t-1$. Similar equations would apply for household income, out-of-pocket medical expenses, and other outcomes. If there are only contemporaneous one-period effects of health events, all lagged values of H_t will be zero.[3]

$\mathbf{X}$ represents a vector of baseline HRS attributes that include baseline measures of birth cohort (or age), marital status, race, ethnicity, education, region of residence, quintiles of family income, and a vector of measures of baseline health. These health measures include dummies for four of the five categories of self-reported health status, the presence of each chronic condition, a set of behavioral risk factors (smoking, exercise, body mass index [BMI], drinking), and a scaled index of functional limitations based on the answers to the ADL questions. Given these extensive sets of baseline health controls, the new onset of chronic conditions in each wave captures the impact of a new health event that is not predicted by (observed) baseline health and to that extent may be labeled news.

While this formulation has been simplified into a single type of new

---

3. All models in this paper are restricted to survivors—those who neither attrited nor died across the waves—so this analysis ignores the relationship of SES to attrition and mortality. Given the age range of HRS respondents, mortality selection, but not attrition, is unlikely to be that critical. That is clearly not the case in the AHEAD sample. For a model that incorporates mortality selection see Adams et al. (2003).

health event (H_{t-1}), different kinds of health changes may have quite different economic consequences (Smith 1999). Health events can be distinguished by their severity, immediacy, impact on functioning, and duration. For example, the onset of hypertension may have no immediate consequences, but it may signal a more difficult future. In contrast, a heart attack or stroke has devastating immediate and future effects on medical expenditures and work effort. At this point in the research effort, I have made only one simple distinction—whether the health event is classified as severe or minor. Further distinctions will be pursued in the future and will largely be an issue of how much data are required.

7.2.1 Medical Expenses and Health Insurance

One quite direct financial impact of a health onset may be the additional medical costs that are incurred. While some combination of private and public health insurance will pay the bulk of these costs, insurance does not cover all of them. Some people may lack health insurance, and even for those who have it not all medical costs are covered, either due to caps or exclusion of certain benefits such as drugs. Table 7.2 presents the distribution of total out-of-pocket medical expenses associated with an onset of a new health condition that took place between the baseline and second wave of HRS. That onset could have been either a major or minor one, and separate OOP expense distributions are presented for each situation. These medical costs are measured over the first five waves of HRS and thus are cumulative across eight years. The reference group in table 7.2 is those HRS respondents who had no medical onset at all across the first five survey waves.

The incremental mean medical expenses associated with a severe health

Table 7.2   **Distribution of out-of-pocket medical expenditures percentiles**

Wave 2 incidence of chronic condition	10th	30th	50th	70th	90th	95th	98th	Mean
Severe	1,007	3,430	6,660	11,011	29,925	43,365	72,266	11,285
Mild	532	2,155	3,187	6,751	15,729	21,199	31,178	7,299
None all five waves	414	1,579	3,164	5,668	12,463	18,356	30,904	5,776
Have health insurance at baseline								
Severe	1,130	3,868	6,672	10,624	25,111	32,382	53,432	10,609
Mild	627	2,265	3,908	6,979	15,748	21,199	35,312	7,570
None all five waves	496	1,633	3,235	5,688	12,170	17,584	30,811	5,738
Have no health insurance at baseline								
Severe	73	1,196	4,867	15,291	43,485	93,982	93,982	16,444
Mild	184	1,247	3,094	5,490	15,008	21,729	30,131	5,674
None all five waves	153	1,138	2,787	5,773	14,958	20,692	39,489	6,168

Source: Calculations by author using HRS—between waves 1 and 5. All data are weighted.

onset are about $5,500, and only about $1,600 if the onset was one I label mild. Given that the time period spans eight years, these are modest sums. However, not all appears modest; there may be considerable financial risks associated with new medical problems. For example, after experiencing a severe onset there is a 10 percent chance that OOP medical expenses over the next year will increase by $17,000, a one-in-twenty chance that they will increase by about $25,000, and a one-in-fifty shot of an increment of more than $40,000. However, these financial risks of additional medical expenses are mostly associated with severe onsets. If the onset was one within the mild category, the mean impact of $1,600 is a reasonably good descriptor of shift in the entire OOP cost distribution. For example, compared to a mean estimate of $1,600, there is a one-in-twenty chance of a $2,800 increase in OOP medical expenses when the new onset was mild.

The cost data contained in table 7.2 describe the cumulative impact of a new onset. To describe year-by-year flows, table 7.3 presents estimates of the mean increase in OOP expenses due to the period-by-period onset of new medical conditions. As described above, these estimates are based on models that control for preexisting health conditions, economic status, and a standard set of demographics. Four sets of models are estimated—one each for the amount of OOP medical expenses that took place between successive waves. Each model includes as covariates all prior-wave health shocks. The rows in table 7.3 represent the wave at which HRS OOP medical costs are measured, and the columns indicate the time of onset of a new health condition. The final row sums these period costs to compute the cu-

Table 7.3   **Impact of new health shock on out-of-pocket medical expenses**

Wave	Major health shock between:			
	W1–W2	W2–W3	W3–W4	W4–W5
2	1,720**			
3	1,037**	2,052**		
4	893**	734**	1,490**	
5	503**	401	607**	1,969**
Total	4,153	3,187	2,097	1,969

Wave	Minor health shock between:			
	W1–W2	W2–W3	W3–W4	W4–W5
2	175			
3	313	766**		
4	160	247	443**	
5	567**	682**	625**	456**
Total	1,215	1,695	1,065	456

**Statistically significant at 5 percent.

mulative (up to wave 5) increase in OOP medical costs associated with each medical event.

Thus, a severe health shock that occurred between waves 1 and 2 of HRS initially increased mean OOP medical expenses by $1,720 during the two-year interval when it happened. This same health event also produced future increases in health costs that were of progressively smaller amounts. By the fifth wave, the mean total cost was a little over $4,000, so that less than half of the incremental costs were borne around the time of the event. Roughly speaking, the same pattern exists for major health events taking place in other HRS waves—an initial mean impact of about $2,000, followed by additional, albeit falling, cost increments in future years. These estimated increases in total OOP medical costs in table 7.3 are not all that different from the simple unadjusted differences displayed in table 7.2, suggesting that these additional costs are due to the actual onset, and not the result of other (measurable) differences at baseline between those who actually experienced a major health event and those who did not.

The primary purpose of health insurance is to reduce this financial risk. The second and third panels of table 7.2 present the same type of data on the distribution of OOP medical expenses, but this time stratified by whether or not the respondent had health insurance at baseline. Health insurance certainly dampens but does not eliminate medical costs due to new major illness. The mean increase in OOP medical costs is around $5,000 among those with health insurance and about twice that amount for those without health insurance. A comparison of the impact of a severe health event by insurance coverage shows that expenditures are actually lower at and below the median respondent without health insurance, but that they become progressively greater for the uninsured in the right tail of the cost distribution. This suggests that there is an impact of insurance on utilization as well as on expenditures. The lower impact of a severe onset below the median for those without health insurance may indicate that those without insurance went without some care costing moderate amounts. But some of the large expenses appear to have been borne by those without health insurance.

The financial risks of health events remain for all HRS respondents. Even for those with health insurance at baseline, there is a one-in-twenty chance of an increase in expenses of about $11,000 and a one-in-fifty of about $23,000 additional outlays. Of course, the situation is far more difficult among those without baseline health insurance, where even the mean effect of a new severe onset is about $10,000. For them, there is a 10 percent chance of $28,000 more in OOP medical costs, and a 5 percent chance of an extra $73,000 in additional expenses. In contrast, the shift in expense distribution induced by a minor onset is not large whether or not the respondent was covered by health insurance.

The data in table 7.2 control for the presence of health insurance at base-

Table 7.4   **Fraction of respondents without health insurance**

	No health onsets	Major health onset by:			
		Wave 1–2	Wave 2–3	Wave 3–4	Wave 4–5
Wave 1	14.0	13.6	14.4	15.1	16.0
Wave 2	12.4	8.0	14.2	12.1	15.6
Wave 3	10.3	6.1	7.8	10.2	13.8
Wave 4	9.4	6.6	7.6	6.0	9.2
Wave 5	7.3	2.6	4.9	3.6	6.5

line. One fear associated with becoming sick is the possibility of losing health insurance, especially if one can no longer work. For those without health insurance, the concern is that it may now be almost impossible to obtain it. Table 7.4 addresses this issue by listing the fraction of HRS respondents who reported no type of health insurance in each wave. As they age into government programs like Medicare, even among those who experienced no new health events across the first five waves, the percent without health insurance fell in half (from 14 percent to 7 percent). Table 7.4 also lists the same data for respondents who experienced a new major health event between each wave. The timing of the new health event is indicated by the placement of the dotted lines in each column. While each of the last four columns shows the same downward trend in noncoverage, in each case there is a noticeable jump at the time the major health event occurred.[4]

Table 7.5 provides a more detailed look at what is happening by listing the types of health insurance held at each wave. At baseline, among those HRS respondents with health insurance the dominant mode by far is employer-provided insurance, but as the waves unfold and retirement comes closer there is a gradual transition toward more government-provided insurance. But with what looks like a one-period lag, this transition is clearly accelerated by a new major event. For example, between the second and fourth waves of data, there is a 25 percentage point drop in employer-only coverage and a 20 percentage point increase in government-only coverage. This compares to only a 10 percentage point drop in employer and 12 percentage point increase in government coverage for those experiencing no new health events. The data in appendix table 7A.1 demonstrate that virtually all of this expansion in government-provided health insurance was Medicare and not Medicaid or Champus—the two other major government programs.

Instead of new major health events raising the prospects of a loss of health insurance, they actually triggered new (earlier) eligibility and lead to an expansion in insurance. This indicates that in terms of the conse-

4. There were no such breaks for new minor health events.

Table 7.5   Changes in type of health insurance

	1	2	3	4	5
No new health event					
No health insurance	12.2	10.8	9.1	8.4	6.1
Employer only	62.8	62.8	60.1	52.0	41.9
Government only	5.2	7.5	13.0	19.4	25.9
Government and employer	4.9	6.6	8.0	11.2	16.1
Personal only	5.9	6.4	9.2	7.3	6.5
All other	9.0	5.0	0.6	1.7	3.5
Severe health event, wave 1–2					
No health insurance	11.9	6.3	5.1	4.9	1.6
Employer only	58.6	57.8	44.8	34.4	23.7
Government only	10.3	16.1	26.0	35.6	41.9
Government and employer	5.1	9.1	16.8	20.7	23.7
Personal only	4.5	3.9	7.4	4.0	1.6
All other	9.6	6.8	0.1	0.4	7.5
Minor health event, wave 1–2					
No health insurance	15.4	13.0	9.9	7.2	5.5
Employer only	59.0	60.5	56.3	47.5	36.0
Government only	6.0	9.7	17.6	23.6	29.1
Government and employer	4.3	5.9	8.3	14.3	21.1
Personal only	6.9	5.1	7.4	6.4	5.6
All other	8.4	5.8	0.5	1.0	2.7

quences of health events, the preretirement years represented by the original HRS cohort might be quite unique and should not be extrapolated to younger people.

7.2.2   Work and Income

New health events can impact the financial well-being of households in other ways as well. Perhaps the most direct is that declining health may make work more difficult. Following the same format used in table 7.3, tables 7.6, 7.7, and 7.8 summarize the estimated effects of new health shocks on changes in the probability of work, changes in the number of hours worked per week (conditional on working), and changes in household income.

Similar to the time pattern of effects documented earlier for OOP medical expenses, a new severe health onset has an immediate and large impact of reducing the probability of working, which is then followed by diminishing ripple-like effects in subsequent waves. To illustrate, a severe health event between the first and second wave of HRS reduced the probability of work by 15 percentage points between the same two waves. Since the average labor force participation rate at baseline among those who were about to experience this major health event was .55, the impact on work is decidedly not trivial. Once again, estimated incremental effects in subsequent years cascade downward, so that by the end of HRS wave 5, the probability of work had declined by about 27 percentage points, due to a major

Table 7.6   **Probability of working**

	Major health shock between:			
Wave	W1–W2	W2–W3	W3–W4	W4–W5
2	–.148**			
3	–.054	–.156**		
4	–.030	–.024	–.091**	
5	–.036	–0.45	–0.49	–.112**
Total	–.268	–.225	–.140	–.112

	Minor health shock between:			
	W1–W2	W2–W3	W3–W4	W4–W5
2	–.041**			
3	–.036**	–.031		
4	–.017	–.022	–.019	
5	–.013	–.004	–.021	–.015
Total	–.107	–.057	–.040	–.015

**Statistically significant at 5 percent.

Table 7.7   **Hours worked per week**

	Major health shock between:			
Wave	W1–W2	W2–W3	W3–W4	W4–W5
2	–4.02**			
3	0.64	–4.31**		
4	–0.60	0.63	–1.96**	
5	0.17	0.16	–0.68	–2.54**
Total	–3.83	–3.50	–2.64	–2.54

	Minor health shock between:			
	W1–W2	W2–W3	W3–W4	W4–W5
2	–1.21**			
3	–0.99	–1.51**		
4	0.40	–0.17	–1.54**	
5	0.30	0.12	0.15	0.07
Total	–1.49	–1.56	–1.39	0.07

**Statistically significant at 5 percent.

health shock between waves 1 and 2. This pattern of a large immediate reduction in the probability of work followed by smaller additional declines in future waves also characterizes major health events that took place between the other waves of HRS. There appears to be a small decline in the absolute size of the impact on work effort, which would not be surprising,

Table 7.8   Impact of health shock on household income

| | Major health shock between: | | | |
Wave	W1–W2	W2–W3	W3–W4	W4–W5
2	–4,033**			
3	–1,258	–737		
4	–698	–3,231	–2,239	
5	–269	–460	–139	–3,601**
Total yearly income loss	–6,258	–4,428	–2,478	–3,601
Cumulative income loss	–36,884	–13,828	–6,856	–3,601
	Minor health shock between:			
	W1–W2	W2–W3	W3–W4	W4–W5
2	–498			
3	–988	20		
4	–44	–3,012**	–1,423	
5	–169	125	–2,680**	351
Total yearly income loss	–1,699	–2,967	–4,103	351
Cumulative income loss	–8,727	–8,811	–6,949	351

**Statistically significant at 5 percent.

as labor force participation is trending down as HRS respondents age. Just as was reported for medical costs, estimated effects are considerably smaller if the health events come under the minor label.

In contrast to these quite dramatic impacts on the probability of work, the estimated effects on my measure of the intensive work margin—weekly hours conditional on work shown in table 7.7—are not only more modest in their immediate impact, but the contemporaneous effects are about the same as the cumulative effects, indicating little spillover to future years. Apparently, the principal way that work is altered by a new severe health event is through the extensive margin of whether one works or not.

Table 7.8 provides estimates of the biannual changes in annual household income that are associated with new health events. While labor force activity refers to the same time as the survey, it is important to remember that household income is for the previous year, so that some part of total income receipts actually predates the onset of the disease. In addition to between-wave household income changes presented in the first four rows of this table, the final two rows provide two summary measures of cumulative change over the first five waves. The first—total yearly income loss— was obtained from summing the column estimates, and thus measures the difference in household income between wave 5 and the wave preceding the new health event. The second—cumulative income loss—measures the total loss in household income associated with the health event.

Table 7.9   **Cumulative effects of new health events**

	W1–W2	W2–W3	W3–W4	W4–W5
Major health event				
HRS—sample				
Cumulative income loss	–36,884	–13,828	–6,856	–3,601
Cumulative income loss + Increase expenses	–48,941	–19,338	–9,805	–5,901
AHEAD—sample				
Cumulative income loss + Increase expenses		–11,346	–3,005	
Minor health event				
HRS—sample				
Cumulative income loss	–8,727	–8,811	–6,949	351
Cumulative income loss + Increase expenses	–11,544	–11,584	–8,610	–316
AHEAD—sample				
Cumulative income loss + Increase expenses		5,926	–6,838	–702

Note: AHEAD sample waves moved over one column.

Not surprisingly, given the labor force results described above, new health events reduce household income with a larger reduction when the shock is major. There is no evidence of any household income recovery in subsequent years, so that the initial income losses persist. In fact, consistent with the labor force participation effects, there are additional diminishing income losses in subsequent waves. These period-by-period income losses, while cumulatively significant, are much smaller than the reductions in work force participation contained in table 7.6. Off their baseline levels, household income declines are in the order of 10 percent or less compared to close to 30 percent for workforce participation. The reasons for this discrepancy in the two related outcomes do not lie so much in offsets in other types of income (for example, I find little evidence of additional work effort of spouses), but instead in different reactions to similar health shocks across the income distribution. Low-income households are much more likely to react to a health shock by exiting the labor force than are higher-income households.

The final row in table 7.8 presents the cumulative household income loss associated with the health event.[5] Evaluated using mean effects, cumulative household income losses are much larger than the cumulative increases in OOP medical expenses described in table 7.3. For example, for the wave 1–2 major health shock, the order of magnitude is ten to one. While less dramatic for the severe health shocks in the other waves, cumulative income losses typically exceed cumulative medical expenses by a large single-digit integer.

Table 7.9 contains my estimates of the sum of cumulative income loss

5. I assume that the health event took place midway between the waves, so that the income loss, coincident with the health event, applies initially for only one year.

plus cumulative medical expenses associated with the onset of a health event derived from these models. The lifetime budget constraint linking consumption, income, assets, and savings implies that this sum of income loss, plus cumulative medical expenses (plus the foregone interest on them), represents an alternative way of measuring the wealth change or savings that took place across the first five waves of HRS.

There are several advantages and disadvantages with this alternative measure of household savings. Since income is arguably measured with much greater accuracy than household wealth, this alternative concept should be less contaminated by measurement error than changes in household wealth are known to be. Second, this alternative measure is also less affected by capital gains, which, during the recent periods of stock market boom and bust, may well dominate changes in household wealth over time. The principal disadvantage is that this alternative measure does not incorporate changes in other components of household consumption besides medical expenses. Invoking standard consumption smoothing arguments may not be a sufficient safe harbor, as standard intertemporal theory suggests that consumption adjustments may be triggered in part by new health events.

With these caveats, the data in table 7.9 indicate that the onset of all major health events should have lead to a reduction in household wealth, with that reduction much larger for major health events compared to the more minor ones. Table 7.9 also includes the same summary measures of household income loss and cumulative medical expenses that were obtained from precisely the same models estimated using the original AHEAD sample. Given the predominance of retirement and virtually universal coverage by Medicare in the AHEAD sample, not surprisingly the implied change in household wealth triggered by a new health event, whether major or minor, is considerably smaller in the AHEAD sample. In the AHEAD sample, there is much less possibility of any income loss, since most respondents' income is either annuitized or is not contingent contemporaneously on changes in health status (see Smith and Kington 1997 for additional evidence).

Table 7.10 lists results of models that use two alternative measures of changes in household wealth—the cumulative income loss and OOP medical expenses plus the implicit foregone interest on them (labeled the cumulative model), and the more direct measure using the change in household wealth between the first and fifth wave of HRS—as the outcome variables. In this formulation, negative coefficients in the cumulative model imply positive household wealth growth, so that the coefficients in the two alternative models should have opposite signs. In most instances this turns out to be the case, and estimated coefficients are often remarkably close, especially as there is nothing at the measurement level tying these two outcomes together.

Table 7.10   **Cumulative income loss and cumulative out-of-pocket medical expenses**

	Cumulative income loss and out-of-pocket medical expenses				Wealth5–Wealth1			
	Estimate	t	Estimate	t	Estimate	t	Estimate	t
Intercept	30,503	0.41	21,124	0.28	91,091	0.48	44,937	0.24
Cohort 1935–37	−34,376	−2.83	−29,081	−2.33	51,748	1.67	59,433	1.90
Cohort 1938+	−91,859	−8.55	−77,832	−7.07	36,613	1.34	56,007	2.04
Health excellent	−23,402	−1.30	−3,574	−0.19	−10,053	−0.22	−10,193	−0.22
Health very good	−18,217	−1.12	−8,747	−0.52	41,862	1.01	39,372	0.94
Health good	−1,984	0.13	5,786	0.37	32,719	0.85	39,605	1.02
Functional limitations scale	476	1.14	378	0.88	86	0.08	215	0.20
Female	29,223	2.93	29,905	2.92	−18,124	−0.72	−17,917	−0.68
African American	9,920	0.72	12,035	0.85	−83,932	−2.42	−62,914	−1.80
Hispanic	20,222	1.13	12,540	0.68	−79,374	−1.75	−59,523	−1.31
Income	2.445	20.6			1.853	6.17	0.3064	1.14
Wealth	−0.2800	37.6	−0.2096	30.8	−0.2152	11.21		
Ed. 12–15	−5,519	−0.48	15,422	1.31	16,398	0.56	15,596	0.53
Ed. college or more	−124,676	−8.20	−58,968	−3.86	134,326	3.47	122,282	3.14
Minor onset wave 2	13,247	0.94	11,128	0.77	−13,364	−0.37	−13,074	−0.36
Major onset wave 2	47,007	2.33	52,158	2.52	−78,266	−1.52	−78,130	−1.51
R^2	.19		.14		.026		.012	

Note: Models also include controls for baseline prevalence of chronic conditions, regions of residence, health risk behaviors, marital status, and the presence of health insurance.

The principal difference between the two models lies in fact in the final row—the R^2—that are more than eight times larger in the cumulative model. The negative consequences of the considerably greater measurement error in household wealth are apparent from the much larger standard errors, lower statistical significance, and somewhat wilder fluctuation in estimated coefficients (when one would think they might be ordered as in baseline self-reported GHS) in the household wealth model compared to the cumulative model.

At least, if only signs are used as the criteria, there are many similarities in the estimates obtained with the two alternative outcome measures. Since these similarities are not forced through measurement, this may encourage at least some of us to assign more credibility to some of the results. For example, both outcome specifications predict that younger HRS respondents experienced greater wealth growth over these eight years, and that wealth growth was somewhat smaller among women, African Americans, and Latinos. Finally, additional years of schooling—and most particularly having a college degree—are associated with larger amounts of wealth accumulation under either definition of the outcome.

The major exception to this theme of overall similarity concerns the household income and wealth variables, which have the same signs in both models in the first and third columns of table 7.10. Since additional financial resources should promote savings, the a priori expectation is that the baseline financial variables should be negative in the cumulative model and positive in the wealth change specification. But this is only the case for wealth in the model where income is included in the outcome (the cumulative model) and household income in the wealth change model. The reason for this confusion stems from the impact of measurement error in both income and wealth, which, when appearing on both sides of the estimated equation, seriously biases the estimated coefficients. The second and fourth columns omit the guilty party from the respective models, and much more sensible estimates are now obtained for the effect of wealth in the cumulative model and the effect of income in the wealth change model. Both estimates now imply reasonable ranges of the marginal propensity to save. By and large the estimated effects of other variables in the model are not sensitive to these alternative specifications.

My principal interest in these models concerns the impact of a new health event. I concentrate only on the impact of new health events between waves 1 and 2. In the cumulative model, the estimates of household savings induced by the major and minor health onset are close to those obtained by summing the individual wave estimates that were summarized in table 7.9—a major health onset lead to a cumulative loss of about $52,000, and a minor one a cumulative loss of about $11,000. Both minor and major health onsets also lead to a cumulative wealth lost when wealth change models are examined. However, estimates now are not terribly precise—a predictable consequence of poorly-measured household wealth in the HRS panel.

I also examined whether or not there were important interaction effects of a new health onset by interacting the two health event onset variables with race, gender, ethnicity, education, income, and wealth. None of these interactions were significant except wealth in the cumulative model and baseline household income in the wealth change model. In both cases, the effects of a major health onset were larger relative to higher baseline wealth or income. For example, the impact of a major health event in reducing wealth growth was larger the higher initial levels of household income. This finding is consistent with a combination of consumption smoothing and liquidity constraints. Lower-income households are forced to absorb more of the wealth change in consumption.

7.3   Predictors of New Health Events

In this section, I reverse the question by examining the ability of baseline SES measures to predict the future onset of disease once one controls for measures of baseline health. I also explore the extent to which innovations in economic status "cause" changes in health.

Table 7.11 contains the results obtained from probit models predicting

Table 7.11   **Probits for future onset of chronic condition**

	Major		Minor	
	Estimate	Chi square	Estimate	Chi square
Intercept	−0.8489	10.14	−1.9624	37.91
Cohort 1935–37	−0.1920	19.78	−0.0799	4.02
Cohort 1938+	−0.1888	24.99	−0.1535	19.35
Health excellent	−0.2314	13.57	−0.2396	16.76
Health very good	−0.1766	9.95	−0.0951	3.17
Health good	−0.0770	2.27	0.0302	0.37
Functional limitations scale	0.0041	8.63	0.0058	18.15
BMI	0.0172	1.47	0.1113	33.25
BMI^2	−0.0002	0.85	−0.0012	14.29
Vigorous exercise	−0.0786	3.94	−0.0266	0.57
Smoker	0.1523	6.68	0.0275	0.25
Number of cigarettes	0.0075	10.69	0.0005	0.06
More than 3 drinks	−0.1583	4.55	−0.0339	0.24
Female	−0.1918	30.12	0.0360	1.25
African American	−0.1245	6.70	0.1396	10.04
Hispanic	−0.2994	20.40	0.0600	1.09
Income	0.0111	0.06	−0.0063	0.03
Wealth	−0.0046	2.26	−0.0005	0.05
Change in stock wealth	−0.0004	0.44	0.0004	0.88
Ed. 12–15	−0.1108	7.78	−0.0912	5.96
Ed. college or more	−0.0844	2.43	−0.1588	10.26

Notes: Models also control for presence of baseline chronic condition, region of residence, health insurance, and missing value indicators. Income and wealth measured in 100,000 of dollars and the change in stock wealth in 10,000 of dollars.

the onset of a major or a minor chronic condition between waves 1 and 5 of HRS. These models include as covariates a vector of baseline health conditions of the respondent—self-reported general health status (excellent, very good, good, with fair and poor the excluded class), the presence of a chronic condition at baseline, a scale measuring the extent of functional limitations (from 0 to 100, with higher numbers indicating poorer functioning). The models also include a standard set of behavioral risk factors (currently a smoker, number of cigarettes smoked), whether one engaged in vigorous exercise, and BMI (entered as quadratic), and a relatively standard set of demographic controls—birth cohort (born between 1935 and 1937, after 1937 with pre-1935, or the older respondents, the excluded group), race (1 = African American), Hispanic ethnicity, and sex (1 = women), and region of residence. My main interest lies in the SES measures that include household income, household wealth, and respondent's education (two dummies—twelve to fifteen years of schooling, sixteen or more years, with less than twelve the excluded group).

Just as one needed innovations in health that were not caused by SES to estimate the impact of health on SES, it is also necessary to isolate innovations in SES that were not caused by health to estimate the impact of SES on health. One opportunity for doing so lies in the large wealth increases that were accumulated during the large stock market run-up during the 1990s. Given the unusually large run-up in the stock market during this decade, it is reasonable to posit that a good deal of this surge was unanticipated and thus captures unanticipated exogenous wealth increases that were not caused by a person's health. If financial measures of SES do improve health, such increases in stock market wealth should be associated with better subsequent health outcomes, at least with a lag.[6]

Putting aside for a moment the central SES results, most of the estimates listed in table 7.11 are as expected. Older respondents are much more likely to experience a new chronic onset, and the likelihood of experiencing a new onset is strongly negatively related to better health status as measured at baseline. There are some suggestions of some to-do's and not-to-do's from the health behavioral risk variables. Even after controlling for an extensive list of baseline health conditions, smoking, excessive drinking, and the absence of vigorous exercise places one at elevated risk for the onset of a new major condition, but appears to have little impact on the minor onsets. Women, Latinos, and, perhaps somewhat surprisingly, African Americans are all of lower risk of a major new onset while only African Americans face a statistically significant higher risk of a new minor onset.

My principal interest in these models is whether prior wave SES predicts the likelihood of new illnesses, and if so, which measures of SES, and if so, why? A pretty consistent generalization can be made for household income—it never predicts future onset on minor or major conditions. While household wealth appears to be only related to a major onset, this effect is not particularly large, and, as we shall see, it will mostly disappear with a single exception when I break out the different types of chronic onset. Finally, my best measure of an exogenous wealth change—the wealth increase from the stock market—is only statistically significant in one instance (arthritis), and there it has the incorrect sign, so that an increase in stock market wealth makes the onset of arthritis more likely. Moreover, in results I do not display in table 7.11, having health insurance also does not predict future onset. In sum, then, SES variables that directly measure or proxy for financial resources of a family are either not related or at best only weakly related to the future onset of disease over the time span of eight years.

This largely negative conclusion is in sharp contrast to the results obtained for the final SES measure—education—and for the gist of the results reported by Adams et al. (2003) for a mostly retired population. Ad-

6. One limitation of using increases in stock market wealth is that these increases are concentrated at the top of the income distribution (see Smith 2000). Obtaining other credible measures of exogenous changes in financial resources that more evenly span the entire income distribution would be very useful.

ditional schooling is strongly and statistically significantly predictive of the new onset of both major as well as minor disease over the first eight waves of the HRS.

To obtain some notion of why all this may be so, table 7.12 lists estimated coefficients for the SES variables, obtained with models for each of the chronic conditions separately. In no single case is the estimated coefficient on household income (which vacillates in sign) statistically significant. While the coefficients on wealth lean toward negative values, in only one case (stroke) is a statistically significant negative result obtained for household wealth. When combined, these results (table 7.12) strengthen the overall conclusion that in a sample of the preretirees, financial measures of SES do not appear to be able to predict future onset of disease across a time horizon of almost a decade.

Once again, however, in all cases except cancer (which looks very much like an equal opportunity disease), the effects of schooling are preventative against disease onset. But here too disease differentiate may eventually be informative as the most powerful protection of education takes place for arthritis and diseases of the lung, with diabetes and heart disease in the next tier.

That leaves us with the most difficult question of all—why does education matter so much? To try to provide at least some partial insight into this question, I ran an expanded version of these models. This expansion involved including some of the more likely prospects that are measured in the HRS—cognition, past health behaviors, early life health and economic environments, parental attributes, and parental health. HRS information on some of these concepts is quite limited, but it does record whether one smoked in the past, whether one was exposed on the job to a health hazard (and the number of years of exposure), the education of parents, whether or not each parent is alive and, if deceased, the age of death, self-assessed general health status as a child (the same five point scale), and an assessment of the economic environment in which one lived during childhood.[7] The results obtained from this expanded model are presented in table 7.13 (for major onsets) and table 7.14 (for minor onsets).

First, let's deal with the easier question—which of these new measures did not seem to matter in this context. Two of the more prominent cognition variables available in the HRS were added to these models—memory word count and the Wechsler scale (a measure of higher-order reasoning). Neither of these cognition variables was statistically significant, and their inclusion had no impact at all on the education variables. The same con-

---

7. The specific question for health was "Consider your health while you were growing up, from birth to age 16. Would you say that your health during that time was excellent, very good, good, fair, or poor?" The specific question for economic circumstances was "Now think about your family when you were growing up, from birth to age 16. Would you say your family during that time was pretty well off financially, about average, or poor?"

Table 7.12   **Probits for future onset of chronic condition**

	Any major		Any minor	
	Estimate	Chi square	Estimate	Chi square
Income	0.0111	0.06	−0.0063	0.03
Wealth	−0.0046	2.26	−0.0005	0.05
Ed. 12–15	−0.1108	7.78	−0.0912	5.96
Ed. college or more	−0.0844	2.43	−0.1588	10.26
Change in stock wealth	−0.0004	0.44	0.0004	0.88

	Cancer		Hypertension	
	Estimate	Chi square	Estimate	Chi square
Income	0.0130	0.05	0.0153	0.11
Wealth	−0.0030	0.53	−0.0032	1.01
Ed. 12–15	0.0008	0.00	−0.0675	2.45
Ed. college or more	0.0567	0.61	−0.0623	1.17
Change in stock wealth	0.0003	0.32	−0.0001	0.11

	Diseases of the lung		Diabetes	
	Estimate	Chi square	Estimate	Chi square
Income	−0.0271	0.12	0.0382	0.40
Wealth	−0.0067	1.13	−0.0023	0.29
Ed. 12–15	−0.1920	10.32	−0.1153	4.82
Ed. college or more	−0.1432	2.67	−0.0777	1.11
Change in stock wealth	0.0006	1.13	−0.0023	1.37

	Heart disease		Arthritis	
	Estimate	Chi square	Estimate	Chi square
Income	−0.0447	0.64	−0.0069	0.03
Wealth	0.0015	0.19	0.0000	0.00
Ed. 12–15	−0.1086	5.10	−0.0819	4.29
Ed. college or more	−0.0519	0.62	−0.1857	12.14
Change in stock wealth	−0.0012	1.36	0.0006	2.41

	Stroke	
	Estimate	Chi square
Income	0.0683	0.70
Wealth	−0.0175	3.83
Ed. 12–15	−0.0390	0.36
Ed. college or more	−0.0746	0.59
Change in stock wealth	−0.0017	0.57

Note: See table 7.11 notes.

Table 7.13   Probits for future onset of major chronic condition

	Major		Major extended	
	Estimate	Chi square	Estimate	Chi square
Intercept	−0.8649	10.14	−0.8963	7.12
Cohort 1935–37	−0.1920	19.78	−0.1778	14.00
Cohort 1938+	−0.1888	24.99	−0.1617	13.66
Health excellent	−0.2314	13.57	−0.2058	8.64
Health very good	−0.1766	9.95	−0.1629	6.79
Health good	−0.0770	2.27	−0.0624	1.18
Functional limitations scale	0.0041	8.63	0.0037	5.31
BMI	0.0172	1.47	0.0199	1.66
BMI^2	−0.0002	0.85	−0.0002	1.01
Vigorous exercise	−0.0786	3.94	−0.0917	4.60
Smoker	0.1523	6.68	0.0997	2.10
Number of cigarettes	0.0075	10.69	0.0103	15.69
More than 3 drinks	−0.1583	4.55	−0.1669	4.22
Female	−0.1918	30.12	−0.1893	20.96
African American	−0.1245	6.70	−0.0556	0.97
Hispanic	−0.2994	20.40	−0.2098	7.34
Income	0.0111	0.06	0.0456	0.93
Wealth	−0.0046	2.26	−0.0040	1.60
Change in stock wealth	−0.0004	0.44	−0.0008	1.06
Ed. 12–15	−0.1108	7.78	−0.0783	2.66
Ed. college or more	−0.0844	2.43	−0.0483	0.52
Ex-smoker			0.0195	0.20
Exposed to hazard on job			0.0200	0.21
No. of years exposed			0.0021	0.99
Memory test			0.0118	2.53
WAIS scale			−0.0001	0.00
Health ex. or VG as child			−0.0870	4.68
Not poor during childhood			−0.0949	6.31
Mother's education			0.0028	0.18
Father's education			−0.0018	0.09
Father alive			−0.1362	1.34
Age of father's death			0.0002	0.01
Mother alive			−0.0743	0.49
Age of mother's death			−.0002	0.01

Note: See table 7.11 notes.

clusion would apply to the ex-smoker variable, the environmental job exposure variable, and parental education.[8]

What did matter was the self-evaluation of childhood health and economic status and parental health as proxied by age of death of each parent.[9] For the major health onsets, a (currently) self-assessed better health

8. When individual chronic conditions were examined separately, the environmental exposure variable has a statistically positive effect on diseases of the lung.

9. For evidence of the role of economic resources during childhood, see Case, Lubotsky, and Paxson (2002), and Wadsworth and Kuh (1997).

Table 7.14   Probits for future onset of minor chronic condition

	Minor		Minor extended	
	Estimate	Chi square	Estimate	Chi square
Intercept	−1.9624	38.19	−1.7780	21.54
Cohort 1935–37	−0.0799	4.06	−0.1122	6.58
Cohort 1938+	−0.1535	19.29	−0.1761	19.12
Health excellent	−0.2396	16.65	−0.2488	14.57
Health very good	−0.0951	2.96	−0.0805	1.83
Health good	0.0302	0.37	0.0224	0.16
Functional limitations scale	0.0058	18.39	0.0060	15.50
BMI	0.1113	32.97	0.1187	31.13
BMI^2	−0.0012	13.99	−0.0013	13.40
Vigorous exercise	−0.0266	0.42	−0.0231	0.38
Smoker	0.0275	0.24	0.0495	0.60
Number of cigarettes	0.0005	0.07	0.0014	0.30
More than 3 drinks	−0.0339	0.30	−0.0271	0.13
Female	0.0360	1.24	0.0704	3.49
African American	0.1396	9.96	0.1366	7.00
Hispanic	0.0600	1.22	0.0614	0.83
Income	−0.0063	0.02	−0.0044	0.01
Wealth	−0.0005	0.00	−0.0001	0.00
Change in stock wealth	0.0004	0.88	0.0003	0.75
Ed. 12–15	−0.0912	6.02	−0.0527	1.38
Ed. college or more	−0.1588	10.46	−0.0927	2.33
Ex-smoker			0.0536	2.12
Exposed to hazard on job			−0.0261	0.44
No. of years exposed			0.0007	0.12
Memory test			−0.0055	0.68
WAIS scale			−0.0035	0.28
Health ex. or VG as child			0.0042	0.01
Not poor during childhood			0.0155	0.20
Mother's education			0.0004	0.00
Father's education			−0.0046	0.72
Father alive			−0.2001	3.32
Age of father's death			−0.0014	0.88
Mother alive			−0.2465	6.51
Age of mother's death			−.00028	4.60

Note: See table 7.11 notes.

status and better economic status during childhood both reduce the risk of incurring a serious health onset in one's fifties and early sixties even after controlling for current health and economic status. There is, of course, ample support for such a finding in the work of Barker (1997) and others who have emphasized the delayed health impact of early childhood exposures. I would currently view these results more cautiously until the disease-specific relevance can be rationalized. For example, when models are estimated on the individual diseases separately, the principal impacts of childhood health appear in heart disease and diseases of the lung (and not cancer). More puzzling, the major impact of childhood economic circumstances appears in cancer, for which a convincing explanation does not immediately jump to mind.

In the minor onset specification in table 7.14, what principally matters are the measures of parental health. Having a living parent or having a parent who was older when they died tend to reduce the likelihood of an onset on new chronic conditions. When these are estimated on a disease-specific basis, the effects are concentrated in hypertension and diabetes and pretty much nonexistent in arthritis. The same caveats mentioned above for the major onsets would apply here as well.

With these additional variables included, the effects of one's own education in predicting onsets appear to be diminished, but the principal impact may have been more on standard errors than on point estimates. My admittedly tentative conclusion would be that collectively these additional factors explain some but not all of the ability of education to predict future onset.[10]

7.4 Conclusions

In this paper, I examined several questions related to the SES health gradient, using a sample of people first observed when they were mostly between ages fifty-one and sixty-one. This research was based on extensive data about baseline health and several dimensions of their SES as well, and the update on this information available from four subsequent follow-ups taking place at two-year intervals. Innovations in health are proxied by the new onset of chronic conditions, a relatively common event in this age group, and innovations in economic status by the change in stock market wealth over this period.

There are some things that appear clear. Among people in their preretirement years, feedbacks from health to labor supply, household income, and wealth are realities that should neither be ignored nor dismissed as of secondary importance. Working is the critical link in this chain, with OOP medical expenses, while not ignorable (especially for distributional analysis) in the second tier. These negative income and wealth consequences of new health innovations do appear to decay with age and are certainly much smaller in an already-retired population. What these consequences would be ten or twenty years earlier in age is an important and yet unanswered question (see Smith 2003). The evidence in this paper, along with that available in other studies (Adams et al. 2003; Smith 1999), means that we can say with more confidence that health has quantitatively strong conse-

---

10. For an alternative explanation of the role of disease self-management in the health education gradient, see Goldman and Smith (2002).

quences for several dimensions of SES, particularly financial ones, in certain age groups.

More tentative conclusions are warranted for the ability of SES measures to predict future onset of disease. Perhaps, most importantly, my evidence does suggest that the role of financial measures of SES—household income, household wealth, or health insurance—is quite weak. To put it most simply, household income never appears to predict any future onset over the horizon of about a decade and there is only weak evidence that levels of change in household wealth help much at all. However, it is not true that SES doesn't matter. Even after controlling for an extensive list of baseline health conditions and status, education still strongly predicts the future onset of disease.

My attempts to explain why education may matter represent the most tentative part of my thinking. There is evidence that the pathways may well be disease-specific, as the predictive power of schooling varies considerably by disease. There is also some evidence that legacy effects from childhood may still matter thirty or forty years later, even when the health outcome is the onset of new disease. Whether or not these legacy effects represent economic, health, or genetic factors is quite uncertain in my view, and requires much more additional research.

Appendix

Table 7A.1   **Types of government insurance**

	1	2	3	4	5
No new health event					
Medicare	37.8	44.5	59.5	75.6	81.4
Medicaid	15.7	13.2	12.0	6.1	4.2
Champus	37.7	30.5	19.5	10.5	5.8
Medicare and Medicaid	3.3	4.1	6.9	5.9	5.7
All other	5.5	7.7	2.1	2.1	2.9
Severe health event, wave 1–2					
Medicare	40.8	50.7	62.7	73.8	74.4
Medicaid	21.8	22.3	16.4	8.1	4.8
Champus	26.2	15.1	6.5	4.7	4.1
Medicare and Medicaid	2.4	7.4	13.1	11.1	15.6
All other	8.8	4.6	1.3	2.4	0.9
Minor health event, wave 1–2					
Medicare	37.3	51.9	62.2	75.1	79.0
Medicaid	19.7	14.8	16.0	6.0	4.7
Champus	28.0	21.4	10.7	7.3	5.5
Medicare and Medicaid	3.8	4.4	9.3	10.1	9.8
All other	11.0	7.5	1.9	1.5	1.1

References

Adams, Peter, Michael Hurd, Daniel McFadden, Angela Merrill, and Tiago Ribeiro. 2003. Healthy, wealthy, and wise? Tests for direct causal paths between health and socioeconomic status. *Journal of Econometrics* 112:3–56.

Barker, David J. P. 1997. Maternal nutrition, fetal nutrition and diseases in later life. *Nutrition* 13 (9): 807–13.

Case, Anne, Darren Lubotsky, and Chris Paxson. 2002. Economic status and health in childhood: The origins of the gradient. *American Economic Review* 92 (5): 1308–34.

Deaton, Angus. 2003. Health, inequality, and economic development. *Journal of Economic Literature* 41 (March): 113–58.

Goldman, Dana, and James P. Smith. 2002. Can patient self-management help explain the SES health gradient? *Proceedings of the National Academy of Sciences; USA (PNAS)* 99 (16): 10929–34.

Kitagawa, Evelyn, and Philip Hauser. 1973. *Differential mortality in the United States: A study in socioeconomic epidemiology.* Cambridge: Harvard University Press.

Marmot, Michael. 1999. Multi-level approaches to understanding social determinants. In *Social epidemiology,* ed. Lisa Berkman and Ichiro Kawachi, 349–67. Oxford: Oxford University Press.

Smith, James P. 1999. Healthy bodies and thick wallets. *Journal of Economic Perspectives* 13 (2): 145–66.

———. 2000. Why is wealth inequality rising? In *Increasing income inequality in America: The facts, causes, and consequences,* ed. Finis Welch, 83–116. Chicago: University of Chicago Press.

———. 2005. Unraveling the SES health connection. *Population and Development Review,* forthcoming.

Smith, James P., and Raynard Kington. 1997. Demographic and economic correlates of health in old age. *Demography* 34 (1): 159–70.

Wadsworth, Michael, and Diane Kuh. 1997. Childhood influences on adult health: A review of recent work from the British 1946 National Birth Cohort Study, the MRC National Survey of Health and Development. *Pediatric and Perinatal Epidemiology* 11:2–20.

Comment   David M. Cutler

It is clear in virtually every data source and measure used that health and socioeconomic status are intimately related: people with more income, education, or wealth are healthier than are people who rank lower on the socioeconomic scale. These differences are quite large. Life expectancy at the top of the income distribution is about seven years greater than life expectancy at the bottom.

David M. Cutler is the academic dean of the faculty of arts and sciences, and a professor of economics in the Department of Economics and the Kennedy School of Government at Harvard University, and a research associate of the National Bureau of Economic Research.

What is less clear is why the two are so strongly associated. Some researchers believe that socioeconomic status (SES) is the driving variable. Higher-SES people may have better access to medical care, more information about appropriate medical practice, less strenuous jobs, or access to more material inputs that improve health, or they may live in more health-promoting environments. Others stress the reverse causality: poor health may lead to lower SES as people lose time at work, do not get promoted, or drop out of the labor force entirely. Still others believe that omitted factors explain both health and socioeconomic differences across individuals. People with lower discount rates may invest more in their own health and in their material circumstances, resulting in the correlation that we observe.

Distinguishing between these theories is very important. If policy seeks to narrow socioeconomic differences in health, as many believe it should, we need to know whether the factor to address is underlying differences in economic circumstances, behavioral differences across people, or patterns of early life investment. To date, there is no consensus among researchers about which is most important.

Jim Smith's paper deals with this thorny set of questions. Smith wades into one of the most vexing topics in public policy and produces new and extremely convincing results showing the impact of health on SES and the reverse. The paper is wonderfully done and very informative.

The most convincing part of the paper is the analysis of the impact of health shocks on income. Using data from the Health and Retirement Study (HRS), Smith follows a cohort of near elderly during the time when major health shocks first begin to occur widely—in their fifties and early sixties. Smith shows that health impairments have a large impact on SES. By ten years after the health event, household wealth is lower by about $40,000.

Interestingly, the lower wealth is not a product of high out-of-pocket medical spending. Household spending on medical care in response to an adverse health shock is relatively low, about $4,000 over the decade. The larger effect is on labor supply and hence earnings. People who suffer health events drop out of the labor force more frequently and work fewer hours. As a result, labor income falls by nearly $4,000 per year.

Because of the nature of the data—panel data collected very thoroughly—and the clarity of the analysis, Smith's results on this point are totally convincing; SES does respond to health.[1] Smith's results will not be easily overturned.

Rather than quibble with the analysis (about which there is little quib-

1. One minor point to note is that these results hold true for income and wealth but not education. Educational attainment is determined long before people reach their fifties. Smith's analysis shows that some dimensions of SES are responsive to health shocks (income and wealth), but not others.

bling to do), I would like to push a little bit on the interpretation. It is clear that people leave the labor force when they experience an adverse health event. But why is that? Consider a few alternatives. The first is that people are essentially unable to work in any meaningful job after a health shock. Their health impairment might affect their ability to get to work, their physical functioning on the job, or their ability to concentrate for long periods of time. A second interpretation is that people could continue to work but choose to retire instead. Health shocks provide information to people that their expected longevity is less than they previously thought. It would be rational for some people to respond by consuming more leisure at a younger age. Finally, some people might be induced out of the labor force by the presence of disability insurance. Those people would have worked otherwise and might be able to work productively, but because of the availability of public coverage they choose to leave the labor force.

The interpretation of the results Smith presents, and the implications for public policy, depend on which of these is correct. Additional work could help differentiate among them. One way to make progress is to combine the information here with data on functional status. How much is the ability to undertake specific activities impaired when a person has an adverse health shock? Do people need specific technical or human aids afterwards? The HRS has some data on this, and it would be valuable to combine them with the results here.

Another way to approach this is to use information about the condition that was responsible for the adverse health shock. Cancer is much less disabling than heart disease, for example. If transitions out of the labor force were caused by significant adverse physical impairment, that should be more true for people with heart disease than cancer. Changes in tastes for work, however, might be affected relatively equally by the onset of these two conditions.

A third way to address this issue is to look at the interaction of health and other factors that would influence retirement. Some people remain at work because they will lose health insurance if they retire before Medicare eligibility. Is the retirement response greater for people with retiree health insurance? What about for those who are near Medicare eligibility age? Additional analysis along these lines could help determine why labor supply responds so strongly to health shocks.

The second part of Smith's paper examines the reverse link—the impact of SES on health. Smith shows that better-educated people, although not higher-income people, are significantly less likely to experience onsets of new health conditions than are less-educated people. In considering why this is the case, Smith shows that the education coefficients decline by only one-third to one-half when a wealth of other measures are included in the regressions. The most important of these other variables are about parental health and health during childhood. Smith concludes that there is tentative evidence for a long-term effect of early life conditions on late-life health.

I have difficulty interpreting these equations for the standard reason—it is hard to know what the education variable is proxying for. For example, education reflects permanent income, and the results would thus show us the importance of permanent income for health (related to Smith's explanation). Alternatively, however, education might be proxying for discount rates, patience, self-control, or other individual attributes that are also related to healthy behavior. In this case, SES by itself is not a factor influencing the onset of adverse health conditions. A third explanation is that better-educated people are more knowledgeable about factors influencing health and as a result take more care of themselves over their lifetime.

The additional measures that Smith includes in the equation do not really differentiate among these explanations. And in fairness, the HRS may not be the most appropriate survey to address these questions. One might want data from a younger age group to determine which type of people continue on with their education and how that is related to factors that subsequently influence health outcomes. I thus consider this part of the paper to be interesting, but not as definitive as the first part.

Overall, however, Smith's article is a wonderful and intriguing look at an extremely important economic issue. Understanding the link between SES and health is vitally important. Jim Smith's paper shows us a first pathway about why the two are linked.

8

Healthy, Wealthy, and Knowing Where to Live
Trajectories of Health, Wealth, and Living Arrangements among the Oldest Old

Florian Heiss, Michael D. Hurd, and Axel Börsch-Supan

8.1 Introduction

Health, wealth, and where one lives are important, if not the three most important material living conditions. This paper investigates the joint evolution of these three conditions. The elderly reach their early postretirement years in an initial status that is characterized by housing wealth, nonhousing bequeathable wealth, annuity income, health status, and family connections. The broad goal of this paper is to describe the trajectories of health, wealth, and living arrangements in older age that start from this initial state; to understand how the trajectories of health status, wealth position, and living arrangements are interrelated with each other; and to be able to predict how health and living arrangements will evolve when economic and other conditions change.

Projecting the trajectories of health, wealth, and living arrangements into the future is not a trivial task. Simple cross-sectional statistics may lead one astray. For instance, we find in cross-section data an increasing propensity for elderly individuals to live with others, especially their children (Börsch-Supan 1988, 1990; Ellwood and Kane 1990; Wolf 1995). But the living arrangements of the oldest may not be a good prediction of the

Florian Heiss is a research associate of the Mannheim Research Institute for the Economics of Aging. Michael D. Hurd is a senior economist at RAND, director of the RAND Center for the Study of Aging, and a research associate of the National Bureau of Economic Research (NBER). Axel Börsch-Supan is a professor of economics at the University of Mannheim, director of the Mannheim Research Institute for the Economics of Aging, and a research associate of the NBER.

We thank Steve Venti for helpful comments. Financial support was provided by the National Institute on Aging (NIA) grant number R01 AG16772, through the NBER. We are also grateful for financial support by the State of Baden-Württemberg and the German Insurers Association (GDV).

241

living arrangement of those just entering their postretirement years. Because of differences in the economic resources of the cohorts, the younger cohorts are likely to reach the oldest ages with more resources, and, assuming that living alone is a superior good, they will have a greater propensity to live alone (Börsch-Supan, Kotlikoff, and Morris 1991; McGarry and Schoeni 1998). Furthermore, the observed age profiles of living arrangements are not followed by any person or couple: because the poorest in a cohort die sooner than the better off, the average value of wealth, health, or housing of a cohort will increase with age even in the absence of any systematic change at the individual or household level.

Yet understanding the age path and determinants of living arrangements is important both from a social point of view and from a scientific point of view. For example, as shown in table 8.1, living with other family members is a substantial economic resource that is frequently ignored in assessing the economic well-being of the oldest old (Cox and Raines 1985; Kotlikoff and Morris 1989; Sloan and Shayne 1993; Grad 1994). This is evidenced, for example, by a much lower poverty rate of elderly widows living with other family members as compared to the poverty rate of widows in the general population.

The frail elderly receive care when living with others, either with a spouse or with children, that can substitute for market-purchased care or for long-term care provided thought public programs such as Medicaid (Wolf 1984, 1994; McGarry and Schoeni 1998). There is even some suggestion that living arrangements affect the health of the elderly person: apparently being cared for in the home of a family member is better for health outcomes than institutionally provided long-term care (Moon 1983; Horowitz 1985; Stone, Cafferata, and Sangl 1987).

From a scientific point of view, the main model of consumption and saving by the elderly, the life-cycle model, is incomplete if it does not recognize the additional resources that may be transferred through joint living (Hurd 1990). For example, it is plausible that the magnitude of such transfers is greater than measured cash transfers to an independently living parent. There are many other examples of close relationships among living arrangements, health, and economic status. For instance, an unexpected

Table 8.1   Poverty and living arrangements: Poverty rates (%)

		Nonmarried women	
Age range	Couples	Live with other family members	Live with no family members
65–74	6	12	24
75–84	7	12	28
85 or over	10	10	31

Source: Grad, 1994.

decline in wealth may trigger a transition to joint living to conserve resources. A decline in health may cause a transition to joint living or into a nursing home for the provision of care. The probability of either transition would be modified by other important covariates. In the first case, health status could act through differences in life expectancy or need for care. In the second case, economic status would be important because of the possibility of purchasing care in the market. In both cases the number and location of children would be important as well as their sex and economic status. For example, a well-to-do son may prefer to transfer cash for the market purchase of services, whereas a daughter may prefer to provide the services directly.

These examples suggest that living arrangements and well-being derived from health and economic status are closely related and that their evolution over the life course should be studied jointly. This is the aim of this paper. We study the relationships among living arrangements, health, and economic status using a microeconometric approach similar to what is known as vector autoregressions (VARs) in the macroeconomics literature.

The economic determinants of living arrangements have had relatively little research attention compared with other aspects of the well-being of the oldest old. For example, the early analyses of the Study of Asset and Health Dynamics of the Oldest Old (AHEAD) did not explicitly consider the choice of living arrangements (Henretta et al. 1997; Wolf, Freedman, and Soldo 1997), although the importance of family care for elderly parents was stressed in both articles.[1] Because research on the economic determinants of living arrangements is not well developed, we are not adequately equipped to understand the decline in the propensity to coreside with children that began in the late 1970s and early 1980s (Börsch-Supan 1990; Ellwood and Kane 1990; Kotlikoff and Morris 1990; Wolf 1995; Costa 1997). It is important to understand how this decrease came about and whether it is related to changes in the economic circumstances of the elderly. Specifically, we would like to understand whether the decrease is related to a change in family linkages or to the increase in Social Security wealth and Medicare benefits, as suggested by Wolf (1995), Costa (1997), and McGarry and Schoeni (1998). This understanding would help to assess the likely impact of future changes in the generosity of Social Security and Medicare benefits, as well as the potential impact of changes in the extent of family links when the members of the baby boom generation will need to support their elderly parents.

We also lack reliable knowledge of some fundamental facts. For example, it is controversial whether the elderly downsize housing in old age and extract equity for nonhousing consumption (Ai et al. 1990; Venti and Wise 1990, 2001; Sheiner and Weil 1992). We do not know the quantitative

---

1. Wolf (1994) provides an extensive survey of the literature.

importance of the progression of care from living independently to coresiding with children to living in a nursing home. We do not know whether coresiding with children changes bequest behavior. The AHEAD data on which this paper is based are well suited to start answering these questions.

Because many fundamental facts are still unclear, our research will proceed in steps. In this paper, we will begin with establishing a reliable account of how living arrangements, health, and economic status evolve as the elderly age and proceed by linking these trajectories to observable covariates. In this sense, this paper is mainly descriptive, although it does use multidimensional regression methods. It extends the analysis by Hurd, McFadden, and Merrill (1998) by a third dimension—namely, living arrangements—and applies a richer methodology. Further research will take account of the considerable heterogeneity in our sample. Accounting for the heterogeneity in order to properly isolate the effects of economic and other covariates will require more advanced econometric methods (e.g., the MPMNP model in Börsch-Supan et al. 1992 and the MIMIC model in Börsch-Supan, McFadden, and Schnabel 1996). Once we have precise estimates of the influence that these covariates exert on living arrangements, health, and economic status, we can compare our estimated coefficients and predicted trajectories to those generated by leading behavioral models. This will be the subject of further research.

The paper is structured as follows. Section 8.2 describes the AHEAD data and presents some central descriptive statistics. Section 8.3 develops our methodology to estimate transition probabilities based on relatively simple first-order Markov processes. Section 8.4 describes our estimation results. Section 8.5 constructs and interprets predicted trajectories of health, wealth, and living arrangements that start at age seventy and go through age ninety. Section 8.6 focuses on a specific aspect of these trajectories, the reduction in home ownership. Section 8.7 briefly concludes.

8.2   Data

Our work is based on the first four waves of AHEAD. This study is particularly well suited for the purposes of this paper because one module was specifically designed to study living arrangements, intergenerational transfers of both money and time help, and how they relate to health and economic status.

The AHEAD survey is a biennial panel that is being collected by the Survey Research Center at the University of Michigan. It is now a part of the U.S. Health and Retirement Survey (HRS). The AHEAD study is nationally representative of the cohorts born in 1923 or earlier with oversampling of blacks, Hispanics, and Floridians. We will focus on age-eligible individuals: that is, those persons from the cohorts of 1923 or earlier who were approximately aged seventy or older at baseline in 1993.

The AHEAD panel is the first data set that permits combining the study of asset decumulation and health with the study of living arrangements of the oldest old. In fact, AHEAD was specifically designed to enable a comprehensive understanding of how health and wealth status affect the well-being of the elderly as they age (Soldo et al. 1997). For instance, the AHEAD survey has much more reliable measures of the wealth of the elderly than the data sets employed in previous analyses, plus more extensive health information, and the AHEAD data identify in a better way family links, in particular the economic resources of the children who, at some point in the future, may coreside with the elderly person.

While the AHEAD data start with a sample of the noninstitutionalized, the panel tracks the elderly when they enter a nursing home or similar institutions. We can observe asset changes at the time of this transition. The AHEAD data supply information on changes in the economic status of children and parents, together with changes in health and changes in housing and living arrangements. The AHEAD data contain a proxy interview after the death of the respondent such that the living arrangement at the time of death can be ascertained.

The AHEAD survey as well as the other cohorts in the HRS have cores with questions in the following broad classes: employment (current and former jobs); health measures, including self-assessed health, performance measures, disease conditions, cognition, mood, and activity of daily living (ADL) and instrumental activity of daily living (IADL) limitations; income and assets; family structure and intergenerational transfers, of both financial help and time help; housing; insurance; and pensions.

In addition to the core content, the survey obtained a roster of the extended family including a number of characteristics of each child of the AHEAD respondent. Of importance for this paper, the characteristics include education, income, home ownership, marital status, and parental status. Children from the family roster were linked during the computer-assisted interview to both financial help and time help given to the AHEAD respondent. This linkage will permit analyses of motivations for transfers such as whether the less well-to-do child receives greater financial transfers from the AHEAD parent and if, in turn, that child provides greater time help. Information about the beneficiaries of life insurance and of wills was obtained. Anticipated bequests were measured by questions about the subjective probability of giving a bequest and its magnitude. Considerable information about housing was obtained at baseline including adaptations of housing to disabilities. This is important since such adaptations offer an alternative to moving when health deteriorates.

The AHEAD survey contains a psychometric battery with questions asking for subjective beliefs such as "Using any number from 0 to 100, where 0 means that you think there is absolutely no chance and 100 means that you think the event is absolutely sure to happen, what do you think are the chances that you will have to give major financial help to family members during the next ten years? . . . that you will receive major financial help from family members during the next ten years? . . . that you will move to a nursing home over the next five years?" In a similar way, subjects who were seventy to seventy-four years old at baseline were asked to give their subjective survival probability to age eighty-five; subjects who were seventy-five to seventy-nine were asked their survival probability to age ninety, and so forth. These subjective survival probabilities are highly predictive of mortality between waves 1 and 2 (Hurd and McFadden 1998).

As in all household-level data sets, the frequency of missing asset items is fairly large in AHEAD. However, AHEAD (as well as HRS) made extensive use of bracketing techniques that converted nonresponses on asset amounts to intervals by a series of questions about the range of the asset amount (Smith 1997). Because the distribution of financial assets in particular is highly skewed, these techniques are very valuable in reducing imputation error. We have spent considerable effort developing and implementing methods to impute missing asset items based on the brackets (Hoynes, Hurd, and Chand 1997). The methods involve using bracket information and covariates in a way that conserves the multivariate distribution of assets and other characteristics. The construction of wealth quartiles in this paper rests on this method.

In the first AHEAD wave in 1993, 8,222 interviews were obtained. We restrict our analysis to those individual who were born before 1924, ignoring 779 younger spouses. In waves 2 (1995) through 4 (1999), no interview could be obtained for 865 of the remaining respondents, leaving 6,578 for our analysis. By wave 4, 2,508 (38 percent) of those respondents have died. In total, 21,296 interviews (on average, 3.2 interviews per respondent) and 14,718 transitions (2.2 per respondent) are available for the analysis.

Table 8.2 shows descriptive statistics of the most important variables for our study. The average age is eighty years, and between two waves 14.6 percent of the respondents die on average. Sixty-two percent of the respondents are female, reflecting the higher life expectancy. Forty-six percent of the respondents are married—85 percent of the others are widowed, the others are either divorced or never married. Seventy-two percent of the interviewees own their home. Seventy-five percent live on their own, and 19 percent coreside with others—mostly with their children and/or grandchildren. Since in wave 1 only noninstitutionalized individuals were interviewed, only respondents who move to nursing homes after that are followed there. This results in only 4.3 percent of interviews in nursing homes. The average respondent has 2.8 children, 1.4 of whom are female. On average, 1.9 of these children are married and 2.3 are single.

Figure 8.1 shows age paths of the most important variables of our analysis. They represent simple averages of these variables for the respondents

Table 8.2   **Variables**

Variable	Mean
Age	80.29
Mortality	0.146
Female	0.619
Married	0.461
Health condition prevalence (heart, stroke, cancer)	0.506
Health condition incidence	0.177
Health status	
Excellent/Very good	0.306
Good	0.303
Fair/Poor	0.391
Home ownership	0.721
Living arrangement	
Alone	0.765
With others	0.192
Nursing home	0.043
No. of children	
Total	2.780
Female	1.416
Married	1.942
With children	2.345

Source: AHEAD, pooled waves 1–4.

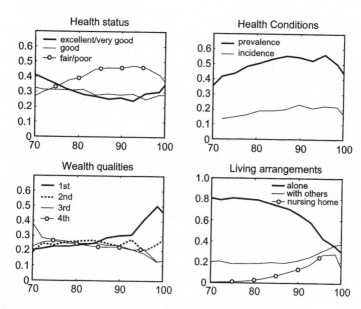

Fig. 8.1   Age patterns in the four pooled cross sections 1993–99
Source: Pooled AHEAD waves 1–4.

of the respective age in a pooled cross section of the AHEAD data, waves 1 through 4. Three effects drive the shape of these curves. The first is cohort differences. The second effect is the evolution of the variables over the life course: older respondents report a worse health status and face a larger threat of health condition incidents. The third effect is differential mortality. It affects the mean characteristics of the (surviving) respondents. This third effect seems to dominate the health measures for the very old: health status and health condition prevalence are actually more favorable for the (very few) centenarians than for those aged around ninety. The share of the respondents in the highest wealth quartiles gradually decreases in the age, whereas the rises of the share of the poorest quartile seems to be more pronounced for those aged eighty-five and above. This is the same age group for which the share of respondents living alone decreases dramatically and both nursing homes and coresidence become important alternatives.

8.3   Estimation of the Transition Probabilities

Health, wealth, housing, and living arrangements are multidimensional concepts. We analyze the joint evolution of the most important dimensions of health, wealth, and living arrangements of elderly Americans. These dimensions are our state variables and comprise the following characteristics:

- Mortality
- Self-reported health status
- Prevalence and incidences of three major health conditions (heart condition, stroke, cancer)
- Wealth quartile (sum of real and financial wealth)
- Owner-occupancy
- Living arrangements (coresidence and nursing homes)

Table 8.3 gives an overview of these state variables and their possible states.

The joint evolution of the state variables is presumably quite complex. We chose a simple strategy to identify basic patterns. We do not aim at pre-

Table 8.3   State variables

Variable	State 1	State 2	State 3	State 4
Mortality	Alive	Dead		
Health condition prevalence	Yes	No		
Health condition incidence	Yes	No		
Health status	Excellent/Very good	Good	Fair/Poor	
Wealth quartile	1st	2nd	3rd	4th
Ownership	Yes	No		
Living arrangement	Alone	With others	Nursing home	

senting a structural model and attach causal interpretations to our findings. Instead, we interpret our approach as a more sophisticated approach to present descriptive evidence. The model can be interpreted like a VAR common in macroeconometrics:

$$\text{(1)} \qquad \mathbf{y}_t = A\mathbf{y}_{t-1} + B\mathbf{x}_t,$$

where $\mathbf{y}$ is a vector of the state or left-hand-side variables detailed in table 8.3 and x represents a set of shift variables. We actually do not estimate a linear relation since most variables in $\mathbf{y}$ are limited dependent in their nature, but it helps to keep the macroeconomic counterpart in mind since our approach shares the same fundamental properties and limitations.

More precisely, a given individual (whose subscript is omitted to ease the notational burden) can assume (almost) each combination of states in table 8.3 at each point in time. Let a_t denote whether the individual is alive ($a_t = 1$) or not ($a_t = 0$) at time t. Let $\mathbf{y}_{1t}$ through $\mathbf{y}_{6t}$ indicate the states of the other variables from table 8.3 at time t. There are $2 \cdot 2 \cdot 3 \cdot 4 \cdot 2 \cdot 3 = 288$ combinations of these other states. Let $\mathbf{y}_t$ denote an indicator of the state defined as a combination of these six variables. Finally, call $\mathbf{x}_t$ a vector of exogenous variables such as age and sex. We are interested in understanding the evolution of the states over time—that is, the probability of the event $a_t = a^*$ and $y_t = y^*$ given the history of y_t and the explanatory variables $\mathbf{x}_t$. We denote this probability by $\Pr(a_t = a^*, \mathbf{y}_t = \mathbf{y}^* \mid \mathbf{y}_{t-1}, \mathbf{y}_{t-2}, \dots, \mathbf{x}_t)$. It is the core explanatory variable.

In this general formulation, it is infeasible to econometrically identify this probability. We therefore have to impose restrictions. As a first step, we impose a first-order Markov structure on our model:

$$\text{(2)} \quad \Pr(a_t = a^*, \mathbf{y}_t = \mathbf{y}^* \mid \mathbf{y}_{t-1}, \mathbf{y}_{t-2}, \dots, \mathbf{x}_t) = \Pr(a_t = a^*, \mathbf{y}_t = \mathbf{y}^* \mid \mathbf{y}_{t-1}, \mathbf{x}_t)$$

This is quite restrictive and could be generalized somewhat. But since we only have four waves of panel data, the dynamic structure that we can identify with these data is quite limited. A test of a more general structure such as a second-order Markov model is planned in the future.

Secondly, the estimation of a 288×288 transition matrix is infeasible with our data (and any other real-world data we can think of). We therefore impose structure on the joint dependencies. We choose a very simple approach by assuming that the outcome probabilities of the state variables are conditionally (on $\mathbf{y}_{t-1}$ and $\mathbf{x}_t$) independent. This allows us to write

$$\text{(3)} \quad \Pr(a_t = a^*, \mathbf{y}_t = \mathbf{y}^* \mid \mathbf{y}_{t-1}, \mathbf{x}_t)$$

$$= \Pr(a_t = a^* \mid \mathbf{y}_{t-1}, \mathbf{x}_t) \cdot \Pr(\mathbf{y}_{1t} = \mathbf{y}_1^* \mid \mathbf{y}_{t-1}, \mathbf{x}_t, a_t = a^*)$$

$$\cdot \Pr(\mathbf{y}_{2t} = \mathbf{y}_2^* \mid \mathbf{y}_{t-1}, \mathbf{x}_t, a_t = a^*) \cdot \dots \cdot \Pr(\mathbf{y}_{6t} = \mathbf{y}_6^* \mid \mathbf{y}_{t-1}, \mathbf{x}_t, a_t = a^*)$$

An alternative feasible approach would be to model correlations between the different state equations with the help of random effects models similar to Börsch-Supan and others (1992). However, this would increase the computational burden substantially since no closed-form solutions for the likelihood function can be derived for these nonlinear simultaneous models.

In addition, we exploit several "natural" restrictions:

- Death is absorbing.
- Health conditions are absorbing: there is no transition from (health conditions = yes) to (health conditions = no).
- Health conditions are preceded by health incidents: if (health conditions$_{t-1}$ = no), then Prob(health conditions$_t$ = yes) = Prob(health incident$_t$ = yes).

Given this structure, the models for the different state variables can be estimated separately. Again, we choose a very convenient approach by assuming conditional independence over time, ignoring the panel structure of our data. This simplifies the analysis even more. In particular, we can simply estimate our models conditional on the first observation for each individual. We specify the separate models as binary logits (health condition incidence, home ownership), ordered logits (health status, wealth quartile), and multinomial logits (living arrangements). Obviously, not a full set of 287 dummy variables for $\mathbf{y}_{t-1}$ is included in the regressions, but simplifications are made. They are described in the following section, which presents our estimation results.

8.4   Estimation Results

Given the independent first-order Markov structure, we can estimate transition probabilities for the categorical variables in table 8.3 conditional on lagged left-hand-side and socioeconomic variables. The results from these regressions are shown in table 8.4. Except for the health incidence equation, all equations feature a satisfactory fit, and the signs of the estimated coefficients—where significant—exhibit no surprises.

The first column shows ordered logit estimates for a combined health status/mortality regression. The dependent variable is coded as (1) excellent/very good health, (2) good health, (3) poor/fair health, (4) deceased. Not surprisingly, health deteriorates with increasing age. This effect accelerates in old age, as the additional slope parameters of the age spline are positive. Being female and being married increases self-reported health. The prevalence of serious health conditions (heart condition, stroke, cancer) negatively affects the self-reported health status. A health condition incident since the previous wave dramatically increases mortality probabilities and decreases the self-reported health status. Health status is

Table 8.4   Regression results

	Health/Mortality (ordered logit)	Health condition incidence (logit)	Wealth (ordered logit)	Ownership (logit)	Live with others (multinomial logit)	Nursing Home (multinomial logit)
Female	-0.192***	-0.245***	-0.023	-0.110	0.093	0.138
	(5.79)	(5.71)	(0.61)	(1.39)	(1.19)	(1.39)
Married	-0.138***	-0.124**	-0.054	0.811***	-0.612***	-0.642***
	(3.26)	(2.22)	(1.34)	(9.57)	(7.18)	(5.67)
Spouse died	-0.021	-0.040	1.814***	-1.074***	1.234***	1.168***
	(0.30)	(0.43)	(21.46)	(7.69)	(8.64)	(6.82)
Age	0.036**	0.034	0.027	-0.001	-0.093**	-0.059
	(2.12)	(1.39)	(1.45)	(0.03)	(2.48)	(0.82)
Age spline > 75	-0.012	0.001	-0.031	-0.105	0.160***	0.220**
	(0.49)	(0.02)	(1.13)	(1.70)	(2.84)	(2.20)
Age spline > 80	0.046**	0.018	-0.001	0.071	-0.060	0.021
	(2.07)	(0.63)	(0.04)	(1.40)	(1.20)	(0.32)
Age spline > 85	0.028	-0.019	0.025	0.039	0.057	-0.078
	(1.02)	(0.58)	(0.77)	(0.63)	(0.92)	(1.29)
Age spline > 90	0.046	-0.002	-0.053	-0.068	0.033	0.047
	(1.36)	(0.05)	(1.26)	(0.88)	(0.44)	(0.72)
Health condition prevalence	0.277***	0.381***	0.010	0.043	-0.182***	-0.043
	(9.65)	(10.38)	(0.32)	(0.64)	(2.74)	(0.55)
Health condition incidence	1.243***		-0.020	-0.388***	0.177**	0.844***
	(33.38)		(0.44)	(4.49)	(2.05)	(9.34)
Health good	1.177***	0.272***	-0.187***	-0.012	-0.055	0.176
	(30.17)	(5.04)	(4.52)	(0.14)	(0.63)	(1.53)
Health poor/fair	2.438***	0.815***	-0.411***	-0.230***	0.330***	0.690***
	(52.91)	(14.56)	(9.53)	(2.61)	(3.84)	(6.42)
Wealth Q2	-0.255***	-0.203***	1.930***	0.518***	-0.018	-0.111
	(5.10)	(3.17)	(34.72)	(5.17)	(0.18)	(0.95)

(continued)

Table 8.4 (continued)

	Health/Mortality (ordered logit)	Health condition incidence (logit)	Wealth (ordered logit)	Ownership (logit)	Live with others (multinomial logit)	Nursing Home (multinomial logit)
Wealth Q3	-0.440***	-0.157**	3.420***	0.624***	0.015	-0.123
	(8.37)	(2.32)	(55.38)	(5.98)	(0.15)	(0.98)
Wealth Q4	-0.565***	-0.229***	5.506***	0.802***	-0.183	-0.255
	(10.31)	(3.22)	(77.63)	(7.33)	(1.62)	(1.91)
Homeowner	-0.010	-0.034	0.560***	4.850***	-0.070	-0.574***
	(0.25)	(0.66)	(11.79)	(58.98)	(0.79)	(5.71)
Live with others	-0.081	-0.123	-0.117***	0.109	4.464***	1.883***
	(0.57)	(0.66)	(2.67)	(1.22)	(60.95)	(16.11)
Nursing home	-1.237***	-1.266***	-0.921***	0.021	1.541***	4.348***
	(3.31)	(2.89)	(5.96)	(0.08)	(4.20)	(20.95)
No. of children					0.274***	-0.047
					(6.00)	(0.61)
No. of female children					0.067	-0.026
					(1.82)	(0.50)
No. of married children					-0.205***	0.037
					(5.52)	(0.66)
No. of children with children					-0.095**	-0.022
					(2.04)	(0.28)
Constant		-4.201**		-2.336	3.703	0.593
		(2.29)		(0.74)	(1.34)	(0.11)
Log-likelihood	-18,998.25	-8,559.63	-14,310.42	-3,315.79	-5,618.71	
Rho²	0.16	0.04	0.29	0.62	0.45	

Note: Absolute value of z-statistics in parentheses.

***Significant at the 1 percent level.

**Significant at the 5 percent level.

persistent over time in the sense that the reported health status in the previous wave is a strong predictor of mortality and current health status. In this health regression, we do not use lagged living arrangements directly. The reason for this is that living arrangements are driven by expectations of future health, leading to a serious endogeneity problem in this regression. Instead, we instrument living arrangements in this regression with detailed characteristics of children.

Many of the results of the health condition incidence regression are similar to the health status/mortality regression. The age coefficients are not individually significant, but a Wald test shows high joint significance ($W = 83.59^{a} \sim \chi^2_{[5]}$). Being in the lowest wealth quartile increases the probability of suffering from a major health incident, but there is no significant difference between the three highest quartiles.

Respondents reporting a positive health status are more likely to be wealthier in the next interview, but the health conditions we included in our measure have no effect on wealth. Marital status is an important determinant of home ownership. Events like the death of the spouse and a major health incident lead to a high number of people selling their home. But variables like self-reported health status and wealth quartile also have important effects. The age spline has a significantly negative slope only for the respondents aged seventy-five to eighty years. For the others, factors like decreasing health seem to drive the further decrease of home ownership.

The results of the living arrangement regression show that living with others and living in nursing homes are in fact substitutes in the sense that the explanatory variables do have similar effects on the probabilities to choose one of these alternatives. Married couples tend to live alone until one spouse dies. The surviving spouse is very likely to move either into a child's home or into a nursing home shortly afterward. Health condition incidents also lead respondents to move in with somebody and—even more so—to move into a nursing home. Similarly, poor or fair health status leads to changes in this direction. Since most cohabitants are own children, their characteristics obviously play an important role in explaining cohabitation. Female children are more likely to live with their parents, whereas married children and those who have children themselves are less likely to do so.

8.5 Simulating Trajectories

According to equation (3), we can rebuild a full 289×289 transition matrix of survival and the six other state variables $\mathbf{y}_t$ for a given set of shift variables $\mathbf{x}_t$. Starting from a suitably chosen initial state, we are thus able to simulate predicted trajectories for our left-hand-side variables.

More specifically, we start these trajectories at age seventy and follow an elderly person through age ninety. A particularly interesting date of observation is age eighty, approximately the conditional life expectancy given survival to age seventy. In the simulations, the estimated transition matrices are interpreted as being valid for two-year transitions in accordance to the biannual nature of the AHEAD data. This is important when interpreting the age variable.

The simulations are done in four steps:

1. Start at initial probabilities (typically 1 for one state, 0 for the others) and a set of shift variables **x** for $t = 0$.
2. Calculate the 289 × 289 transition matrix as described above.
3. Predict probabilities for $t = 1$.
4. Repeat steps 2–3 until age ninety is reached.

We will perform several exercises. First, we predict whole system for different initial conditions, taking account of all (implicit) interactions. Second, in subsections 8.5.1 through 8.5.3, we look at various dimensions separately (like wealthy vs. poor, healthy vs. sick, etc.). For instance, how does survival, how do living arrangements, change with initial health, with initial wealth? Third, in subsection 8.5.4, we decompose the observed effects by leaving some of the left-hand-side variables at their starting values. This amounts to setting some off-diagonal elements in the transition matrix to zero and therefore annihilates interaction effects. Note that we painfully avoid any notion of causality—these exercises should be interpreted as simulations of persons under different circumstances and initial conditions. Finally, in subsection 8.5.5, we simulate shocks such as the onset of a health condition and look at the resulting response pattern. This last exercise is well known in the macroeconomics literature as "response analysis."

To warm up to our methodology, we start with figure 8.2, which shows the trajectories of two very different people. The top figure shows a poor single person in bad health, while the bottom figure depicts a rich married person in good health. Good health is defined by a self-reported health status of excellent or very good, bad health by a self-reported health status of poor or fair. The rich person is in the highest wealth quartile, while the poor person is in the lowest one. All other characteristics are identical. Both persons are male, have no children, have no previous health conditions, and live independently in an owner-occupied home.

The figure presents the evolution of our seven state variables, each represented by a line that starts at an initial probability and then moves from that initial probability as the two people age. The first five state variables start at identical initial values for both persons. The solid line depicts the survival probability, starting with 1 and declining with age. The small-dotted line shows the probability of a health condition, starting with zero and increasing with age. The line with triangles is the probability of home ownership. It starts at 1 and declines with age. The line with circles repre-

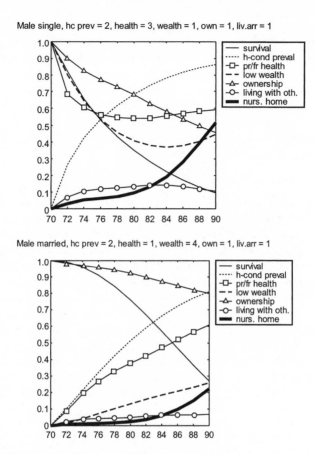

Fig. 8.2   **Trajectories of two very different people**

sents the probability of living with others, the thickest solid line living in a nursing home. Both start at zero and increase with age. Finally, two state variables start at different values, namely wealth, represented by a large-dotted line, and self-reported health, depicted by a line with squares.

Quite clearly, survival at age eighty is much higher (about 40 percent) for the healthy, rich, and married person. The probability of ending up in poverty is, as expected, also much lower. Note that the trajectories eventually converge. In the long run, we are all dead. Mathematically speaking, the outcome of the Markov process will eventually be independent of the initial state and converge on a state solely defined by the transition matrix. For a given age, this matrix depends on "shift" variables such as sex, the number of children, and so on—that is, the $\mathbf{x}_t$ in equation (2).

It is worthwhile to look at various details in figure 8.2 to understand which mechanisms are picked up by our estimated transition probabilities.

For instance, it is noticeable that the probability of reaching the lowest quartile in the wealth distribution increases again for the poorer person past age eighty-four, which probably reflects nursing home costs—the poorer single person of worse health has a much higher likelihood of living in a nursing home than the richer married person of good health.

We now analyze the state variables separately and investigate their interaction with other state variables. Subsection 8.5.1 looks at survival and health, subsection 8.5.2 at wealth and home ownership, and subsection 8.5.3 at living arrangements of the elderly.

8.5.1   Survival and Health

We begin with survival and relate it to initial wealth and initial health. Figure 8.3 shows the probability of survival as a function of two initial health characteristics, self-reported health ("would you rate your health as fair/poor vs. excellent/very good") and the existence of at least one previous serious health condition ("has a doctor ever told you . . ."), where serious conditions include heart problems, stroke, and cancer. The survival curves remain essentially parallel whether such a condition exists or not, while the effect of the self-rated health assessment is strong, maybe measuring other conditions, such as arthritis or diabetes, that are making life difficult without being immediately life threatening.

Figure 8.4 shows survival stratified by initial wealth. Survival at age eighty, given survival until age seventy, is about 15 percent higher in the highest wealth quartile as compared to the lowest wealth quartile. The bot-

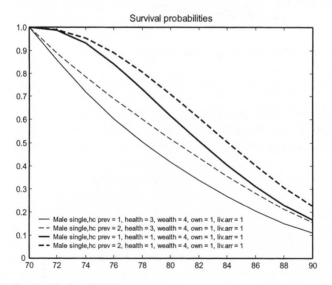

Fig. 8.3   Survival by health status

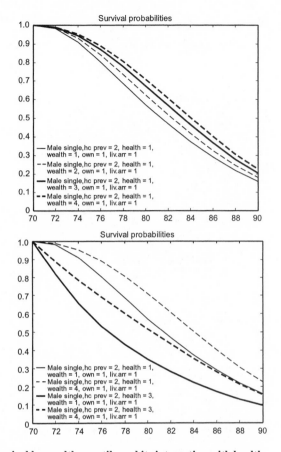

Fig. 8.4   Survival by wealth quartile and its interaction with health

tom part of the figure shows the interaction of wealth and health in determining survival, and the relative magnitudes of the effects: survival, while clearly dependent on initial wealth, is influenced much more strongly by initial health.

Similar to survival, health is quite clearly influenced by initial economic status. Figure 8.5 shows the evolution of two dimensions of health over time, each stratified by whether the person is initially in the lowest or the highest wealth quartile. The top part of the figure depicts self-reported health, the bottom part the prevalence of a serious health condition. Being wealthy decreases the likelihood of feeling in bad health by about 12 percentage points at age seventy-five relative to being in the lowest wealth quartile. This wealth effect is much smaller for an actual occurrence of a serious health condition.

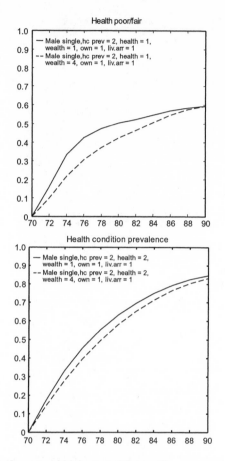

Fig. 8.5   Health by lowest and highest wealth quartile

8.5.2   Wealth and Home Ownership

We now turn to wealth and home ownership, starting with the latter. Home ownership declines slowly but steadily as people age (see figure 8.6). The decline in home ownership follows from the tendency of the system to converge. Hence, its speed is the interesting observation, since this relates to our regression estimates of section 8.4. Quite clearly, home ownership declines much less for married elderly people than for single ones. It also declines faster for the poor (more precisely, those with total wealth in the lowest quartile) than for the rich (highest wealth quartile). We will investigate this decline more closely in section 8.6.

The tendency of the system to converge is also clearly visible in figure 8.7, which depicts the evolution of wealth. The top part of this figure shows a poor person (lowest wealth quartile) and the probability of staying in this

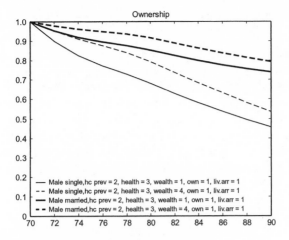

Fig. 8.6 Home ownership by wealth and marital status

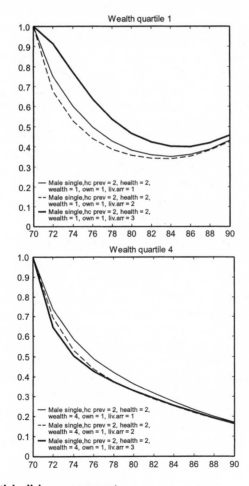

Fig. 8.7 Wealth by living arrangement

quartile. This probability declines, but increases again, most likely due to nursing home costs. Figure 8.7 stratifies this decline by initial living arrangement. Staying in the poor quartile is most likely when an elderly person lives in a nursing home, and least likely when this person lives with others.[2] The bottom part of figure 8.7 shows the reversed patterns as it looks at the probability of staying in the highest wealth quartile. For the initially wealthy, living with others decreases the expected future wealth relative to living alone. This is consistent with the notion that cohabitation implies intrafamily transfers to the needy.

8.5.3   Living Arrangements

We now turn to the main topic of this paper—namely, living arrangements. We distinguish three living arrangements: living alone (or as a couple), living with others (mainly with adult children), and living in a nursing home. Figure 8.8 depicts the probability of the first two living arrangements and shows the effect of additional children, in this case three daughters. Figure 8.9 adds the probability of living in a nursing home. The figures compare a single male, who has no previous health conditions, who rates his health as fair or poor, who is in the lowest wealth quartile, and who has one son with a similar male who has, in addition, three daughters.

Having daughters substantially decreases the probability of being alone at age eighty (by about 20 percent) and living in a nursing home (by about 10 percent) in favor of living with others—that is, being taken in by one of the daughters (by almost 30 percent). Interesting is the gender-specific effect of additional children. As shown in many other papers, daughters reduce the likelihood of living in a nursing home substantially more than sons (see figure 8.9).

8.5.4   Decomposing the Effects: Keep Some Dimensions Fixed

The next experiment separates direct and indirect effects. In the previous simulations, all left-hand-side variables in equation (1) were predicted using the full transition matrix. Now we hold certain dimensions constant. As an example, we show the evolution of the survival probabilities (figure 8.10) and the probability of being in the highest wealth quartile (figure 8.11). The figures show how the interaction effects in the full model dampen the effects that would be predicted without the interactions.

We begin with the survival probabilities in figure 8.10. The solid line shows the trajectory using the full model with all interactions. In all other lines, the occurrence of a serious health condition is fixed at "no occurrence." This shifts, as expected, the survival probabilities up (light-dotted line). If we also assume that self-reported health stays fixed at "excellent or

---

2. Remember that this finding should not be interpreted in a causal fashion: we only know that the two processes (wealth decumulation and where to live) are correlated, not which process causes which other process to change.

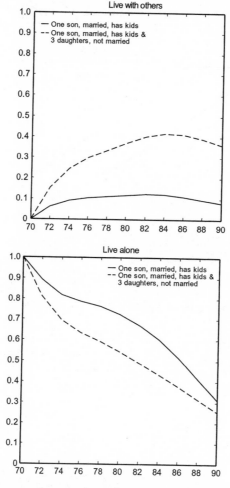

Fig. 8.8 **Probability of living alone or with another person in the community**

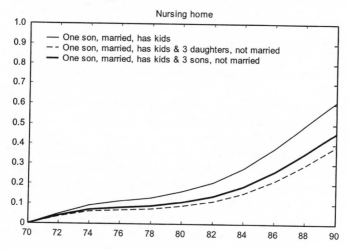

Fig. 8.9 **Probability of living in a nursing home**

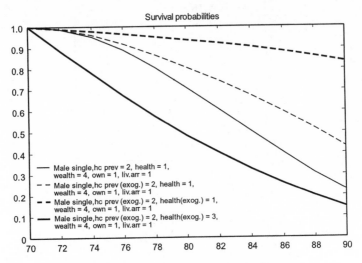

Fig. 8.10   Decomposing survival probabilities by health effects

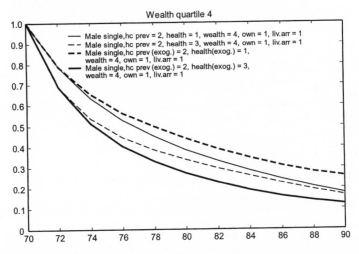

Fig. 8.11   Decomposing the probability of being wealthy

very good," survival rates stay very high and decline only slowly (dark-dotted line). Fixing self-reported health at a "poor or fair" level, of course, creates the opposite effect (thick solid line).

Figure 8.11 performs a similar exercise with the probability of being in the highest wealth quartile. The solid and the light-dotted lines show initial trajectories using the full model with all interactions. The solid line starts with a healthy individual (self-rated health "excellent or very good"), the light-dotted one with an unhealthy elderly individual (self-rated health "poor or fair"). Note that the two lines eventually merge—there is no long-run effect of health on wealth, although at age seventy-five the probability of being in the highest wealth quartile is substantially higher for the initially healthy individual.

If we now keep the initial health status fixed (thick-dotted and thick solid lines), the trajectories stay apart. The probability of staying in the highest wealth quartile is about 15 percent higher for the elderly individual, who stays healthy through age ninety.

8.5.5 Dose and Response Analysis

Finally, we look at the behavior of the multidimensional system in response to shocks. Figure 8.12 depicts the survival probability after a health shock ("doctor told person about one of the following three conditions: heart problem, onset of cancer, or stroke"). We compare this thick solid trajectory to the one generated by the full model (with all interactions, solid line) and to two variants in which the health condition is kept fixed, as we did in the previous subsection. We fix it at "no conditions" (light-dotted line) and at "some conditions exist at the age of seventy, but no further incidents occur" (thick-dotted line).

Figure 8.12 shows that the survival probabilities in the aftermath of a health shock follow pretty much the long run paths. There are no over-shooting or other complex dynamic effects. This is quite different for the self-reported health status; see figure 8.13. We apply the same shock but focus on self-reported health as outcome variable. The thick solid line depicts the typical "overshooting" after a shock vis-à-vis the trajectory where this condition has happened in the past. After a while, the health status perception variable returns approximately to the long-run path.

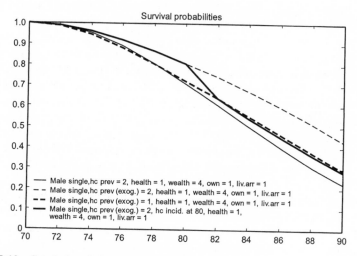

Survival probabilities

— Male single,hc prev = 2, health = 1, wealth = 4, own = 1, liv.arr = 1
- - Male single,hc prev (exog.) = 2, health = 1, wealth = 4, own = 1, liv.arr = 1
▪ ▪ Male single,hc prev (exog.) = 1, health = 1, wealth = 4, own = 1, liv.arr = 1
▬ Male single,hc prev (exog.) = 2, hc incid. at 80, health = 1,
    wealth = 4, own = 1, liv.arr = 1

Fig. 8.12   Survival probabilities in response to a health shock

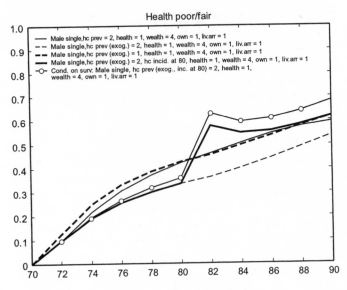

Fig. 8.13   Self-rated health in response to a health shock

Part of this effect, however, is a selection effect due to differential mortality. If we also keep the survival variable fixed at probability one (see the line with circles in figure 8.13), subjective health stays worse for a long time past the occurrence of the shock for those who actually survive.

8.6   Do the Elderly Downsize Housing?

In the preceding section, we found that home ownership decreases with age. We noted that the Markov process has the built-in property of convergence; hence, declining home ownership is, to some extent, an artifact built into the model. We did, however, detect some significant differences in the speed of decline depending on the initial characteristics of the elderly person. This suggests that there are elderly in our sample who systematically decumulate housing. This section looks closer at the issue of home ownership. We note that ownership is somewhat different from housing equity, which can be influenced by mortgage repayment, housing price changes, or neglect of maintenance. Venti and Wise (1990, 2001) found that in general the elderly to not reduce home equity except at the death of a spouse.

Table 8.5 shows cross-section housing and living arrangements by age bands. About 82 percent of those seventy to seventy-four years old were owners, and most of them lived "alone," either with a spouse only or singly. The table shows a slow but accelerating decline in ownership with age and a corresponding increase in renting, although until age eighty-five or over

Table 8.5   **Home ownership and living arrangements, percent distribution**

	70–74	75–79	80–84	85+
Own home	81.6	77.2	70.7	57.6
Alone	66.4	64.0	57.3	43.1
With others	14.7	12.1	11.5	9.0
Nursing home	0.5	1.1	1.9	5.5
Rent home	14.0	16.3	18.1	22.2
Alone	11.1	13.7	15.7	18.7
With others	2.9	2.6	2.4	3.5
Neither own nor rent	4.3	6.0	9.5	13.1
Not own, nursing home	0.2	0.6	1.8	7.0
All	100.0	100.0	100.0	100.0
N	4,099	7,157	5,427	4,535

Source: AHEAD pooled cross-sections (four waves).

Table 8.6   **Home ownership and living arrangements, percent distribution: Married**

	70–74	75–79	80–84	85+
Own home	90.4	88.6	85.5	77.1
Alone	76.7	77.8	75.3	67.1
With others	13.3	10.2	8.8	5.9
Nursing home	0.4	0.6	1.4	4.1
Rent home	7.7	8.6	10.0	14.0
Alone	6.5	7.2	9.2	13.2
With others	1.2	1.4	0.8	0.8
Neither own nor rent	1.9	2.5	4.2	5.8
Not own, nursing home	0.0	0.2	0.4	3.0
All	100.0	100.0	100.0	100.0
N	2,555	3,733	2,238	1,232

Source: AHEAD pooled cross-sections (four waves).

the increase is small. Most notable in the table is the increase in "other," which includes neither renting nor owning (mostly living with children in their house) and living in a nursing home, especially at age eighty-five or over.

Because of differential mortality we would expect a greater decline in owning in panel than we see in cross section, although cohort differences could obscure this decline.

Table 8.6 has cross-section housing and living arrangements for married persons. The patterns are similar to the patterns in table 8.5, but there is a much slower reduction in ownership with age. By age eighty-five or over the ownership rate is 13 percentage points lower than at seventy to seventy-four, whereas in table 8.5 it is 24 percentage points lower. In the oldest group about 7 percent live in a nursing home.

Table 8.7   Home ownership and living arrangements, percent distribution: Singles

	70–74	75–79	80–84	85+
Own home	66.8	64.7	60.1	50.3
Alone	49.2	48.9	44.5	34.1
With others	17.0	14.2	13.4	10.2
Nursing home	0.6	1.6	2.2	6.0
Rent home	24.6	24.5	23.8	25.3
Alone	18.8	20.7	20.3	20.8
With others	5.8	3.8	3.5	4.5
Neither own nor rent	8.2	9.8	13.3	15.9
Not own, nursing home	0.5	1.0	2.8	8.5
All	100.0	100.0	100.0	100.0
N	1,544	3,420	3,178	3,298

Source: AHEAD pooled cross-sections (four waves).

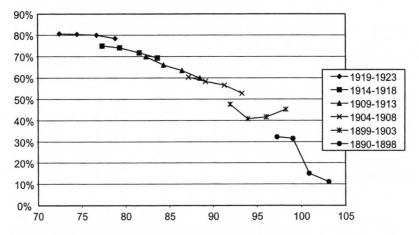

Fig. 8.14   Home ownership rates in six cohorts: Percentages
Source: AHEAD pooled cross sections (four waves).

Table 8.7 has similar results for singles. The levels of ownership are lower and decline at a greater rate with age. By age eighty-five or over 14.5 percent live in nursing homes and 15.9 percent neither own nor rent.

Figure 8.14 has the average ownership rates by cohort. For example, approximately 75 percent of the cohort of birth years 1919–23 owned a house in wave 1 of AHEAD (when the cohort was approximately seventy-seven), and the ownership rate of the cohort declined to 69 percent when the cohort was about eighty-four in 2000. The figure shows that cohort differences are relatively minor: holding age constant, cohort ownership rates are approximately the same.[3] The cohort comparisons include differential

3. But the sample sizes are small in some cases.

Table 8.8   **Home ownership transition rates: Survivors only (%)**

Marital transition	Age	Lagged ownership	Number	Ownership status	
				Own	Not own
Married to married	70–74	Own	2,013	98.3	1.7
		Not own	179	9.5	90.5
	75–79	Own	2,142	97.0	3.0
		Not own	259	11.2	88.8
	80–84	Own	1,068	94.4	5.6
		Not own	160	12.5	87.5
	85+	Own	419	93.8	6.2
		Not own	114	10.5	89.5
Single to single	70–74	Own	929	94.6	5.4
		Not own	449	8.9	91.1
	75–79	Own	1,568	91.8	8.2
		Not own	858	8.2	91.8
	80–84	Own	1,201	90.0	10.0
		Not own	762	4.2	95.8
	85+	Own	855	89.0	11.0
		Not own	817	5.4	94.6
Married to single	70–74	Own	146	93.2	6.8
		Not own	34	8.8	91.2
	75–79	Own	223	86.1	13.9
		Not own	55	12.7	87.3
	80–84	Own	155	85.2	14.8
		Not own	44	0.0	100.0
	85+	Own	86	79.1	20.9
		Not own	28	7.1	92.9

Source: AHEAD pooled cross-sections (four waves).

mortality, the tendency for renters to die sooner than owners. Differential mortality causes average ownership to increase even if there is no reduction in ownership in the panel.

Table 8.8 shows panel transitions among survivors. Among marrieds in the youngest age group, there were very low rates of transition out of ownership, and some transitions into ownership. But the predominant flow is out because of high rates of ownership. The transition rate out of ownership increases with age.

From the flows the steady-state rate of ownership (the ownership rate were the transition rates into and out of ownership to remain constant for the indefinite future) is given by

$$\frac{T}{1 + T},$$

where $T = (1 - P_{00})/(1 - P_{11})$, P_{00} is the transition probability from not owning to not owning, and P_{11} is the transition probability from owning to owning. Among those married in both waves t and $t + 1$ and in the age band seventy to seventy-four the steady-state rate of ownership is 84.8 percent and the actual average is 91.8 percent. Thus, there is a trend out of ownership among marrieds, but the trend is slow. Among marrieds aged eighty-five or over, the steady-state rate is 62.9 percent and the average is 78.6 percent, also showing a downward trend in ownership.

Among those who were single in two adjacent waves the transition rate out of ownership increases with age. The steady-state rates decline from 62.2 percent in the age band seventy to seventy-four to 32.9 percent in the age band eighty-five or over.

Widowing is associated with considerably higher rates of transition out of ownership: for example, among those aged seventy to seventy-four who were widowed between adjacent waves the transition rate out of ownership was 6.8 percent, compared with just 1.7 percent among surviving couples. This rate increases sharply with age.

We ask whether the panel transitions can explain the cross-section patterns of ownership that are in table 8.5. Figure 8.14 indicated that cohort differences are not important, but we must still address differential mortality. The average risk (holding age constant) of a renter's dying compared with an owner's dying is about 1.39: said differently, the age-adjusted mortality rate of renters is about 39 percent higher than the mortality rate of owners. In that renters die more frequently than owners, the average rate of ownership by a cohort will increase over time even if there are no transitions into or out of ownership in panel among survivors. However, the rate of ownership is high so that differential mortality will not increase the average ownership rate substantially as a cohort ages. Under the assumption that owners and renters have the same mortality risk, the average over all groups, the home ownership rate would decline by about 0.4 percent per year more than the observed cohort rate. The difference is shown in figure 8.15: it shows the cross-section ownership rates averaged over four waves of AHEAD data, the rates predicted from the panel ownership transitions reported in table 8.8 (panel), and the rates predicted both from the panel and from differential mortality (panel accounting for differential mortality).

The cumulative effects of differential mortality can be seen by comparing the two panel lines: after about fifteen years the simulation that accounts for differential mortality is about 5 percentage points above the simulation that does not. The cross section is very closely matched by the simulation that accounts for differential mortality showing that cohort effects are not very important and that the transition rates over the period of our sample (mid- to late 1990s) have been stable for a considerable time.

The difference between the time paths of ownership by singles and by couples and the effects of widowing on ownership are shown in figure 8.16. The top curve, for couples, and the bottom curve, for singles, are derived

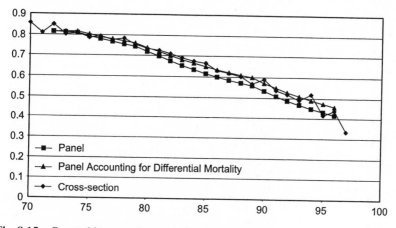

Fig. 8.15   Ownership rates: Cross section and simulation
Source: Own computations based on AHEAD.

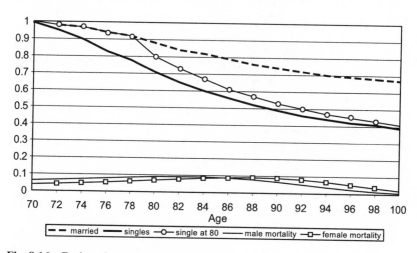

Fig. 8.16   Projected ownership rates
Source: Own computations based on AHEAD.

from the estimated transition rates in ownership in table 8.4 beginning with an ownership rate of 100 percent at age seventy. The curves are conditional on survival and so have the interpretation of anticipated lifetime probabilities of owning. Thus, if both members of a couple survive to ninety, the probability of owning will decline to about 75 percent. Among singles who are owners at age seventy the rate of decline is considerably greater, and the probability of owning at age ninety less than 50 percent. The middle curve shows predicted rates of ownership of couples who are owners at age seventy, but where one spouse dies between seventy-eight and seventy-nine.

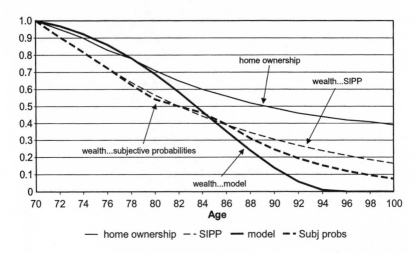

Fig. 8.17   Home ownership and wealth
Source: Own computations based on AHEAD.

During the one-year transition period to widowhood the probability of owning declines sharply, as shown in table 8.4, and then the probability follows the path of singles but at a higher level.

The two curves at the bottom of figure 8.16 show the probability of males and of females dying at each age conditional on reaching age seventy. The most likely age for males to die is eighty-two, and it is eighty-eight for females. The figure suggests that 50–60 percent of couples who are owners at age seventy will be owners at the death of the surviving spouse, and that a somewhat lower fraction of singles will be owners. These percentages are not much different from the estimates of Sheiner and Weil (1992), who estimated that among couples who were owners at age sixty-five, just 41 percent of the last survivor would die still owning.

The life-cycle model (LCM) predicts that wealth will be decumulated as people age, and in figure 8.17 we compare the wealth paths predicted in three different ways with the rate of ownership among singles. The objective of the comparison is to find whether the path of ownership as an indicator of housing wealth is broadly consistent with wealth paths as predicted by the LCM. The first wealth forecast (labeled wealth . . . SIPP) uses observed wealth change in the 1984–85 Survey of Income and Program Participation (SIPP) panel. The second (labeled wealth . . . subjective probabilities) is based on the subjective probability of bequests as elicited in the HRS. Hurd and Smith (2002) compared them with actual bequeathable wealth to estimate annual rates of anticipated dissaving, which we use to construct the curve. The third (labeled wealth . . . model) uses an LCM estimated over the 1969–79 Retirement History Survey to predict the path of bequeathable wealth (Hurd 1989).[4] The rates of decumulation of bequeathable wealth are broadly consistent with each other. They predict that a single person who survives into his or her nineties will have consumed three-fourths or more of bequeathable wealth.

The path of home ownership initially follows the path of bequeathable wealth, but after about ten years it is higher than all of them. The lower rate of decline probably reflects a number of ways in which housing wealth is treated differently from nonhousing wealth. There are substantial transaction costs in moving from home ownership to renting, so that there will be a tendency to retain housing beyond what would be optimal were adjustment costless. People have a sentimental attachment to a particular house, which increases the transaction costs. There is risk associated with renting, such as inflation in rental costs, whereas, except for property tax and maintenance, owned housing is a way of purchasing a stream of real consumption.

We can find whether the increase with age in the rate transitions out of owning is a pure age effect or is associated with characteristics such as health or economic circumstances. Our method is to estimate the probability of owning in wave $t + 1$ as a function of characteristics and economic circumstances as well as ownership status in wave t. Using four waves of AHEAD, we have three transitions. Table 8.9 shows the ratio of the probability of owning to not owning (the risk of owning) of someone with one of the characteristics displayed in the first column divided by the risk of owning of someone in the reference group. These results are estimated by multivariate logit over the three transitions. Thus, someone who is married has a risk of owning in wave $t + 1$ that is 124 percent higher than the risk of someone who is not married, and the difference is significant at less than the 0.001 level.

The covariates with substantial explanatory power and statistical significance are the death of a spouse, which reduces the likelihood of owning in the next wave; the incidence of a health event; baseline health of fair or poor; and measures of wealth, as well as ownership itself. Of note is that age per se is not associated with an accelerating transition out of home ownership. This implies that the increased transition rates by age band that are in table 8.8 are due to worsening health and possibly reductions in wealth that occur with age.

---

4. We would like to use the AHEAD wealth data for this comparison, but two problems prevent its use: stock ownership was apparently underreported by about 10 percentage points in the 1993 wave, leading to a very large increase in measured wealth between 1993 and 1995 (Rohwedder, Haider, and Hurd 2004). There is no obvious way to correct for this data error. The 1995 wave of AHEAD was followed by the stock market boom, leading to wealth increases that were likely unanticipated and do not reflect planned life-cycle wealth accumulation.

Table 8.9   **Relative risk for home ownership, logit estimates**

	Risk	*p*-value
Female	0.90	0.169
Married	2.24	0.000
Spouse died	0.34	0.000
Age splines		
70	1.00	0.994
75	0.90	0.090
80	1.07	0.174
85	1.04	0.526
90	0.93	0.377
Health condition	1.05	0.484
Health incident	0.68	0.000
Health good	0.99	0.936
Health fair/poor	0.79	0.006
Housing wealth quartile lowest	0.60	0.000
Quartile 2 and 3		
Highest	1.19	0.063
Nonhousing wealth quartile lowest	0.87	0.094
Quartile 2 and 3		
Highest	1.32	0.002
Home owner	101.67	0.000
Live with others	1.09	0.359
Nursing home	1.13	0.607

Source: Own computations based on AHEAD.

We have included two wealth measures: housing wealth and nonhousing wealth. For each we define three categories: the lowest wealth quartile, the second and third quartiles, and the highest quartile. Both types of wealth are associated with higher levels of ownership. That is, those with more housing wealth and those with more nonhousing wealth tend to retain ownership. We had anticipated that high housing wealth combined with low nonhousing wealth would be associated with an elevated probability of selling the home, but the four interactions were neither economically nor statistically significant.

In summary, we find that home ownership is reduced with age but that the rate of reduction is less than the rate of reduction of nonhousing wealth. The lower rate of decline is likely due to a mixture of causes: housing may be held for a precautionary motive, as in Skinner (1996); it may be held until health makes ownership infeasible, whereas health should not affect the ability to hold financial wealth; and in that its sale is often associated with widowing, as in Venti and Wise (2001), it may be used to cover costs associated with widowing.

Some of these explanations are consistent with an LCM extended to include precautionary saving: poor health or a health event are predictors of reduced life expectancy, which should accelerate the decumulation of wealth. However, the interaction of health with the requirements of home ownership makes the study of ownership more complex than the study of nonfinancial wealth.

8.7 Conclusions

This paper investigated the interaction among health, wealth, and where elderly persons live. We reproduce the finding that wealth and health are strongly related to each other. Wealthier persons live longer and are healthy longer. This interaction is moderated by where elderly persons live. Remaining in the lowest wealth quartile is most likely when an elderly person lives in a nursing home and least likely when this person lives with others. The reversed pattern is true for the probability of remaining in the highest wealth quartile. For the initially wealthy, living with others decreases the expected future wealth relative to living alone. This is consistent with the notion that cohabitation implies intrafamily transfers to the needy. For those who remain living independently, home ownership declines, but the speed of reduction is slower than we would expect for financial wealth.

Results in this paper are descriptive and imply no causality. Further research will apply more sophisticated econometric methods in order to identify patterns of causality.

References

Ai, C., J. Feinstein, D. McFadden, and H. Pollakowski. 1990. The dynamics of housing demand by the elderly: User cost effects. In *Issues in the economics of aging,* ed. D. Wise, 33–88. Chicago: University of Chicago Press.

Börsch-Supan, A. 1988. Household dissolution and the choice of alternative living arrangements. In *The economics of aging,* ed. D. Wise, 119–50. Chicago: University of Chicago Press.

Börsch-Supan, A. 1990. Elderly Americans: A dynamic analysis of household dissolution and living arrangement transitions. In *Issues in the economics of aging,* ed. D. Wise, 89–120. Chicago: University of Chicago Press.

Börsch-Supan, A., V. Hajivassiliou, L. Kotlikoff, and J. Morris. 1992. Health, children, and elderly living arrangements: A multiperiod-multinominal probit model with unobserved heterogeneity and autocorrelated errors. In *Topics in the economics of aging,* ed. D. Wise, 79–108. Chicago: University of Chicago Press.

Börsch-Supan, A., L. Kotlikoff, and J. Morris. 1991. The dynamics of living arrangements of the elderly, health and family support. In *The economics of care of the elderly,* ed. J. Pacolet and C. Wilderom, 114–36. Aldershot, England: Avebury.

Börsch-Supan, A., D. McFadden, and R. Schnabel. 1996. Living arrangements, health and wealth effects. In *Advances in the economics of aging,* ed. D. Wise, 193–218. Chicago: University of Chicago Press.

Costa, D. L. 1997. A house of her own: Old age assistance and the living arrangements of older nonmarried women. NBER Working Paper no. 6217. Cambridge, MA: National Bureau of Economic Research.

Cox, D., and F. Raines. 1985. Interfamily transfers and income redistribution, horizontal equity, uncertainty and economic well-being. In *Horizontal equity, uncertainty, and economic well-being,* ed. Martin David and Tim Smeeding, 393–421. Chicago: University of Chicago Press.

Ellwood, D. T., and T. J. Kane. 1990. The American way of aging: An event history analysis. In *Issues in the economics of aging,* ed. D. Wise, 121–48. Chicago: University of Chicago Press.

Grad, S. 1994. Income of the population 55 or older, 1992. pub. no. SSA 13-11871. Social Security Administration, U.S. Department of Health and Human Services. Washington, DC: U.S. Government Printing Office.

Henretta, J. C., M. S. Hill, W. Li, B. J. Soldo, and D. A. Wolf. 1997. Selection of children to provide care: The effect of the earlier parental transfers. *The Journals of Gerontology* Series B (52B): 110–19.

Horowitz, A. 1985. Family caregiving to the frail elderly. In *Annual review of gerontology and geriatrics,* ed. C. Eisdorfer, M. P. Lawton, and G. L. Maddox, 194–246. New York: Springer.

Hoynes, H. W., M. D. Hurd, and H. Chand. 1998. Household wealth of the elderly under alternative imputation procedures. In *Inquiries in the economics of aging,* ed. D. Wise, 229–57. Chicago: University of Chicago Press.

Hoynes, H. W., and D. McFadden. 1998. The impact of demographics on housing and non-housing wealth in the United States. In *The economic effects of aging and the United States and Japan,* ed. M. Hurd and N. Yashiro, 153–94. Chicago: University of Chicago Press.

Hurd, M. D. 1989. Mortality risk and bequests. *Econometrica* 57 (4): 779–813.

———. 1990. Issues and results from research on the elderly, economic status, retirement, and savings. *Journal of Economic Literature* 28:565–637.

Hurd, M. D., and D. McFadden. 1998. Predictors of mortality among the elderly: Wealth, income, education and subjective survival probabilities. Paper presented at the American Economic Association Annual Meeting. 3–5 January, Chicago.

Hurd, M. D., D. McFadden, and A. Merrill. 1998. Healthy, wealthy and wise? Socioeconomic status, morbidity and mortality among the elderly. University of California, Berkeley, Department of Economics. Mimeograph, April.

Hurd, M. D., and J. P. Smith. 2002. Expected bequests and their distribution. NBER Working Paper no. 9142. Cambridge, MA: National Bureau of Economic Research.

Kotlikoff, L. J., and J. Morris. 1989. How much care do the aged receive from their children? A bimodal picture of contact and assistance. In *The economics of aging,* ed. D. Wise, 151–76. Chicago: University of Chicago Press.

———. 1990. Why don't the elderly live with their children? A new look. In *Issues in the economics of aging,* ed. D. Wise, 149–72. Chicago: University of Chicago Press.

McGarry, K., and R. F. Schoeni. 1998. Social Security, economic growth and the rise in independence of elderly widows in the 20th century. RAND Labor and Population Program Working Paper Series no. 98-01. Santa Monica, CA: RAND.

Moon, M. 1983. The role of the family in the economic well-being of the elderly. *The Gerontologist* 23:45–50.

Rohwedder, S., S. Haider, and M. Hurd. 2004. Increases in wealth among the elderly in the early 1990s: How much is due to survey design? NBER Working Paper no. 10862. Cambridge, MA: National Bureau of Economic Research.

Sheiner, L., and D. Weil. 1992. The housing wealth of the aged. NBER Working Paper no. 4115. Cambridge, MA: National Bureau of Economic Research.

Skinner, J. 1996. Is housing wealth a sideshow? In *Advances in the economics of aging,* ed. D. Wise, 214–74. Chicago: University of Chicago Press.

Sloan, F. A., and M. W. Shayne. 1993. Long-term care, Medicaid, and impoverishment of the elderly. *Milbank Memorial Fund Quarterly* 71 (4): 575–97.

Smith, J. P. 1997. Wealth inequality among older Americans. *The Journals of Gerontology* Series B (52B): 74–81.

Soldo, B., M. D. Hurd, W. Rodgers, and R. Wallace. 1997. Asset and health dynamics among the oldest old: An overview of the AHEAD study. *The Journals of Gerontology* Series B (52B): 1–20.

Stone, Robyn, Gail Lee Cafferata, and Judith Sangl. 1987. Caregivers of the frail elderly: A national profile. *The Gerontologist* 27 (5): 616–26.

Venti, S., and D. Wise. 1990. But they don't want to reduce housing equity. In *Issues in the economics of aging,* ed. D. Wise, 13–32. Chicago: University of Chicago Press.

———. 2001. Aging and housing equity: Another look. NBER Working Paper no. 8608. Cambridge, MA: National Bureau of Economic Research.

Wolf, D. A. 1984. Kin availability and the living arrangements of older women. *Social Science Research* 13:72–89.

———. 1994. The elderly and their kin: Patterns of availability and access. In *Demography of aging,* ed. L. G. Martin and S. A. Preston, 146–94. Washington, DC: National Academy Press.

———. 1995. Changes in the living arrangements of older women: An international study. *The Gerontologist* 35 (6): 724–31.

Wolf, D. A., V. Freedman, and B. J. Soldo. 1997. The division of family labor: Care for elderly parents. *The Journals of Gerontology* Series B (52B): 102–9.

Comment   Steven F. Venti

Whether elderly persons live independently, live with others, or live in an institution has important implications for their well-being. There seems little doubt that the choice of living arrangements is closely related to the past financial resources and the health status of elderly persons. It is also likely that living arrangements will have an effect on future health and, possibly, wealth as well. Disentangling the complicated relationships between these outcomes is a formidable task. This paper takes a modest first step by carefully describing the relationships among some of the key variables that affect the well-being of the elderly without delving into the complex problem of identifying causality.

The first part of this paper describes how the "state" variables—health (prevalence, incidence, and self-reported measures), wealth (four quar-

Steven F. Venti is a professor of economics and the DeWalt Ankeny Professor of Economic Policy at Dartmouth College, and a research associate of the National Bureau of Economic Research.

tiles), home ownership, living arrangements (alone, with other, nursing home), and survival—evolve after retirement. This is done by estimating first-order transition probabilities among the state variables, controlling for a set of exogenous variables. The authors are up-front about the limitations of this procedure. There is no claim of causality in the estimated relationships. The use of a first-order process leads to a mechanical tendency for the simulated age profiles to converge over time, so in many simulations the rate of convergence is more important than the level at which simulated profiles eventually converge. The first-order assumption also imposes conditional independence over time. Thus, for example, ownership in the current period, but not length of tenure in an owned home (ownership in previous periods), affects outcomes in the next period. The assumption also implies that a health "shock" will only have a one-period direct effect on other outcomes, although indirect effects may persist through effects on other state variables.

Despite these limitations, the estimates and simulated trajectories based on the estimates provide a rich description of the relationship between the state variables. Given the number of state and control variables, there are almost an infinite number of scenarios the authors could simulate. The key scenarios of interest involve living arrangements—both the effects of other variables on living arrangements and how living arrangements affect other outcomes. The parameter estimates suggest strong persistence of living arrangements: previous location strongly predicts current location. However, there are other significant factors that can lessen this persistence. Marriage is associated with higher rates of ownership and lower rates of the other arrangements. Death of a spouse or a decline in health produces the opposite result. Wealth is positively related to ownership but is unrelated to the likelihood of other living arrangements. None of this is much of a surprise; it implies that healthy, wealthy persons with stable family structures are more likely to own and to continue owning.

Sections 8.2 through 8.4 simulate the interactions between health, wealth, and living arrangements by fixing the control variables, setting initial values of state variables, and letting these state variables vary freely in subsequent periods. Essentially, this procedure allows for complete interaction among the state variables. First is the age profile of home ownership by wealth. Elderly households with lower *initial* wealth discontinue ownership at a faster rate than elderly households with high *initial* wealth. It is important to emphasize that state variables, such as the incidence of a health problem or nursing home entry, are not held constant in the simulated age profile of ownership. Thus, low-initial-wealth households end up with lower rates of ownership than high-initial-wealth households, but other state variables may be indirectly responsible for the decline.

Another issue to keep in mind is that the parameter estimates are average effects. A conditional logit of ownership in the current period on ownership and other state variables in the previous period is the basis for the simulated age-profile of ownership. This methodology yields the *average* ownership profile in the population. Of course, it may be that few individuals behave like an "average" person, particularly when many of the state variables, such as ownership, are discrete. Thus, the authors' observation that "home ownership declines slowly but steadily as people age" is a description of average behavior but not necessarily of individual behavior. We will return to this point.

Another set of simulations considers the trajectory of wealth for households with different initial living arrangements. Again, full interaction among the state variables is allowed. Households initially in nursing homes are more likely to remain poor, and households initially living with others are least likely to remain poor. The probability of remaining poor for all three living arrangements decreases from ages seventy to eighty-five and then begins to rise. Perhaps a large fraction of initially poor households—regardless of their initial living arrangement—eventually face the financial burden of nursing home costs. This peculiar result deserves further analysis.

Perhaps the most interesting results pertain to the effect of the control variables. As expected, marriage and home ownership are positively related. The sex composition of children is startlingly powerful. Having daughters substantially increases the likelihood of living with others and decreases the probability of other living arrangements.

To isolate the effects of individual state variables, the authors fix some of the state variables at their initial values and let the others vary. The simulations consider survival and wealth trajectories when some of the health variables are fixed. As expected, the probabilities of remaining alive and remaining in the highest wealth quartile are higher when persons are assumed to remain healthy. This technique is useful to sort out the relationships between the state variables, but unfortunately it is not applied to either home ownership or living arrangements. A final set of simulations looks at the effect of health shocks on age profiles for survival and self-reported health status.

The second part of the paper shifts the focus to a more detailed analysis of the decline in home ownership. This has been widely studied (Merrill 1984; Sheiner and Weil 1992; Feinstein and McFadden 1989; Venti and Wise 1990, 2004; Megbolugbe, Sa-Adu, and Shilling [1997]), and the results are broadly consistent: households that experience shocks such as death of a spouse, change in health, or nursing home entry have a higher likelihood of discontinuing ownership. Elderly households that do not experience these shocks tend to stay put and may even increase home equity on average. For example, Venti and Wise (2004), also using the AHEAD, find annual percentage declines in home equity (not ownership) of 0.1 percent among continuing two-person households, 1.2 percent among continuing one-person households, and 7.8 percent among households that suffer the death of a spouse or in which a member enters a nursing home. Among all households combined, the decline in home equity is 1.8 percent per year.

The results in this paper are broadly consistent with these findings. The projected rate of home ownership for married couples declines from 100 percent to 75 percent between the ages of seventy and ninety, or about 1.4 percent per year. For continuously single households the projected annual rate of decline is 3.4 percent. The overall rate of ownership decline for *all* households is about 2.5 percent per year. These estimates are slightly higher than the Venti-Wise estimates, but there are three important differences. First, the Venti-Wise estimates pertain to home equity, so rising real house prices as well as declining mortgage balances suggest that equity will fall more slowly than ownership. Second, the studies also differ in their treatment of households in which a member entered a nursing home. These households have a very high rate of exit from ownership. The Venti-Wise estimates for one-person and two-person households exclude these nursing home entrants and are expected to be lower. Finally, the changes in home equity reported by Venti-Wise include not only the decline in home equity among households that discontinue owning, but also the change in home equity among initial owners who buy another home. On average, this latter group of owners "trades up," thus offsetting, in part, the decline in equity for households moving out of ownership. In light of these differences, the authors' overall rate of ownership decline for *all* households of about 2.5 percent per year is of comparable magnitude to the 1.8 percent per year decline in home equity found by Venti and Wise. Interestingly, the logit estimates presented in table 8.9 show that significant reductions are associated with death of a spouse and incidence of a health event (as well as initial housing and nonhousing wealth quartiles), but once these shocks are accounted for, there is no tendency for ownership to decline with age.

Although the authors' empirical results are consistent with prior findings, the interpretation of these results is not. The authors compare their findings to the rate of decumulation predicted by the life-cycle model and to observed rates of decumulation of nonhousing wealth. They hope to establish "whether the path of ownership as an indicator of housing wealth is broadly consistent with wealth paths predicted by the LCM." The authors compare their ownership projections to wealth change in the 1984–85 SIPP, to the subjective probability of bequests elicited in the HRS, and to the predicted path of bequeathable wealth based on a life-cycle model using data from the 1969–79 Retirement History Survey. The authors conclude that their results are "broadly consistent" with these wealth paths, although it is clear that the decline in ownership in the AHEAD is less pronounced than any of the three comparison wealth profiles.

I find it odd that the authors compare the decline in home ownership obtained from the 1992–98 AHEADs to declines in wealth estimated from the 1984 SIPP and the 1969–79 Retirement History Survey. More recent data are available for this comparison. The 1996 panel of the SIPP shows little decline in nonhousing wealth through age eighty (authors' estimates), and the AHEAD shows dramatically increasing nonhousing wealth among the older old (Hurd 2002). The authors are aware of the AHEAD results but argue that "the 1995 wave of AHEAD was followed by the stock market boom, leading to wealth increases that were likely unanticipated, and do not reflect planned life-cycle wealth accumulation."

The same reasoning can be used to argue that the decline in home ownership observed in the AHEAD does not reflect life-cycle motives. Most, or perhaps all, of the decline in ownership is accounted for by changes in health status or the death of a spouse. Elderly households that do not face these shocks (likely unplanned and unanticipated) decumulate very little of their housing wealth, if any. This suggests that most elderly persons desire to continue owning their homes for as long as they can. In the absence of shocks, housing wealth is not used to finance general consumption in retirement, as implied by the LCM. This unwillingness to downsize may be rooted in emotional and psychological attachment to homes, or it may reflect the conscious decision to keep the house as a form of insurance against catastrophic events. Survey evidence suggests that, with the possible exception of an end-of-life hospital stay, the members of most households plan, desire, and expect to die in their homes (American Association of Retired Persons 2000). Their "plan" is not to decumulate housing wealth, and, for the large fraction of the population that does not experience these events, the decline in ownership looks nothing like the profile predicted by the LCM. Of course, some fraction of the population experiences some sort of shock, and these households decumulate dramatically. Thus, as noted earlier, the "average" profile may bear some resemblance to a life-cycle path, but the experience of individual households does not.

Overall, this paper is a promising start to disentangling the complicated relationship between health, wealth, and living arrangements. The relationships are so complicated that it is difficult to even develop a methodology to describe them in a systematic and coherent way. The vector autoregression structure used here does quite a good job. The initial results are informative, although I yearn for more simulations of ownership and living arrangements that hold fixed other outcomes. Such simulations help to isolate the effects of these key state variables. I look forward to further efforts to extend this methodology.

References

American Association of Retired Persons. 2000. Fixing to stay: A national survey of housing and home modification issues. Washington, DC: AARP.

Feinstein, J., and D. McFadden. 1989. The dynamics of housing demand by the elderly: Wealth, cash flow, and demographic effects. In *The economics of aging,* ed. D. Wise, 55–86. Chicago: University of Chicago Press.

Hurd, M. 2002. Portfolio holdings of the elderly. In *Household portfolios,* ed. L. Guiso, M. Haliassos, and T. Jappelli, 431–71. Cambridge: MIT Press.

Megbolugbe, I., J. Sa-Aadu, and J. Shilling. 1997. Oh, yes, the elderly will reduce housing equity under the right circumstances. *Journal of Housing Research* 8 (1): 53–74.

Merrill, S. 1984. Home equity and the elderly. In *Retirement and economic behavior,* ed. H. Aaron and G. Burtless, 197–238. Washington, DC: Brookings.

Sheiner, L., and D. Weil. 1992. The housing wealth of the aged. NBER Working Paper no. 4115. Cambridge, MA: National Bureau of Economic Research.

Venti, S., and D. Wise. 1990. But they don't want to reduce housing equity. In *Issues in the economics of aging,* ed. D. Wise, 13–32. Chicago: University of Chicago Press.

———. 2004. Aging and housing equity: Another look. In *Perspectives on the economics of aging,* ed. D. Wise, 127–80. Chicago: University of Chicago Press.

Institutions and Saving for Retirement
Comparing the United States, Italy, and the Netherlands

Arie Kapteyn and Constantijn Panis

9.1 Introduction

This paper analyzes retirement saving and portfolio choice in the United States, Italy, and the Netherlands. In addition to relying on public retirement provisions, households prepare for retirement through tax-sheltered and after-tax savings. They may invest these funds in a wide variety of assets, including housing, stocks, bonds, savings accounts, and so on. These asset types differ in their risk, return, and liquidity characteristics as well as in their fiscal treatment. Economic theory postulates that households allocate their portfolios according to their risk aversion, time horizon, uncertain out-of-pocket medical expenditures, income risk, informal (family) risk-sharing arrangements, and more. While the literature has tested various parts of the theory, both testing and quantification of the theory are hampered by the fact that some of the major variables do not exhibit sufficient variation within a country to establish their relative importance for portfolio choice, or, more generally, for retirement saving and investment. This paper partially fills that gap by exploring three countries with widely varying institutional arrangements for retirement income.

Portfolio allocation behavior is important for a number of reasons (e.g.,

Arie Kapteyn is an economist at RAND and director of the Labor and Population Program at RAND. Constantijn Panis is a manager at the economic consulting practice of Deloitte & Touche, LLP.

This paper benefited greatly from the expert input of Rob Alessie and Luigi Guiso throughout the course of the conceptualization and analysis. We are also very grateful to Nicholas Souleles and Andrew Samwick for their thoughtful comments and to Delia Bugliari for her excellent research support. This research was sponsored by the Department of Labor, Employee Benefits Security Administration, under Contract J-9-P-7-0045. We thank Patricia Willis for her encouragement and support.

Bertaut and Starr-McCluer 2000). Returns vary across asset types, so portfolio composition has important implications for the pace of wealth accumulation and the degree of retirement preparedness; risks vary across asset types, so portfolio composition has important implications for the distribution of retirement income; portfolio decisions illuminate how tax policy affects household spending and saving; portfolio decisions illuminate how macro variables (interest rates, stock prices, inflation, unemployment) affect household spending and saving; also, understanding households' portfolio decisions may provide deeper insight into theories of consumption and saving behavior.

This paper is organized as follows. Section 9.2 poses a brief theoretical framework. Section 9.3 highlights relevant aspects of the legal and institutional environments of the three countries under study. Section 9.4 describes the three countries' microdata that we use. Section 9.5 draws together the theoretical framework and the institutional differences to formulate four hypotheses about expected patterns in the microdata from the different countries. Section 9.6 presents the empirical analysis with particular emphasis on section 9.5's hypotheses. Section 9.7 concludes.

9.2   Theoretical Framework

Our point of departure to study retirement savings is the life-cycle hypothesis (LCH) formulated by Modigliani and Brumberg (1954). The basic tenet of the LCH is that rational consumers will try to smooth consumption over the life cycle in such a way that the marginal utility of consumption is equalized across periods. Since individuals usually have a life-cycle income pattern that is inversely U-shaped (at young ages, earnings are modest but grow until roughly retirement, after which income declines), the life-cycle pattern of wealth is also inversely U-shaped. In its simplest form, sometimes referred to as a "stripped-down" version (Browning and Lusardi 1996), the LCH fails to explain several well-known facts. Several extensions have therefore been introduced. These include the incorporation of uncertainty, bequest motives, borrowing constraints, precautionary motives, transaction costs associated with the reshuffling of portfolios, taxes, and lack of financial sophistication. We draw on several of these extensions below, insofar as they shed light on the portfolios of the (near-)retired. Our interest is primarily in the implications of institutional arrangements for individuals' wealth accumulation and profile.

9.3   Legal and Institutional Environments

Kapteyn and Panis (2002) provide a detailed discussion of legal issues and institutional features that affect retirement income in the United States, Italy, and the Netherlands. This section highlights the features that are relevant for our purposes. In separate subsections, we highlight the three legs of the proverbial retirement income stool: social security, occupational pensions, and private savings.[1] We then discuss capital market imperfections (transaction costs and liquidity constraints) and exposure to financial risks in retirement.

9.3.1   Social Security

In the United States, social security is mainly provided as Old-Age and Survivors Insurance (OASI).[2] It makes cash payments to retired workers, spouses of retired workers, and widows and children of deceased workers. A separate program, Supplemental Security Income (SSI), makes cash payments to, among others, needy elderly. The Italian social security program, Programma Nazionale di Sicurezza Sociale, makes cash payments to retired workers and widow(er)s of deceased workers; it also guarantees a minimum benefit for the poor. The Italian program does not have a spousal benefit. In the Netherlands, cash payments are made to elderly individuals—regardless of their work history—on the basis of the General Old-Age Act (Algemene Ouderdoms Wet [AOW]). We use the term "social security" to refer to all programs that pay cash benefits to the elderly, regardless of whether the entitlement originates from contributive insurance or social assistance.

All three social security programs are predominantly funded on a pay-as-you-go basis. The United States maintains a buffer in the form of an OASI trust fund. There is no trust fund in Italy. Italian social security outlays currently exceed contributions by about 8–17 percent of payroll (Brugiavini 1999); the difference is funded from general tax revenues. The Netherlands instituted a trust fund in 1996.

In all three countries, participation in social security is mandatory, and coverage is nearly universal. Almost all elderly are eligible to receive some benefits.

Table 9.1 gives an indication of the generosity of social security in the three countries. The first column shows social security expenditures as a percentage of gross domestic product (GDP). Italy spent approximately 15.7 percent of GDP on social security in 1999, far higher than the United

---

1. Laws and institutions are changing continuously. As a general rule, we describe the status around the time of our household surveys, that is, from roughly 1995 to 1999, and note major changes over time only where relevant. All amounts are in 1998 currencies, unless stated otherwise. We converted all amounts in Dutch guilders (NLG) or Italian liras (ITL) into euros (€) at the exchange rates that were irrevocably fixed at the euro's conceptual introduction in the beginning of 1999: €1 = NLG 2.20371 = ITL 1936.27. On 1 January 1999 the exchange rate of the euro and the U.S. dollar was $1 = €0.857. The dollar exceeded parity with the euro for several years but had returned to its initial level of $1 = €0.857 by June of 2003. For purposes of comparing purchasing power, an exchange rate of one to one is probably a reasonable approximation.

2. Unless noted otherwise, our discussion does not extend to public support for the disabled and their dependents.

Table 9.1   Social security outlays and dependency ratios

	(1) Social security outlays as percentage of GDP (1999)	(2) Population age 65+ as percentage of population age 25–64 (1994)	Ratio of (1) and (2)
United States	3.9	24.8	0.156
Italy	15.7	29.6	0.523
The Netherlands	5.0	24.4	0.208

Sources: Board of OASI Trustees (2001); Social Security Administration (2000); Franco (2000); Kapteyn and De Vos (1999); Bureau of the Census (2001).

States (3.9 percent in 2000) and the Netherlands (5.0 percent in 1999). This is in minor part explained by the age structure of its population. The second column shows the elderly dependency ratio, that is, the size of the population that is at least sixty-five years old as a fraction of the working-age population. Italy again tops the list, but the differences are not large.[3] The third column shows the ratio of social security outlays as a fraction of GDP and the dependency ratio. It may be interpreted as a measure of the generosity of each country's social security program. Italy remains far above the other two countries. This is largely because occupational pensions, which play a significant role in the United States and the Netherlands, are negligible in Italy—see below. In addition, until recently, early retirement was very widespread in Italy, especially in the public sector. Several categories of public employees could retire after fifteen to twenty years of contributions. Early retirement essentially increases the dependency ratio.

Social security benefits are paid in the form of a lifelong annuity in all three countries.

In the United States, OASI benefits are a function of historical earnings, retirement age, and marital status. They may be claimed at age sixty-two; delayed claiming results in higher benefits according to a schedule that is roughly actuarially fair. In 2001, average retired worker benefits were $845 per month. Aged couples received an average of $1,410 per month, and single elderly widow(er)s $811. Benefits are adjusted annually for inflation. The replacement rate for unmarried individuals with average wages was approximately 44 percent. The nationwide average replacement rate, including spousal and other derived benefits, was approximately 56 percent in 1995 (Blöndal and Scarpetta 1998). There is no minimum OASI benefit. However, regardless of their earnings history, elderly individuals (and couples) are eligible for a monthly SSI benefit of $530 ($796 for couples).

3. Italy's fertility rate was very low during the 1990s, well below the replacement level. While the dependence ratio is only somewhat larger in Italy than in the United States and the Netherlands, the difference is expected to increase markedly in the future.

In Italy, private-sector workers may retire with full benefits at age sixty (men) or fifty-five (women) or after thirty-five years of social security tax payments, whichever is earlier.[4] For public-sector employees, only twenty (men) or fifteen (women) years of tax payments are required. Benefits are a function of number of years worked and so-called pensionable earnings. For private-sector employees, pensionable earnings are equal to the average earnings of the last five years prior to retirement. (For public-sector employees, pensionable earnings are based on the last paycheck only.) Pensionable earnings are converted into social security benefits by applying a 2 percent factor (referred to as the rate of return) for each year of social security tax payment up to a maximum of forty years (Brugiavini 1999). A worker can thus get at most 80 percent of his pensionable earnings. Earnings that enter the calculation of pensionable earnings are capped. Benefits are therefore also capped, at approximately €6,000 per month in 2000. Contributions are not subject to any maximum. There is no actuarial adjustment for retirement age.[5] There are no spousal benefits in Italy. However, the entire benefit becomes payable to a surviving spouse upon death of the retiree. In 2000, the benefit was never lower than a means-tested minimum benefit of approximately €370 per month. A substantial fraction of retirees receive this minimum benefit. Benefits are adjusted regularly for nominal wages.

In the Netherlands, social security benefit rules are very simple. Earnings history does not play a role: the benefits are almost exclusively a function of marital status and residency history. In 2001, unmarried individuals age sixty-five or older received €883 per month; married couples with both spouses at least age sixty-five received €1,206 per month. Married couples with one spouse below age sixty-five received between €603 and €1,206, depending on the younger spouse's income (Social Insurance Bank 2000). The eligibility age is sixty-five, and there is no provision for early retirement.[6] There is no link between labor force participation and entitlement to social security. The full benefits apply to residents who have lived their entire working life (age fifteen to sixty-four) in the Netherlands; benefits are reduced by 2 percent for every year spent abroad (Kapteyn and de Vos 1999). Benefits are adjusted annually for nominal wage growth.

---

4. Italian social security benefit calculations changed materially in 1992 and, to a lesser extent, in 1995. The changes will be phased in over a long period. Workers with at least eighteen years of contributions in 1995 will receive benefits computed on the basis of the rules applying before the 1992 reform (Franco 2000). For purposes of our analysis, which focuses on individuals aged fifty and older, the pre-1992 regime therefore applies.

5. The 1992 and 1995 reforms made fundamental changes to benefit calculations. Benefits are now uncapped but progressive, and there is an actuarial adjustment for retirement age. On average, the new rules will reduce benefits by 27–29 percent (Beltrametti 1996; Rostagno 1996).

6. Occupational pensions often offer bridge benefits between the (early) retirement age and age sixty-five.

Table 9.2   **Contribution and replacement rates**

| | Contribution rate (% of taxable income) | | | |
	Employer	Employee	Total	Average replacement rate
United States	5.26	5.26	10.52	56.0
Italy	18.93	8.34	27.27	80.0
The Netherlands	0.00	17.90	17.90	45.8

Source: Blöndal and Scarpetta (1998).

Table 9.3   **Importance of occupational pensions (late 1990s)**

	Funds (% of GDP)	Percent of retirees receiving pension	Percent of working population covered
Italy	Negligible	Negligible	0.02
The Netherlands	118	76 (men) 23 (women)	90
United States	66	48 (men) 26 (women)	44

Source: Johnson (1999).

Table 9.2 summarizes social security contribution rates and average replacement rates for the three countries. The replacement rates are the average over four scenarios and may therefore differ from the average nationwide replacement rates.[7]

9.3.2   Occupational Pensions

Occupational pensions are retirement income schemes that are sponsored by employers. The United States, Italy, and the Netherlands vary widely in the role of occupational pensions. They are widespread, well funded, and generous in the Netherlands; largely immaterial for most Italians (except for so-called severance pay arrangements; see below); and on roughly equal footing with social security in the United States. Table 9.3 shows pension assets as a percentage of GDP, the percentage of retirees with any pension benefits, and the percentage of the working population that is covered by a pension plan.

Traditionally, employer-sponsored pensions in the United States have been of the defined benefit (DB) type. The plans are specific to individual employers, not to industry groups—such as is mostly the case in the

7. The replacement rates are computed as averages of four scenarios: two earnings levels (average and two-thirds of average), and two household compositions (single worker and worker with a dependent spouse). The earnings profile is assumed to be flat, and earnings are revalued according to changes in average earnings. The rates refer to basic pensions, means-tested supplements, and mandatory occupational pensions only. See Blöndal and Scarpetta (1998).

Netherlands.[8] Given that there are tens of thousands of different plans, their features vary widely. Portability is very limited. The benefit is typically fixed in nominal terms upon job separation. An increasing fraction of DB plans—64 percent in 1993—offers the option of a lump-sum distribution upon job separation (Scott and Shoven 1996). Workers who take that option may leave the distribution tax-sheltered by investing it in an individual retirement account (IRA) or they may cash it out (Hurd, Lillard, and Panis 1998).

In 1978, 38 percent of American workers were covered by a DB pension, compared to only 21 percent in 1997 (Department of Labor 2001). Instead, defined contribution (DC) plans are becoming more widespread (up from 7 percent in 1978 to 25 percent in 1997). Under DC plans, retirement income depends on the level of contributions and the rate of return earned on those contributions. Workers typically decide on the allocation on their plan balance and bear the investment risk.

In Italy, the social security program was traditionally intended to provide comprehensive retirement income. In light of its social security program's dire financial outlook, Italy established DC pension plans in 1992. These plans are still in their infancy. As of March 1999, only approximately 400,000 workers were enrolled in a DC plan, and total assets represented only 0.015 percent of GDP (Banca d'Italia 1999). With few exceptions, there are no DB plans.

While not strictly a pension plan, so-called severance pay arrangements have long played an important role in Italian retirement income security. They are somewhat similar to DC plans but are paid out upon job separation, regardless of age. Employers contribute 6.9 percent of workers' wages into a self-administered fund (Franco 2000). Workers earn a legally determined return on those funds of 1.5 percent plus three-fourths of the inflation rate. While this severance entitlement is accruing, the worker has a secure but uncollectable credit with his employer, who retains full discretionary powers over the funds (Franco 2000). Upon job separation, there is a lump-sum severance payment. Severance pay credits comprised 5.2 percent of household financial wealth in 1997 (authors' calculations, based on the 1998 Survey of Household Income and Wealth [SHIW]).

In the Netherlands, occupational pensions are widespread and large. Plans are organized by industry sectors and administered by industrial organizations. Virtually all pensions are DB pensions. They are easily ported across employers. If a worker's previous and new employers belong to the same industrial organization, portability is merely an administrative issue. If the employers belong to different industrial organizations, the plan administrators settle internally such that the previous administrator dis-

---

8. The Pension Benefit Guaranty Corporation, a federal agency, guarantees pension payments to retirees whose pension plan ended.

Table 9.4   **After-tax median replacement rates**

	Replacement rate
Italy	75
The Netherlands	91
United States	41

Source: Gruber and Wise (1999).

burses a lump sum to the new administrator. The employee receives credit for accumulated pension rights as part of the new pension.[9] All benefits are paid in the form of a lifelong annuity; lump-sum distributions upon job termination are not allowed.

Of course, what matters for individual households is the combined replacement rate resulting from the combination of social security and occupational pensions. Table 9.4 provides an estimate of the after-tax replacement rates in the three countries for a typical (median) household. Clearly, the replacement rate is highest in the Netherlands and lowest by far in the United States.[10] Based on microdata from the three countries, we calculate and report below an alternative measure of replacement rate.

9.3.3 Private Savings

In addition to claims on social security and occupational pensions, individuals build up private savings to support them during retirement. Private savings may take many forms. They may be held in financial instruments, in real estate, or other. They are not restricted to after-tax funds. Specifically, we include IRAs, universal life insurance, and similar tax-sheltered accounts among private savings. The largest differences in private saving across the United States, Italy, and the Netherlands lie in opportunities to save in tax-sheltered instruments.

Americans may accumulate retirement savings in IRAs. Individuals may contribute up to $2,000 annually to IRAs.[11] In traditional IRAs, contributions are tax deductible; distributions (including interest) are taxed at the time of the distribution. Contributions are fully tax deductible only for per-

---

9. For example, suppose someone worked for twelve years under a plan that promises a benefit equal to 1.5 percent of last earned salary for every year worked. His new plan promises 2.0 percent of last earned salary per year worked. The worker receives credit in his new plan for $(12 \cdot 1.5) 2.0 = 9$ years of work, as if those years were worked at the new employer under the new pension plan.

10. There are many ways to calculate replacement rates. Table 9.4 is therefore not directly comparable to table 9.2. However, within each table, the rates are computed in the same manner.

11. Individuals who separate from a job with a pension plan may often take a lump-sum distribution of their pension rights. Such distributions may be rolled over into an IRA and remain tax sheltered. There is no limit on the amount that may be contributed to IRAs in this manner.

sons whose income falls below certain phaseout levels, which depend on whether the person is covered by an occupational pension. Since 1997, so-called Roth IRAs allow for after-tax contributions; distributions (including interest) are tax-free. By the end of 1999, the assets in IRAs amounted to $2.47 trillion (Copeland 2001). By comparison, assets of private DB and DC pension plans amounted to $2.14 trillion and $2.53 trillion, respectively (Federal Reserve 2001).

There is no Italian equivalent of IRAs. However, all Italians are eligible for universal life insurance contracts that are hybrids of term life insurance and savings plans: they pay out a benefit upon death or reaching a specific age, whichever comes first. The general principle of taxation on these contracts is very favorable: both contributions and benefits are partially tax exempt. The value of such life insurance contracts comprised 5.5 percent of household financial wealth in 1997 (authors' calculations, based on the 1998 SHIW).

The situation is similar in the Netherlands. Dutch law does not recognize IRAs but offers tax advantages for universal life insurance policies. The limit up to which contributions are tax deferred has fluctuated widely. Prior to 1992 the limit was €7,300, fixed in nominal terms. In 1992 the limit was lowered. For the year 2000 it was €5,600 for a married couple. (Starting in 2001 the limit is lower yet, at only €1,000; it is higher for individuals with income over which no pension rights are accumulated, such as the use of a company car.) Dutch universal life insurance payments must take the form of a lifelong or fixed-term annuity. The annuity benefits are subject to income tax.

Rates of return in the stock market have varied substantially across the three countries. Consider the Morgan Stanley Capital International (MSCI) index, representative of large companies and computed consistently over time and across countries. Between 1970 and mid-2001, the overall annual rate of return, including reinvested dividends, was highest in the Netherlands (13.8 percent nominal, 10.9 percent real), followed by the United States (11.9 percent nominal, 8.3 percent real), and Italy (11.2 percent nominal, 2.3 percent real). The Italian market exhibited markedly more volatility. For example, the standard deviation of annual nominal returns in Italy was 34.4 percent, compared to 16.6 percent in the United States and 21.7 percent in the Netherlands.

9.3.4 Capital Market Imperfections

Access to capital markets for households varies across the three countries. We discuss housing transactions, mortgages, and transaction costs of stock purchases.

Transaction costs of housing in the United States consist largely of real estate agent fees (approximately 6 percent of the house price) and legal fees (roughly 2 percent). Transfer taxes are negligible in most areas. In the

Netherlands, transaction costs are largely real estate agent fees (typically 1.5 percent of the house price) and a transfer tax of 6 percent. Legal fees are minimal by comparison. House transaction costs are higher in Italy than in the United States and the Netherlands. Real estate agent fees are 8–10 percent, and a transfer tax of 6–7 percent applies.

There is a well-developed mortgage market in the United States, including a standardized secondary market. Buyers may choose variable or fixed interest rate loans of up to thirty years' maturity. The typical down payment is 10 or 20 percent of the value of the house, but full financing is available. Interest payments are generally fully deductible for income tax purposes. The mortgage market is much less developed in Italy, perhaps due to banks' limited ability to sell the house in case of default on mortgage payments. Anecdotal evidence suggests that the associated legal proceedings may take as long as ten years. Banks therefore typically require a down payment of 40 to 50 percent of the price of the house. In the Netherlands the mortgage market is well developed, with a wide variety of loan options available. Many mortgage products are tied to universal life insurances, largely to take maximal advantage of the tax deductibility of mortgage interest. In principle, there are no down payment requirements. To cover the transaction costs of buying a house, mortgages of up to 110 percent of the transaction price are available and common. In 1998, per capita mortgage debt in the United States ($15,421) and the Netherlands (€14,167) was almost identical, and about ten times as large as in Italy (€1,415) (De Nederlandsche Bank 2000; Federal Reserve 2001).

The three countries may also face different transactions costs for the purchase and sale of stocks. An informal Internet search in March 2002 revealed roughly comparable fees for unassisted stock transactions via online brokers. In the United States, E-Trade (us.etrade.com) charges $14.95–19.95 per transaction, and Charles Schwab (www.schwab.com) charges $29.95 for up to 1,000 shares. In the Netherlands, Robeco (www.robecodirect.nl) charges 0.3–0.4 percent of the total transaction, often with a €15 minimum. In Italy, Twicetrade (www.twicetrade.it) charges €12 plus the lower of €0.019 per share and €19. The differences are not large. However, they reflect current online trades only. Actual average commissions during our analysis period (mid- to late 1990s), when online banking was far less developed, are likely much higher. We do not have comparable information on trends in transactions costs.

9.3.5   Exposure to Financial Risks Before and After Retirement

We now turn to financial risks before and after retirement. Before retirement, the main source of financial risk is earnings uncertainty. Casual observation would suggest that in the United States, earnings uncertainty is considerably larger than in Italy or the Netherlands. Social insurance programs (unemployment, sickness, disability) in the two European countries are generally more generous than in the United States, and employment protection laws make it relatively hard to fire employees in Italy and the Netherlands. An interesting piece of direct evidence on earnings uncertainty comes from a common question asked in household surveys in the three countries. The question asks respondents directly for the amount of income uncertainty they face. Guiso, Jappelli, and Pistaferri (1999) analyzed the coefficient of variation of income uncertainty for the United States, the Netherlands, and Italy. They found that income uncertainty across respondents had about the same distribution in Italy and the Netherlands. By contrast, U.S. respondents reported much more income uncertainty than the respondents in the two European countries.

Loss of earnings due to disability is another important financial risk before retirement. In all three countries, workers may count on long-term disability insurance in case of disability. Generally, public disability insurance schemes are more generous in Italy and the Netherlands than in the United States. In many cases, workers are covered by private disability insurance in all three countries.

After retirement, the main source of financial risk is health related. Americans face greater risks of large out-of-pocket medical expenses than their Dutch or Italian counterparts. In the Netherlands, virtually all elderly are covered by comprehensive health insurance with negligible out-of-pocket expenses. In Italy, the public health system grants essentially free assistance to the entire population in case of illness. However, only inpatient assistance is provided, implying substantial out-of-pocket expenses for the elderly in case of a serious illness that requires little hospital care. In the United States, the elderly may face serious out-of-pocket medical expenses, depending on their insurance coverage. Elderly with low income and financial assets are typically eligible for Medicaid, which offers fairly comprehensive insurance, including for deductibles. The risks are also limited for elderly that are covered by both private health insurance and Medicare, a public health insurance program for the elderly and disabled. However, American elderly who rely only on Medicare face substantial risks of large out-of-pocket expenses. Medicare consists of two components. Coverage for part A is almost universal; it covers inpatient expenses in hospitals and skilled nursing facilities. Most elderly also have supplemental (part B) coverage, purchased at subsidized rates. Medicare requires copayments that can be substantial, especially in the case of long hospital stays.

9.4 Data

Our analysis is based on microdata on individuals aged fifty and older from each country. For the United States, we use the Health and Retirement Study (HRS); for Italy, the SHIW; and for the Netherlands, the SocioEconomic Panel (SEP). We briefly describe each survey.

For the United States, we use the HRS, including all its cohorts. The HRS is a national longitudinal sample of households with at least one person born in 1931–41 (fifty-one to sixty-one years old at the 1992 baseline) or 1923 or before, that is, with at least one person aged seventy or over in 1993. The 1998 interview added the 1924–30 and 1942–47 birth cohorts, so that the most recent data cover all individuals over age fifty. We use the 1998 data and rely on other waves (1992–2000) where longitudinal information is needed. The principal objective of the HRS is to monitor economic transitions in work, income, wealth, and changes in health status. The first wave of data was collected in 1992 (1993 for the pre-1923 birth cohort), with follow-ups fielded at approximately two-year intervals. Blacks, Hispanics, and Florida residents were oversampled at a rate of two to one. The 1998 HRS contained 21,351 respondents: 8,949 men and 12,402 women.

The main wealth data for Italy is the SHIW, collected by the Banca d'Italia, Italy's central bank. Its main purpose is to collect detailed data on demographics, household consumption, income, and balance sheets. This survey is representative of the Italian population and has been fielded biannually since 1984. Financial wealth data have only been publicly available since 1989. Beginning in 1989, some but not all of the households were re-interviewed in subsequent panels. The panel component has increased over time—in 1989, 29 percent of the households were re-interviewed and by 1995, 45 percent were re-interviewed. The sample size is about 8,500 households. The SHIW contains questions on detailed asset and debt categories.

For the Netherlands, we rely on the SEP, a representative panel survey conducted by Statistics Netherlands. The SEP covers about 5,000 households and is representative of the noninstitutionalized Dutch population. It contains detailed information about a number of household demographic characteristics and collects data on household income and wealth. The SEP has been collected annually since 1984. It is a panel data set. Since 1987, the SEP contains a wealth module with fairly detailed questions on asset and debt categories. These categories have varied somewhat during the course of the panel. Because of problems collecting the data, no asset and debt information has been collected on the self-employed since 1990. In 1997, the SEP contained 8,904 respondents: 4,385 men and 4,519 women.

9.5   Method and Hypotheses

The aim of this paper is to exploit institutional variation across countries to shed light on the effect of different policies on the wealth accumulation and portfolio choices of households near or in retirement. Since, at this stage, we are only considering three countries, we have in a sense only three data points to generalize from. Thus, if we were to take a completely atheoretical approach we would have very few degrees of freedom to establish any empirical regularity with reasonable confidence. We therefore take a different approach. Drawing on the theoretical framework of the life-cycle hypothesis and the description of institutional differences across countries we formulate a number of stylized predictions, which are next confronted with the data at hand. The more these predictions are corroborated by the microdata, the more confident we can be that the policies in the different countries help explain the differences in wealth accumulation and portfolio composition that we observe.

An important caveat in our analysis will be that we generally assume that policies are exogenous. Thus, for example, we exclude the possibility that social security benefits are generous because citizens of a country have an innate tendency to save too little for retirement.

We briefly characterize a number of stylized facts that we expect to hold in the microdata across the three countries as a result of their institutional differences and the theoretical framework. We formulate our "predictions" as rather informal hypotheses, with generally a ceteris paribus clause to account for other counteracting institutional effects.

Hypothesis 1: The Displacement Effects of Retirement Benefits

A straightforward implication of the LCH is that more generous retirement benefits will induce less saving for retirement. We will therefore consider replacement rates at retirement in the three countries and predict that the country with the lowest replacement rate will be the country with the highest saving rate, ceteris paribus. Based on the discussion above we expect retirement savings to be most prominent in the United States and least prominent in the Netherlands, at least at the median.

Hypothesis 2: The Role of Earnings and Consumption Uncertainty

The LCH, extended to incorporate uncertainty, predicts that the introduction of additional uncertainty increases an agent's saving if and only if the agent is "prudent" (Kimball 1990; Gollier 2001).[12] Empirical work suggests that generally an increase in risk leads to more saving, but the estimated magnitude varies considerably across studies (e.g., Dynan 1993; Guiso, Jappelli, and Terlizzese 1992; Lusardi 1997; Hubbard, Skinner, and Zeldes 1994a,b, 1995; Banks, Blundell, and Brugiavini 2001).

Saving for precautionary reasons should be most prominent in a country with the highest earnings uncertainty. We will invoke subjective infor-

12. A necessary and sufficient condition for prudence is that an agent's marginal utility of future consumption is convex (Gollier 2001, Proposition 60). Prudence is related to, but is not the same as, risk aversion. A consumer is prudent if absolute risk aversion is decreasing in wealth; in the special case of constant relative risk aversion, (relative) prudence is equal to (relative) risk aversion + 1.

mation on earnings uncertainty to support the assumption that earnings uncertainty is highest in the United States and hence that we would expect to have the highest level of precautionary saving in the United States, again under ceteris paribus conditions. In addition to earnings uncertainty, consumption uncertainty may be important as well. A prime example of consumption uncertainty would be the possibility of unforeseen large out-of-pocket medical expenses. It appears that this kind of consumption risk is considerably larger in the United States than in Europe. Hence, even after retirement, when earnings uncertainty presumably does not play a role anymore, we would still expect precautionary motives to lead to a stronger desire to hold bequeathable wealth in the United States than in Italy or the Netherlands.

Hypothesis 3: The Role of Capital Market Imperfections

In the basic, stripped-down version of the LCH, consumers may be borrowing to finance consumption at a young age and enter middle age with negative wealth. Only after earnings exceed optimal lifetime consumption will saving become positive. Clearly such a pattern will not be observed if capital market imperfections prevent substantial borrowing at young ages. A point in case is the possibility to obtain home mortgages. As observed above, the typical minimum down payment requirement in the United States is 10–20 percent. In Italy the minimum down payment is on the order of 40–50 percent. In the Netherlands one can buy a house with a negative down payment up to 10 percent (i.e., one can borrow 110 percent of the market value of the house). Aspiring homeowners will thus need to save the most in Italy and the least in the Netherlands. From a liquidity constraints perspective, the risk of an adverse income shock yields the same result. Without liquidity constraints, the consumption effects of an adverse income shock may be spread out over many periods by borrowing to pay for current consumption and reducing consumption in all future periods by a little bit, rather than immediately cutting consumption by the total shortfall in income. Liquidity constraints limit the possibility to spread out the consumption shortfall over many periods. The only way to reduce the risk of such a forced reduction in consumption is to save more. Savings then act as a "buffer stock" (Deaton 1991; Carroll 1992, 1997). Liquidity constraints thus increase saving, even if they are not binding in the current period.

Differences in capital market structure in the three countries thus predict that Italy should have the highest saving rate and the Netherlands the lowest. In addition, when considering net household wealth, Italy should be the country where net wealth, as a percentage of gross wealth, is highest.

Hypothesis 4: Portfolio Composition

The preceding hypotheses imply higher levels of private wealth in Italy and the United States upon retirement than in the Netherlands. The implications for stock ownership and the share of wealth that is held in stocks are not clear-cut. Standard theory predicts that all agents should invest at least some fraction in stocks. The data clearly do not support this prediction, possibly because of the cost of acquiring information about stocks, transaction costs, and minimum investment requirements (Haliassos and Bertaut 1995; Vissing Jørgensen 2000). Standard theory further predicts that, under the usual assumption of constant relative risk aversion, the share of risky assets does not vary with wealth. However, economies of scale in portfolio management costs would induce a positive correlation between the share of risky assets and wealth. Empirically, people with more wealth own more risky assets, such as stocks (e.g., Hochgürtel 1998; Barsky et al., 1997; Carroll 2001; Hurd 2001).

The above suggests that stock ownership in Italy and the United States should be higher than in the Netherlands. On the other hand, the less well-developed capital market in Italy may reduce stock ownership in Italy. Similarly, the existence of more earnings and consumption uncertainty (e.g., medical expenses) in the United States may depress stock ownership in favor of more secure assets. We hypothesize that stock ownership in the Netherlands will be the lowest among the three countries, because of the lowest level of private wealth. In the United States, the combination of a well-developed capital market and a high level of private wealth for retirement and precautionary purposes should induce a relatively high level of stock ownership.

9.6 Empirical Analysis

We begin by presenting a number of relevant descriptive statistics for the three countries. We then discuss the evidence in favor of (or against) the hypotheses we have formulated above. Most of the analyses are in simple tabular form, with sometimes an excursion to multivariate analyses.

9.6.1 Descriptive Statistics

For Italy and the Netherlands, we restrict our analysis to households with a head over age fifty. For the United States, we consider the entire 1998 HRS, representative of the population age fifty-one and older. Table 9.5 presents data for 1998 for the United States and Italy and 1997 for the Netherlands. The table indicates that the age distributions in the three countries are very similar, with samples roughly equally split between heads of household under and over age sixty-five. Italian and Dutch respondents are somewhat more likely to be married than American respondents. Based on the educational distributions reported in table 9.5, U.S. respondents appear to be somewhat better educated than their Italian and Dutch counterparts. The comparison should be interpreted with caution, though, because the schooling systems differ greatly across the three countries.

The mean noncapital after-tax household income in the United States was higher than in Italy and the Netherlands, whereas median income was

Table 9.5   Demographics and income (unit of observation: household)

	United States	Italy	The Netherlands
Number of households	14,147	4,200	1,487
Age household head			
50–59	35.1	38.0	33.0
60–64	13.7	16.8	15.4
65+	51.2	45.2	51.6
Household structure			
Couple	53.4	67.4	60.8
Single male	11.1	8.8	10.6
Single female	35.5	23.8	28.7
Education household head			
Elementary	33.0[a]	51.8	30.6
Some high school		24.8	18.4[b]
High school	29.2	16.5	32.2[c]
Some college	37.8	7.0	18.8[d]
Household noncapital income			
Mean	$26,500	€24,000	€24,600
Median	$18,800	€20,400	€21,300

[a]less than high school
[b]lower vocational/junior high school
[c]middle vocational
[d]at least high school

lower.[13] The pattern reversal reflects a more equal income distribution in Italy and the Netherlands compared to the United States.

Our hypotheses are couched in terms of accumulated savings and allocation into risky assets. Given the information in the microdata, we define risky assets as stock and bond holdings. An intuitive measure of risky asset allocation is the ratio of risky assets to net worth. Unfortunately, nonnegligible subsamples report zero or negative net worth, so that the ratio of risky assets to net worth cannot be determined or is very difficult to interpret. Instead, we define two related measures. Consider households' balance sheets in table 9.6.

We decompose the ratio of risky assets to net worth as follows:

$$\frac{R}{NW} = \frac{R}{GW}\frac{GW}{NW} = \frac{\dfrac{R}{GW}}{\dfrac{NW}{GW}} = \frac{\text{Exposure}}{\text{Solvency}}.$$

13. The American HRS collects gross income data, whereas the Italian SHIW and Dutch SEP ask for after-tax income. We estimated tax liabilities to convert the American income data to be net of taxes. Since the state of residence and many financial details are unknown, we assume standard deductions and account for federal taxation only. This includes federal income tax and Federal Insurance Contributions Act (FICA) liabilities. Incomes after state income tax, where applicable, are therefore slightly lower than reported in table 9.5.

Table 9.6   **Stylized household balance sheet**

Assets		Liabilities	
Safe (cash, savings accounts)	S	Net worth	NW
Risky (stocks, bonds)	R	Debts (mortgage and other)	D
Gross housing (housing equity + mortgage debt)	H		
Other	O		
Gross wealth	GW	Gross wealth	GW

Very few respondents report having no gross wealth at all. Both *exposure,* defined as the ratio of risky assets to gross wealth, and *solvency,* defined as the ratio of net worth to gross wealth, are therefore straightforward to construct.

Table 9.7 characterizes the size and composition of bequeathable household wealth in the three samples. The American and Italian figures are based on 1998 HRS and SHIW, the Dutch on the 1997 SEP. As predicted, the Netherlands has by far the lowest level of private household wealth, both in the mean and in the median. Partly this reflects the lower home ownership rate in the Netherlands for these older cohorts. Stock or bond ownership is highest in the United States (33 percent) and lowest in the Netherlands (19 percent). Following table 9.6, we aggregated assets in four broad categories: (a) safe assets (saving and checking accounts, cash); (b) risky assets (stocks and bonds); (c) housing and other real estate; and (d) other. Since the Dutch sample excludes the self-employed, we have excluded business equity in all countries. U.S. households clearly hold the most risky assets, both in absolute value and as a fraction of gross wealth. Dutch households hold more of their gross wealth in safe assets than the Americans and Italians. Again, this partly reflects the lower home ownership rate in the Netherlands for this age group. In both the United States and the Netherlands, the share of risky assets increased between 1992 and 1997–98 (not shown). The average solvency ratios are large and negative in the United States and Italy, because the ratios are dominated by households with negative net worth that is large relative to their reported gross wealth.

9.6.2   Empirical Evidence for the Hypotheses

Hypothesis 1: The Displacement Effects of Retirement Benefits

Although we have provided some evidence that replacement rates at retirement are lowest in the United States and highest in the Netherlands, it is useful to exploit our microdata to shed further light on this. The replacement rates given in section 9.3.2 were based on hypothetical (median) individuals in the three different countries and on plausible institutional

Table 9.7   Assets and asset allocation (unit of observation: household)

	United States	Italy	The Netherlands
Gross wealth			
Mean	276,200	168,100	95,300
Median	130,000	96,500	45,200
Net worth			
Mean	253,400	166,200	79,300
Median	105,000	95,000	33,500
Owns house (%)			
Mean	76.8	71.8	46.5
Median	100	100	0
Owns stocks/bonds (%)			
Mean	33.0	26.8	18.7
Median	0	0	0
Exposure (R/GW)			
Mean	0.079	0.051	0.039
Median	0	0	0
Solvency (NW/GW)			
Mean	−51.8	−18.3	0.62
Median	1	1	1
Housing equity (if owner)			
Mean	128,200	121,800	111,600
Median	95,000	100,000	95,800
Stocks/bonds (if owner)			
Mean	169,500	54,483	45,700
Median	45,000	20,000	16,900
Portfolio shares (%)			
Safe (S/GW)			
Mean	20.4	29.4	43.4
Risky (R/GW)			
Mean	7.9	5.1	3.9
House (H/GW)			
Mean	45.6	53.2	38.6
Other (O/GW)			
Mean	26.0	12.3	14.0

Note: Monetary values in $ for the United States and in € for Italy and the Netherlands.

parameters. Here we take a different approach. We exploit the longitudinal nature of the data to consider incomes in the waves before and after a respondent first reports being retired to gauge the actual change in income experienced by those who retire. For example, if someone first reports being retired in 1994, we consider incomes as reported in 1993 and 1995. (In the American HRS and Italian SHIW data, the waves are two years apart, except three years for the 1995–98 SHIW.) This approach avoids contamination from part-year employment. We consider *household* noncapital income before and after *individual* retirement. This assumes resource sharing within a household, so that, for instance, a transfer of resources by other household members compensates for a drop in the new retiree's income.

Table 9.8   **Empirical replacement rates, wealth accumulation, and income growth in the
United States**

	N	Mean	10th percentile	Median	90th percentile
Newly retired					
Preretirement household noncapital income	1,953	36,600	6,900	30,600	69,500
Postretirement income	1,797	26,100	6,500	21,200	47,300
Postretirement income + annuity value of wealth	1,797	44,100	9,000	34,100	83,100
Replacement rate (%)	1,749	147.1	28.7	75.7	175.2
Generalized replacement rate[a]	1,749	261.0	47.6	111.4	271.6
Not newly retired					
Noncapital household income $t - 2$	29,442	36,800	7,000	30,000	69,200
Noncapital household income $t + 2$	28,894	35,900	6,300	29,500	68,700
Income ratio $(t + 2)/(t - 2)$ (%)	19,463	213.1	33.5	97.8	179.6
Newly retired					
Preretirement household net worth	1,982	215,200	1,100	115,600	491,600
Postretirement household net worth	1,815	254,900	1,000	124,700	594,500
Wealth growth (%)	1,746	41.9	−85.1	2.2	169.0
Not newly retired					
Net worth $t - 2$	29,735	246,400	2,500	113,200	552,200
Net worth $t + 2$	29,204	267,700	3,200	119,900	588,000
Wealth growth (%)	19,936	114.3	−83.2	6.6	192.8

Note: N = number of observations.

[a]Postretirement noncapital household income + annuity value of wealth divided by preretirement noncapital household income. The annuity value assumes a 3 percent interest rate.

This assumption acknowledges the joint nature of retirement decisions (e.g., Zweimüller and Winter-Ebmer 1996; Gustman and Steinmeier 1994; Maestas 2001). Finally, we consider after-tax income,[14] expressed in constant 1998 dollars.

The top panel of table 9.8 presents empirical after-tax replacement rates for the United States based on the 1992–2000 HRS. The table compares incomes in the wave before retirement and the wave after retirement,[15] that is, at $t - 2$ and $t + 2$. Postretirement income is substantially lower than preretirement income, both in the mean and the median.[16] The average re-

14. See note 13.
15. For the United States and Italy, retirement is defined based on respondent's own report of (complete) retirement status. For the Netherlands, retirement is defined as receiving some form of income transfer (pension, disability, or unemployment benefits), being over fifty years old, and not doing any work for pay.
16. In order to exploit the longitudinal feature of the HRS, the sample consists of original HRS respondents, that is, those born in 1931–41 and their spouses. The sample is thus younger than the sample used in table 9.5, which included all HRS cohorts. This explains why mean and median income levels in table 9.8 exceed those in table 9.5.

placement rate is well above unity, but this is driven by a small number of respondents with particularly low preretirement income. The median replacement rate is 75.7 percent. There is large variation: at the 10th percentile, income dropped by three-quarters after retirement, whereas it increased by three-quarters in real terms at the 90th percentile.

To put these findings in perspective, compare the income changes between the year before retirement and the year after retirement with income changes of individuals who did not retire (i.e., who worked in years $t-2$, t, $t + 2$, or who were retired in all three waves). We observe that the latter individuals also experienced a decline in real income, at least at the median. The decline in income is far smaller at the median (2.2 percent) than the median decline among newly retired individuals (24.3 percent).

The replacement rate improves if we assume that individuals who retire can annuitize their wealth and consume the annuity. Adding the annuity value of bequeathable wealth to postretirement income, possible consumption levels exceed preretirement income for most households. We define the generalized replacement rate as the sum of postretirement income and annuity value of private wealth divided by preretirement income. At the median, the generalized replacement rate is above one (111.4 percent). Even at the 10th percentile, postretirement consumption may be sustained at almost half the level of preretirement income.

The bottom part of table 9.8 presents a similar analysis for household net worth around retirement and compares changes to wealth changes of households in which no retirement takes place. Most households experience wealth growth, but wealth grows somewhat faster for households who do not have a recently retired member. At the median, the increase is 2.2 percent among households that transitioned through retirement and 6.6 percent among those who did not.

Similar to table 9.8, table 9.9 documents income replacement rates, wealth accumulation, and income growth in Italy, based on 1987–98 data. Table 9.8 was in 1998 dollars; table 9.9 in 1998 euros. As in the United States, real household noncapital income tends to drop after retirement. However, the declines are milder. At the median, postretirement Italian household incomes replace 85.9 percent of preretirement income, about 10 percentage points above the median U.S. replacement rate. While there is substantial variation, the differences are smaller than in the United States. For example, at the 10th and 90th percentile, postretirement incomes are about 50 percent below and above their preretirement levels, compared to three-quarter differences in the United States. At the median, real incomes among households that did not transition through a retirement remained almost exactly constant. Naturally, the replacement rates increase when including the annuity value of net worth. The median generalized replacement rate for new retirees in Italy is 124.5 percent, again greater than in the United States (111.4 percent).

Table 9.9   **Empirical replacement rates, wealth accumulation, and income growth in Italy**

	N	Mean	10th percentile	Median	90th percentile
Newly retired					
Preretirement household noncapital income	402	33,800	15,300	30,150	55,300
Postretirement income	402	30,300	11,600	26,150	51,800
Postretirement income + annuity value of wealth	402	46,100	14,000	39,100	79,500
Replacement rate (%)	402	97.3	49.1	85.9	147.5
Generalized replacement rate[a]	402	143.7	65.5	124.5	231.9
Not newly retired					
Noncapital household income $t - 2$	5,682	25,300	9,800	21,500	45,100
Noncapital household income $t + 2$	5,682	26,000	9,600	21,400	46,300
Income ratio $(t + 2)/(t - 2)$ (%)	5,673	112.0	57.9	100.8	170.0
Newly retired					
Preretirement household net worth	402	187,200	7,700	122,650	435,200
Postretirement household net worth	402	225,000	11,100	153,650	515,400
Wealth growth (%)	398	320.8	−68.4	24.0	350.6
Not newly retired					
Net worth $t - 2$	5,682	154,600	3,800	87,900	350,600
Net worth $t + 2$	5,682	189,900	4,400	110,000	431,500
Wealth growth (%)	5,595	305.2	−73.3	14.5	373.2

Note: N = number of observations.

[a]Postretirement noncapital household income + annuity value of wealth divided by preretirement noncapital household income. The annuity value assumes a 3 percent interest rate.

Italian households enjoyed greater wealth gains than American households during the mid- and late 1990s. At the median, net worth among households with a new retiree increased by 24 percent. This gain exceeds the gain among households that did not experience a retirement (14.5 percent), probably because of severance payments (see above).

Table 9.10 shows the same set of statistics for the Netherlands, based on 1984–97 income reports and 1987–97 wealth data. Income and wealth values are in 1998 euros. Dutch replacement rates generally exceed those of both the United States and Italy. At the median, fully 102.3 percent of real preretirement income is replaced. The spread is narrower than in the other two countries. At the 10th and 90th percentile, only about one-third of preretirement income is lost or gained, compared to one-half in Italy and three-quarters in the United States. Dutch households without a new retiree also fared well—at the median, their real household noncapital income rose by 8.1 percent. The spread is again small, much smaller than in the United States and Italy. (This is in part explained by the fact that the Dutch income and wealth figures refer to survey waves that are only two years apart; the Dutch SEP survey is conducted annually, whereas Ameri-

Table 9.10   Empirical replacement rates, wealth accumulation, and income growth in the Netherlands

	N	Mean	10th percentile	Median	90th percentile
Newly retired					
Preretirement household noncapital income	772	22,200	10,500	18,800	38,600
Postretirement income	772	21,900	10,900	18,600	37,400
Postretirement income + annuity value of wealth	772	26,900	12,100	22,900	49,700
Replacement rate (%)	772	113.9	68.0	102.3	138.3
Generalized replacement rate[a]	772	137.1	80.8	114.5	187.2
Not newly retired					
Noncapital household income $t - 1$	52,333	27,300	12,600	25,900	43,200
Noncapital household income $t + 1$	52,333	29,600	13,000	28,100	47,000
Income ratio $(t + 1)/(t - 1)$ (%)	52,333	124.3	81.8	108.1	138.9
Newly retired					
Preretirement household net worth	802	63,400	600	23,400	172,600
Postretirement household net worth	802	67,000	800	23,000	175,400
Wealth growth (%)	800	−82.0	−61.2	4.5	128.3
Not newly retired					
Net worth $t - 1$	55,995	47,900	100	23,300	121,500
Net worth $t + 1$	55,995	57,100	400	31,100	141,100
Wealth growth (%)	55,995	118.2	−79.7	12.5	164.2

Note: N = number of observations.

[a]Postretirement noncapital household income + annuity value of wealth divided by preretirement noncapital household income. The annuity value assumes a 3 percent interest rate.

can HRS and Italian SHIW waves are generally two years apart.) Adding in the annuity value of net worth increases the replacement rates, though not by very much. This reflects the small average wealth holdings among Dutch households.

In the Netherlands, households with a newly retired member enjoyed an increase of 4.5 percent in net worth, far lower than in Italy but somewhat higher than in the United States. The increase among households without a retiring member was one-eighth in two years time, more than the comparable American and Italian figures.

In summary, replacement rates are lowest in the United States and highest in the Netherlands, with a gap at the median of 26.6 percentage points. However, American households accumulate far more private savings than their Dutch counterparts. The replacement rate gap narrows to just 3.1 percentage points when we include the annuity value of net worth in the calculations. This is fully consistent with a life-cycle model in which retirement saving is crowded out by institutional old age pension provisions in the Netherlands, but much less so in the United States.

Clearly, we do not control for the endogeneity of the retirement decision in the empirical analysis. One would expect that, other things being equal, an individual facing a low replacement rate and with little bequeathable wealth to be less likely to retire than an individual with a high replacement rate and substantial bequeathable wealth. By working longer one may be able to increase one's wealth. This will tend to improve the generalized replacement rate. Hence, the relatively small observed differences in generalized replacement rates between the United States and the Netherlands may partly be due to the fact that Americans have a stronger incentive to work longer. Thus, the relatively modest differences in generalized replacement rates across the United States and the Netherlands may be the result of at least two behavioral reactions to differences in replacement rates: these affect both saving decisions and retirement decisions.

Hypothesis 2: The Effect of Earnings and Consumption Uncertainty

Above we argued that Americans face greater financial risks, both before and after retirement. A problem in a cross-country context with the data at hand is that we do not have individual information on the amount of uncertainty faced by the individuals in our sample. Since there are at least two different strong incentives for households in the United States to accumulate more private wealth than in Italy or the Netherlands (precaution and to provide for retirement), it is probably impossible to disentangle the relative influence of the two different incentives. We have argued above that in any case retirement provisions provide a powerful explanation for the difference in wealth accumulation between the United States and the Netherlands. Providing further insight into the patterns of wealth accumulation in Italy, the Netherlands, and the United States, table 9.11 presents results of a regression of household net worth on a number of household characteristics.

Since both household income and net worth have a skewed distribution, we have applied a loglike transformation to these variables. A direct logarithmic transformation is not possible, since both variables can take on negative values. Hence we adopted the inverse hyperbolic sine: $h(x) = \log(\sqrt{x^2 + 1} + x)$. For values of x not too close to zero, $h(x)$ is approximately equal to $\log(2x)$ for positive x and $-\log(2x)$ for negative x. The function $h(x)$ is antisymmetric: $h(x) = -h(-x)$. The drawback of the inverse hyperbolic sine in comparison to the logarithm is that it is not invariant to a change of units. The regressions reported involve both quantities measured in U.S. dollars and quantities measured in euros. If we were to use logs of the monetary variables, the currency differences would simply be absorbed in the country-specific intercepts. For the inverse hyperbolic sine, that is only approximately true.[17]

Table 9.11 presents two regressions. The first regression involves full in-

---

17. We measure net worth in dollars and euros, so that the outcome is far from zero for most respondents with nonzero net worth. At zero, there is no scale issue.

Table 9.11   **Cross country regressions for net worth**

	Separate age functions	IT/NL same age function
Dummy SEP1992	541.482	4.479***
	(0.74)	(6.26)
Dummy SEP1997	541.655	4.673***
	(0.74)	(6.49)
Dummy HRS1992	622.872	−41.788
	(0.86)	(0.56)
Dummy HRS1998	622.080	−42.579
	(0.85)	(0.57)
h(noncapital household income)		
US	0.308***	0.308***
	(17.61)	(17.61)
IT	0.668***	0.668***
	(11.80)	(11.81)
NL	0.031	0.024
	(0.72)	(0.56)
Dummy retired		
US	−0.697***	−0.697***
	(11.52)	(11.52)
IT	0.907***	0.933***
	(5.21)	(5.57)
NL	0.530**	0.648***
	(2.05)	(3.15)
High school, US	1.073***	1.073***
	(8.68)	(8.68)
More than high school, US	1.682***	1.682***
	(18.07)	(18.06)
Some high school, IT	0.900***	0.916***
	(4.73)	(4.86)
High school, IT	1.529***	1.550***
	(6.89)	(7.03)
Some college, IT	2.016***	2.017***
	(6.47)	(6.48)
Lower vocational/junior high, NL	1.034***	1.009***
	(4.02)	(3.94)
Middle vocational, NL	2.044***	1.989***
	(8.92)	(8.82)
Some college, NL	2.829***	2.788***
	(10.42)	(10.41)
No. of observations	21,517	21,517
R^2	0.08	0.08

Notes: Dependent variables: Inverse hyperbolic sine h($\cdot$) of household net worth. Absolute value of *t*-statistics in parentheses. US = United States; IT = Italy; NL = the Netherlands.
***Significant at the 1 percent level.
**Significant at the 5 percent level.

teractions of all variables with country dummies, which is equivalent to having separate equations for each country. It turned out that the age functions of Italy and the Netherlands are quite similar, an impression that was confirmed by a statistical test. Hence, the regression was repeated with identical age functions for the Netherlands and Italy. We specified the effect of age on wealth accumulation as a fifth-degree polynomial. Rather than presenting the estimated coefficients of the polynomials, we sketch the estimated age functions in figure 9.1.

Figure 9.1 shows that after age fifty, American households keep accumulating wealth at a brisk pace, whereas the age profile in the Netherlands and Italy is approximately flat or slightly downward sloping. This would be consistent with the prevalence of a precautionary motive to guard against high out-of-pocket medical costs in the United States as compared to Italy and the Netherlands. Here, and repeatedly in subsequent analyses, we have to offer the caveat that we are not controlling for cohort effects, so that the age effects we observe may be (and probably are) contaminated by cohort effects. Disentangling age and cohort effects is beyond the scope of the current study.

Since the definitions of education levels differ substantially across the three countries, all education dummies are country specific. The lowest education category is always the reference category. Net worth increases monotonically with education in all three countries.

The effect of being retired differs substantially across the three countries, with a negative effect in the United States and positive effects in the Netherlands and Italy. We should be somewhat careful in interpreting these results, as retirement status is correlated with age. In particular, the negative effect of being retired on net worth in the United States should be considered jointly with the strong positive age effect on net worth, shown in fig-

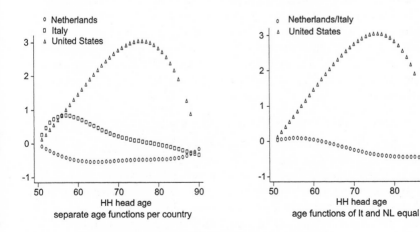

Fig. 9.1   Estimated age functions in the net worth regressions

ure 9.1. More important, retirement may be partly endogenous in the sense that retirement is more likely for individuals with more wealth. Thus, the positive sign of the retirement dummy in Italy and the Netherlands may simply reflect that people with more wealth are more likely to retire. With this interpretation, the sign of the retirement dummy in the United States is harder to understand.

Household income has a positive influence on capital accumulation. However, the strength of the effect varies substantially across the three countries. In the Netherlands the effect of income is very small and not statistically significant. In Italy and the United States it is much bigger and very significant. The discussion of the next hypothesis interprets this pattern.

Hypothesis 3: The Role of Capital Market Imperfections

The implications of the differences in capital markets in the United States, the Netherlands, and Italy are that, ceteris paribus, Italy should have the highest saving rate and the Netherlands the lowest. In addition, when considering net household wealth Italy should be the country where net wealth, as a percentage of gross wealth, should be highest. The former implication is hard to test directly, because of other factors influencing saving rates, but the latter implication is easy to verify.

Table 9.7 shows that median solvency (net worth divided by gross wealth) is equal to one in all three countries. The ratios of median net worth and median gross wealth in table 9.7 are 0.81 in the United States, 0.98 in Italy, and 0.74 in the Netherlands. Thus, for a given level of net worth Italian households borrow considerably less money than households in the United States and the Netherlands. The weaker borrowing constraints in the latter countries induce lower private capital accumulation.

Somewhat tentatively, we interpret the high coefficient of noncapital income in the wealth regressions in table 9.11 for Italy as another indication of the relevance of borrowing constraints. Conceivably, the harder it is to borrow money to invest in profitable undertakings (e.g., real estate or stocks), the more important income becomes as a source of capital for investment. Thus, ceteris paribus, the connection between income and wealth accumulation would be stronger in Italy than in the United States or the Netherlands.

Hypothesis 4: Portfolio Composition

We hypothesized that stock ownership in the Netherlands will be the lowest among the three countries, because it has the lowest level of private wealth. In the United States, the combination of a well-developed capital market and a high level of private wealth for retirement purposes should induce a relatively high level of stock ownership. Italy should be in between, because it has a relatively high level of private wealth but a less-developed capital market. To shed light on the plausibility of these hypotheses, table 9.12 presents results from cross-country regressions of the

Table 9.12   **The share of risky assets across countries**

	(1)	(2)	(3)
Dummy HRS1992	−43.591	0.205**	0.062***
	(0.63)	(2.45)	(4.19)
Dummy HRS1998	−43.554	0.244***	0.101***
	(0.63)	(2.92)	(6.47)
Dummy SEP1992	−29.098	−0.437***	−0.643***
	(0.42)	(3.60)	(7.54)
Dummy SEP1997	−29.077	−0.415***	−0.631***
	(0.42)	(3.39)	(7.28)
h(noncapital income)			
US	0.015***	0.015***	
	(9.17)	(9.24)	
IT	0.018***	0.019***	
	(2.83)	(2.91)	
NL	0.004	0.004	
	(1.00)	(0.96)	
h(net worth)			
US	0.052***	0.052***	
	(32.30)	(32.36)	
IT	0.060***	0.061***	
	(12.01)	(12.14)	
NL	0.109***	0.109***	0.105***
	(15.32)	(15.30)	(14.67)
Dummy retired			
US	−0.000	0.001	0.001
	t(0.00)	(0.17)	(0.17)
IT	0.075***	0.067***	0.068***
	(4.89)	(4.87)	(4.95)
NL	0.031	0.047**	0.050**
	(1.10)	(2.39)	(2.50)
High school, US	−0.005	−0.006	−0.006
	(0.43)	(0.52)	(0.54)
More than high school, US	0.075***	0.074***	0.074***
	(9.45)	(9.34)	(9.29)
Some high school, IT	0.085***	0.089***	0.093***
	(5.14)	(5.49)	(5.80)
High school, IT	0.143***	0.146***	0.155***
	(7.83)	(8.09)	(8.91)
Some college, IT	0.154***	0.156***	0.169***
	(6.31)	(6.38)	(7.35)
Lower vocational/junior high, NL	−0.011	−0.015	0.003
	(0.33)	(0.46)	(0.10)
Middle vocational, NL	0.088***	0.084***	0.094***
	(3.38)	(3.22)	(3.55)
Some college, NL	0.170***	0.169***	0.182***
	(6.09)	(6.10)	(6.49)
h(noncapital income)			0.015***
			(9.67)
h(net worth)			0.053***
			(34.39)
No. of observations	21,447	21,445	21,344
Pseudo R^2	.21	.21	.21

Notes: Dependent variables: share of risky assets in gross wealth. Absolute value of *t*-statistics in parentheses. US = United States; IT = Italy; NL = the Netherlands.

***Significant at the 1 percent level.

**Significant at the 5 percent level.

share of risky assets (stocks and bonds) in gross wealth. The approach is similar to the approach in table 9.11. We start with separate analyses by country and then simplify the model by imposing equality of parameters allowed by the data. Since shares are between zero and one by construction, we use a two-limit tobit model to estimate the equation, with a lower limit equal to zero and an upper limit equal to one.

The first column presents estimates of the unrestricted equations. A test for equality of the age functions across countries is far from rejection and hence the second column imposes equal age functions. A test of equality of the income coefficients across the three countries is almost rejected at the 5 percent level ($F[2,21419] = 2.83, p = .0590$). Similarly, we cannot reject the hypothesis that the net worth coefficients of the United States and Italy are equal ($F[1,21419] = 2.73, p = .0984$) at the 5 percent level. The last column presents estimation results with these equalities imposed. Figure 9.2 sketches the estimated age function, which turns out to be fairly flat in the age range where most of the data points are.

For convenience, we restrict a discussion of table 9.12 to the last column. Household income has a relatively small but significant direct influence on the share of risky assets held. Its influence is positive, which would be consistent with a model where income can be used to buffer risks incurred by investing in the risky assets (i.e., having a higher noncapital income reduces background risk in some informal sense). Of course, there is also an indirect effect of income via its effect on total net worth, as discussed with re-

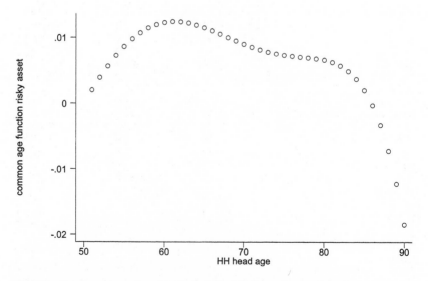

Fig. 9.2   A common age function to explain risky asset share across the three countries

spect to table 9.11. Net worth has a positive effect on the share of risky assets in all three countries, as expected.

The share of risky assets in gross wealth increases with education in all countries (except the difference between high school and less than high school in the United States; the difference between these two education levels is not statistically significant). This can be interpreted in at least two different ways: (a) owning stocks or bonds requires a certain level of knowledge which is more likely to be present among the higher-educated; (b) a higher education level reduces risks in the labor market and this reduction in background risk makes an individual less risk-averse.

We note that the indicator for being retired is insignificant in the United States and significantly positive in both Italy and the Netherlands. A possible interpretation is that after retirement income and consumption risks have essentially disappeared in Italy and the Netherlands, whereas in the United States consumption risk associated with adverse health shocks becomes more important. This risk reduction after retirement in Italy and the Netherlands would allow households to take on more risk in the stock market.

It is tempting to interpret the country- and wave-specific dummies as propensities to hold risky assets, after controlling for the variables listed in table 9.12. One should note, however, that in general the values of the dummies are sensitive to the scaling of the monetary variables. If, for instance, we switch from dollars and euros to thousands of dollars and euros, then to a good approximation all monetary variables are reduced by $\ln(1,000) = 6.91$. Since the monetary variables have different coefficients for different countries, such changes in monetary units affect country- and wave-specific dummies differentially, without changing the underlying model. The only valid comparison in table 9.12 is between Italy and the United States in the last column, because we have restricted the coefficients of net worth and household income to be equal. We notice that the dummies for the United States are significantly positive, consistent with the notion that a more developed capital market in the United States facilitates stock and bond ownership, controlling for education, wealth, and demographics.

9.7 Conclusion

The analysis in this paper is a first attempt at consistently exploiting institutional variation across countries to improve our understanding of wealth accumulation and portfolio choice of households at or near retirement. The number of countries considered is limited, as is the amount of detail in the data that we have been able to use. The stylized facts that we are able to glean from the microdata are certainly consistent with the hypotheses that we formulated. In summary, their main implications are as follows:

- Americans should save more for retirement than the Dutch or the Italians.
- Americans should save more due to more exposure to uninsurable income and consumption risk.
- Italians should save more due to severe borrowing constraints in their country.
- The Dutch should have relatively low stockholdings due to the low level of private wealth.
- Stock ownership in the United States should be higher than in Italy because of more developed capital markets in the United States.

While each of these implications is borne out by the data, we cannot rule out alternatives to our stochastic life-cycle framework. Further, it is in general not possible to establish the relative magnitude of factors influencing wealth accumulation or portfolio choice. For instance, both low replacement rates at retirement and higher consumption and income risk in the United States imply that Americans should save more than Europeans. To further disentangle the relative effect of these factors one possibility would be to exploit variation in risk and replacement rates across individuals in the datasets, for example, along the lines of Carroll and Samwick (1998). However, such an approach is vulnerable to the criticism that individuals select into occupations that are more or less risky according to their risk preferences. Assuming that such self-selection is more difficult across countries, analyzing a substantial larger number of countries would appear to be preferable.

It is worthwhile to extend the analysis in two main directions. First, it is very desirable to add countries to have more institutional variation that can be exploited, as the problem of disentangling the roles of replacement rates and risk illustrates. Yet, second, the current data can be analyzed more extensively and more information can be brought to bear on the hypotheses formulated. In particular, one could exploit the longitudinal nature of the data more, for example, to disentangle age and cohort effects, but also to exploit time series variation in addition to cross-sectional and cross-country variation. This will also permit addressing such endogeneity issues as the timing of retirement.

References

Banca d'Italia. 1999. *Relazione Annuale.* Rome: Bozze di Stampa.
Banks, J., R. Blundell, and A. Brugiavini. 2001. Risk pooling, precautionary saving and consumption growth. *The Review of Economic Studies* 68:757–79.
Barsky, R. B., F. T. Juster, M. S. Kimball, and M. D. Shapiro. 1997. Preference pa-

rameters and behavioral heterogeneity: An experimental approach in the Health and Retirement Study. *Quarterly Journal of Economics* 112:537–79.

Beltrametti, L. 1996. *Il debito pensionistico in Italia.* Bologna: Il Mulino.

Bertaut, Carol, and Martha Starr-McCluer. 2000. Household portfolios in the United States. Washington, DC: Federal Reserve Board of Governors. Mimeograph.

Blöndal, S., and S. Scarpetta. 1998. The retirement decision in OECD countries. OECD Economics Department Working Paper no. 202. Paris: Organization for Economic Cooperation and Development.

Board of OASI Trustees. 2001. The 2001 Annual Report of the Board of Trustees of the Federal Old-Age and Survivors Insurance and Disability Insurance Trust Funds. Government Printing Office: Washington, DC.

Browning, M., and A. Lusardi. 1996. Household saving: Micro theories and micro facts. *Journal of Economic Literature* 34:1797–1855.

Brugiavini, A. 1999. Social Security and retirement in Italy. In *Social Security and retirement around the world,* ed. J. Gruber and D. A. Wise, 181–237. Chicago: Chicago University Press.

Bureau of the Census. 2001. Resident population estimates of the United States by age and sex: April 1, 1990 to July 1, 1999, with short-term projection to November 1, 2000. Washington, DC: U.S. Census Bureau.

Carroll, C. D. 1992. The buffer-stock theory of saving: Some macroeconomic evidence. *Brookings Papers on Economic Activity* Issue no. 2:61–156.

———. 1997. Buffer stock saving and the life cycle/permanent income hypothesis. *Quarterly Journal of Economics* 112:3–55.

———. 2001. Portfolios of the rich. In *Household Portfolios,* ed. L. Guiso, M. Haliassos, and T. Jappelli, 389–429. Cambridge: MIT Press.

Carroll, C. D. 1998. How important is precautionary saving? *The Review of Economics and Statistics* 80:410–19.

Copeland, Craig. 2001. IRA assets continue to grow. *Employee Benefit Research Institute Notes* 22:1.

De Nederlandsche Bank. 2000. *Het Bancaire Hypotheekbedrijf Onder de Loep.* Amsterdam: De Nederlandsche Bank.

Deaton, A. 1991. Saving and liquidity constraints. *Econometrica* 59:1221–48.

Dynan, K. E. 1993. How prudent are consumers? *Journal of Political Economy* 101:1104–13.

Federal Reserve. 2001. Flow of funds accounts of the United States: Fourth quarter 2000. Washington, DC: Board of Governors of the Federal Reserve System. Available at [http://www.federalreserve.gov/releases/Z1].

Franco, Daniele. 2000. Italy: A never-ending pension reform. Paper presented at the NBER-Kiel Institute Conference, 20–21 March, Berlin.

Gollier, C. 2001. *The economics of risk and time.* Cambridge: MIT Press.

Gruber, J., and D. A. Wise, eds. 1999. *Social security and retirement around the world.* Chicago: University of Chicago Press.

Guiso, L., T. Jappelli, and L. Pistaferri. 1999. What determines earnings and employment uncertainty? Center for Economic Policy and Research. Discussion Paper no. 2043. London: Centre for Economic Policy and Research.

Guiso, L., T. Jappelli, and D. Terlizzese. 1992. Earnings uncertainty and precautionary saving. *Journal of Monetary Economics* 30:307–37.

Gustman, A. L., and T. L. Steinmeier. 1994. Retirement in a family context: A structural model for husbands and wives. NBER Working Paper no. 4629. Cambridge, MA: National Bureau of Economic Research.

Haliassos, M., and C. C. Bertaut. 1995. Why do so few hold stocks? *The Economic Journal* 105:1110–29.

Hochgürtel, S. 1998. *Household portfolio choices.* Ph.D. diss. Tilburg University.
Hubbard, G. R., J. Skinner, S. P. Zeldes. 1994a. Expanding the life-cycle model: Precautionary saving and public policy. *American Economic Review* 84:174–79.
———. 1994b. The importance of precautionary motives in explaining individual and aggregate saving. *Carnegie-Rochester Conference Series on Public Policy* 40: 59–125.
———. 1995. Precautionary saving and social insurance. *Journal of Political Economy* 103:360–99.
Hurd, M. D. 2001. Portfolio holdings of the elderly. In *Household Portfolios,* ed. L. Guiso, M. Haliassos, and T. Jappelli, 431–72. Cambridge: MIT Press.
Hurd, M. D., L. Lillard, and C. Panis. 1998. An analysis of the choice to cash out pension rights at job change or retirement. RAND Working Paper no. DRU-1979-DOL: Santa Monica, CA.
Johnson, P., ed. 1999. *Older getting wiser.* London: Institute for Fiscal Studies.
Kapteyn, A., and K. de Vos. 1999. Social security and retirement in the Netherlands. In *Social Security and retirement around the world,* ed. J. Gruber and D. A. Wise, 269–303. Chicago: Chicago University Press.
Kapteyn, A., and C. Panis. 2002. The size and composition of wealth holdings in the United States, Italy, and the Netherlands. RAND Working Paper no. DRU-2767-DOL, March 2002: Santa Monica, CA.
Kimball, M. S. 1990. Precautionary saving in the small and in the large. *Econometrica* 58:53–73.
Lusardi, A. 1997. Precautionary saving and subjective earnings variance. *Economics Letters* 57:319–26.
Maestas, N. 2001. Labor, love and leisure: Complementarity and the timing of retirement by working couples. University of California, Berkeley, Department of Economics. Mimeograph.
Modigliani, F., and R. Brumberg. 1954. Utility analysis and the consumption function: An interpretation of the cross-section data. In *Post-Keynesian economics,* ed. K. Kurihara, 388–436. New Brunswick: Rutgers University Press.
Rostagno, M. 1996. *Il percorso della riforma, 1992–1995: Nuovi indicatori di consistenza e di sostenibilità per il Fondo Pensioni Lavoratori Dipendenti.* Rome: Banca d'Italia.
Scott, J., and J. Shoven. 1996. Lump sum distributions: Fulfilling the portability promise or eroding retirement security? EBRI Issue Brief. Washington, DC: Employee Benefit Research Institute, October.
Social Insurance Bank. 2000. *Bedragen AOW per 1 januari 2001.* Netherlands: The Hague.
U.S. Department of Labor. 2001. Abstract of 1997 Form 5500 Annual Reports. *Private Pension Plan Bulletin* no. 10 (Winter). Washington, DC: U.S. Department of Labor, Pension and Welfare Benefits Administration, Office of Policy and Research.
Vissing Jørgensen, A. 2000. Towards an explanation of household portfolio choice heterogeneity: Nonfinancial income and participation cost structures. University of Chicago, Department of Economics. Working Paper.
Zweimüller, J., and R. Winter-Ebmer. 1996. Retirement of spouses and social security reform. *European Economic Review* 40:449–72.

Comment   Andrew A. Samwick

This chapter provides a systematic examination of the level and composition of wealth holdings across three developed countries. It is similar in spirit to cross-country comparisons in volumes by Poterba (1994) on saving and Gruber and Wise (1999) on retirement, in which micro-level data from several countries were harmonized to examine a specific issue. The analysis is organized around a set of motives for saving or stock ownership, with predictions made for the ranking of countries based on the institutions in each one. The goal of such an undertaking is to assess the validity of each motive as a separate component of a general life-cycle model.

This objective is for all practical purposes beyond the reach of a study that uses only macroeconomic data for each country, unless there were a long time series on aggregate saving with exogenous changes in the institutions of one country relative to the others. The use of microeconomic data is therefore a sensible area for current research. However, the same caveat regarding identification applies with microeconomic data as with macroeconomic data—to what extent are the differences across subgroups of the population due *only* to the institutions related to the specific motive in question? It is in this regard that more work needs to be done in this line of inquiry.

The authors' results are briefly summarized in table 9C.1.

The authors consider each of four savings and portfolio motives in turn: retirement saving, based on differences in replacement rates; precautionary saving, based on presumed differences in postretirement out-of-pocket health expenditures; liquidity constraints, particularly with respect to purchasing a home; and stock ownership, given the differences in wealth levels that decrease the household's aversion to holding risky assets. In general, the authors conjecture that households in the United States face lower replacement rates and higher postretirement uncertainty and should therefore hold more wealth. This, along with very well-developed equity markets, allows them to allocate more of their wealth to stock ownership. Italian households face more severe borrowing constraints in financial markets, particularly related to home ownership, and thus are conjectured to hold greater wealth to accumulate down payments or less debt relative to their assets.

The first hypothesis pertains to retirement saving. The authors set up a comparison between the raw replacement rates provided by social security and pensions and the generalized replacement rate, including the annuity

Andrew A. Samwick is a professor of economics and director of the Nelson A. Rockefeller Center at Dartmouth College, and a research associate of the National Bureau of Economic Research.

Table 9C.1   Relative strength of saving or portfolio motives, by country

Motive	United States	Italy	The Netherlands
Retirement	High	Low	Low
Uncertainty	High	Low	Low
Liquidity constraints	Low	High	Low
Stock ownership	High	Low	Low

Note: Each cell reports the predicted relative amount of saving (or stock ownership) in each country due to the specified motive based on prevailing institutions.

Table 9C.2   Raw and generalized replacement rates, by country

Motive	United States	Italy	The Netherlands
Raw	75.7	85.9	102.3
Generalized	111.4	124.5	114.5

Notes: Each cell reports the ratio of postretirement noncapital income to preretirement income. The generalized replacement rates also include the annuity value of household wealth in the numerator.

value of wealth. Table 9C.2 shows the comparisons at the medians. The authors' argument receives some support—in the Netherlands, where raw replacement rates are highest, the annuity value of wealth accumulated privately is smaller than in the United States and Italy.

There are two important caveats to this conclusion. First, because the comparisons are done using actual retirements that are observed during the sample, there is a potential for sample selection to exaggerate the results. Households that have the highest replacement rates are more likely to retire. The bias may go in either direction—depending on whether it is the high raw replacement rate or the high annuity value of wealth that more strongly correlates with retirement behavior. This correlation must be estimated empirically for each country. Second, for Italy and the Netherlands, sample sizes are in the hundreds (largely because the surveys are for the whole population rather than just a cohort nearing retirement). Standard errors should be reported to determine whether the replacement rates are significantly different in each case.

The second hypothesis rests on the authors' assertion that households in the United States should save more to confront uncertainty in preretirement income and old-age health expenditures. The main finding is that Americans save more after age fifty. This could be evidence in favor of precautionary saving, but it could also be due to many other factors, including a stronger bequest motive. Much more could be done in this aspect of the paper. Other authors examining the relationship between income uncertainty and wealth (see, for example, Carroll and Samwick 1997) have tested whether households in higher-risk occupations, industries, or education groups actually save more. The authors should include in their analysis proxies for the actual risks faced to determine if precautionary motives are in fact responsible for the disparities in saving.

The third hypothesis pertains to the effect of liquidity constraints on saving. In general, the possibility of being liquidity constrained in a future period generates higher saving in the current period. The authors approach this possibility by noting that Italy, where access to credit is more limited than in the other countries, has the highest ratio of net wealth to total wealth. This is also supportive of the hypothesis. One caveat to the comparison is that a sample of households near retirement age is not the most effective place to examine borrowing constraints, as a life-cycle model suggests very little borrowing at these ages in any country. Since most of the borrowing would occur earlier in life when the household first attempts to become a home owner, it would be better to make the comparison using a sample of younger households.

The last hypothesis considers portfolio choice, based on the results of the first three. Since risk aversion is thought to decrease as wealth increases, the higher wealth holdings in Italy and especially the United States should lead to higher stock ownership. This conjecture is empirically verified. However, there are several caveats to the interpretation. First, many other factors that differ at the country level may contribute to different degrees of stock ownership. For example, Poterba and Samwick (2003) show that marginal tax rates influence the ownership and allocation of financial assets in the United States. The finding that older households in the United States hold more stock in their portfolios could reflect a larger capital gains tax or estate tax preference for equities relative to the tax preferences in other countries. Second, I disagree with the underlying assumption that there is a single, global market for all securities—the supply of securities in each country will influence the portfolios of that country's households. There is no necessary reason why the aggregate debt-equity ratio in each country will be the same. High stock ownership in the United States may simply reflect a greater supply of corporate equity relative to the other countries. Third, in equilibrium, the holdings of a particular cohort (e.g., those nearing retirement) may be a passive response to the portfolio needs of another cohort. For example, younger households in the Netherlands may be more willing to hold stock than their contemporaries in other countries. The younger households would bid up the price of equities in the Netherlands, causing older households to hold less stock. The authors should take more care to control for these confounding possibilities in making their conclusions.

Overall, the authors achieve some degree of success in exploiting variation in institutions across countries to test hypotheses about saving. Certainly nothing in the chapter suggests a reason to doubt a straightforward stochastic life-cycle model. Future work needs to consider more carefully the other factors that influence saving at the country level to ensure that the comparisons are truly identified.

References

Carroll, Christopher D., and Andrew A. Samwick. 1997. The nature and magnitude of precautionary wealth. *Journal of Monetary Economics* 40:41–72.

Gruber, Jonathan, and David A. Wise, eds. 1999. *Social security and retirement around the world.* Chicago: University of Chicago Press.

Poterba, James M., ed. 1994. *International comparisons of household saving.* Chicago: University of Chicago Press.

Poterba, James M., and Andrew A. Samwick. 2003. Taxation and household portfolio composition: U.S. evidence from the 1980s and 1990s. *Journal of Public Economics* 87:5–38.

Household Saving in Germany
Results of the First SAVE Study

Axel Börsch-Supan and Lothar Essig

10.1 Introduction

This paper takes a fresh look on the saving behavior of German households. It exploits newly collected data, the first wave of the so-called SAVE panel. It is a preliminary look, since many aspects of saving can only be understood using longitudinal data—savings, after all, is an intertemporal decision. Further waves of the SAVE study will be collected in 2005. This paper reports on the initial wave that was collected in 2001.

While the topic of savings is by no means uncharted territory—see the recent comprehensive surveys by Deaton (1992), Browning and Lusardi (1996), and Attanasio (1999)—the savings behavior of households is still not well understood. This is astonishing, since the allocation of available income into spending and saving is one of the most important economic decisions made by a household. The intertemporal aspect of saving is fundamental for our understanding of how a household plans for the long term. How far ahead and how accurately do households look into the future? To what extent do they plan at all? Which rules and mechanisms do

Axel Börsch-Supan is a professor of economics at the University of Mannheim, director of the Mannheim Research Institute for the Economics of Aging, and a research associate of the National Bureau of Economic Research. Lothar Essig is a research associate of the Mannheim Research Institute for the Economics of Aging.

We are grateful to Anette Reil-Held, Bernd Katzenstein, Klaus Kortmann, and Joachim Winter for most helpful comments, and to the interviewers for their commitment in implementing this study. We would also like to thank the German Science Foundation (DFG) and the European Commission, which financed most of the survey through the "Sonderforschungsbereich 504" and the Training and Mobility of Researchers (TMR) Grant "Savings, Pensions and Portfolio Choice." Finally, we thank Volker Zimmermann for translating parts of this paper from German to English. The usual disclaimers apply.

households employ when they decide about saving? These are the core questions that we try to answer in this paper.

Saving behavior encompasses not only the sober economic thinking by perfectly informed planners but also (often only seemingly) unstructured reactions deeply rooted in human psychology and sociocultural norms. Actual behavior may deviate (e.g., Thaler and Shefrin 1981; Laibson 1997; O'Donoghue and Rabin 1999) from the models that economists are used to working with (e.g., Kotlikoff 1989; Hurd 1990; Jappelli and Modigliani 1998). To understand saving, it therefore helps to be open for economic as well as psychological and sociological explanations. The SAVE panel attempts to collect a large set of variables that shed light on many household characteristics. Moreover, saving behavior, whether soberly planned or driven by intuition and conventions, is shaped by the institutional and political environment, notably the social safety net, tax rules, and capital market regulations (see Poterba 1994 and Börsch-Supan 2003). To understand saving, it therefore helps to exploit institutional variation. This paper on German saving behavior should therefore be seen in connection with—as well as in contrast to—the large literature on saving behavior of U.S. households.

Our poor understanding of saving behavior has far-reaching consequences for economic policy. We do not understand well, for instance, to what extent saving must be encouraged so that enough savings are available for financing the investment that forms the basis for long-term growth of our economy. Payments toward a saving scheme increase the after-tax interest rate and thus the return on the funds saved. If the substitution effect prevails, measures designed to encourage saving will achieve what they are meant to do. However, there is also an income effect. If households have a specific target in mind—say, an automobile, a foreign trip, a house, or a certain sum for their old age—then a higher return only means that the state is now helping and that they themselves have to save less to achieve the same goal. In this case, savings subsidies are only a windfall; they do not increase savings within the economy as a whole and may even reduce aggregate savings, if the taxes necessary to finance the subsidies are raised with inefficiencies.

A particular case in point is retirement saving and its role in pension reform. In fact, we do not have a reliable empirical basis on which to assess whether the recent German pension reform named after former labor secretary Walter Riester will be successful in creating new saving. As with other multipillar pension reforms, Riester reduced the generosity of pay-as-you-go pensions and hoped that households would fill the so-created pension gap by saving in individual accounts, which are heavily subsidized. There are several unresolved issues here. First, the substitution between pay-as-you-go "virtual" saving and the "real" saving in these new accounts: will such saving exactly compensate for the reductions in pay-as-you-go pensions? Or will substitution be less than perfect? Second, will the

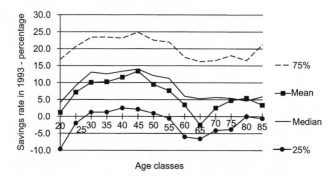

Fig. 10.1   Saving rates according to income quartile and mean value, 1993 income and expenditure survey
Source: Börsch-Supan et al. (2001) based on income and expenditure surveys 1978–1993.

new retirement saving simply displace other saving? Will the increase in savings made in life insurance and pension funds coincide with a reduction of saving, for example, in home ownership and real estate? We do not have good answers to these questions. One purpose of the SAVE panel is to shed light on them during an important transition period, when the new multi-pillar pension system in Germany will slowly replace the monolithic pay-as-you-go pension system, in which 85 percent of retirement income was the state-provided pension.

Germany is an interesting country in which to study household saving behavior since it appears to contradict the familiar textbook version of the life-cycle theory of consumption and saving. Figure 10.1 shows the saving rate of Germans according to their age and income. It is based on data from the Income and Expenditure Survey conducted by the Federal Statistical Office, which collects data from a very large number of households (approximately 50,000). The saving rate is calculated as net expenditure on wealth formation (expenditure for real estate and financial assets, including capital repayment but minus borrowings), divided by the net income of the household.[1] The Income and Expenditure Survey is carried out every five years. Figure 10.1 relates to 1993, the last year for which detailed information that can be compared with the previous year is available.[2]

Figure 10.1 shows the average saving rate, which is constructed from flow data: sum of purchases of assets within a year, minus sales of assets during this year, divided by net household income in the year under review. Figure 10.1 also shows the saving rate of three income levels, the median income and the lower and upper quartile.

1. Cf. Börsch-Supan et al. (1999).
2. An analysis of the 1998 German income and expenditure survey (EVS) has not been made because comparison is difficult. See text for details.

Two aspects do not match the pattern predicted by naive textbook theory. First, we do not see borrowings from young households—they are clearly constrained. This may not be particularly surprising. Second, and more striking, is that nearly everyone—whether in the middle income bracket or richer—also saves substantial amounts in old age. Only households that earn less than 25 percent of average income spend more between the ages of sixty and seventy-five than they save.

An important purpose of the SAVE panel is therefore to shed light on the many facets of saving behavior that can enrich the life-cycle hypothesis to make it fit actual behavior better. Extensions in four directions appear particularly promising:

- Pay more attention to the complex institutional background, in particular the social insurance system.
- Study the approximation properties when households use rules of thumb in place of perfect economic optimization, and understand the welfare loss involved.
- Try to measure the influence of psychological factors such as risk aversion and self-control.
- Understand how households learn about saving decisions from their family and social environment.

Along these lines, this paper highlights first and large descriptive results of the first wave of the SAVE study. Section 10.2 describes this new survey. Section 10.3 reports on methodological aspects such as representativity and item-nonresponse patterns. Sections 10.4 to 10.6 present the substantive results: section 10.4, qualitative and quantitative saving measures; section 10.5, saving motives; and section 10.6, saving rules. Section 10.7 concludes with some preliminary suggestions relevant to public policy.

10.2   The SAVE Survey

In Germany there is currently no survey that records detailed savings data in conjunction with sociological and psychological characteristics. The socioeconomic panel (SOEP) only records rough indicators, such as "Did you spend all of your income last year or was there anything left over?" and "Do you have a savings book?" and so on, but it does not cover the quantitative composition and any change in the amount of wealth. The position was similar for the "debit and credit" surveys, which contain binary data (yes/no) on portfolio composition; they detailed a large set of investment forms but did not quantify the portfolio shares.

The EVS, conducted every five years by the Federal Statistical Office, with its detailed information on the amount and composition of income, expenditure, and wealth, is the main source of data on the savings behav-

Table 10.1   **Structure of the questionnaire of the SAVE survey**

Part 1: Introduction, determining which person will be surveyed in the respective household
Part 2: Basic socioeconomic data of the household
Part 3: Qualitative questions concerning saving behavior, income, and wealth
Part 4: Budget balance: Quantitative questions concerning income and wealth
Part 5: Psychological and social determinants of saving behavior
Part 6: Conclusion: Interview situation

ior of households in Germany.[3] The 1993 EVS also contains the most important sociodemographic characteristics for all persons living in the household, while other surveys only contain information on the reference person. In the light of the squeeze on public funds, the 1998 EVS has again been slimmed down drastically, and in some areas it bears very little resemblance to earlier surveys. It still covers a very large number of households, but several variables that are important for savings behavior are now missing. Sociological and psychological characteristics as well as many economic characteristics important for an understanding of savings are absent, because these expensive surveys are primarily intended for the administrative work of the Federal Statistical Office and not for research purposes.

Weaknesses of existing data material can only be rectified by new surveys. We departed from the Dutch CentER Panel and the U.S. Health and Retirement Survey as examples and cooperated with the Mannheim Center for Surveys, Methods, and Analyses (ZUMA) and Infratest-Burke (Munich) to produce a questionnaire consisting of six parts. The questionnaire has been designed in such a way that the interview should not exceed forty-five minutes. On average, households took between thirty-one and thirty-two minutes. Table 10.1 provides an overview of the SAVE questionnaire.

The brief first part explains the purpose of the questionnaire and describes the precautions that have been taken in respect of data protection. We feel that this introduction is important because the survey deals with sensitive issues such as personal finances. The interviewer then asks to speak to a member of the household who knows about income and assets. If this person is not at home, the interviewer must make a return visit—up to five times, if necessary.

Part 2 lasts about fifteen minutes and is the standard initial interview, in which questions are asked about the composition and socioeconomic

---

3. Papers using these data include Börsch-Supan (1992, 1994a,b), Reil-Held (1999), and Schnabel (1999).

structure of the household, including age, education, and participation in the labor force of the person surveyed and his or her partner.

Part 3 contains qualitative questions on saving behavior, such as the importance of a series of savings motives, whether there is actually anything left over to save, how regularly savings are made, and so on. Questions are also asked about decision processes, possible rules of thumb, and past patterns of behavior, as well as their parents' attitude to money.

Part 4 is the critical part of the questionnaire because this is where a complete balance sheet of the household is ascertained. A detailed survey is made of income according to source, changes in income, the level of assets according to the various kinds of wealth, and changes in the types of wealth over the last year. Apart from financial assets, the questions also cover private and company pensions, ownership of property, and business assets. Questions are also asked about debt. Part 4 is kept separate from the other parts. We will come back to this feature.

Part 5 contains questions about psychological and social factors. It includes the social environment, expectations about the economic situation, health and possible future events, life expectancy, and general attitudes to life.

Part 6 ends the interview with standard questions about the interview situation and leaves both the person surveyed and the interviewer considerable scope for their own comments. We received comments about confidentiality as well as the length and accuracy of the questionnaire. Questions are also asked about Internet access and willingness to participate in future waves of the survey, as required under German law.

A survey of this kind is an experiment in Germany. Apart from the income and expenditure survey, no German survey to date has attempted to produce such a detailed assessment of income, savings, and wealth. When one combines this economic information with the questions about psychological and social factors, the survey provides a multifaceted picture of the household surveyed. We think that only such a detailed picture will help us understand the savings behavior of a household. The price of this complex picture is a questionnaire that demands considerable patience and willingness on the part of the household to answer the questions.

The survey was carried out in five different variants (see table 10.2). The variants in this initial wave were designed in order to find the best possible combination of accurate answers and willingness to answer. Later waves will use only one variant. The first four variants were computer-aided personal interviews (CAPIs) carried out by Infratest-Burke (Munich) on a representative quota-sample. The quotas were in proportion to current official population statistics (the 2000 microcensus) and related to age, whether the respondent is a wage earner or a salaried employee, and household size. The sample augmentation in the 2005 wave will be random-route

Table 10.2   Survey variants: Sampling and interview techniques

	CAPI		CAPI-D		Access panel
	Numeric	Categorical	Via pick-up service	Via mail	
Interview technique	CAPI	CAPI	CAPI	CAPI	PAPI
Type of random sample	Quota sample	Quota sample	Quota sample	Quota sample	Access panel
Questions concerning income and fortune	In DM	Brackets	In DM	In DM	In DM
Design of part 4	Part of CAPI	Part of CAPI	Drop-off (via pick-up)	Drop-off (via mail)	Part of PAPI
No. of interviews	295	304	294	276	660

samples. In contrast, the fifth survey method was a conventional paper-and-pencil questionnaire (PAPI), given to a so-called Access Panel operated by the Test Panel Institute (TPI) Wetzlar. Both surveys recorded information from households where the head of the household is between eighteen and sixty-nine years old.

The only difference among the first four variants lies in part 4 of the questionnaire. In variants 1 and 2 of this part, all questions are answered in the presence of the interviewer. The difference between variants 1 and 2 is that the quantitative questions were presented once in numerical form as deutsche mark (DM) amounts ("How high do you estimate your household income is in DM?") and once as categories in specified ranges, disguised in such a way that it would be difficult for the interview to interpret them: "Does your income fall within range R?" in which case the respondent is given a picture in which range R, say around DM 2,000–2,500, has been defined.

Because many of these questions relate to intensely personal matters of income and wealth, we went one step further in variants 3 and 4. Here the entire part 4 was skipped in CAPI and left with the respondent (termed "drop off," abbreviated below as CAPI-D), so that the respondents could fill it out at their leisure and without their answers being seen by the interviewer. With variant 3, the interviewer came back personally and collected that part of the questionnaire; with variant 4, the questionnaire had to be returned by mail. If this was not done within a specified number of days, the respondent was reminded of this by telephone several times.

Table 10.2 summarizes these five survey variants. In total, 1,829 households were surveyed. The survey took place in early summer 2001. The fieldwork for the personal interviews took place between May 29 and June 26, 2001, whereas the fieldwork for the Access Panel (cf. below) took place between June 29 and July 24, 2001.

10.3   Quality of the SAVE Data

This section discusses the quality and representativity of the SAVE data, in particular item nonresponse. To what extent do those surveyed refuse to answer the sensitive questions? Can we keep within the agreed interview time, or do the respondents lose interest in the survey after the assessment of income and wealth in part 4? How representative are the 1,829 successful interviews? Do the results in these surveys reflect the areas also covered by official statistics? And naturally: which variant of the survey proved to be the most successful for larger-scale studies of this kind?

10.3.1   Response Rate and Representative Nature of the Survey

The response rate for part 4 of the surveys, which was left with respondents in the CAPI-D survey variant, was surprisingly high. In the version where the interviewer collected this part of the survey personally, only 2 percent of those surveyed refused to return the completed part 4. However, even when this part had to be returned by mail, nearly 91 percent of respondents did as requested.

Willingness to participate in a repeat survey on the same subject was also high for German households. This figure was between 59 percent and 66 percent for the CAPI variants and 90 percent for the Access Panel. It is therefore entirely feasible to establish a panel, in particular because second-stage panel mortality is typically very low. Finally, it can be seen from the comments in the box provided for "Comments on the interview" that the vast majority of those surveyed found the subject matter of the interview interesting and the questions to be acceptable, in spite of the fact that they were often of a personal nature.

Table 10.3 shows how representative the SAVE sample is in comparison with the 2000 microcensus. The figures in this table compare the proportion of households in an age and income class with the comparable proportion of the same type of households in the microcensus. A figure of 1.2 means that the microcensus covers 20 percent more households of this type than are present in our random sample. If we take the microcensus as the benchmark, a figure of less than 1 indicates underrepresented household types and figures over 1 indicate overrepresented household types.

In comparison to the microcensus, our random sample contains considerably more middle-aged households but fewer older households. This applies to both sample groups (CAPI variants and Access Panel). Young households are represented approximately correctly. With regard to income, we can see a really pronounced shift toward richer households. This is particularly pronounced in the Access Panel: here the microcensus indicates four times as many households with a monthly net income of less than DM 2,500 (approximately 1,300 euros) than in our sample group but

Table 10.3   **Representativity of the SAVE quota sample**

Age	Low income (up to 2,500 DM)		Average income (2,500–5,000 DM)		High income (over 5,000 DM)		All income categories	
	CAPI variants	Access panel	CAPI variants	Access panel	CAPI variants	Access panel	CAPI variants	Access panel
Up to 35 years	1.24	3.43	0.78	0.74	2.63	2.61	0.88	1.06
	(77)	(17)	(120)	(77)	(52)	(32)	(249)	(126)
35–55	1.14	3.33	0.76	0.71	0.69	0.44	0.79	0.67
	(67)	(14)	(226)	(148)	(198)	(190)	(491)	(352)
55+	3.28	6.45	1.09	1.36	0.86	0.70	1.41	1.62
	(58)	(18)	(182)	(89)	(94)	(70)	(334)	(177)
All age categories	1.79	4.51	0.88	0.90	0.72	0.52		
	(202)	(49)	(528)	(314)	(344)	(292)		

Notes: Relative frequency in the micro-census 2000 divided by relative frequency in the SAVE random sample. Number of observations are shown in parentheses. Currency during the survey was the DM. 2,500 (5,000) DM equal 1,280 (2,550) Euros. One Euro is roughly about $1 in terms of purchasing power parity.

only half as many households with an income of over DM 5,000 (approximately 2,600 euros). In order to compensate for this "distortion," we are weighting all the results of the tables and graphics in sections 10.5 and 10.6 using the figures in table 10.3.

10.3.2   Refusal to Answer Individual Sections

One of our main concerns was that the persons surveyed would refuse to answer precisely those questions that were most important for understanding savings behavior, since these were, at the same time, also the questions that were the most difficult and/or most personal for the respondents.

Systematic refusal to answer was not a problem in respect of household income. In all variants of the survey, we initially tried to ask about income in deutsche marks. Approximately 14.4 percent of those surveyed did not want to answer this. These respondents were then shown size classifications in which 63.3 percent of those surveyed indicated an income range. Consequently, information on income was available for 94.7 percent of households. When it came to providing information on wealth, the number of those refusing to answer was considerably higher. In fact, the refusal rates for individual questions ("item nonresponse") vary greatly between individual items and between survey variants—a very important outcome of this experimental survey in terms of the methodology. Details are shown in the appendix; they can be summarized as follows:

- As a rule, the rate at which households refused to respond was between a quarter and a third. These levels reflect the situation in surveys in

Great Britain and the United States. This clearly refutes the frequently held view that, in contrast to those countries, you cannot ask about financial matters in Germany.

- An important exception was the CAPI variant in which the respondents had to disclose to the interviewer their wealth in deutsche marks. Here the refusal to answer was very high. This confirms the obvious: anonymity is extremely important.
- A second exception was the question about a private insurance. This concept was clearly not understood by the majority of households.

10.3.3   Quality of Answers

Ultimately, it is important to understand the quality of the answers in respect of the range of fluctuations and outliers, and the extent to which they concur with related sets of data. This, too, is covered in detail in the appendix. Compared to official statistics, the age of the respondents is lower than the age of the head of household recorded there. There are two reasons for this bias (in spite of weighting; see table 10.3). First, in many cases the persons responding to our survey are the wives of the heads of household recorded in the 2000 microcensus and the 1998 income and consumption survey and, in a typical German marriage, wives are approximately three years younger than their husbands. Second, our random sample does not cover households in which the heads of household are substantially older than sixty-nine.[4]

With regard to the size of the household, it is noticeable that the Access Panel contains considerably more households made up of a husband and wife with children than do the four CAPI variants. However, overall the household size of the SAVE random sample agrees exactly with the size of household in the 2000 microcensus.

A good match has also been achieved for the household's net income vis-à-vis the familiar sets of data that are often used. In all types of the survey, respondents were initially asked to give their household income as a figure. If they refused, respondents then chose categories for their answers, which would then be anonymous for the interviewer. There was, therefore, no difference between the survey variants in recording income.[5]

Table 10.4 shows that the mean value of the net income recorded in the SAVE study is in very close agreement with the net household income recorded in the 2000 microcensus. It is only slightly higher than the figure in the SOEP and lower than the figure in the EVS.

A comparison of financial assets is more difficult, because only very little

---

4. According to the terms of reference in respect of the quota, the survey should only cover respondents aged between eighteen and sixty-nine (cf. section 10.3). In actual fact, there are a few respondents in the random sample who are younger and a few who are older.

5. In twenty-one cases the monthly income was confused with the annual income, and the coding was corrected accordingly.

Table 10.4   **Comparison of mean household net income (euros)**

	SAVE 2001	MZ 2000	SOEP 1999	EVS 1998
Mean	2,020	1,995	1,896	2,247
Median	1,841		1,636	1,900
Standard error	28.8		16.0	6.9

Notes: The SAVE value is the mean of all variants of the SAVE Study. The MZ 2000 value is the average across grouped numbers. EVS 1998 figures based on own calculations.

Table 10.5   **Comparison of the mean total wealth (euros)**

	CAPI		CAPI-D		Access panel	SAVE	EVS 1998
	Numeric	Categorial	Pick-up	Mail			
Mean	73,823	102,521	100,756	105,473	143,828	112,773	113,639
Median	7,792	19,940	18,867	36,813	51,129	26,178	38,685
Standard error	12,052	15,489	18,419	13,118	14,619	7,180	810
No. of households	119	202	176	168	328	993	49,720

Notes: All values of the SAVE-Study weighted according to table 10.3. The SAVE value is the mean across all variants of the SAVE Study. EVS values based on own calculations.

official statistical data is available. We define financial wealth as the value of all financial investments (total of deposits in savings accounts, amounts saved under a building society savings agreement, the market value of whole life insurance policies and private pension schemes, bonds, equities, mutual funds, investment funds, and real estate investment trusts). This includes all individual items ascertained in part 4 of the questionnaire.[6]

In contrast to net household income, the questions relating to wealth were asked differently in the individual variants of the survey, as described in table 10.2. We are therefore interested in whether outcomes differ according to variant (see table 10.5).

In view of the high standard error—wealth fluctuates widely between households—the mean figures for wealth are statistically identical in the majority of CAPI survey variants. However, in the survey variant that was not anonymous (first column: "CAPI numerical"), overall wealth was considerably lower. Here the answer is often a series of zeros, which tends to indicate that the respondents wished to conceal the fact that they were refusing to answer rather than the fact that they do not have available the specific details on their assets. The households that make up the Access Panel are considerably wealthier—or it may be that we manage to make a better record of their wealth than we do in the other households. In other

---

6. Two individual items had to be recoded as "missing" because it was clear that they were implausible.

respects, the mean values are considerably higher than the medians, due to the well-known asymmetry of the wealth distribution.

How do the data on wealth compare with the figures given in the official statistics? This can be seen in the last two columns of table 10.5. Overall, both the mean value and the median of wealth in the SAVE study are lower than the figures recorded in the 1998 EVS. The difference is, however, only barely statistically significant and concurs with the higher income of EVS households.

Finally, we compared the saving rate in the SAVE study with the EVS saving rate (see table 10.6). The saving rate is defined as the sum of savings that were the subject of direct questions ("Can you tell me how much money you and your partner saved in total in the year 2000?") divided by the net income. New borrowings are deducted from this figure; repayments are added to the savings. These savings do not contain real savings—in other words, expenditure on durable consumer goods, housing, and so forth. In view of the considerable influence outliers have on saving rates, we use more robust medians and avoid means.

The median saving rate in our SAVE study (i.e., calculated across all survey variants) was 12 percent. As would be expected in view of the higher wealth of the Access Panel—as compared with the other respondents— the saving rate of the Access Panel is also higher. In other respects, the difference in the saving rates in the CAPI variants of the SAVE study is not statistically significant. The saving rate of SAVE respondents was 1.1 percentage points higher than the saving rate in the sample group of the EVS income and consumption survey (10.9 percent). However, this difference is not statistically significant.

The SAVE and EVS saving rates are, however, substantially higher than the saving rate calculated by the German Bundesbank and cited in official statistics, which was 9.8 percent in 1999. The reason for this is that the Bundesbank "saving rate of private households" also includes private nonprofit organizations (such as trade unions and churches), whereas households in the SAVE study and the EVS are only private households in the strict sense of the word.

Table 10.6   **Comparison of saving rates (%)**

	CAPI		CAPI-D		Access panel	SAVE	EVS 1998
	Numeric	Categorial	Pick-up	Mail			
Median	11.7	11.4	10.7	9.6	14.2	12.0	10.9
Standard error	1.2	0.9	1.1	1.4	1.2	0.6	0.0
No. of households	126	153	114	126	349	868	45,375

Notes: All values of the SAVE Study weighted according to table 10.3. EVS values based on own calculations.

10.3.4   Lessons for Further Waves

Germans are prepared to give information about their wealth and how they save, not much different from U.S. households. However, measures must be put in place during both the interview and subsequent analysis to provide a credible assurance that the respondents' anonymity will be preserved.

The information from the SAVE study corresponds closely with the information that we have obtained from the official statistics (here, in particular, the 2000 microcensus and the 1998 income and consumption survey) and the SOEP. This applies to demographic indicators such as age and size of household, as well as for the most important economic values of this study—in other words, income, wealth, and saving rate.

Which variant of the survey proved to be the best? If we take as our benchmark the attitude as regards refusing to answer and the representative nature of the information, the CAPI in combination with one part handled on a drop-off basis appeared to be the best method. While the Access Panel delivered excellent results in respect of accuracy and willingness to answer, this panel appears to be substantially self-selected toward larger and richer households.

10.4   Qualitative and Quantitative Saving Measures

While the primary purpose of the initial wave was methodological, we also evaluated the answers of the respondents in order to understand which substantive results can be expected from a panel survey. We first turn to the qualitative saving questions. In general, the households gave a rather positive assessment of their situation in life: most households surveyed have adequate income available to save ("saving capability"), and they appear to have a sufficiently positive view of the future to also want to save ("willingness to save"). In brief: the majority of Germans save, and the Germans who do so put away substantial amounts.

10.4.1   Qualitative Information on Savings

We begin with the "warm-up question" on how the households surveyed manage to balance income and expenditure in general. Table 10.7 shows the questions and different responses for those households in the upper and lower income brackets. Approximately half of those surveyed had "some money left at the end of the month," whereas the number of households who "always had a lot of money left" or "only had some money left if additional one-off revenues came in" were about the same.

Nearly two-thirds of German households and over three-quarters of households in the richer half of the income bracket are "capable of saving." However, approximately one in five households states that the money was

Table 10.7   Saving capability (%)

"If you think back, how well did you get along with your revenues in the year 2000? Which of the following best describes your experience?"

	All households	Income below median	Income above median
At the end of the month, there was always a lot of money left.	14.6	7.0	22.1
At the end of the month, there was often some money left.	49.4	45.7	53.1
There was only some money left if additional one-off revenues came in.	14.8	16.7	12.9
Often, there was not enough money left at the end of the month.	17.1	24.3	9.9
At the end of the month, there was never enough money left.	4.3	6.4	2.1

Note: Weighted averages across survey variants, see table 10.3.

"often" or "never" enough—and surprisingly this also includes 12 percent of households whose income puts them in the richer bracket of German households.

10.4.2   Quantitative Information on Saving

These qualitative answers can be translated into hard figures. We first ascertain a rather broad and vague number of the total amount saved ("Can you tell me how much money you and your partner saved in total in the year 2000?"). Borrowings are then deducted from this; debt repayments are added to savings. The median saving rate of 12 percent is approximately the same as the figure we know from the EVS—as we have already established in table 10.6. Table 10.8, which shows the saving rate as a function of the saving capability listed in table 10.7, shows that the answers are intuitively plausible. The households with savings capability save at a rate that is nearly three times as high as those households where funds are always short.

It is interesting that even in households who say that "there was never enough money left at the end of the month," the saving rate was over 7 percent. This is an interesting finding. One explanation is that contractual saving—such as building society contributions, parts of the premium to whole life insurance contracts, or debt repayments which are typically paid by automatic withdrawal from checking accounts in Germany—is not counted in this one-item question. We see evidence for this explanation in the course of the paper.

Table 10.9 presents euro amounts of saving and its components. In 2000 the households in our SAVE sample saved nearly €4,850, in a colloquial

Table 10.8   **Saving rate and saving capability (%)**

	At the end of the month, there was always a lot of money left.	At the end of the month, there was often some money left.	There was only some money left if additional one-off revenues came in.	Often, there was not enough money left at the end of the month.	At the end of the month, there was never enough money left.	All
Mean	22.8	13.8	11.9	10.4	7.4	14.8
Median	20.2	11.6	9.4	8.7	7.8	12.0
Standard error	1.3	0.8	1.2	1.6	2.9	0.6

Note: Weighted averages across survey variants, see table 10.3.

Table 10.9   **Gross and net savings**

	Gross savings	Net new debt	Net savings
	Absolute values for 2000 (euros)		
Mean	4,842.1	−179.8	5,338.6
Median	2,556	0	3,068
Standard error	401.1	335.2	643.4
No. of households	1,039	1,534	905
	Saving rates (%)		
Mean	13.2	−1.9	14.8
Median	10.2	0	12.0
Standard error	0.3	1.3	0.6
No. of households	1,001	1,486	868

Notes: Weighted averages across survey variants, see table 10.3. Saving rates are monthly savings divided by monthly net income. Medians are not additive.

sense of the word (gross savings, i.e., purchase of new savings investments minus the sale of old savings investments) and on average paid off around €180 more of debts than they took out in new borrowings. Net new debt is therefore negative, and savings in an economic sense (i.e., the net savings) is greater than gross saving. However, many households do not have any outstanding debt, hence the low mean value and a median of zero. Among the approximately 900 households for which current data on borrowings and savings formation were available, the net savings were around €5,350 in 2000. This corresponds to a saving rate of 14.8 percent.

The medians are substantially below the mean values, which indicates that the distribution is skewed: many households save very little, but some households save a great deal. Even so, half of households saved €3,070 net in 2000—in other words, more than 12 percent of net income.

Figure 10.2 provides more detailed information about the distribution of the saving rate. The majority of households save between 8 and 12 percent of their net household income. Only around 4 percent state that they liqui-

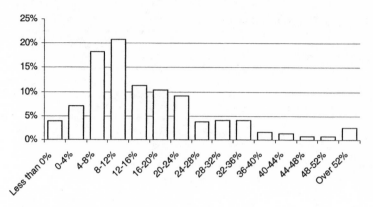

Fig. 10.2   Distribution of net savings

Notes: Weighted averages across survey variants, see table 10.3. The saving rates are monthly savings divided by net income per month.

date more savings than they invest in other savings instruments. The proportion of high saving rates is extraordinary. Around 11 percent of households maintain that they save a third or more of their net income. Out of the nearly 3 percent of particularly high saving rates (over 50 percent of net income) at the right-hand extremity of the distribution chart, some are likely to be implausible, although it is quite possible that a considerable amount is saved in the case of lump-sum receipts (such as an inheritance). We will look at this again later on.

10.4.3   Assets

These savings accumulate to the stock of assets. We differentiate between financial and real estate assets. Financial wealth is defined as the value of all financial investments (the total of deposits in savings accounts, amounts saved under a building society savings agreement,[7] the market value of whole life insurance policies and private pension schemes, bonds, equities, mutual funds, investment funds, and real estate investment trusts). Real estate assets are made up from the value of self-used real estate, the value of other property, business assets, and other assets (jewelry, antiques, etc.). Total wealth is ultimately the sum of financial assets and real estate assets minus any outstanding loans.

If individual parts of questions were not answered, total wealth could not be reconstructed without making further assumptions. In these cases, total wealth was coded as "missing." A total of 993 households provided a complete set of data on assets, that is, 54 percent of all respondents.

Over 80 percent of households were able to give a figure for the wealth

---

7. Building society savings contracts are an important savings vehicle in Germany. See Börsch-Supan and Stahl (1991b) for a description and analysis.

they possess (i.e., a positive amount; see table 10.10). Around 46 percent of SAVE households state that they own property, generally a residential property they use themselves. This figure lies between the official statistics (EVS 1998: 47 percent) and the SOEP (approximately 41 percent). Around 44 percent of households have debt. For the majority of households, these are mortgages or building loans on their owned home.

In the case of 82 percent of households who held positive wealth, this figure was around €143,000. Financial assets were only around €32,000. In contrast, the average value of the property owned was €208,000. The value of residential property correlates closely to the value of financial assets, as table 10.11 shows. Households with high financial assets also live in expensive houses, whereas households who rent their accommodation also

Table 10.10   **Total wealth and single asset types**

	Total wealth	Financial assets	Self-used real estate	Debt	Business assets
Proportion of households that own this kind of wealth (%)	82.4	83.5	45.8	43.6	4.0
Households that own this asset type:					
Number	818	900	793	728	71
Mean (euros)	142,284	31,878	208,279	52,768	213,305
Median (euros)	64,934	13,294	191,734	19,429	40,903
Standard error (euros)	8,512	1,864	6,292	2,857	40,890

Notes: Weighted averages across survey variants, see table 10.3. "Owning" of an asset type means that the household lists a positive amount for this asset type. Total wealth was only calculated for those households which provided data on all asset types. Since some households listed certain asset types (i.e., financial assets), but refused to provide information about others, the proportion of households with positive total wealth lies below the proportion of households with positive financial assets.

Table 10.11   **Correlation between financial and housing wealth**

	Value of owner-occupied housing				
	Not applicable	Below 128k Euro (250k DM)	128–256k Euro (250–500k DM)	256–512k Euro (500–1,000k DM)	Above 512k Euro (1 million DM)
Mean	15,900	19,303	35,485	58,963	1,286,517
Median	3,681	10,226	18,560	29,655	132,936
Standard error	1,440	3,582	3,125	9,210	35,828
No. of households	582	84	266	118	13

Note: Weighted averages across survey variants, see table 10.3.

Table 10.12   Wealth and saving capability (euros)

	At the end of the month, there was always a lot of money left.	At the end of the month, there was often some money left.	There was only some money left if additional one-off revenues came in.	Often, there was not enough money left at the end of the month.	At the end of the month, there was never enough money left.
Mean	277,642	115,187	75,636	43,014	21,531
Median	155,944	53,123	11,862	1,636	0
Standard error	37,547	6,959	10,974	6,982	7,512

Note: Values weighted across survey variants, see table 10.3.

have the least financial assets. These types of assets are therefore not substitutes but complementary forms of investment.

The distribution of wealth is very skewed. Many households have few assets, but some households have very considerable assets. If one looks at the distribution of wealth by income group, we obtain the following picture: The poorer half of earners only own just under 20 percent of total wealth, whereas the 10 percent of households in our SAVE study with the highest incomes own approximately 33 percent of total wealth. As expected, there is a high correlation between qualitative saving capability and wealth (see table 10.12). In the case of households in which "there was never enough money left" at the end of the month, the average total wealth was around €22,000. More than half of these households stated that they did not have any assets at all, whereas households who "always had a lot of money left" had assets of €280,000 on average, and more than half owned more than €156,000.

10.4.4   Age Structure of Savings

Since this only one cross section, we cannot distinguish age from cohort effects in saving. We thus cannot make inferences on life-cycle behavior, but at least we can say something about how the elderly save or dissave in the year 2001.

Table 10.13 shows us that a majority of older households in 2001 "always have a lot of money left" or "often have some money left" at the end of the month, actually considerably more often than is the case for younger households. On average, at least, old age is currently not a time in life when German savers have a bad time. When we look at actual savings, the figures also do not provide evidence for dissaving in old age. Figure 10.3 shows the saving rate (thicker bars) and absolute savings (thinner bars). While older (earlier born, if one prefers the cohort interpretation) households save less than younger ones, both the saving rate and absolute saving remain positive.

Table 10.13   **Who is able to save? Age pattern (%)**

Saving capability	Age		
	Under 30	30–59	60 and over
At the end of the month, there was always a lot of money left.	9.7	13.2	14.5
At the end of the month, there was often some money left.	47.2	45.0	58.0
There was only some money left if additional one-off revenues came in.	14.3	17.8	10.8
Often, there was not enough money left at the end of the month.	23.1	19.5	12.9
At the end of the month, there was never enough money left.	5.8	4.5	3.8

Note: Weighted averages across survey variants, see table 10.3.

Savings and saving rates

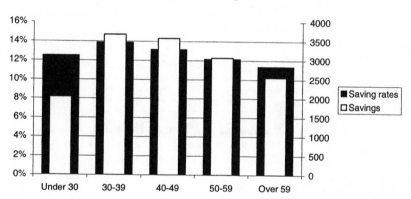

Fig. 10.3   Age pattern of savings
Notes: Values weighted according to table 10.3. Amounts in euros.

10.5   Savings Motives

There are many reasons for saving a portion of one's income, including short-term reasons, such as saving for next summer's vacation, and long-term reasons, such as saving for retirement.[8] Figure 10.4 shows the importance which the households in our survey attached to nine reasons for saving:

8. The literature on savings motives is extensive. This is not the place to review it. Among economists, most attention has been given to retirement savings (Modigliani and Brumberg 1954; Feldstein 1974), precautionary savings (Abel 1985; Carroll 1992; Carroll and Samwick 1998; Lusardi 1997), and bequest motives (Bernheim, Schleifer, and Summers 1985; Hurd 1987).

Purchase of Real Estate for yourself

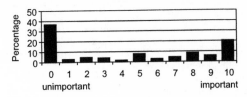

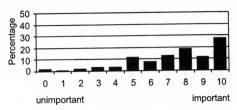

Precautions for Unexpected Events

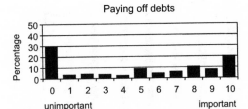

Paying off debts

Fig. 10.4   Reasons for saving
Note: Weighted averages across survey variants, see table 10.3.

- Saving to buy their own home
- Saving as a precaution for unexpected events
- Saving to pay off debts
- Old-age provision
- Saving to go on vacation
- Saving to make a major purchase (car, furniture, etc.)
- Saving for education or for supporting children and/or grandchildren
- Saving to provide bequests for children or grandchildren
- Saving to take advantage of state subsidies (e.g., a subsidy for building society savings)

Each reason for saving had to be rated on a scale from 0 (no importance) to 10 (very important).

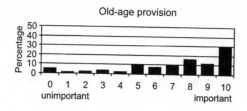

Old-age provision

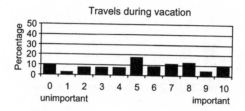

Travels during vacation

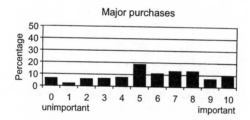

Major purchases

Fig. 10.4   (cont.)

What is immediately noticeable are qualitative differences. Some motives have a clear maximum at 10, others at 0, and a third group is bimodal. In the case of buying a home and repaying debts, the emphasis is on the two extremes—nearly all households consider that these two reasons for saving are either of absolutely no importance or are really important. The reason is obvious: "saving to buy one's own home" is an important reason for saving, either for those who already own their own home or for those who want to become a home owner. Equally, the answer in respect of "repaying debts" is almost exclusively linked to the current debt situation of the households.

Nearly all households rated "saving as a precaution" and "saving for old age" as important. The number of households who considered saving for unforeseen events to be of lesser importance (rated between 0 and 4 on the 10-point scale) was only 4.0 percent, and the number of households who felt the same about savings as provision for old age was only 8.6 percent.

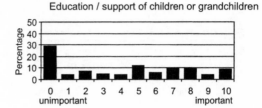

Education / support of children or grandchildren

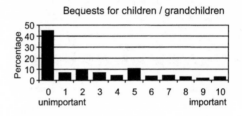

Bequests for children / grandchildren

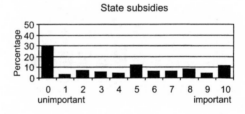

State subsidies

Fig. 10.4   (cont.)

Conversely, saving for educating or supporting children or grandchildren was only accorded secondary importance, as was—surprisingly—saving to provide an inheritance to children or grandchildren. With regard to inheritance, nearly 40 percent of households were of the opinion that this was an absolutely unimportant reason (classification of 0). Exploiting state incentives to save also did not turn out to be a primary reason for saving. This prompts doubts concerning the effectiveness of the various savings policies, including the huge new incentives to take out a private pension and home ownership subsidies. This must be seen in the context of respondents' answers on saving for old-age provision and for acquiring their own home: it is apparent that the primary reason (adequate income in old age, owning one's own home) is considerably more important than the secondary reason (tax incentives). If tax incentives are only a secondary reason for saving, the danger of windfalls is high. Further evidence is needed, however, to make a sound judgment on this finding.

Figure 10.4 contains declarations of intent. Are these intentions also credible? A particular opportunity to verify savings intentions is offered by unexpected lump-sum payments (e.g., inheritances or gifts), because they—according to economic theory—are supposed to be mainly used for saving and less for consumption. Table 10.14 shows what households did who received a particularly high lump sum. The column "Frequency of the investment" shows the percentage of households who used the lump-sum payment for the purpose indicated in the first column. For example, 11.2 percent of households paid part of their lump sum into a savings account (or a similar form of investment). As multiple answers could be given and the households often divided the lump sum for different purposes, these percentages often add up to more than 100 percent.

Table 10.14   **Use of large lump sum payments**

"In 2000, did you or your partner receive extraordinarily high revenues or inheritance of over 1,000 DM? What did you and/or your partner do with the money? Which of the following applies? Please only list amounts of at least DM 500."

	Frequency of the investment (%)	Number	Median expenditure share (%)	Number	Average expenditure share (%)	Number
Dedicated savings[a]	11.2	57	40.0	42	7.0	46
Other financial saving[b]	24.8	119	72.7	103	19.3	108
Purchase of real estate[c]	6.0	25	91.3	15	24.6	19
Renovation or expansion[d]	21.9	114	51.3	95	11.9	109
Purchase of commodities[e]	25.4	129	42.9	112	9.4	122
Travel[f]	26.6	134	44.4	115	3.9	130
Articles for everyday life[g]	34.0	171	26.3	132	2.5	145
Paying off debt[h]	21.7	111	60.0	95	8.8	104
Other[i]	8.7	41	71.4	33	12.6	36

Note: Weighted averages across survey variants, see table 10.3. "Median expenditure share" is the median of the expenditure ratio (expenditure for the respective use divided by lump sum). "Average expenditure share" is the total sum of expenditures for the respective use divided by the total sum of investments (total sums across all respondents).

[a]Dedicated saving account (building society, whole life insurance, individual pension)
[b]Other financial saving (e.g., purchase of stocks or securities)
[c]Purchase of an apartment or a house
[d]Renovation or expansion of an apartment or a house
[e]Purchase of commodities (e.g., a car or furniture)
[f]Travels during vacation
[g]Articles for everyday life
[h]Paying off debt
[i]Other

The column "Median of the expenditure share" describes the percentage of lump sums used for the respective purpose (we are using the more robust median rather than the mean value). The number "40%" in the first line thus means that, of those who have paid part of their lump sum into a savings account, the median share used for that purpose was 40 percent. This column therefore describes the intensity of a usage for those who selected that usage.

Finally, the penultimate column ("Average expenditure share") shows what happened to the overall sum of all lump-sum payments—these percentages therefore add up to 100 percent. If we come back to the example given in the first line, in total only 7 percent of the total amount received as lump sums found its way into savings accounts, whereas 93 percent was used for other purposes. This last column therefore states what is important for the economy as a whole.

While the most frequently stated use of the lump sum (34 percent) was for "articles for everyday life," households who stated this spent only around a quarter of the lump sum on it. From an aggregate point of view, this usage category thus only played a secondary role, with 2.5 percent of the overall total lump sum spent on it. Other short-run expenditure is money spent on vacations—in total, around 4 percent. Thus, less than 10 percent of lump-sum income is spent on short-term consumption.

From this aggregate view, investment in real estate, shares and securities—in other words, savings in the form of property and financial assets—play a much more important role. What is noticeable with these investments is that those households who operate them concentrate on them to a very great extent. More than 90 percent of the lump-sum payments is used for real estate if this type of usage is chosen. Including conventional savings investments, building society savings agreements, whole life insurance policies, and private pensions, more than half of the lump-sum income is used directly for savings. On top of this, renovations and repayment of debts account for around a further 20 percent. Consumer durables fall in the gray area between consumption and investment, and account for just under 10 percent of the total additional income.

Hence, although table 10.14 is based on relatively few households—so the results must be interpreted cautiously—a rather clear overall picture emerges. It confirms that the proportion of additional revenue used for consumption is negligible, while most goes toward savings.

We now return to the initial question and ask ourselves whether the intentions in figure 10.4 correspond to actual behavior. They do, at least as shown in table 10.15, in which we compare the actual use of unexpected lump-sum payments (here coded as "yes" or "no," according to whether the lump sum has been used for purpose x) with the corresponding savings motives (here coded in three categories: purpose x was an "important" or "indifferent" or "unimportant" reason to save).

Table 10.15 Consistency of words and actual behavior (importance of saving reason by actual use of lump sum)

Reason for saving:

	Travel		Pay off debt		Purchase of own home		Larger purchases (cars, furniture)	
	Use of lump sum for:							
	Vacation		Pay off debt		Purchase of real estate		Durables (cars, furniture)	
	No	Yes	No	Yes	No	Yes	No	Yes
Unimportant	22.9	4.4	34.5	4.2	35.4	5.0	12.5	6.7
Indifferent	55.4	47.9	22.9	29.6	18.7	19.8	55.0	68.1
Important	21.7	47.6	42.6	66.1	45.9	75.3	32.6	25.2
No. of households	364	134	387	111	473	25	369	129

Reason for saving:

	Old-age provision		Unexpected events		Old-age provision		Unexpected events	
	Use of lump sum for:							
	Dedicated savings (Whole life insurance, individual pension)		Unexpected events		Old-age provision		Other savings (stocks, securities)	
	No	Yes	No	Yes	No	Yes	No	Yes
Unimportant	5.1	4.0	2.7	2.1	4.9	5.4	2.6	2.8
Indifferent	28.8	15.4	36.3	40.9	27.5	26.7	38.1	32.8
Important	66.1	80.6	61.0	57.0	67.6	67.9	59.3	64.4
No. of households	441	57	441	57	379	119	379	119

Note: Weighted averages across survey variants, see table 10.3.

Example: Of those respondents who did not use their lump sum for vacation spending, 22.9 percent assessed travel as an unimportant reason for saving.

Among those who listed "vacation" as an important reason for saving, more than twice as many households actually spent a lump-sum payment on vacation trips (47.6 percent vs. 21.7 percent). A similar correlation exists for repayment of debts (66.1 percent vs. 42.6 percent) and for purchasing real estate (75.3 percent vs. 45.9 percent).

The preference for old-age provision is also quite clearly reflected in the type of investment selected. Over 80 percent of households who state that old-age provision is an important reason for saving invest a portion of their lump-sum payment in a whole life insurance policy or a private pension. This contrasts with a figure of 45.9 percent for those who "save as a precaution" (households that save for nonspecific and unforeseen events). These households tend to invest the unexpected lump-sum amounts in shares and securities (64.4 percent). It is only when it comes to purchasing consumer durables that this picture becomes less clear. Overall, therefore, intentions are quite well backed up by actual deeds, at least among those who received an unexpected lump-sum payment.

The saving motives have a clear age and income structure, as can be seen in table 10.16.

Older and richer households find saving for unforeseen events more important than do younger people (67.7 percent vs. 57.9 percent vs. 54.7 per-

Table 10.16   **Saving motives, by age and income (%)**

	Age group (year)			Income group (DM)		
	Under 35	35–54	>55	Under 2,500	2,500–<5,000	>5,000
Saving for unexpected events						
Unimportant	3.8	4.6	1.9	6.9	2.8	2.8
Indifferent	41.5	37.4	30.4	41.1	35.8	35.9
Important	54.7	57.9	67.7	52.0	61.5	61.4
Saving for old-age provision						
Unimportant	7.6	7.1	18.0	11.9	8.3	5.5
Indifferent	37.3	31.7	21.9	32.7	31.5	32.6
Important	55.1	61.2	60.1	55.4	60.1	61.9
Purchase of own home						
Unimportant	26.4	48.3	55.6	54.2	44.1	31.8
Indifferent	28.8	18.6	10.2	23.9	20.1	16.9
Important	44.8	33.1	34.3	21.9	35.8	51.3
Travel and vacation						
Unimportant	14.8	21.1	22.1	26.7	18.0	14.4
Indifferent	55.2	50.5	49.2	47.1	50.5	58.6
Important	30.0	28.4	28.7	26.2	31.5	27.1
Larger purchases						
Unimportant	7.5	14.5	26.5	24.8	11.0	7.5
Indifferent	58.0	56.0	48.8	51.0	55.3	59.8
Important	34.5	29.4	24.7	24.3	33.7	32.7

Note: Weighted averages across survey variants, see table 10.3.

cent) and poorer people (61.4 percent vs. 61.5 percent vs. 52.0 percent). The differences in income may be surprising, because richer households would find it easier to finance unforeseen events from their regular income. The income effect is also reflected in saving for old-age provision: richer households place more emphasis on this than do poorer households (61.9 percent vs. 60.1 percent vs. 55.4 percent). Finally, and as one would expect, saving for one's own home is reflected in a very distinct age and income profile: considerably more younger (44.8 percent) and, above all, richer (51.3 percent) households save for their own home. The picture is very similar with respect to major purchases (34.5 percent and 32.7 percent).

10.6   Saving Rules

In many regards, this section is the core section of this paper. It reports on our attempt to use direct and indirect questions to shed light on how German households save; that is, which rules they apply to determine the amount of savings. The section investigates saving behavior in a very fundamental sense (see Lettau and Uhlig 1999).

10.6.1   Direct Questions about Saving Behavior

Table 10.17 lists the answer to the question "Which of the following sentences best describes your own personal saving behavior?" The households were asked to choose one alternative. They were only allowed to select one option so that the result would produce a clear rating.

Table 10.17 shows that the largest proportion of households—around 40 percent—save a fixed amount, and they do this regularly. A further fifth also save regularly, but they adjust the amount they save to the circumstances. Thus, nearly 60 percent of all households save on a regular basis.

Table 10.17   **Self-assessment of saving behavior (%)**

	I regularly save fixed amount.	I regularly save, but the amount is flexible.	I save only if there is money left to save.	I do not have the financial capability to save.	I do not save. I would rather enjoy life.
All	40.1	18.4	23.1	16.0	2.4
Age					
Under 35	49.2	13.8	20.8	15.3	0.9
35–55	38.3	18.4	23.8	17.7	1.8
55 and older	29.7	27.2	25.0	10.1	8.1
Income					
Up to 2,500 DM	18.8	11.5	33.5	33.8	2.4
2,500–5,000 DM	43.7	20.6	21.3	11.8	2.8
Over 5,000 DM	58.6	21.7	13.9	4.9	1.2

Note: Weighted averages across survey variants, see table 10.3.

For just under a quarter of households the decision whether to save any-thing is primarily guided by available income. Sixteen percent of the house-holds state that they do not have sufficient financial capacity to save, and only a very few accord themselves the freedom of just living for the day.

We have deliberately asked about the primary behavioral pattern in or-der to force the households to give a clear answer. However, the fact that one of the category headings in table 10.18 has been selected does not rule out that actual behavior may be more complicated, and may consist of sev-eral behavioral patterns. For instance, a household may save a fixed amount on a regular basis but also save additional sums if the amount of income they receive turns out to be particularly high.

The extraordinary point about the answers in table 10.17 is how many households emphasize the regular nature of their savings. Rather than just making use of short-term fluctuations in income, they make savings from long-term elements of income; a fixed amount is then frequently saved for a long period.

This regularity is extraordinary—particularly among young people: Nearly half (49.2 percent) of those under thirty-five save a fixed amount on a regular basis. Hardly any households in this age group state that they only enjoy life (0.9 percent), whereas a more than proportionally large number of older households do this. In spite of this, the majority of these older households (56.9 percent) save something—again a confirmation of the fact that older households in Germany do not dissave.

Household income plays the role one would expect. The rich are more likely to save regularly, while a third of those households that have an in-come of under DM 2,500 state that they do not have the financial capabil-ity to save.

Part of the striking regularity of German saving behavior can be ex-plained by a small set of firm savings objectives. This is shown in table

Table 10.18   **Fixed savings targets**

		Saving goal (euros)		Time (years)	
	Percentage	Mean	Median	Mean	Median
All	25.5	53,515	15,339	6.5	4
Age					
Under 35	30.1	79,516	25,565	6.5	5
35–55	24.3	45,999	15,339	7.3	4
55 and older	21.5	15,481	5,113	2.8	5
Income					
Up to 2,500 DM	23.4	15,049	5,113	4.5	2
2,500–5,000 DM	24.6	40,799	11,760	6.4	2
Over 5,000 DM	29.4	89,862	51,129	8.3	6

Notes: Weighted averages across survey variants, see table 10.3. Only households that save ac-cording to the first three columns in table 10.17 (1,555 households in total).

10.18. A good quarter of the 81.6 percent of households who answered the above question by stating that they saved in some form (either regularly or irregularly) have a set savings objective in mind.

Young people have more often than average a fixed savings goal in mind (30.1 percent). The amount is rather high (€79,250 average, €25,564 median). We speculate that the main reason is the purchase of their own home. Among those aged fifty-five and over, the time scale is relatively short term. The savings goal is more likely to be an expensive holiday immediately after retirement. The income pattern is as expected: richer households aim to save more and look further into the future than is the case for households with lower incomes.

10.6.2   Indirect Questions about Saving Behavior

The discipline noticeable in table 10.18 is also reflected in the fact that more than one in six households kept a record of household expenditure. This is almost exactly the same proportion as those respondents whose parents had a housekeeping book, at least according to the information provided by the households. It is noticeable that richer households are more likely to keep a record of expenditure than households with lower incomes (see table 10.19).

Keeping a record of household expenditure appears to be an inheritable trait that is passed from one generation to another. The proportion of those households who kept a record of expenditure is almost five times higher among those respondents whose parents kept such a record than among those whose parents did not (see table 10.20).

Table 10.19   **Keeping record of the household budget, by income (%)**

"Do you or your partner maintain a book of all household expenditures?"

	Below 2,500 DM	2,500–<5,000 DM	>5,000 DM	All	Parents
No	87.9	82.4	79.7	83.1	83.0
Yes	12.1	17.6	20.3	16.9	17.0

Note: Weighted averages across survey variants, see table 10.3.

Table 10.20   **Inheritance of record keeping (%)**

	Record keeping by parents	
Record keeping by respondents	No	Yes
No	89.8	53.7
Yes	10.2	46.3

Notes: Weighted averages across survey variants, see table 10.3. The correlation coefficient is 0.37.

10.6.3 How to Invest

The way in which savings are invested in Germany is extremely conservative. Figure 10.5 shows that over 70 percent of households have conventional savings accounts and around 40 percent have building society savings contracts and whole life insurance policies. On the other hand, fewer than 20 percent of households have bonds or a private pension in their portfolio. Thirty percent of households state that they hold shares, equities, or real estate funds.

Portfolio choice fluctuates considerably according to age and income, as can be seen in table 10.21.

Younger households are much more likely to have building society savings contracts, whole life insurance policies, a private pension, and equities. An age or life-cycle effect most probably explains the investment in building society savings and whole life insurance policies, while the higher investments in equities and funds are more likely due to a cohort effect. Persons born later have become familiar with new types of financial investments at an earlier age than their parents, who grew up in a Germany that used passbook savings as the main instrument of savings. While Germany had a stock and bond market fever between the two world wars, hyperinflation and World War II changed investment behavior back to a very conservative portfolio, until quite recently. Wealthier households have larger holdings of all financial investments. This effect is especially pronounced in the case of whole life insurance policies and stocks and shares.

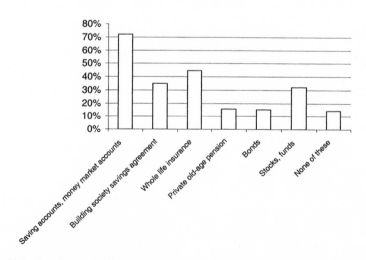

Fig. 10.5 Investment of financial assets

Notes: Portion of households that own a certain asset type. Weighted averages across survey variants, see table 10.3.

Table 10.21   **Investment of the financial assets, by age and income (%)**

	Savings accounts, money market accounts	Building society savings agreements	Whole life insurance	Private old-age pension	Bonds	Stocks, funds	None of these
Age							
Under 35	71.7	48.0	46.2	22.0	13.2	41.7	12.5
35–54	71.0	33.3	47.7	15.6	16.3	30.1	14.9
Over 54	79.3	15.4	26.3	3.0	16.0	19.5	13.0
Income							
<2,500 DM	53.9	22.7	21.9	12.0	7.9	15.1	32.5
2,500–5,000 DM	77.9	35.0	49.8	13.4	14.6	26.7	8.1
≥5,000 DM	83.7	49.0	61.6	23.1	24.1	54.9	3.2

Notes: Portion of households that own a certain asset type. Weighted averages across survey variants, see table 10.3.

10.7   Conclusions

Overall, our findings show a savings pattern that is extraordinarily stable and sound. Germans save regularly, in a manner that is planned, and often with a clearly defined purpose in mind. German households appear not to save in order to balance out transitory income fluctuations. Rather, they appear to save also out of income components that are stable in the long run. It is worth noting at this point that German labor income has less individual variation than U.S. earnings have (see Börsch-Supan and Lusardi 2003). This should reduce the precautionary savings motive, all else being equal, relative to the United States. In addition, German public pension replacement rates are much higher than those of the U.S. social security systems. This should reduce the savings motive for old-age provision relative to the United States. Our findings on German savings motives, however, contradict these predictions: we found that precaution and old-age provision are the two most important savings motives in Germany. These motives are still taken seriously. In connection with less-developed credit markets (see Jappelli and Pagano 1989), this may explain the high saving rate relative to the United States in spite of "objectively" less uncertainty.

We finish this paper with a few remarks on what we can learn about economic policy. One of the greatest challenges that Germany will face in the future is demographic change. In thirty years' time, for each person aged twenty-five to sixty there will be over twice as many people over sixty than exist today. Will higher or lower amounts be saved in the wake of this demographic change? Should we be concerned about overall economic growth because older households do not wish to save? The SAVE survey shows that the tendency to save, even in old age, is still great. Older households save nearly as enthusiastically as households in the thirty to sixty age range. If one applies today's age-specific saving rates to the age structure of the population as it will be in the future, demographic change will have negligible effects on the aggregate household saving rate. Hence, if—and this is a big if—there is no behavioral change, saving will not be a concern. Other concerns about the effect of an aging population on overall economic growth will be more important—for instance, the burden of social security contributions, or the dramatic reduction in the available workforce. Changes in behavior, however, cannot be ruled out, and they might be precipitated by the current pension reform process, since more funded retirement saving is likely to induce a more pronounced hump-shaped saving profile and actual dissaving in old age.

The German pension reform of 2001 enacted by Riester will place more emphasis on private provision. To what extent must saving be encouraged to achieve this? Our results show that hardly any households save primarily because they are given subsidies to do so. The original reason—provision for old age—is, in contrast, emphasized as an important primary reason by nearly all households. In a country like Germany, which has a high saving rate—quite different from the United States—tax incentives might therefore have considerable windfall effects, in particular for the middle class.

Finally, a time-honored crucial policy question is whether pension reform will create new savings or simply displace old savings. For instance, will the amount by which investments in life insurance policies and pension funds increase be offset by a parallel drop in assets in other types of investments—housing, for example? We will need the 2003 and 2005 panel waves to answer this important question. It cannot be answered with a single cross section because it is necessary to observe changes; that is, potential movements of funds from one form of saving into other types of investment. This paper shows that the first wave of the SAVE study has produced interesting data with reasonable item response rates, comparable to U.S. surveys. It has shown that the impossibility of collecting data on wealth in Germany is a myth. It is fruitful, therefore, to focus further research activities on establishing a panel of saving data in Germany.

Appendix

Item Nonresponse and Data Quality

This appendix documents the extent to which those surveyed refused to answer specific questions ("item nonresponse").

Table 10A.1 shows the extent to which individuals refused to answer

Table 10A.1   **Item nonresponse: Financial assets (%)**

	CAPI		CAPI-D		
	Numeric	Categorial	Pick-up	Mail	Access panel
Existence of financial assets	1.7	0.7	2.7	1.2	0.5
Nonresponse rate: Value of the following components of financial assets:					
Savings accounts	47.0	18.1	25.4	18.8	17.9
Building societies	44.7	16.9	27.8	30.1	24.4
Whole life insurances	57.1	30.3	35.1	30.1	37.8
Individual pensions	76.8	39.2	54.5	45.6	50.4
Bonds	48.7	23.8	46.1	33.7	35.1
Stocks and mutual funds	53.1	22.2	25.0	19.1	20.0

Note: Portion of households that gave account of which types of assets were existent (first line) and how great the assets were (other lines, in relation to asset type).

Table 10A.2   **Item nonresponse: Value of the owner-occupied dwelling (%)**

	CAPI		CAPI-D		
	Numeric	Categorial	Pick-up	Mail	Access panel
No information about housing situation	0.0	0.0	3.1	0.0	0.9
Value of the owner-occupied dwelling	23.5	6.2	4.4	5.8	2.3

Note: Portion of the households that provided valid information.

questions about assets and borrowings. The first question asks which types of financial assets are held by the household. This is a simple yes/no question for six broad categories of financial assets. There were hardly any households who could not or would not provide any information on this topic in the presence of an interviewer and with the Access Panel. Refusal to answer was at a similarly low level among households who were asked to complete the questionnaire themselves and send it back. Of the nearly 91 percent who complied with the request, the willingness to provide information was very high in all areas. The same phenomenon can also be seen in the questions about home ownership (table 10A.2) and the situation as regards loans (table 10A.3).

However, there were then also a high percentage of households who did not know or were unwilling to divulge the amount in DM of one or other type of asset. Failure to provide information was noticeably high in the case of private pensions and in the case of survey variant 1, in which respondents were asked to give an exact figure in DM during the oral interview (CAPI numerical). Whereas the latter can be attributed to the lack of privacy, the fact that they did not know is more likely to be a reason for the

Table 10A.3   Item nonresponse: Loans and mortgages (%)

	CAPI		CAPI-D		
	Numeric	Categorical	Pick-up	Mail	Access panel
No information about credit history	1.4	0.3	3.4	1.6	1.1
No information about types of loans	0.3	0.0	2.1	0.0	0.2
Refusal rate: Amount of the following types of loans:					
Building society loan	37.0	19.2	11.5	14.7	6.5
Mortgages	18.9	25.0	4.3	6.05	2.9
Consumer loans	8.7	15.6	6.8	4.8	9.8
Intrafamiliar loans	28.6	33.3	27.4	0.0	9.7
Other	11.1	25.0	10.1	12.5	7.0

Note: Portion of households that provided information about whether there are loans to be paid off (first line), which kinds of loans are existent (second line), and how high the loans were (other lines, in relation to type of the loan).

high numbers who refused to answer in the case of the private pension. The reason for assuming this is that refusal to answer was high both in the second variant too, in which respondents were asked to reply in the form of coded ranges (CAPI categorical), and in the case of forms that respondents completed themselves.

Apart from the CAPI survey variant with missing numerical data and data on a private pension, the item nonresponse rates are within the usual range. In particular, they broadly correspond to the item nonresponse rates of surveys in the United States and Great Britain. This disproves the assumption that is often made that, in contrast to these countries, it is impossible to conduct surveys in Germany about money matters.

Table 10A.2 shows the refusal rate in respect of the value of the home owned by the respondent and in which he or she lives. Apart from the survey variant in which the respondent has to disclose the value of the house to the interviewers (CAPI numerical), the rate of refusal is very low.

The picture for the level of debt is also similar. Item response rates are highest for the two survey variants completed entirely using CAPI technology. The figures fluctuate more because only around 41 percent of SAVE households have outstanding loans.

References

Abel, A. 1985. Precautionary saving and accidental bequests. *American Economic Review* 75:777–91.

Attanasio, O. 1999. Consumption. In *Handbook of macroeconomics,* ed. J. Taylor and M. Woodford, 741–812. Amsterdam: Elsevier Science.

Bernheim, D., A. Schleifer, and L. Summers. 1985. The strategic bequest motive. *Journal of Political Economy* 93:1045–75.

Börsch-Supan, A. 1992. Saving and consumption patterns of the elderly: The German case. *Journal of Population Economics* 5:289–303.

———. 1994a. Savings in Germany—part I: Incentives. In *Public policies and household saving,* ed. J. M. Poterba, 81–104. Chicago: University of Chicago Press.

———. 1994b. Savings in Germany—part II: Behavior. In *International comparisons of household saving,* ed. J. M. Poterba, 207–36. Chicago: University of Chicago Press.

Börsch-Supan, A., ed. 2003. *Life-cycle savings and public policy.* New York: Academic Press.

Börsch-Supan, A., and A. Lusardi. 2003. Saving: A cross-national perspective. In *Life-cycle savings and public policy,* ed. A. Börsch-Supan, 1–31. New York: Academic Press.

Börsch-Supan, A., A. Reil-Held, R. Rodepeter, R. Schnabel, and J. Winter. 2001. The German savings puzzle. *Research in Economics* 55 (1): 15–38.

Börsch-Supan, A., and K. Stahl. 1991a. Do dedicated savings increase personal savings and housing consumption? An analysis of the German Bausparkassen system. *Journal of Public Economics* 44:265–97.

———. 1991b. Life-cycle savings and consumption constraints. *Journal of Population Economics* 4:233–55.

Browning, M., and A. Lusardi. 1996. Household saving: Macro theories and micro facts. *Journal of Economic Literature* 34:1797–1855.

Carroll, C. 1992. The buffer-stock theory of saving: Some macroeconomic evidence. *Brookings Papers on Economic Activity,* Issue no. 2:61–156.

Carroll, C. D., and A. A. Samwick. 1998. How important is precautionary saving? *Review of Economics and Statistics* 80 (3): 410–19.

Deaton, A. 1991. Saving and liquidity constraints. *Econometrica* 59:1221–48.

Deaton, A. 1992. *Understanding consumption.* Oxford: Oxford University Press.

Feldstein, M. 1974. Social Security, induced retirement and aggregate capital accumulation. *Journal of Political Economy* 82 (5): 905–26.

Guiso, L., M. Haliassos, and T. Jappelli. 2001. *Household portfolios.* Cambridge, MA: MIT Press.

Hurd, M. D. 1987. Savings of the elderly and desired bequests. *American Economic Review* 77:298–312.

———. 1990. Issues and results from research on the elderly, economic status, retirement, and savings. *Journal of Economic Literature* 28:565–637.

Jappelli, T., and F. Modigliani. 1998. The age-saving profile and the life-cycle hypothesis. CSEF Working Paper no. 4. University of Salerno, Centre for Studies in Economics and Finance.

Jappelli, T., and M. Pagano. 1989. Consumption and capital market imperfections: An international comparison. *American Economic Review* 79:1088–1105.

Kotlikoff, L. 1989. *What determines savings?* Cambridge: MIT Press.

Laibson, D. 1997. Golden eggs and hyperbolic discounting. *Quarterly Journal of Economics* 112:443–78.

Lettau, M., and H. Uhlig. 1999. Rules of thumb versus dynamic programming. *American Economic Review* 89 (1): 148–74.

Lusardi, A. 1997. Precautionary saving and subjective earnings variance. *Economics Letters* 57:319–26.

Modigliani, F., and R. Brumberg. 1954. Utility analysis and the consumption function: An interpretation of cross-section data. In *Social cognitive development frontiers and possible futures,* ed. J. H. Flavell and L. Ross. Cambridge: Cambridge University Press.

O'Donoghue, T., and M. Rabin. 1999. Doing it now or later. *American Economic Review* 89:103–24.

Poterba, J., ed. 1994. *International comparisons of household savings.* Chicago: University of Chicago Press.

Reil-Held, A. 1999. Bequests and aggregate wealth accumulation in Germany. *The Geneva Papers on Risk and Insurance* 24:50–63.

Schnabel, R. 1999. *Ersparnisbildung und rentenversicherung—eine empirische analyse für die Bundesrepublik Deutschland.* Habilitation, University of Mannheim, Mannheim, Germany.

Thaler, R., and H. Shefrin. 1981. An economic theory of self-control. *Journal of Political Economy* 89:392–406.

Comment   Andrew A. Samwick

This is a fascinating chapter about a new survey of saving in Germany. The authors are to be commended for producing an original approach to the study of household saving. Rather than attempting to infer the models, methods, or motivations that govern household saving behavior from data on household budget sets, the SAVE survey asks them questions to elicit the answers directly. It represents a useful first step in forming a more complete understanding of the extent to which households systematically plan their savings over the life cycle and ultimately how faithfully those plans are realized.

My starting point differs from the one expressed by the authors in the motivating statement "The savings behavior of households is not well understood." I will certainly stipulate that we do not know everything about savings behavior, but I believe it is time for researchers to consider what we do know about saving in motivating and framing their further work. For example, I started working in this literature about a dozen years ago, and my current understanding of savings has evolved over that time into a mixture that is equal parts Deaton (1991, 1992), Carroll (1992, 1994), and Laibson (1997). Here is what we know. The model is forward looking, with precautionary motives and impatience for the typical household. Households may implement the model through various approximations or rules of thumb. Households make systematic mistakes in processing information and in adhering to plans. There is also evidence that heterogeneity in

Andrew A. Samwick is a professor of economics and the director of The Nelson A. Rockefeller Center at Dartmouth College, and a research associate of the National Bureau of Economic Research.

preferences, such as the rate of time preference, is also important (see Samwick 1998a, for example).

Fortunately, the SAVE survey is so broad in its choice of questions that it likely includes novel information for researchers who have widely different current views about how households save. Of the many novel tabulations in the paper, I will summarize three that I found particularly interesting, given my own background in savings and portfolio research in the United States.

The first is that financial planning is an acquired taste. Table 10.13 reports the answers to a question about whether there is typically money left over at the end of the month, separately for those under thirty, thirty to fifty-nine, and sixty and over. The comparisons are suggestive that the probability of having money left over increases with age. Further evidence on the main point was presented in an earlier version of the chapter, which reported that households were over four times more likely to keep a record of household expenditures if their parents did. The comparisons would be more persuasive if the authors conditioned on income and included standard errors, so that statistical significance might also be inferred. Both comparisons should nonetheless give pause to economists who typically leave the process by which households learn how to match expectations with outcomes out of their models.

The second is that there are considerable differences by age in the savings patterns of German households. For example, table 10.17 shows that saving at regular intervals is more a characteristic of households under thirty-five than households between thirty-five and fifty-five years of age. Table 10.18 reports a higher frequency of target saving behavior among younger households as well. These facts are true despite the correlation of regular saving and target saving with income, which is (presumably) positively correlated with age. Table 10.21 gives an indication that some of these disparities could be related to the types of portfolio investments that typify each age group. The youngest group of households has a greater likelihood of participating in a building society saving arrangement or a private old-age pension. This is true despite the positive relationship between these investments and income.

The same age patterns are evident for ownership of stocks and mutual funds. Households under thirty-five are twice as likely as households over fifty-four to own stocks, again despite the positive correlation of income with both age and stock ownership. These age profiles for pensions and stocks are opposite of what researchers have found in the United States (see, for example, Poterba and Samwick 2001) and suggest the need for a more careful study of cohort or cultural factors in saving behavior.

The third finding that I think is useful is that while not all households save for the same specific reasons, the number of unique motives is relatively small. Figure 10.4 presents histograms of the strength of each of nine possible motivations for saving. Retirement, uncertainty, and housing are prominent motives. In the United States (which has a lower saving rate overall), similar questions also yield "education" as a less important but nontrivial motive. Specifically enumerating household reasons for saving leads to several important insights.

First, different motives can lead to different behavior. Saving for education, housing, and to a large extent uncertainty (early in the life cycle) may take the form of target saving. For target saving, income effects due to interest rate changes are likely to overwhelm substitution effects. As discussed in Samwick (1998b), large income effects suggest a negative effect of tax preferences on total saving.

Second, specific questions on savings motives are a useful way to track changes in the population. In the U.S. Survey of Consumer Finances, similar questions are asked about the relative importance of savings motives. Comparing the results in Samwick (1998b) for the 1992 survey with those in Samwick (2000) for the 1998 survey shows that motives shifted over time. In 1992, uncertainty is reported as the most important motive for all ages under fifty-five. In 1998, retirement is the most important motive at all ages before retirement. Since the tabulations condition on age, they are not the result of a demographic shift. Some explanations are seasonal, such as the change in the level and direction of the stock market at the time. Others are more systematic, such as the greater availability of investor-directed 401(k) plans over time. Identifying the factors that generate these changes could help in formulating tax policy that more effectively promotes household saving.

Finally, the presence of multiple reasons for saving highlights an important shortcoming in the current saving literature. Almost no one writes down a model of saving in which there is more than one motive for saving apart from traditional life-cycle concerns. The current state of the art is a stochastic life-cycle model, in which both retirement and uncertainty motives are included, perhaps with a detailed budget set that includes both taxable and tax-deferred savings accounts. With the continuing improvements in computer power, it is now feasible to also add housing and education purchases to the model. The key aspects of these two motives are that they occur early in the life cycle and may have characteristics of target saving. One element of savings behavior that really is poorly understood is the interaction of savings motives over the life cycle, and surveys such as SAVE can be used to guide future modeling efforts.

References

Carroll, Christopher D. 1992. The buffer-stock theory of saving: Some macroeconomic evidence. *Brookings Papers on Economic Activity,* Issue no. 2:61–156.
———. 1994. How does future income affect current consumption? *Quarterly Journal of Economics* 109:111–48.
Deaton, Angus. 1991. Saving and liquidity constraints. *Econometrica* 59:1221–48.
———. 1992. *Understanding consumption.* Oxford: Oxford University Press.
Laibson, David. 1997. Golden eggs and hyperbolic discounting. *Quarterly Journal of Economics* 112:443–78.
Poterba, James M., and Andrew A. Samwick. 2001. Portfolio allocations over the life cycle. In *Aging issues in the United States and Japan,* ed. Seiritsu Ogura, Toshiaki Tachibanaki, and A. David Wise, 65–103. Chicago: University of Chicago Press.
Samwick, Andrew A. 1998a. Discount rate heterogeneity and Social Security reform. *Journal of Development Economics* 57:117–46.
———. 1998b. Tax reform and target saving. *National Tax Journal* 51:621–35.
———. 2004. The effects of Social Security reform on private pensions. In *Private pensions and public policies,* ed. William G. Gale, John B. Shoven, and Mark J. Warshawsky, 189–213. Washington, DC: Brookings Institution Press.

Caste, Culture, and the Status and Well-Being of Widows in India

Robert Jensen

11.1 Introduction

Issues in aging are becoming of increasing importance in India. While this may seem paradoxical because of the low life expectancy (about sixty-four years for women and men), these numbers are somewhat misleading because they reflect in part very high infant mortality rates. Conditional on surviving to age sixty, male life expectancy in India is about sixteen years for men and seventeen years for women (Irudaya Rajan, Mishra, and Sankara Sarma 1999), which is not much less than the eighteen to twenty years for most developed countries. India currently has the world's second largest population of elderly persons, with over 70 million persons aged sixty or above (though India still has a relatively young population, in that this represents only about 7 percent of the total population). This population is projected to grow to about 160 million within two decades, which will represent about 12 percent of the total population at that time. Thus, the elderly present an extremely large and rapidly growing population in India.

Research on the elderly in India has increasingly focused on the well-being of widows in particular (Chen 2000; Drèze and Srinivasan 1997; Chen and Drèze 1995). About 55 percent of women aged sixty and above are widowed, compared to about 15 percent widowers among men (Irudaya Rajan, Mishra, and Sankara Sarma 1999); this difference reflects in

Robert Jensen is an associate professor of public policy at the Kennedy School of Government, Harvard University, and a faculty research fellow of the National Bureau of Economic Research.

The support of the National Bureau of Economic Research (NBER) Center for Aging and Health Research for this project is graciously acknowledged.

part the large husband-wife age gap (six years) as well as a greater inci-dence of remarriage among widowers compared to widows. Widowhood is generally thought to represent a particular economic vulnerability for women. In rural areas, most earnings opportunities involve strenuous physical labor, such as in agriculture, which becomes increasingly difficult with age. Caste norms also often discourage women, and widows in par-ticular, from working, and in many cases women face difficulties in retain-ing control of their husband's land upon his death. Further, private pen-sions are not common, and there is little in the way of public support for the elderly.[1] Drèze and Srinivasan (1997) find that, even with a range of adjustments for equivalence scales, widows are no more likely to live in poverty than nonwidows, but because widows tend to live in households with fewer members, even small adjustments for economies of scale result in widows' being significantly worse off than average. However, almost all studies of the well-being of the elderly are unable to examine the distribu-tion of resources within households, using household income or expendi-ture per capita as a proxy for the resources available to the elderly person, and there is ample evidence to suggest that widows often do not receive an equal share within the household (Chen 2000).

Beyond the economic difficulties faced by widows, authors have also pointed to social, cultural, and political limitations widows often en-counter. For example, Chen (2000) points out that social mores often dis-courage widows from remarriage and dictate changes in their diet and be-havior, and widows are often unwelcome at social events and religious festivals and avoided by others because they are considered bad luck. More generally, there are a variety of customs, norms, practices, beliefs, and in-stitutions that affect the economic, social, and political opportunities and the social status of the elderly, especially widows (the most infamous, though perhaps least widespread, of which is *sati*, or self-immolation on the husband's cremation pyre). These practices are important not just be-cause of the economic constraints they may place on widows, but in their own right as well, as part of a broader conception of well-being that ex-pands beyond purely economic terms (e.g., Sen 1999).

In this paper, we examine how these norms, attitudes, and practices vary

1. In principle, public support for the elderly is a joint responsibility of the state and na-tional governments. There is a national pension scheme for impoverished elderly persons aged sixty-five or older. Coverage is not extensive, eligibility is limited to only persons with no surviving sons and below a (very low) income threshold, and states have statutory maxi-mum outlays. As a result, very few elderly persons participate. For example, Chen (2000) finds that only 10 percent of widows in her sample, and 23 percent of those with no adult sons, re-ceive pensions. Pension levels are low, typically about 100 rupees (about U.S. $2) per month, though some states have supplemental programs. There is a mandatory pension system for firms with more than twenty employees and a separate system for civil servants. However, about 90 percent of all workers are in the uncovered, informal sector (though a few states have implemented limited schemes for this sector).

across groups in India and how they affect the well-being of the elderly. We first examine the influence of caste on well-being. Caste is a social organization prevalent in India that creates a well-defined social ordering (see appendix for a brief note about caste). Caste is highly correlated with other measures of socioeconomic status (SES), with those from higher castes typically better off along most dimensions than those from lower castes. Castes also differ in terms of behavior, practices, and norms; most relevant for the present case, higher castes often place *more* restrictions on and assign lower status to women, and widows in particular. Thus, caste offers two potentially opposing influences on the well-being of women. Our objective is to examine the net consequences for widows, using indicators for individual nutritional status and health rather than relying on household income or expenditure per capita.

The second theme of this paper is examining whether social and cultural institutions and the status of widows have any underpinnings in economic factors. In particular, we explore whether the presence in the village of residence of crops for which women and the elderly are likely to have a comparative advantage, namely those that are less strength intensive (i.e., crops not based on draft plough agriculture), means that women and the elderly are able to make larger economic contributions (and have improved opportunities outside the household) and thus the status and treatment of widows, and women more generally, will be more favorable. This exercise also carries larger lessons about the potential role of economic factors in the determination and evolution of social or cultural institutions and practices.

11.2 Widowhood and Remarriage

Before beginning the analysis, it is useful to explore the broad patterns relating to widowhood and remarriage across various groups. To do so, we make use of data from the 1998–99 National Family Health Survey (NFHS),[2] a nationally representative survey of 90,303 ever-married women aged fifteen to forty-nine (which can be weighted to generate statistics representative at the state and national levels). The survey collects data on a range of demographic, social, and (to a lesser extent) economic variables for the household and its various members, as well as a village-level survey with information on agricultural, economic, and social conditions and infrastructure. These data do not contain a great deal of detail on elderly persons, but data from the household roster can be used to describe the patterns of widowhood.

2. The NFHS is the Indian implementation of the Demographic and Health Surveys (DHS; now Measure DHS). The data, questionnaires, and additional information are available at http://www.measuredhs.com.

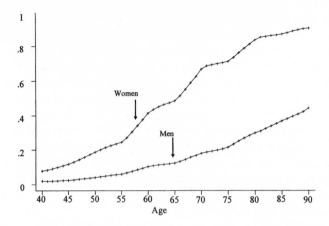

Fig. 11.1   Current widowhood by age
Source: NFHS 1988–89.

Figure 11.1 shows NFHS data on the incidence of *current* widowhood by age for men and women. At all ages the incidence is much higher for women than men. About 40 percent of women aged sixty are widowed compared to 12 percent of men, and the gap grows to 69 and 19 by age seventy. The large disparity at each age is the result of the large average husband-wife age gap (six years) and the greater incidence of remarriage among men.[3] Despite popular perception, remarriage is not prohibited by any caste or religious group in India (Chen 2000). Unfortunately, the NFHS only collects more information on marital histories for female respondents aged fifteen to forty-nine, including whether they have had a previous marriage (but not separately indicating whether the first marriage ended due to marriage or divorce).[4] We focus on women aged forty-five to forty-nine, to capture the oldest population available. Table 11.1 shows data on the incidence of widowhood and remarriage, disaggregated by religious and caste groupings. The data reveal that 15 percent of women of this age have ever been widowed or divorced, and 11 percent of ever-widowed/divorced women are currently married. The greatest incidence of ever-widowhood is among women of scheduled tribes, at nearly one in five.

3. Very few data sets, and no national-level data sets, collect information on remarriage. However, a few studies for specific villages or regions have collected this information. For example, Chen's (2000) sample reveals a remarriage rate of 10 percent among widows, while Drèze (1990) finds 15 to 20 percent. Agarwala (1970) finds that 60 percent of widowers in Delhi remarry, compared to 37 percent for women, and United Nations (1961) estimate the rates at 60 and 10 percent respectively in rural Mysore (Karnataka). Bhat and Kanbargi (1984) estimate 63 and 34 percent remarriage rates for men and women across all India, using information on current marital status and applying a cohort-based inferential technique to census data.

4. However, divorce is not very common in India, significantly less so than widowhood.

Table 11.1   Widowhood and remarriage, women aged 45–49 (%)

	Ever widowed	Ever widowed and remarried	Currently widowed
All India	.15	.11	.13
	(.01)	(.01)	(.01)
Scheduled tribe	.18	.21	.14
	(.01)	(.03)	(.01)
Scheduled caste	.16	.11	.14
	(.01)	(.02)	(.01)
Other backward caste	.15	.11	.13
	(.01)	(.02)	(.01)
Forward caste	.12	.07	.11
	(.01)	(.01)	(.01)
Muslim	.15	.17	.13
	(.01)	(.03)	(.01)
Christian	.18	.19	.15
	(.02)	(.04)	(.01)

Source: Author's calculation from the NFHS.

Notes: Standard errors in parentheses. The NFHS data only indicate whether a woman has been previously married, and do not indicate whether the first marriage ended due to widowhood or divorce. However, divorce is very uncommon in India.

Reflecting underlying economic differentials, there is a gradient by caste, with the higher (forward) castes having only two-thirds the widow rate of the scheduled tribes. However, the rate of remarriage is significantly higher for the scheduled tribes, at nearly three times the rate among the higher castes, and almost twice that of scheduled castes and other backward castes (OBCs). Thus, in terms of current widowhood, there is not a significant gradient by caste. Muslims and Christians have similar widowhood and remarriage rates as the scheduled tribes.

For Hindus, within castes,[5] two general factors are thought to affect the likelihood of remarriage. First, the likelihood of remarriage (and social approval of remarriage) declines with age, and becomes extremely rare after age forty. An additional important factor is whether the woman has had any children, in particular sons, in her first marriage. In general, even controlling for age, those who have no children and especially no sons will be more likely to remarry. This distinction is motivated in part by choice (for example, a woman may fear a new husband would treat her children poorly, or she may feel less of a need to remarry because the son can help support her) and in part by constraint (no one will remarry a widow with children, or society may not condone it). The NFHS data reveal that conditional on having been ever widowed or divorced, having had a child from

5. There is a limited notion of caste among Muslims in India, even more limited among Christians. However, caste for non-Hindus is often much less overt and does not connote the same divisions as among Hindus.

the first husband decreases the likelihood of remarriage by about 43 percent, and conditional on having had a child, women with at least one son are 23 percent less likely to remarry than women with only daughters (results not shown).

11.3 Socioeconomic Status, Caste, and Well-Being

Given the widespread incidence of widowhood, especially among older women, it is important to examine the well-being of widows. Unfortunately, the NFHS provides only very limited data on SES; while there is some information on employment status and assets owned, there is no information on income or expenditure. Further, even if household income were available, the measurement of poverty among the elderly is very sensitive to assumptions on economies and scale and costs of children (Deaton and Paxson 1998), as well as assumptions on the intrahousehold allocation of resources. However, as an initial investigation, the NFHS data do provide information on whether individuals work, either outside the household for pay or in self-employment. Table 11.2 provides information on female employment for both widows and nonwidows aged forty-five to forty-nine, with a distinction drawn between land-owning and landless households. Female employment rates among nonwidows are low overall, at 20 percent among those owning land and 40 percent among the landless. In general, employment rates are higher among the scheduled tribes and castes relative to the OBCs and forward castes (even though land ownership is highest among the scheduled tribes). For all castes and reli-

Table 11.2   Employment among women aged 45–49, by widowhood status, NFHS

	Nonwidows			Widows		
	Work for pay	Own land	Work for pay (landless)	Work for pay	Own land	Work for pay (landless)
All India	.20 (.01)	.52 (.01)	.40 (.02)	.39 (.01)	.43 (.01)	.48 (.05)
Scheduled tribe	.29 (.01)	.72 (.01)	.43 (.02)	.53 (.04)	.60 (.04)	.54 (.05)
Scheduled caste	.31 (.01)	.44 (.03)	.35 (.01)	.50 (.03)	.34 (.03)	.43 (.01)
Other backward caste	.21 (.01)	.58 (.01)	.26 (.01)	.43 (.02)	.45 (.02)	.47 (.03)
Forward caste	.14 (.01)	.52 (.01)	.24 (.01)	.30 (.02)	.46 (.02)	.32 (.02)
Muslim	.11 (.01)	.42 (.01)	.14 (.01)	.23 (.03)	.31 (.03)	.30 (.04)
Christian	.33 (.01)	.47 (.01)	.41 (.02)	.43 (.04)	.36 (.04)	.48 (.06)

Source: Author's calculation from the NFHS.

Table 11.3   **Expenditure per capita, body mass index (BMI) and caste, widows and nonwidows, SARI**

	Expenditure per capita		BMI	
	Nonwidows	Widows	Nonwidows	Widows
Scheduled tribe	323	251	18.9	19.1
	(193)	(213)	(.48)	(.57)
Scheduled caste	424	348	19.3	19.4
	(131)	(159)	(.32)	(.38)
Other backward caste	593	502	19.5	19.3
	(110)	(201)	(.32)	(.34)
Forward caste	715	577	20.6	19.4
	(198)	(228)	(.58)	(.51)

Source: Author's calculations from SARI data.

gious groups, employment rates are higher among women currently widowed, for both landed and landless households. Over one-half of widowed scheduled tribe women work, compared to only one-third among the forward castes (though, in percentage terms, the difference between nonwidows and widows is greater for the forward castes). Of course, selection into widowhood is nonrandom,[6] and that selection may differ across these groups, and we don't have panel data to examine the prewidow employment rates of current widows. Therefore, these results should only be seen as descriptive and suggestive.

For a more in-depth investigation of the relationship between caste and well-being, we apply data from the Survey of Aging in Rural India (SARI), a survey of 1,477 households, each containing a person aged fifty or older, conducted by the author in 2002 in five states or Union Territories (Delhi, Jharkhand, Haryana, Kerala, and Tamil Nadu).[7] Several sections of this survey were modeled to be compatible with other demographic surveys for India, including the NFHS. The survey collected information on a range of (current and past) demographic, health, social, and economic variables. In addition, a village-level survey was conducted in each sample cluster, gathering information on economic and social conditions and infrastructure, as well as the prevailing customs and norms relating to the elderly.

Table 11.3 shows data on household expenditure[8] per capita (with no adjustments for economies of scale or adult equivalence) for widows and

6. Selection into ownership of land and retention of land after widowhood is also non-random.

7. The sample of households for the survey was selected in two stages. In the first stage, village administrative areas, or *panchayat,* were selected at random from district lists. In the second stage, within each *panchayat* households were chosen through a random sampling procedure based on registration lists. There was an average of about fifteen households in each of 103 sampling units selected.

8. Land-owning households were asked the quantity and market value of any consumption from own production.

nonwidows in the SARI sample. Across all caste groups, expenditure per capita is lower for widows than nonwidows, with differences of 20 to 25 percent (though, again, selection into widowhood is nonrandom, and it is likely that currently widowed women had lower prewidow expenditures than nonwidows). And across both widows and nonwidows, there is a clear gradient in expenditure per capita, with scheduled tribes worst off on average, having expenditures per capita less than one-half of that among forward castes.

However, as mentioned above, such data are not entirely indicative of the consumption or well-being of individuals within households. Instead, we explore a reduced-form measure of consumption and nutritional status by examining the body mass index (BMI),[9] constructed from physical measurements conducted for all respondents in the survey. The last two columns of table 11.3 provide data on BMI across caste groups. Focusing first on nonwidows, there is a clear gradient in BMI by caste that mirrors that of expenditure per capita, with the scheduled tribes or castes having the lowest BMI and the forward castes having the highest (approximately 10 percent higher than the scheduled tribes). However, comparing widows and nonwidows within each caste group reveals interesting differences. In particular, for the scheduled tribes and castes, widows are no worse off in terms of BMI than nonwidows. However, there are large differences between widows and nonwidows for OBCs and especially the forward castes. While forward-caste widows still have a slightly higher BMI than widows in the scheduled tribes, they no longer differ from the scheduled castes or OBCs. There is no longer any discernible gradient with caste, and in fact none of the across-caste group differences in BMI are statistically significant. In part, this lack of a gradient likely reflects the fact that there are stronger restrictions on employment among forward-caste women, as suggested by table 11.2, and may also indicate that widows in forward-caste households are not given as large a share of total household consumption as they are in lower-caste households. Thus, wealthier, upper-caste widows are no better off in terms of nutritional status than poorer but more equally treated lower-caste widows. Of course, the possibility of differential selection into widowhood across these groups cannot be ruled out.[10] Table 11.4 presents comparable data on BMI across caste groups for the NFHS, for all currently not-pregnant widows and nonwidows aged forty-five to forty-nine. Similar patterns emerge in the SARI data, though a distinction arises between landed and nonlanded households. A similar weakening of the BMI gradient is seen among widows, and among landless widows the gradient is essentially absent.

9. BMI is weight (in kilograms) divided by squared height (in meters).
10. Of course, in all cases, we are unable to distinguish whether the lower consumption among widows is by choice or the result of an allocation of resources within the household over which they have no choice.

Table 11.4   Body mass index, widows and nonwidows aged 45+, NFHS

	Landed		Landless	
	Nonwidows	Widows	Nonwidows	Widows
Scheduled tribe	20.2	20.2	20.1	20.5
	(.13)	(.31)	(.18)	(.47)
Scheduled caste	20.4	20.7	19.8	20.1
	(.12)	(.33)	(.12)	(.31)
Other backward caste	21.2	20.7	20.5	20.3
	(.09)	(.24)	(.12)	(.34)
Forward caste	22.9	21.7	21.3	20.3
	(.10)	(.26)	(.18)	(.44)
Muslim	21.8	22.6	20.5	20.4
	(.19)	(.55)	(.20)	(.67)
Christian	21.9	21.8	21.4	20.9
	(.20)	(.46)	(.24)	(.50)

Source: Author's calculations from NFHS data.

11.4 Institutions, Customs, Norms, and Practices

There are many important institutions, behaviors, and practices surrounding widowhood that affect the well-being of widows, such as whether the widow is discouraged from remarrying, whether she retains full control of her husband's land upon his death, and whether she works. While widows' rights in all of these cases are protected by law, actual outcomes are likely to be shaped by societal constraints, traditions, and practices. Further, there are a variety of other social practices, customs, attitudes, and beliefs that affect the status and well-being of widows. For example, following the death of their husband, women are often expected to undergo a period of seclusion (remaining in a remote room in the home), followed by confinement to the home (or village) for a period of time, as well as permanently changing their diets (in particular, avoiding "heating" foods (*garam,* including meat, eggs, alcohol, onions, and garlic) in favor of "cooling" foods (*thanda,* including yogurt, rice, milk, and honey; Chen 2000). Widows are often also unwelcome at social events, ceremonies, and rituals, and avoided socially because they are considered bad luck, in part because of their association with death. *Sati* is the most extreme example of such practices, although the evidence suggests it is extremely uncommon and in fact has never been very widespread.

The various norms and practices, and more generally the status of the elderly and widows in particular, vary widely across India. Many authors have noted that women fare better in the south relative to the north along many dimensions of well-being, such as infant mortality, life expectancy, and education (e.g., Visaria 1967; Bardhan 1974; Miller 1981). Two explanations have typically been suggested for these patterns. The first is that wheat is the dominant crop in the north whereas rice is dominant in the south, and the latter allows women to make a greater economic contribution, which in turn affects women's status. Consistent with a link between economic status and the treatment of women, Rosenzweig and Schultz (1982) find that differences in expected lifetime earnings for men and women are associated with differentials in male-female survival rates among children in India. The second explanation offered is the cultural and historical differences between the populations of the north and south of India. In particular, the northern populations are the descendents of Aryans that invaded northern India around 1500 BCE, whereas the dominant population in the south consists of descendents of the Dravidians who were either originally residing in the south or pushed from the north when the Aryans arrived. It is generally believed that the Dravidians and Aryans had widely varying social customs, practices, and organization.[11] However, this historical-cultural explanation only pushes the analysis one step back, and it then becomes important to ask why the Dravidians and Aryans had differing norms and customs (or why those norms and practices evolved differently once the Aryans arrived).

Our motivating hypothesis focuses around the first explanation, namely that there are certain economic conditions that differentially affect the comparative advantage of men and women (and the elderly and the young). For example, there are some crops, such as rice and tea, that are less strength intensive than others, such as wheat and other ploughed crops. Because women and the elderly are able to make a larger economic contribution in areas growing less strength-intensive crops, we might expect their status to be greater.[12] (Though it is also important to take into consideration that some crops, although strength intensive in their planting and harvesting, potentially provide secondary employment opportunities for women and the elderly in processing those crops, such as the grinding of wheat into flour).[13] It should be emphasized that we are not arguing for a model of "norms" in the sense of a set of behaviors or attitudes based on shared social beliefs and enforced through social and emotional sanctions and rewards, rather than as part of self-interested behavior; the greater status of women and the elderly could arise through a model of bar-

11. For example, it is believed that the Aryans brought caste with them to India, though it is also possible that the Aryans created caste at the time of their arrival in India, perhaps as a system to place the Aryans in positions of advantage and prevent intermarriage. Unfortunately, there are no recorded sources to determine whether the Aryans had different attitudes toward women at the time they invaded or whether those attitudes evolved afterward.

12. We are distinguishing the comparative advantage women or the elderly may have in particular crops from the idea of whether crops are "gendered." For example, especially in West Africa, some crops are considered female crops and others male crops. It often has less to do with the nature of the crop than with whether the crop is grown for own-household consumption (female crops) or as a cash crop (male crops).

13. Of course, it must also be kept in mind that norms could evolve the other way around, such that norms of respect and care for the elderly arise in places where they are less able to fend for themselves or live independently.

gaining within the household.[14] Empirically, the two are difficult to distinguish. Therefore, we do not argue in favor of one interpretation over the other, but instead focus on the reduced-form evidence relating the status of widows to the strength intensity of locally grown crops.

To test this hypothesis, we will explore how various indicators of the status and well-being of widows vary with indicators for whether the dominant crop grown in a village is "female" in the sense that women and the elderly have a comparative advantage in these crops over other crops. While the choice is somewhat arbitrary,[15] the following crops were considered not conducive to women or the elderly: wheat, maize, and other cereals. Crops considered more amenable to women or the elderly include rice, tea, tobacco, cotton, and pulse.

Regarding the status of widows, in addition to measures of consumption and health, the SARI gathered information from respondents regarding institutions, practices, and customs relating to women, the elderly, and widows. For example, respondents were asked whether they feel welcome at ceremonies or "connected" to the society around them. Some questions regarding status and treatment were asked retrospectively of widows, regarding changes in status and treatment around the time of widowhood. Our empirical analysis surrounds two primary specifications. We first examine indicators of women's well-being that vary as a function of widowhood in male versus female crop areas, estimating:

$$(1) \quad W_i = \gamma_0 + \gamma_1 \text{Widow}_i + \gamma_2 \text{FEMCROP}_i + \gamma_3 \text{Widow}_i \cdot \text{FEMCROP}_i + \sum_c \phi_c \text{CASTE}_i + \xi \mathbf{X}_i + \eta_i,$$

where W_i is an indicator of status or well-being and $\mathbf{X}_i$ is a vector of individual, household and village level covariates. The coefficient of interest is γ_3, the interaction term on widow and female crop—in other words, whether the difference in W_i for widows and nonwidows differs across male and female crop areas.[16] As indicators of welfare, we use the BMI, self-assessed health status (1 to 5, with higher numbers indicating better

14. In particular, where higher threat point utilities of women or the elderly improve their allocation within the household. It should be noted that threat points are often considered as the utility attainable if an individual left the household. While divorce is not common in India, it is not necessary to invoke leaving the household, since it could be that the woman instead threatens not to work or to work at less than her capacity.

15. It is possible to define crops that provide greater female employment opportunities as those in which we see a larger percent of female labor. However, that strategy introduces an element of circularity, since working outside of the household is in itself an indicator of women's status.

16. In order to allay concerns that crops are chosen in order to accord with the status of women, in additional specifications we use historical means and variability of rainfall and temperature as well as soil properties (pH, potassium, nitrogen, phosphorous, salinity, stoniness, and soil type) as instruments for crops grown in the village. However, we cannot rule out the possibility that groups migrate to places where the nature of agriculture and the opportunities for women are more consistent with their preexisting views on women's status.

health), whether they feel they are respected by others in the community, and how connected to society they feel (the last two of which also range from 1 to 5, with higher numbers indicating more respect and more connection). We also include a set of caste dummy variables (scheduled tribe, scheduled caste, and OBC), and indicators for whether the widow lives alone (about 11 percent) or with her children (about 56 percent).[17] As additional covariates, we also include age, education, income, household size, and whether the respondent is the head of the household. As stated, this is a difference-in-differences estimator, comparing the difference in the outcome of interest between widows and nonwidows in female crop areas relative to the difference in male crop areas. Unfortunately, the data are cross-sectional, and it is not possible to track individuals over time or examine selection into widowhood (which in itself could differ across male and female crop areas). Our goal will simply be to focus on whether the differences between widows and nonwidows vary with the crops grown locally. Further, we are only examining differences upon entering into widowhood in these areas: it is likely that women may be treated worse in male crop areas even when they are not widows, in which case we might not expect a large differential change at widowhood.

To examine the practices and changes in well-being, treatment, and status surrounding widowhood in male versus female crop areas, we estimate

$$(2) \qquad W_i = \gamma_0 + \gamma_1 \text{FEMCROP}_i + \sum_c \phi_c \text{CASTE}_i + \xi X_i + \eta_i,$$

which has the advantage of explicitly examining changes in treatment and status in the two types of areas, rather than comparing widows and nonwidows. As indicators of changes in welfare following widowhood we examine the following: whether, at the time of their husband's death, there was change in treatment by the husband's family (1: better, 2: about the same, 3: worse); whether they lost control of their husband's land (0,1 conditional on having owned land); whether they noticed a change in their status among other people in the village (1: better, 2: about the same, 3: worse); whether they feel less welcome at ceremonies and events such as weddings or births (0,1); how long they remained inside the household after the death of their husband (in months); and whether they changed their diet (0,1) toward *thanda* foods. While these are imperfect measures and do not capture the full complexity of well-being, they are useful proxies for treatment and status along key dimensions following widowhood.

The results of regression (1) are presented in table 11.5. Across all four measures, BMI, self-assessed health, respect from others in the village, and sense of connectedness, widows are worse off than nonwidows. Body mass

17. Of the remainders, about 30 percent live with their deceased husband's family, 3 percent with other people.

Table 11.5   **Change in status and well-being indicators, widows vs. nonwidows, NFHS**

	BMI (1)	Self-assessed health (2)	Respect from others in village (3)	Connectedness (4)
Widow	−1.10	−.29	−.65	−.56
	(.49)	(.15)	(.27)	(.31)
Female crop	−.29	−.07	−.27	−.12
	(.16)	(.10)	(.08)	(.06)
Female crop × widow	.69	.24	.30	.48
	(.21)	(.13)	(.11)	(.19)
Age	−.008	−.005	−.003	−.01
	(.005)	(.003)	(.003)	(.01)
Education	.14	.13	.021	.16
	(.01)	(.01)	(.007)	(.05)
Scheduled tribe	−.68	−.31	.34	.57
	(.16)	(.10)	(.08)	(.06)
Scheduled caste	−.79	−.39	.35	.56
	(.15)	(.09)	(.07)	(.05)
Other backward caste	−.34	−.27	.29	.33
	(.15)	(.09)	(.07)	(.05)
North	−.27	−.10	.08	.08
	(.12)	(.07)	(.06)	(.04)

Notes: All results from the SARI data set. Sample restricted to women. The number of observations is 1,249. The dependent variable in column (1) is the body mass index (BMI). Self-assessed health status in column (2) is an indicator ranging from one to five (1 = very bad, 2 = bad, 3 = about average, 4 = good, 5 = very good). Respect from others in the village and connectedness also range from 1 to 5, with higher numbers indicating more respect and more connection to the village.

index is also statistically significantly higher in female crop areas, though this may in part not reflect an intrahousehold allocation issue as much as the fact that areas with male crops tend to be slightly better off on average. But in all four cases, the interaction term on female crop and widow suggests that the difference between widows and nonwidows is much larger in areas that do not have female crops. In fact, for self-assessed health and the sense of connectedness with the community, while widows are worse off in male crop areas, we cannot reject the hypothesis that widows are no worse off than nonwidows in female crop areas. Women in the lower castes generally have lower BMI and self-assessed health, as would be expected given the socioeconomic differentials by caste. However, interestingly, lower-caste groups feel more respect and social connectedness, which seems inconsistent with the view that lower castes explicitly have lower status under the caste system. However, it is possible that lower castes feel more respect or connection to others in the village of the same caste, since residence is often segregated by caste; unfortunately, the question did not make this distinction or specify the group meant by "the village."

Table 11.6   **Comparative change in status and well-being indicators, widows**

	Δ Treatment husb. family (1)	Δ Diet (2)	Lost land (had before) (3)	Δ Status in village (4)	Less welcome (5)	How long stay inside (6)
Female crop	−.31	−.18	−.21	−.16	−.13	−.94
	(.15)	(.06)	(.08)	(.06)	(.07)	(.39)
Scheduled tribe	−.25	−.06	−.12	−.10	−.039	−3.2
	(.06)	(.05)	(.07)	(.05)	(.05)	(.27)
Scheduled caste	−.19	−.10	−.03	−.08	−.034	−3.1
	(.05)	(.04)	(.06)	(.04)	(.04)	(.21)
Other backward	−.04	−.13	−.09	.005	.018	−1.7
caste	(.05)	(.04)	(.06)	(.04)	(.04)	(.28)
Education	−.01	.002	−.001	−.005	−.002	−.13
	(.006)	(.004)	(.001)	(.004)	(.004)	(.02)

Notes: All results from the SARI data set. Sample restricted to ever-widowed women. The number of observations is 978 for all columns except column (5), where it is 453 because the sample is restricted to those who owned land before widowhood and who have not remarried (since nearly all of those who remarry report losing their original land). In column (1), the dependent variable is whether the respondent feels her husband's family treated her 1) better, 2) about the same, or 3) worse following the death of her husband. In column (2), it is an indicator for whether the wife changed her diet following the death of her husband. In column (4), it is whether other people in the village treated her 1) better, 2) about the same, or 3) worse following the death of her husband. In column (3), the dependent variable is whether the widow lost access to her husband's land after his death. In column (5), it is an indicator for whether she felt less welcome at ceremonies such as weddings or births, and in column (6), the dependent variable is how long (in months) the woman stayed inside her husband's household following his death ceremony.

Table 11.6 further confirms that there are fewer adverse consequences of widowhood in female crop areas relative to male crop areas, using widows' self-reports of changes in indicators of welfare. Widows are less likely to report having experienced a decline in their relationship with their husband's family following the death of their husband, and among those who have not remarried, they are less likely to have lost their land (typically, to the family of the husband) in cases where they had owned land. In terms of social connectedness, they also are less likely to report feeling less welcome at public events or having experienced an overall decline in their status in the village since becoming widowed. Finally, in terms of individual behavior, widows are significantly less likely to have changed their diet in female crop areas (which could also account for some of the smaller decline in BMI in female relative to male crop areas) and spent on average about a month less confined to their deceased husband's home following his death.

The results on caste are also consistent with the view that widows are treated better and have higher status among the lower castes relative to the higher castes. In particular, relative to widows from forward castes, widows from scheduled tribe and scheduled caste groups are significantly less likely to have experienced a decline in the relationship with their husband's family or their status in the village upon widowhood. They are also less likely to have changed their diet and remained in their husband's home for significantly less time.

11.5   Conclusion

There are two primary lessons from this paper. The first is that issues of intrahousehold allocation are essential for assessing individual well-being, especially for the elderly. While this has been widely appreciated in economics for some time, very little is done about it in practice, and most studies focus only on household per capita measures in assessing living standards. This observation also has implications for studies on the relationship between SES and health. Further, the results also show that the relationship between SES and health or nutrition in India is more complex than simply the purchasing power potentially implied by income or expenditure; in particular, other factors, such as the treatment of individuals within the household, mediate this relationship. In particular, we find that widows are much better off in forward-caste households when measured in terms of per capita expenditure, but when BMI is used as a crude proxy for consumption of the elderly, forward-caste persons are no better off than lower-caste households, suggesting the share of household resources is not well proxied by expenditure per person.

The second lesson of this paper is that the status, treatment, and well-being of widows have a foundation in potential economic value, either through bargaining power within households or through a cultural underpinning to the evolution of cultural norms. Of course, this is not to claim that economic factors are the only, or even the largest, determinant of "culture" or to argue that factors such as history and lineage are not important. However, the evidence indicates that economic factors do appear to play at least some role in influencing the well-being and status of widows. The implication is that programs such as microenterprise ventures that expand economic opportunities for women or the elderly, attempts to minimize age or gender discrimination in private-sector employment, or gender- or age-sensitive hiring schemes for public projects, especially in places where the state employs a significant number of people, may improve women's and widows' status.

Appendix

A Brief Note on Caste in India[18]

Throughout India, caste is a social structure that is pervasive, highly visible, and an influence on most aspects of life, including employment and social opportunities, access to resources, customs, diet, occupation, and relations with others. Caste is transmitted through birth, though it is com-

---

18. This section draws broadly from Dumont (1980).

plex, dynamic, and changing: through marriage or changing some activities or practices, some castes move up or down. In general, there is a great deal of caste segregation regarding marriage and residential patterns.

The system referred to as caste today has its roots in the earlier *varna* (color) system. In the early Vedic period, society was said to be organized into four broad social groups, called *varnas*. The *varnas* represented a social hierarchy based on notions of purity and pollution. Some kinds of work are pure and some are impure or polluted, and the *varna* system was organized around the principle of delegating the various activities to particular groups, in particular to allow religious clerics to remain ritualistically pure. At the top of the hierarchy are the *Brahmins* (priests and teachers); then come the *Kshatriyas* (rulers and warriors), the *Vaishras* (traders and farmers), and the *Shudras* (servants or menial workers; more commonly referred to today as other backward castes [OBCs]). There is a fifth group outside this categorization, called by a variety of names such as the Outcastes, *Dalits, Harijans,* Untouchables, or the Scheduled Castes. For India, 15 percent of the population comes from the upper or forward castes, 15 percent are scheduled castes, and 8 percent scheduled tribes, with the remaining bulk of the population the *Shudras* or OBCs. Over time, the *varna* system evolved into or combined with the *jati* system, which is what is generally meant today by caste. *Jatis* are smaller categories that vary widely from place to place in India and can roughly be categorized to correspond to the *varnas* (or the scheduled caste category). The system has evolved over time, and there currently are over 3,000 castes and 20,000 subcastes, with a fairly well-defined social ranking.

References

Agarwala, S. N. 1970. *A demographic study of six urbanising villages.* Bombay: Asia Publishing House.
Bardhan, Pranab. 1974. On life and death questions. *Economic and Political Weekly* 9:1293–1304.
Bhat, M., and R. Kanbargi. 1984. Estimating the incidence of widow and widower re-marriage using census data. *Population Studies* 3 (1): 89–103.
Chen, Martha Alter. 2000. *Perpetual mourning: Widowhood in rural India.* New Delhi: Oxford University Press.
Chen, Martha Alter, and Jean Drèze. 1995. Widowhood and well-being in rural North India. In *Women's health in India: Risk and vulnerability,* ed. Monica Das Gupta, Lincoln Chen, and T. N. Krishnan, 245–88. New Delhi: Oxford University Press.
Deaton, Angus, and Christina Paxson. 1998. Measuring poverty among the elderly. In *Inquiries in the economics of aging,* ed. David Wise, 169–200. Chicago: University of Chicago Press.
Drèze, Jean. 1990. Widows in rural India. Department of Economics Research Program paper no. 26. London: London School of Economics.

Drèze, Jean, and P. V. Srinivasan. 1997. Widowhood and poverty in rural India: Some inferences from household survey data. *Journal of Development Economics* 54:217–34.

Dumont, Louis. 1980. *Homo heirarchicus: The caste system and its implications.* Chicago: University of Chicago Press.

Irudaya Rajan, S., U. S. Mishra, and P. Sankara Sarma. 1999. *India's elderly: Burden or challenge?* New Delhi: Sage Publications.

Miller, Barbara D. 1981. *The endangered sex: Neglect of female children in rural North India.* Ithaca, New York: Cornell University Press.

Rosenzweig, Mark, and T. Paul Schultz. 1982. Market opportunities, genetic endowments and intrafamily resource distribution: Child survival in rural India. *American Economic Review* 72 (4): 803–15.

Sen, Amartya. 1999. *Development as freedom.* New York: Anchor Books.

United Nations. 1961. *The Mysore population study.* New York: United Nations.

Visaria, Pravin M. 1967. *The sex ratio of the population of India.* Census of India 1961, Vol. 1, Monograph #10. New Delhi.

Comment   Esther Duflo

The plight of widows in India is the focus of a growing literature. Widows are eminently vulnerable for several reasons: they are women; they are often relatively old (although women who married older men and did not remarry after their spouse's death can be young widows); and norms and usages restrict their mobility, the exercise of their property rights, and even the food they can eat and the dress they can wear.

This paper uses existing and original data from India to cast new light on two important issues: whether the treatment of widows is affected by their castes, and whether it is affected by their potential "usefulness." The main result of the first part is that, while widows from "forward" castes live in richer households than those in "backward" castes (which reflects the general correlation between caste and economic status), their own health status, reflected in their BMI, is no higher in forward than in backward castes. This is not true for nonwidows, who have a higher BMI in households from richer castes. The author interprets this evidence as suggesting that widows in high-caste households actually get a smaller share of a bigger cake, reflecting the more conservative habits of so-called forward castes. This is not the only possible interpretation, however: the sample does not seem to be restricted to older women, since, at least in the NFHS, most measurements are only obtained for women aged fifteen to forty-nine. If it is not, it might be that the differential caste gradient for widows and non-widows just reflects a differential caste gradient for older women than for younger women, perhaps indicating a differential impact of food intake on

Esther Duflo is professor of Economics at the Massachusetts Institute of Technology and a research associate of the National Bureau of Economic Research.

BMI in older women, or that older women develop different priorities as they grow older, so that when they are better treated, they feed their grandchildren more. For example, Duflo (2003) shows that when the bargaining power of grandmothers increased in South Africa (as they received a substantial old age pension), their granddaughters were better fed. More information would be useful in sorting out some of Jensen's evidence: What is the caste gradient in self-reported health measures (used later in the paper)? What is the income gradient for widows and nonwidows? Does the differential caste gradient persist even after controlling for age? Does the income gradient differ by caste group? Is there a caste gradient in reported norms and usages?

The second part of the paper seeks to explain differences in the treatment of widows across regions. It hypothesizes that widows would be better treated in regions where women are more productive. The main result is that widows are better treated, relative to nonwidows, in places that grow rice (or other crops intensive in "women's labor") than in places that grow wheat (or other crops intensive in "men's labor"). This shows up in two types of variables: direct measure of health (BMI and self-reported health status) and report of constraints (on food, dress, mobility) associated with becoming a widow.

There is a bit of a theoretical lapse between the initial argument and the actual results: the argument involves the comparative advantage of women in general, not of widows in particular. Yet the regressions show that widows are doing better in regions where women have a comparative advantage relative to nonwidows. This is somewhat surprising, in view of the initial argument, since one would think that widows are less productive than other women and thus lose part of their comparative advantage vis-à-vis men. It is also very difficult to ignore the fact that the comparison essentially boils down to a comparison of different types of regions: as the author himself points out, there is a little bit of circularity in defining which crops are naturally more suited to women than to men, and to take the crop mix (or even the geographical suitability) as exogenous in a regression that seeks to explain longstanding customs. It might well be that communities that treat women more equally have evolved technology for production of crops which gives an important role to women. Perhaps if Dravidians had lived in the north instead of the south, wheat growing would actually be female intensive and rice would not. Instrumenting with weather or suitability would address this issue.

In this context, the positive difference-in-difference becomes more troubling than reassuring: since there are no theoretical reasons to expect one (in fact, a technological argument would lead one to expect the opposite), perhaps it comes precisely from these omitted variables. This is made even more troubling by the fact that, in general, women actually do not seem to be better off in rice-producing regions.

That being said, the main insight of the paper, that the treatment of widows, even if ostensibly governed by timeless norms, may actually respond in part to economic motives, is very important. The evidence provided here, while far from definitive, is certainly tantalizing. Chen and Drèze (1995) provide related evidence when they report that the presence of a widow's pension protects the widow from poor treatment. Abhijit Banerjee, Angus Deaton, and I hope to test this idea directly: widows in India are eligible for a pension, subject to certain conditions. The Panchayat is in charge of identifying potential beneficiaries. However, very few potentially eligible people actually receive the pension. This is probably due in part to the difficulties of navigating the system, establishing one's rights, and following through until the pension is actually delivered. We are planning to evaluate the work of Seva Mandir, a local nongovernmental organization, in one rural district in Rajasthan that will provide assistance to eligible widows to receive their pension. By comparing the treatment of widows who have received this assistance to those who have not, we might be able to provide a further test of the very interesting hypothesis brought forward in this paper.

References

Chen, Martha, and Jean Drèze. 1995. Widowhood and well-being in rural North India. In *Women's health in India: Risk and vulnerability,* ed. Monica Das Gupta, Lincoln Chen, and T. N. Krishnan, 245–88. New Delhi: Oxford University Press.
Duflo, Esther. 2003. Grandmothers and granddaughters: Old age pension and intra-household allocation in South Africa. *World Bank Economic Review* 17 (1): 1–25.

Individual Subjective Survival Curves

Li Gan, Michael D. Hurd, and Daniel McFadden

12.1 Introduction

Many economic models are based on the forward-looking behavior of economic agents. Although it is often said that "expectations" about future events are important in these models, it is the probability distributions of future events that influence the models. For example, an individual's consumption and saving decisions are believed to depend upon concerns regarding future interest rates, the likelihood of dying, and the risk of substantial future medical expenditures. According to our theories, decision makers have subjective probability distributions about these and other events in their lives and, moreover, use them to make decisions about their saving practices.

A typical objective of empirical models on intertemporal decision making is to estimate responses to changes in variable levels, such as changes in saving due to an anticipated change in the interest rate. A second objective is to find the extent of an individual's risk aversion; namely, what is his or her response to changes in outcome variability? For instance, do changes in the variability of future income lead to changes in saving practices?

Li Gan is an assistant professor of economics at the University of Texas, Austin, and a faculty research fellow of the National Bureau of Economic Research. Michael D. Hurd is a senior economist at RAND, director of the RAND Center for the Study of Aging, and a research associate of the National Bureau of Economic Research. Daniel McFadden is the E. Morris Cox Professor of Economics at the University of California, Berkeley, 2000 Nobel Laureate in Economics, and a research associate of the National Bureau of Economic Research (NBER).

We gratefully acknowledge the research assistance from Malathi Velamuri, Victoria Vernon, and especially Guan Gong. Research support for this paper was provided to NBER by a grant from the National Institute of Aging. The views expressed in this paper are those of the authors and not necessarily those of NBER.

These are worthwhile objectives due to the importance of choices that depend on uncertain future events in our society. For example, poverty in old age depends partly on an individual's consumption choices at a younger age. Consequently, how is consumption influenced by mortality risk and the uncertainty of medical expenditures? Why do some individuals purchase adequate insurance against unfavorable outcomes while others do not? Why do many reach retirement age with inadequate financial provisions for postretirement living expenses? Is it due to misperceptions about the probabilities of reaching old age? Do people maintain excessive housing into old age as a hedge against inflation risk? The answers to these and similar questions depend on our understandings of decision maker reactions to future uncertainty. Moreover, creating policies that alleviate the consequences of such decision-making processes depends on answers to the aforementioned questions.

In a few economic models, we have data on probability distributions that are assumed to approximate those required by decision-making models under uncertainty. Life-cycle models of consumption, in which mortality risk helps determine savings, have been estimated by assuming that individuals have subjective probability distributions on mortality risk that are the same as those found from life tables (Hurd 1989). A precautionary motive for saving thus depends on the risk of future medical outlays. It therefore seems reasonable that the distribution of outlays as estimated from microdata represents a good approximation of the subjective probability distributions used by decision makers (Hubbard, Skinner, and Zeldes 1995). More generally, Manski (1993) has proposed using observed outcome probabilities in panel data as estimations of the subjective probability distributions for individuals on the panel, on the grounds that the sampling exercise can itself be taken as a model of the subjective probability process.

In most applications, however, we do not have adequate data for probability distributions—thus requiring the use of unverifiable assumptions in estimations. For example, in macroeconomic models expectations are assumed to be rational. Yet the rationality assumption cannot be tested outside of the model's immediate context. In life-cycle models on saving, a cohort's average mortality risk may not be well approximated by the mortality risk found on life tables since the cohort may not believe that the mortality experience of older cohorts will be the same as his or her own. Furthermore, individuals within the same cohort will have different subjective evaluations of probability distribution and its influence on their behavior, even if it is systematically incorrect. However, such evaluations are not generally observable. These individual heterogeneities often become problematic in parameter estimates. For example, consider a typical individual utility function,

$$u(c_t) = \frac{c_t^{1-\gamma}}{1-\gamma},$$

where c_t is the consumption at time t, and γ is the risk aversion parameter. The first-order condition in a common formulation is

$$\frac{1}{c_t} \cdot \frac{dc_t}{dt} = \frac{-h_t + r - \rho}{\gamma} + \beta' X_t,$$

where h_t is the individual subjective hazard rates, while X_t represents certain sociodemographic variables. In this framework, if h_t is not observed but correlated with X_t, we will have a typical endogeneity problem. If h_t is poorly measured, estimations of γ will subsequently be biased.

Previous studies have typically obtained individual mortality risks through two different approaches: either by using life tables or by using well-known variations in mortality rates by economic status. Since mortality risk life tables only vary by age, race, and sex, there are not enough variations from which to calculate mortality risks. If subjective mortality risks of individuals with different economic status vary in the same way as observed mortality rates, model estimations using standard life tables will lead to biased estimates. Moreover, forecasts of economic status distributions will be incorrect such that poorer individuals who believe that their mortality risk is higher will spend money faster than what is predicted by the model. Although mortality risk variations can, in principle, be calculated from some given variables, individuals surely have subjective probability distributions that are only partly related to observable variables.

Two recent surveys have posed questions regarding individual subjective probabilities, including Asset and Health Dynamics among the Oldest Old (AHEAD) and the Health and Retirement Survey (HRS). Hurd and McGarry (1995) reveal that average survival probabilities are very close to those presented in life tables. In a more recent paper, Hurd and McGarry (2002) use panel data from HRS and find that respondents modify their probabilities in response to new information, such as the onset of a new illness. Their findings are consistent with an earlier study of Hamermesh (1985), who surveys a selected sample of economists about their survival probabilities. On average, self-reported survival probabilities are consistent with life tables; at the personal level, however, these probabilities face a serious problem. In all age groups, we find that a large fraction of respondents give what we call focal-point responses: 0.0 and 1.0. These responses cannot represent the respondents' true probabilities, as the distribution of true probabilities should be continuous, and moreover, true probabilities cannot literally equal 0 or 1. Thus, the main focus of this paper is to recover the true subjective survival curve for each respondent. To do so, we develop a Bayesian update model to accomplish this objective.

In our model, for individuals at age a, we let the prior survival probability distribution at a future point in time $(a + t)$ be a truncated normal between 0 and 1 (we do not include 0 and 1). The conditional density of the observed survival probability is assumed to be a censored normal between 0 and 1, allowing for the focal points. In addition, we suggest two approaches that model the deviations of each individual's belief from the life table.

We use the posterior density mean as an individual's estimated subjective survival probabilities, and estimate the model using the observed death record. Our model produces optimistic indices to measure the deviation of his or her subjective belief from the life table. Consequently, the survival curves for each individual produced by the optimistic indexes do not encounter problems associated with focal points and have considerable variations. These subjective survival curves are readily applicable to life-cycle models and other economic models that require individual subjective mortality risk.

The remainder of the paper is organized as follows: section 12.2 introduces the self-reported subjective survival probabilities including their consistency with the life table and problems associated with individual responses. Next, section 12.3 introduces a Bayesian method that helps us to recover underlying subjective survival curves. Section 12.3 also introduces two approaches that are used to represent individual deviations from life tables. In section 12.4, we estimate the model and conduct the out-of-sample prediction. Lastly, we present the paper's conclusions in section 12.5.

12.2   Individual Subjective Mortality Risk

In the AHEAD sample, each respondent is asked a series of questions about how likely it is that various presented future events will occur. These future events include an income that is consistent with changes in inflation, major medical expenses, leaving a bequest, receiving financial help from family members, moving to a nursing home, and surviving for another ten to fourteen years.[1] In particular, the survival probability question AHEAD posed to respondents is as follows:

> [Using any] number from 0 to 100 where "0" means that you think there is absolutely no chance and "100" means that you think the event is absolutely sure to happen . . . What do you think are chances that: You will live to at least A? (A is an age that is 11–15 years older than the respondent's current age.)

To examine whether these survival probabilities carry useful informa-

---

1. Bassett and Lumsdaine (2001) find that all responses contain a common component.

Table 12.1   **Self-reported and life table survival probabilities**

	Target age									
	Male					Female				
	80	85	90	95	100	80	85	90	95	100
					Wave 1					
Means										
AHEAD	0.557	0.510	0.382	0.332	0.302	0.570	0.510	0.386	0.307	0.289
Life table	0.593	0.422	0.252	0.114	0.037	0.716	0.605	0.432	0.232	0.081
Median										
AHEAD	0.500	0.500	0.400	0.250	0.100	0.500	0.500	0.450	0.100	0.100
Life table	0.593	0.422	0.252	0.115	0.037	0.723	0.603	0.433	0.232	0.076
N	90	951	631	436	175	575	1,334	978	664	309
					Wave 2					
Means										
AHEAD	0.524	0.279	0.622	0.278	0.574	0.516	0.283	0.692	0.296	0.559
Life table	0.614	0.457	0.284	0.138	0.078	0.736	0.633	0.464	0.260	0.138
Median										
AHEAD	0.500	0.200	0.600	0.200	0.600	0.500	0.200	0.600	0.200	0.600
Life table	0.629	0.456	0.285	0.140	0.051	0.746	0.632	0.465	0.261	0.100
N	95	1,044	675	451	223	620	1,436	1,090	807	498

Note: N = number of observations.

tion, we compare the subjective survival probabilities with the life tables. Table 12.1 lists the average and median survival probabilities from AHEAD and the 1992 life tables for the target ages used in the AHEAD survival questions, as calculated by the first two waves of AHEAD (e.g., eighty-five years of age for subjects aged seventy to seventy-four, ninety years of age for subjects aged seventy-five to seventy-nine, etc.). In general, younger AHEAD respondents have average subjective probabilities that closely mirror life table averages, while older respondents have averages that are substantially higher.[2] In general, AHEAD medians are closely related to those in the life table.

Table 12.2 lists the percentage of those respondents who gave continuous responses, focal responses, and no responses in the two waves. Table 12.2 also lists the transition probabilities of different response modes between the two waves. In wave 1, only 50 percent of respondents gave continuous responses, with about 25 percent of them providing either 0 or 1 as their answers. The subjective probabilities for the remainder of the population are not available. In wave 2, about 53 percent of respondents who

2. Several reasons are suggested in Hurd, McFadden and Gan (1998) for this finding. One reason is that the AHEAD survey does not include respondents who reside in nursing homes or other institutional care facilities. Thus, AHEAD represents a healthier population than is represented by a life table.

Table 12.2   **Focal responses**

	Wave 2					
	Continuous	0	1	Dead	n.a.	Total
Wave 1						
Continuous	2,728	223	327	227	592	4,097
	(66.6)	(5.4)	(8.0)	(5.5)	(15.5)	(49.9)
0	508	329	44	178	265	1,324
	(38.4)	(24.9)	(3.3)	(13.4)	(20.0)	(16.1)
1	306	18	244	35	119	722
	(42.4)	(2.5)	(33.8)	(4.9)	(16.4)	(8.8)
n.a.	403	106	78	372	1,116	2,075
	(19.4)	(5.1)	(3.8)	(17.9)	(53.8)	(25.3)
Total	3,945	676	693	812	2,092	8,218
	(48.0)	(8.2)	(8.4)	(9.9)	(25.5)	

Note: Numbers in parentheses are percentages. n.a. = not available.

were alive gave continuous responses, whereas approximately 19 percent of the population responded either 0 or 1. A continuous respondent in wave 1 is much more likely to give continuous response again in wave 2. If a respondent gave focal response of 1 in wave 1, he or she is much more likely to give a focal response of 1 than 0 in wave 2. A person who is a nonrespondent in wave 1 is more likely to be a nonrespondent again in wave 2. Finally, a person who gave a focal response of 0 in wave 1 is much more likely to die than other persons, indicating that responses themselves do carry information about the actual survival probabilities, as suggested in Hurd and McGarry (1995, 2002). Thus the prevalence of focal-point responses indicates that subjective probability measurements in AHEAD cannot represent the respondents' true probabilities. Without correcting for focal responses of 0 or 1, it is impossible to derive a survival curve that varies over time. In the next section, we develop a Bayesian update model to correct focal responses.

12.3   Modeling Individual Subjective Survival Curves

Before we present the model, it is necessary to define the notations that we use throughout this paper.

- a: age
- t: time at risk
- $L_0(t)$: life table survival probability from birth
- $S_{0a}(t) = L_0(a + t)/L_0(a)$: life table survival probability from age a
- $\Lambda_0(t)$: life table integrated mortality hazard rate
- $\lambda_0(t)$: life table mortality hazard rate

- T: an age at which $L_0(T) = 0$, say $T = 108$
- i: individual
- $S_{ia}(t)$: personal survival probability from age a to target age $a + t$ for subject i. Since survival probabilities differ for different people at the same age a, we let $S_{ia}(t)$ be a random variable with a density $\pi(s_{ia}[t])$, or $\pi(s_{iat})$
- $\Lambda_{ia}(t)$: personal integrated mortality hazard rate at age a
- $\lambda_{ia}(t)$: personal mortality hazard rate at age a
- τ: time at risk in interview survival question
- p_{iat}: response to interview survival question. We assume that p_{iat} is measured with an error. The density of p_{iat}, conditional on personal survival probability from age a to age $a + t$, is given by $f(p_{iat} \mid S_{ia\tau} = s_{ia\tau})$

By definition, an individual i's survival curve is

$$(1) \qquad s_{ia}(t) = \exp[-\Lambda_{ia}(a + t) + \Lambda_{ia}(a)] = \exp\left[-\int_0^t \lambda_{ia}(a + r)dr\right].$$

It is first necessary to specify the plausible families of $\lambda_{ia}(a + t)$ that satisfy this equation. We propose to use the population hazard function $\lambda_{0a}(a + t)$ as a base, while minimally modifying it to calculate individual $\lambda_{ia}(a + t)$. Two alternative ways to specify the $\lambda_{ia}(a + t)$ function include

$$(2) \qquad \lambda_{ia}(a + t) = \gamma_i \lambda_{0a}(a + t).$$

The parameter γ_i is an individual "optimism" parameter. In comparison with the life table, if $\gamma_i > 1$, then the person is "pessimistic"; if $\gamma_i < 1$, then the person is "optimistic." Since this model in equation (2) scales the population hazard, we will refer to it as a "hazard-scaling" model from now on.

The second model specification is given as

$$(3) \qquad \lambda_{ia}(a + t) = \lambda_{0a}\left(a + \frac{t}{\gamma_{ia}}\right)\frac{1}{\gamma_{ia}}.$$

This model represents an accelerated failure time frame where the individual thinks of himself or herself as aging forward from his or her current age more or less rapidly than the average person. If a large γ_i corresponds to slow future aging, that is, $\gamma_i > 1$, then the person is "optimistic"; if $\gamma_{ia} < 1$, then the person is "pessimistic." Similarly, we refer to the model in equation (3) as the "age-scaling" model, as it scales ages to represent individual optimism.

If $p_{ia\tau}$ has no response error or focal bias, the models in equations (2) and (3) are accurately identified with no free parameters. We can then take these models as actual survival information and subsequently decide which model works best. Since a response error or focal bias in $p_{ia\tau}$ is present, the personal survival curve is not forced through $p_{ia\tau}$ at age $a + \tau$. To solve this problem, we use a model of Bayesian update.

The prior belief for the personal survival curve density S_{iat} in the Bayesian model is $\pi(s_{iat})$. The mean for prior density is $\exp(-\psi\Delta\Lambda_{0at})$, where ψ represents a parameter for measuring the population's average subjective optimistic degree. When $\psi = 1$, the mean of prior distribution S_{iat} corresponds with the life table value. Given $S_{iat} = s_{iat}$, the self-reported survival probability p_{iat} has a conditional density of $f(p_{iat} | s_{iat})$. The difference between the self-reported survival probability p_{iat} and the subjective survival probability S_{iat} is the measurement error.

The primary objective of this paper is to use the observed $p_{ia\tau}$ to update the prior density $\pi(s_{ia\tau})$ and to obtain the posterior density $\pi(s_{ia\tau} | p_{ia\tau})$. After we observe $p_{ia\tau}$, the posterior density of s_{iat} is given by

$$\pi(s_{ia\tau} | p_{ia\tau}) = \frac{f(p_{ia\tau} | s_{ia\tau})\pi(s_{ia\tau})}{f(p_{ia\tau} | s_{ia\tau})\pi(s_{ia\tau})ds_{ia\tau}}.$$

If the loss function is given by $L(S_{it}, \hat{S}_{it}) = E(S_{it} - \hat{S}_{it})^2$, the best estimator for $S_{i\tau}$ is $\hat{S}_{i\tau} = E(S_{i\tau} | p_{ia\tau})$. We apply $\hat{S}_{i\tau}$ to the observed death record to obtain the model's parameter values. The log-likelihood function is given by

$$(4) \qquad \ln L = \sum_{\text{alive}} \ln \hat{S}_{it} + \sum_{\text{dead}} \ln(1 - \hat{S}_{it}).$$

Maximizing the likelihood function in equation (4) requires specifying the distribution functions. For the population of agents who share the same age a, their surviving probabilities to age $a + t$ are different. The random variable S_{iat} is used to represent such differences. Let the prior distribution for the random variable S_{iat}, $\pi(s_{ia\tau})$ be the truncated normal distribution with the truncation range being $0 < s_{ia} < 1$. We also let the mean of S_{iat} be $\exp(-\psi\Delta\Lambda_{0at})$, variance σ_2^2. The prior distribution is given by

$$(5) \qquad \pi(s_{ia}; \psi) = \frac{\dfrac{1}{\sigma_2}\phi\left(\dfrac{s_{ia} - \nu_{ia}}{\sigma_2}\right)}{\Phi\left(\dfrac{1 - \nu_{ia}}{\sigma_2}\right) - \Phi\left(-\dfrac{\nu_{ia}}{\sigma_2}\right)},$$

where ν_{ia} and σ_2 satisfy the equation

$$\exp(-\psi\Delta\Lambda_{0at}) = \nu_{iat} - \sigma_2\eta(0,1,\nu_{iat},\sigma_2).$$

The right-hand side of equation (6) represents the mean of the truncated normal in equation (5). The functional form of $\eta(0,1,\nu_{iat},\sigma_2)$ in equation (6) is provided in equation (A2) in the appendix. We let the conditional density of the responses to interview survival questions follow a censored normal distribution (including 0 and 1).

$$f(p_{ia\tau} \mid s_{ia\tau}) = \phi\left(\frac{p_{ia\tau} - \mu_{ia\tau}}{\sigma_1}\right) \text{ when } 0 < p_{ia\tau} < 1;$$

$$\Pr(p_{ia\tau} = 0 \mid s_{ia\tau}) = 1 - \Phi\left(\frac{\mu_{ia\tau}}{\sigma_1}\right) \text{ and } \Pr(p_{ia\tau} = 1 \mid s_{ia\tau}) = 1 - \Phi\left(\frac{1 - \mu_{ia\tau}}{\sigma_1}\right).$$

Furthermore, we assume that the expectation of the conditional distribution is s_{ia}. Thus, μ_{ia} and σ_1 satisfy the following equation:

$$s_{ia} = \left[\Phi\left(\frac{1 - \mu_{ia}}{\sigma_1}\right) + \Phi\left(\frac{\mu_{ia}}{\sigma_1}\right) - 1\right][\mu_{ia} - \sigma\eta(e, f, \mu_{ia}, \sigma_1)]$$

$$+ \left[1 - \Phi\left(\frac{1 - \mu_{ia}}{\sigma_1}\right)\right]$$

The formula for the mean of the censored normal is given in equation (A3) in the appendix. The censored normal captures the idea that many observations may be at 0 or 1. Given $p_{ia\tau}$, the posterior distribution is given by

(7) $$\pi(s_{ia} \mid p_{ia\tau}) = \frac{\phi\left[\dfrac{p_{ia\tau} - \mu_{ia}(s_{ia}, \sigma_1)}{\sigma_1}\right]\phi\left[\dfrac{s_{ia} - v_{ia}(\psi, \sigma_2)}{\sigma_2}\right]}{\displaystyle\int \phi\left[\dfrac{p_{ia\tau} - \mu_{ia}(s_{ia}, \sigma_1)}{\sigma_1}\right]\phi\left[\dfrac{s_{ia} - v_{ia}(\psi, \sigma_2)}{\sigma_2}\right]ds_{ia}}.$$

The distribution in equation (7) is no longer a normal or a censored normal. The best estimator for s_{ia} under a mean square loss function is its mean:

(8) $$\hat{S}_{ia} = \int_0^1 s_{ia}\pi(s_{ia} \mid p_{ia\tau})ds_{ia}$$

$$= \frac{\displaystyle\int_0^1 s_{ia}\phi\left[\dfrac{p_{ia\tau} - \mu_{ia}(s_{ia}, \sigma_1)}{\sigma_1}\right]\phi\left[\dfrac{s_{ia} - v_{ia}(\psi, \sigma_2)}{\sigma_2}\right]ds_{ia}}{\displaystyle\int \phi\left[\dfrac{p_{ia\tau} - \mu_{ia}(s_{ia}, \sigma_1)}{\sigma_1}\right]\phi\left[\dfrac{s_{ia} - v_{ia}(\psi, \sigma_2)}{\sigma_2}\right]ds_{ia}}.$$

When $p_{ia\tau} = 0$, we have

$$\Pr(s_{ia} < s \mid p_{ia\tau} = 0) = \frac{\int_0^s \Pr(p_{ia\tau} = 0 \mid s_{ia})\pi(s_{ia}; \psi)ds_{ia}}{\int_0^1 \Pr(p_{ia\tau} = 0 \mid s_{ia})\pi(s_{ia}; \psi)ds_{ia}}$$

$$= \frac{\displaystyle\int_0^s \left\{1 - \Phi\left[\dfrac{\mu_{ia}(s_{ia}, \sigma_1)}{\sigma_1}\right]\right\}\phi\left[\dfrac{s_{ia} - v_{ia}(\psi, \sigma_2)}{\sigma_2}\right]ds_{ia}}{\displaystyle\int_0^1 \left\{1 - \Phi\left[\dfrac{\mu_{ia}(s_{ia}, \sigma_1)}{\sigma_1}\right]\right\}\phi\left[\dfrac{s_{ia} - v_{ia}(\psi, \sigma_2)}{\sigma_2}\right]ds_{ia}}.$$

Thus, the posterior distribution S_{ia} given $p_{ia\tau} = 0$ is

$$\pi(s_{ia} \mid p_{ia\tau} = 0) = \frac{\left\{1 - \Phi\left[\dfrac{\mu_{ia}(s_{ia}, \sigma_1)}{\sigma_1}\right]\right\}\phi\left[\dfrac{s_{ia} - \nu_{ia}(\psi, \sigma_2)}{\sigma_2}\right]}{\displaystyle\int_0^1 \left\{1 - \Phi\left[\dfrac{\mu_{ia}(s_{ia}, \sigma_1)}{\sigma_1}\right]\right\}\phi\left[\dfrac{s_{ia} - \nu_{ia}(\psi, \sigma_2)}{\sigma_2}\right]ds_{ia}}.$$

Then, the best predictor for S_{ia} when $p_{ia\tau} = 0$ is

$$(9) \qquad \hat{S}_{ia} = \frac{\displaystyle\int_0^1 s_{ia}\left\{1 - \Phi\left[\dfrac{\mu_{ia}(s_{ia}, \sigma_1)}{\sigma_1}\right]\right\}\phi\left[\dfrac{s_{ia} - \nu_{ia}(\psi, \sigma_2)}{\sigma_2}\right]ds_{ia}}{\displaystyle\int_0^1 \left\{1 - \Phi\left[\dfrac{\mu_{ia}(s_{ia}, \sigma_1)}{\sigma_1}\right]\right\}\phi\left[\dfrac{s_{ia} - \nu_{ia}(\psi, \sigma_2)}{\sigma_2}\right]ds_{ia}}.$$

Similarly, when $p_{ia\tau} = 1$,

$$\pi(s_{ia} \mid p_{ia\tau} = 1) = \frac{\left\{1 - \Phi\left[\dfrac{1 - \mu_{ia}(s_{ia}, \sigma_1)}{\sigma_1}\right]\right\}\phi\left[\dfrac{s_{ia} - \nu_{ia}(\psi, \sigma_2)}{\sigma_2}\right]}{\displaystyle\int_0^1 \left\{1 - \Phi\left[\dfrac{1 - \mu_{ia}(s_{ia}, \sigma_1)}{\sigma_1}\right]\right\}\phi\left[\dfrac{s_{ia} - \nu_{ia}(\psi, \sigma_2)}{\sigma_2}\right]ds_{ia}},$$

with the best predictor being given by

$$(10) \qquad \hat{S}_{ia} = \frac{\displaystyle\int_0^1 s_{ia}\left\{1 - \Phi\left[\dfrac{1 - \mu_{ia}(s_{ia}, \sigma_1)}{\sigma_1}\right]\right\}\phi\left[\dfrac{s_{ia} - \nu_{ia}(\psi, \sigma_2)}{\sigma_2}\right]ds_{ia}}{\displaystyle\int_0^1 \left\{1 - \Phi\left[\dfrac{1 - \mu_{ia}(s_{ia}, \sigma_1)}{\sigma_1}\right]\right\}\phi\left[\dfrac{s_{ia} - \nu_{ia}(\psi, \sigma_2)}{\sigma_2}\right]ds_{ia}}.$$

In equations (8), (9), and (10), we obtain the predicted $\hat{S}_{ia}$ given the observed subjective survival probability of $p_{ia\tau}$. In the next section, we discuss how to estimate our model. We also present the estimation results and out-of-sample predictions.

12.4 Estimation and Out-of-Sample Prediction

Since respondents are interviewed every two years, we update information regarding whether they are still alive, accordingly. The likelihood function in equation (4) should be changed to: $\ln L = \Sigma_{\text{alive}} \ln \hat{S}_{ia2} + \Sigma_{\text{dead}} \ln(1 - \hat{S}_{ia2})$. However, the self-reported survival probability is not the survival probability during a two-year period. Rather, it typically represents a survival probability ten to fifteen years in the future.

To derive a survival probability in two years, it is necessary to get individual optimistic indexes γ_i. First, we consider the hazard-scaling model in equation (2). Plug equation (2) into equation (1), and we get

(11) $$s_{ia}(t) = \exp[-\gamma_i \Lambda_{0a}(t)].$$

In equation (11), by letting $t = \tau$, we can solve for the individual optimistic index γ_i:

(12) $$\hat{\gamma}_i = -\frac{\ln(\hat{S}_{ia\tau})}{\Delta \Lambda_{0a\tau}}.$$

If we plug equation (12) into equation (11), but let $t = 2$, we can get the survival probability in a two-year period:

(13) $$\hat{S}_{ia2} = \hat{S}_{ia\tau}^{\Delta \Lambda_{0a2}/\Delta \Lambda_{0a\tau}},$$

Therefore, the log-likelihood function in equation (4) should be rewritten to accommodate the observed data. The new log-likelihood function is given by

(14) $$\ln L = \sum_{\text{alive}} \ln \hat{S}_{ia\tau}^{\Delta \Lambda_{0a2}/\Delta \Lambda_{0a\tau}} + \sum_{\text{dead}} \ln(1 - \hat{S}_{ia\tau}^{\Delta \Lambda_{0a2}/\Delta \Lambda_{0a\tau}}).$$

Second, we consider the age-scaling model in equation (3). Although we cannot arrive at the explicit expression of γ_i, we can numerically solve the following equation to obtain the value of γ_i for each individual:

(15) $$\hat{S}_{ia\tau} = \exp\left[-\Lambda_0\left(a + \frac{\tau}{\gamma_i}\right) + \Lambda_0(a)\right].$$

Similarly to the hazard-scaling model, the numerically obtained $\hat{\gamma}_i$ is then used to calculate the survival probability in a two-year period:

(16) $$\hat{S}_{ia2} = \exp\left[\Lambda_0\left(a + \frac{\tau}{\hat{\gamma}_i}\right) - \Lambda_0\left(a + \frac{2}{\hat{\gamma}_i}\right)\right]\hat{S}_{ia\tau}.$$

Plugging equation (16) into equation (14), we have a likelihood function. Maximizing the likelihood function yields the parameter estimates of the model.

In sum, we let the prior survival probability distribution from age a to age $a + t$ be a truncated normal (between 0.0 and 1.0). The conditional density of observed survival probabilities is assumed to be a censored normal, allowing for the focal points 0.0 and 1.0. The posterior density of the survival probabilities has, therefore, a distribution that does not allow for the focal points 0.0 and 1.0. In order to obtain the model's parameter values, we apply the posterior distribution mean to actual death records between wave 1 and wave 2 in order to estimate a person's survival probability.

Both the hazard-scaling model in equation (2) and the age-scaling model in equation (3) are estimated. In each model, we first let $\psi = 1$, constrain-

Table 12.3   **Estimation results**

	Hazard-scaling		Age-scaling	
	$\psi = 1$	ψ is a parameter	$\psi = 1$	ψ is a parameter
Standard deviation of conditional density: σ_1 (censored normal)	.3255 (.1197)	.1837 (.0154)	.5434 (.0012)	.2793 (.0312)
Standard deviation of prior density: σ_2 (truncated normal)	.2045 (.0045)	.1165 (.0176)	.3159 (.0000011)	0.1083 (.0304)
Average optimistic parameter: ψ		.7226 (.0507)		0.6590 (.0011)
Maximum likelihood value[a]	−1,495	−1,483	−1,500	−1,491
Log likelihood for out-of-sample prediction[b]	−1,692.9	−1,532.4	−1,644.1	−1,533.4

Note: Standard errors are in parentheses.

[a]The likelihood value calculated from life table survival rates is −1,533.4.

[b]The likelihood value for out-of-sample prediction using life table survival rates is −2,559.0.

ing the mean of the prior density to be the same as that of the life table. Whenever we do this, we refer to the model as the constrained model. In addition, we let ψ be an estimated parameter. In this case, we let the data determine if the prior density mean is the same as the life tables. We refer to such a model as an unconstrained model. Table 12.3 lists the results of four different specifications: constrained hazard-scaling model, unconstrained hazard-scaling model, constrained age-scaling model, and, finally, unconstrained age-scaling model. All four specifications yield reasonable estimates that are highly significant. Moreover, likelihood ratio tests favor unconstrained models over constrained models.

Since we use a survey that currently has three waves of data available, we can apply the estimated parameters to actual survival experiences in wave 3 observations and compare the log-likelihood of each model for model selection. We select the sample that comprises individuals who are still alive in wave 2, then calculate the log-likelihood values separated by those who are alive in wave 3 and those who are dead between waves 2 and 3. The log-likelihood from the out-of-sample prediction is given by

$$\ln L = \sum_{\text{alive in wave 3}} \ln \hat{S}_{ia4} + \sum_{\text{dead b/w waves 2\&3}} \ln(1 - \hat{S}_{ia4}).$$

The log-likelihood values from the out-of-sample predictions are reported in table 12.3. The two unconstrained models perform much better than the corresponding two constrained models. Between the two unconstrained models, the hazard-scaling model yields slightly better likelihood values than the age-scaling model. Finally, we calculate the maximum likelihood value if the life-table survival rates are used. The value is −1,533.4, much smaller than any of the four specifications. Further, using the life table survival rates to predict the observed survival experience yields the maximum likelihood of $-2,599.0$. Again, this value is much smaller than the likelihood values from out-of-sample predictions from any of the four specifications in this paper. Clearly, the subjective survival probabilities can predict the observed survival record much better than the life tables.

For each specification, we calculate the optimistic indexes γ_i for each individual. The formula to calculate γ_i in the hazard-scaling model is given by equation (12), while the implicit formula to calculate γ_i in the age-scaling model is provided in equation (15). Table 12.4 presents the summary statistics of the indexes and the correlation coefficients from the four different models' indexes.

From table 12.4, we find that the correlation coefficients among different indexes are very high. The lowest correlation coefficient between the unconstrained hazard-scaling model and the age-scaling model is $-.8975$. The negative signs for the correlation coefficients between the two models are expected; that is, in the hazard-scaling model, the larger the index, the less optimistic a person is. The inverse result can be found for the age-scaling model: namely, the larger the index, the more optimistic a person is. The highest correlation coefficient between the unconstrained and the constrained hazard-scaling models is $.9887$, which is very close to 1.

Although the correlations among the four different specifications are very high, the means of estimated γ_i from the four different models differ significantly. These means are also reported in table 12.4. The estimated $\hat{\gamma}_i$ for unconstrained specifications portrays a more optimistic picture than those for constrained specifications. In the hazard-scaling model, the average $\hat{\gamma}_i$ in the constrained specification is 1.020, indicating that an individual's subjective survival probability on average is very close to the life table.

Table 12.4   **Correlation coefficients among four optimistic indexes**

	Hazard-scaling		Age-scaling	
	Constrained	Unconstrained	Constrained	Unconstrained
Hazard-scaling (constrained)	1	.9887	−.9000	−.9019
		(.00024)	(.0014)	(.0018)
Hazard-scaling (unconstrained)		1	−.8975	−.9284
			(.0017)	(.0016)
Age-scaling (constrained)			1	.9479
				(.0015)
Age-scaling (unconstrained)				1
Means	1.040	.822	1.051	1.271
	(.375)	(.296)	(.227)	(.186)

Notes: "Constrained" indicates $\psi = 1$; "unconstrained" indicates ψ is a parameter to be estimated. Standard errors are in parentheses, calculated from bootstrapping 1,000 times of the sample.

In the unconstrained version of the hazard model, the average $\hat{\gamma}_i$ is .822, indicating that people are generally optimistic about their survival probabilities. Similar patterns occur in the two specifications of the age-scaling model.

In the constrained specification, the means of the prior densities (truncated normal) are constrained according to life-table survival probabilities. The Bayesian update model only changes its σ_2, that is, the standard deviation of the original normal density that generates the truncated normal density (see equations [5] and [6]). Although updating σ_2 may have some effects on the means of the prior densities, the effects are relatively small. Therefore, it is not surprising to see that the constrained versions of both models are very similar to life tables. In the unconstrained specification, in addition to obtaining the value of σ_2, the updated Bayesian model also changes the mean of the prior density through ψ.

Although different specifications yield different levels of optimistic indexes, an important feature of all these indexes is that a significant heterogeneity exists among all individuals. The individual heterogeneity in γ_i can be summarized by a simple regression that uses the optimism indexes to regress certain demographic variables. In this regression, four different optimism indexes represent dependent variables, while independent variables include a constant, the person's age, a male dummy, an African American dummy, a Hispanic dummy, a marriage status dummy, a high school graduate dummy, a some-college dummy, a college (including postcollege) dummy, mother's age at the time of death, father's age at the time of death, and lastly, the wealth level at wave 1 in $1,000. The last column in table 12.5 lists the summary statistics of the variables we used in the regression. The first four columns in table 12.5 report the estimation results.

From the estimates reported in table 12.5, the coefficients for African American dummies are negative for the hazard-scaling model specifications and positive for the age-scaling model specifications. All coefficients indicate that African Americans are more optimistic than white respondents. No difference exists between Hispanic and White respondents in terms of their optimism indexes. Neither does a person's marriage status make any difference in his or her optimism indexes. Another pattern that can be found in all four specifications is that male respondents are more optimistic than female respondents. In addition, older respondents are generally more optimistic than younger respondents in three specifications. The only exception is the unconstrained age-scaling model, where the age coefficient is insignificant. Parents' ages of death also affect people's subjective optimistic indexes: people whose parents died at older ages are more optimistic than people whose parents died at younger ages. Finally, as expected, richer people are more optimistic than poorer people.

Tables 12.6 through 12.9 provide the predicted survival probabilities of four different specifications, the stated survival probabilities, and the life

Table 12.5   **Summary regressions of four optimistic indices**

	Hazard-scaling		Age-scaling		Summary statistics
	Constrained	Unconstrained	Constrained	Unconstrained	
Constant	2.193	1.738	.638	.809	
	(.071)	(.056)	(.044)	(.035)	
Age	−.0116	−.0093	.0037	.0045	75.46
	(.00081)	(.00064)	(.0005)	(.0004)	(6.09)
Male	−.173	−.130	.100	.088	.371
	(.010)	(.0079)	(.0062)	(.0051)	(.483)
Black	−.085	−.068	.066	.052	.107
	(.015)	(.012)	(.0094)	(.0076)	(.309)
Hispanic	.039	.024	.0078	.0038	.045
	(.022)	(.018)	(.014)	(.011)	(.207)
Married	.0153	.014	−.012	−.00074	.579
	(.010)	(.0082)	(.0064)	(.0052)	(.494)
High school graduate	−.031	−.021	.0037	.0066	.323
	(.011)	(.0089)	(.0070)	(.0057)	(.468)
Some college	−.059	−.043	.0172	.0168	.166
	(.014)	(.011)	(.0085)	(.0069)	(.372)
College graduate	−.070	−.051	.0157	.0186	.136
	(.015)	(.012)	(.0093)	(.0075)	(.343)
Mom's age of death	−.0012	−.00096	6.13E-04	5.08E-04	72.08
	(.00031)	(.00024)	(1.90E-04)	(1.53E-04)	(14.83)
Dad's age of death	−.00124	−.00098	5.80E-04	4.48E-04	74.04
	(.00029)	(.00024)	(1.76E-04)	(1.42E-04)	(15.97)
Wealth/1,000 in wave 1	−4.34E-05	−3.64E-05	1.03E-05	1.51E-05	192.3
	(1.24E-05)	(9.82E-06)	(7.69E-06)	(6.21E-06)	(383.0)
No. of observations	6,092	6,092	6,092	6,092	6,092
R^2	.109	.104	.069	.092	

Note: Standard errors are in parentheses.

table survival probabilities. The predicted survival probabilities in the unconstrained specifications are higher than those based on constrained specifications. This derives from the fact that the unconstrained specifications produce indexes that indicate more optimism than those based on constrained specifications.

In figure 12.1, we produce two fitted probability histograms for males and females between the ages of seventy and seventy-four at the time the survey is conducted for the constrained hazard-scaling model. The histograms for all other age groups and all other models are the same save for their location. From this figure, all focal responses of 0 and 1 have moved away from 0 and 1. For example, for males who are between seventy and seventy-four years old at the time of the survey, the predicted probabilities of surviving to age eighty-five are .22 and .61 if the responses are 0 and 1, respectively. Figure 12.2 has various survival curves for both males and fe-

Table 12.6　　　　　　　**Fitted survival probabilities (constrained hazard-scaling model)**

Age group	Target age	Life table	Nonfocal respondents Predicted	Nonfocal respondents Stated	Focal respondents $p_{ia\tau} = 0$ (predicted)	Focal respondents $p_{ia\tau} = 1$ (predicted)	All respondents Predicted	All respondents Stated
Female								
70–74	85	0.5880	0.5565 (0.0696)	0.5001	0.3571 (0.0218)	0.7592 (0.0213)	0.5604 (0.1215)	0.5095
75–79	90	0.4250	0.4426 (0.0745)	0.4616	0.2486 (0.0155)	0.6584 (0.0348)	0.4107 (0.1319)	0.3885
80–84	95	0.2240	0.2904 (0.0666)	0.4139	0.1398 (0.0176)	0.4806 (0.0213)	0.2485 (0.1113)	0.3029
Male								
70–74	85	0.3970	0.4293 (0.0680)	0.4845	0.2270 (0.0225)	0.6342 (0.0250)	0.4383 (0.1199)	0.5103
75–79	90	0.2500	0.3086 (0.0651)	0.4127	0.1466 (0.0133)	0.5091 (0.0446)	0.2936 (0.1079)	0.3820
80–84	95	0.1130	0.1848 (0.0543)	0.3960	0.0771 (0.0119)	0.3208 (0.0561)	0.1645 (0.0845)	0.3324

Note: Standard errors are in parentheses.

Table 12.7　　　　　　　**Fitted survival probabilities (unconstrained hazard-scaling model)**

Age group	Target age	Life table	Nonfocal respondents Predicted	Nonfocal respondents Stated	Focal respondents $p_{ia\tau} = 0$ (predicted)	Focal respondents $p_{ia\tau} = 1$ (predicted)	All respondents Predicted	All respondents Stated
Female								
70–74	85	0.5880	0.6266 (0.0708)	0.5001	0.4659 (0.0193)	0.8062 (0.0207)	0.6322 (0.1084)	0.5095
75–79	90	0.4250	0.5171 (0.0769)	0.4616	0.3602 (0.0169)	0.7069 (0.0323)	0.4927 (0.1162)	0.3885
80–84	95	0.2240	0.3634 (0.0790)	0.4139	0.2117 (0.0242)	0.5551 (0.0158)	0.3213 (0.1167)	0.3029
Male								
70–74	85	0.3970	0.5042 (0.0710)	0.4845	0.3339 (0.0304)	0.6838 (0.0227)	0.5129 (0.1092)	0.5103
75–79	90	0.2500	0.3814 (0.0750)	0.4127	0.2224 (0.0199)	0.5777 (0.0377)	0.3667 (0.1109)	0.3820
80–84	95	0.1130	0.2673 (0.0771)	0.3960	0.1191 (0.0171)	0.4503 (0.0380)	0.2390 (0.1146)	0.3324

Note: Standard errors are in parentheses.

Table 12.8   Fitted survival probabilities (constrained age-scaling model)

Age group	Target age	Life table	Nonfocal respondents Predicted	Nonfocal respondents Stated	Focal respondents $p_{ia\tau} = 0$ (predicted)	Focal respondents $p_{ia\tau} = 1$ (predicted)	All respondents Predicted	All respondents Stated
Female								
70–74	85	0.5880	0.5561 (0.0565)	0.5001	0.5589 (0.1167)	0.7554 (0.0195)	0.5589 (0.1167)	0.5095
75–79	90	0.4250	0.4452 (0.0611)	0.4616	0.2516 (0.0141)	0.6629 (0.0342)	0.4136 (0.1276)	0.3885
80–84	95	0.2240	0.2917 (0.0524)	0.4139	0.1505 (0.0165)	0.4750 (0.0249)	0.2529 (0.1024)	0.3029
Male								
70–74	85	0.3970	0.4306 (0.0552)	0.4845	0.2320 (0.0209)	0.6399 (0.0250)	0.4407 (0.1154)	0.5103
75–79	90	0.2500	0.3112 (0.0524)	0.4127	0.1572 (0.0132)	0.5070 (0.0476)	0.2974 (0.0998)	0.3820
80–84	95	0.1130	0.1788 (0.0431)	0.3960	0.0850 (0.0123)	0.2879 (0.0646)	0.1602 (0.0717)	0.3324

Note: Standard errors are in parentheses.

Table 12.9   Fitted survival probabilities (unconstrained age-scaling model)

Age group	Target age	Life table	Nonfocal respondents Predicted	Nonfocal respondents Stated	Focal respondents $p_{ia\tau} = 0$ (predicted)	Focal respondents $p_{ia\tau} = 1$ (predicted)	All respondents Predicted	All respondents Stated
Female								
70–74	85	0.5880	0.6689 (0.0384)	0.5001	0.5850 (0.0202)	0.7728 (0.0241)	0.6733 (0.0606)	0.5095
75–79	90	0.4250	0.5531 (0.0446)	0.4616	0.4720 (0.0184)	0.6592 (0.0369)	0.5413 (0.0649)	0.3885
80–84	95	0.2240	0.3825 (0.0457)	0.4139	0.3007 (0.0286)	0.4864 (0.0179)	0.3598 (0.0662)	0.3029
Male								
70–74	85	0.3970	0.5342 (0.0394)	0.4845	0.4427 (0.0351)	0.6329 (0.0258)	0.5392 (0.0613)	0.5103
75–79	90	0.2500	0.4043 (0.0458)	0.4127	0.2812 (0.0684)	0.5122 (0.0429)	0.3956 (0.0657)	0.3820
80–84	95	0.1130	0.2715 (0.0488)	0.3960	0.1738 (0.0239)	0.3719 (0.0417)	0.2509 (0.0728)	0.3324

Note: Standard errors are in parentheses.

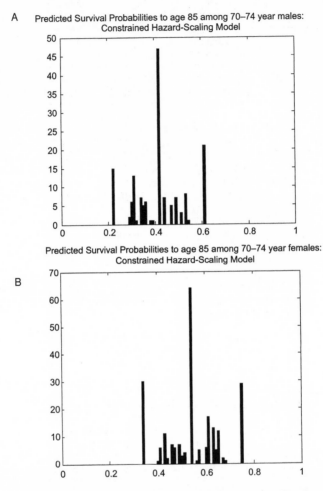

Fig. 12.1   **Histograms of predicted survival probabilities:** *A,* **predicted survival probabilities to age 85 among 70–74 year males (constrained hazard-scaling model);** *B,* **predicted survival probabilities to age 85 among 70–74 year females (constrained hazard-scaling model)**

males at age seventy for both constrained and unconstrained specifications in the hazard-scaling model. Graphs based on other models at other age categories look similar. In figure 12.2, the lines "personal-$p = 1$" and "personal-$p = 0$" represent the survival curves if the response is 1 and 0, respectively. The line "personal-$p = $ Average" represents the survival curve if the response represents the average of all responses. Not surprisingly, a person whose response is 1 typically has the highest survival curve, thus demonstrating the highest survival probabilities, while a person whose response is 0 has the lowest survival curve.

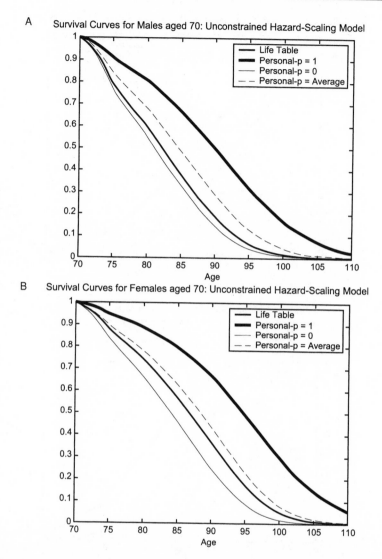

Fig. 12.2   Survival curves: *A,* survival curves for males aged 70 (unconstrained hazard-scaling model); *B,* survival curves for females aged 70 (unconstrained hazard-scaling model); *C,* survival curves for males aged 70 (constrained hazard-scaling model); *D,* survival curves for females aged 70 (constrained hazard-scaling model)

The densities of prior and posterior distributions are illustrated in figure 12.3. The first panel in figure 12.3 shows the prior and posterior densities if the response is 1, with the posterior density lying to the right of the prior density. Similarly, in the second panel in figure 12.3, the posterior density lies to the left of the prior density if the response is 0. This is

C   Survival Curves for Males aged 70: Constrained Hazard-Scaling Model

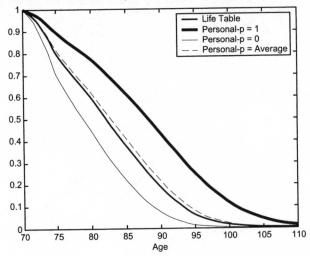

D

Survival Curves for Females aged 70: Constrained Hazard-Scaling Model

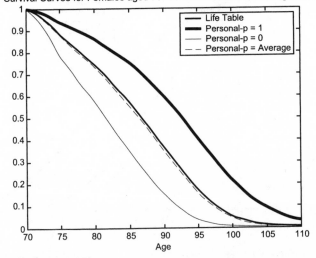

Fig. 12.2 (cont.) Survival curves: *A,* survival curves for males aged 70 (uncon-strained hazard-scaling model); *B,* survival curves for females aged 70 (uncon-strained hazard-scaling model); *C,* survival curves for males aged 70 (constrained hazard-scaling model); *D,* survival curves for females aged 70 (constrained hazard-scaling model)

A   Prior and Posterior Densities for Males Aged 70 with P = 1: survival rate = 0.5654

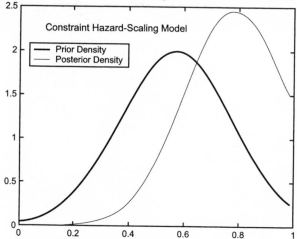

B   Prior and Posterior distributions for Males Aged 70 with P = 0: survival rate = 0.5654

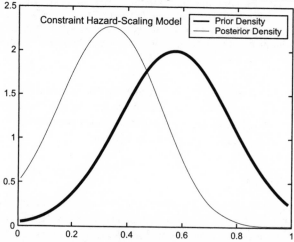

Fig. 12.3 Densities of prior, conditional, and posterior distributions: *A,* prior and posterior densities for males aged 70 with $P = 1$: survival rate = 0.5654; *B,* prior and posterior distributions for males aged 70 with $P = 0$: survival rate = 0.5654; *C,* prior and posterior densities for males aged 70 with $P = 0.5$: survival rate = 0.5654

what one would expect from the Bayesian update model. The third panel in figure 12.3 illustrates a case where the response is 0.5. In this case, it is unclear a priori that the response would pull the prior to the left or the right.

Finally, we produce histograms of the estimated optimistic parameters γ_i

C   Prior and Posterior Densities for Males Aged 70 with P = 0.5: survival rate = 0.5654

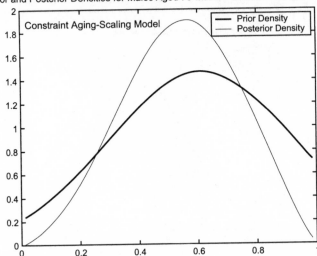

Fig. 12.3   (cont.) Densities of prior, conditional, and posterior distributions: *A*, prior and posterior densities for males aged 70 with $P = 1$: survival rate = 0.5654; *B*, prior and posterior distributions for males aged 70 with $P = 0$: survival rate = 0.5654; *C*, prior and posterior densities for males aged 70 with $P = 0.5$: survival rate = 0.5654

for all four models in figure 12.4. The average and standard deviations of γ_i are also given in the histograms. There are significant variations between these indexes. The significant variations in optimistic indexes produce significant variations in individual survival curves.

12.5   Conclusions

Many economic models are based on forward-looking behavior on the part of economic agents. Surveys such as HRS and AHEAD ask individuals for their expectations on the probability of given future events' occurring in their lifetime. On average, the subjective probability of a future event is consistent with the observed probability that the event does occur. For example, average individual survival probabilities are consistent with those from the life tables.

However, at the micro level, the subjective probability responses in HRS and AHEAD suffer serious problems of focal responses of 0.0 and 1.0. Consequently, applications of subjective probabilities will be extremely limited if "true" subjective survival probabilities are not recovered.

In this paper, we suggest a Bayesian update model to account for problems caused by focal responses of 0.0 and 1.0. As a result, individual sur-

A   Histogram for optimistic index: unconstrained hazard-scaling model
mean = 0.8229, standard deviation = 0.2956

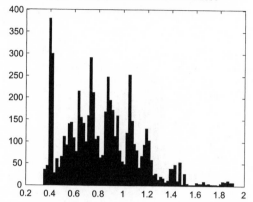

B   Histogram for optimistic index: constrained hazard-scaling model
mean = 1.0398, standard deviation = 0.3752

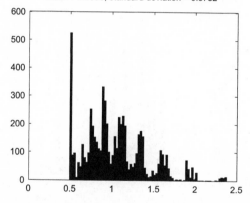

Fig. 12.4   Histogram for optimistic indices: *A*, histogram for optimistic index: unconstrained hazard-scaling model (mean = 0.8229, standard deviation = 0.2956); *B*, histogram for optimistic index: constrained hazard-scaling model (mean = 1.0398, standard deviation = 0.3752); *C*, histogram for optimistic index: unconstrained age-scaling model (mean = 1.2708, standard error = 0.1855); *D*, histogram for optimistic index: constrained age-scaling model (mean = 1.0617, standard deviation = .2049)

vival curves derived from the model do not suffer the problems of focal responses. We also propose two approaches to model the individual heterogeneities of their subjective survival curves. One approach modifies the life table hazard rates, while another approach models the subjective aging process, which is different from the life table aging process. The model is estimated from the observed survival information of our sample. From the

C   Histogram for optimistic index: unconstrained age-scaling model
mean = 1.2708, standard error = 0.1855

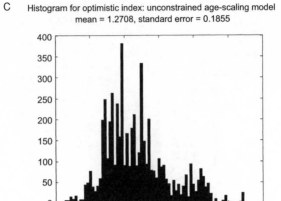

D   Histogram for optimistic index: constrained age-scaling model
mean = 1.0617, standard deviation = .2049

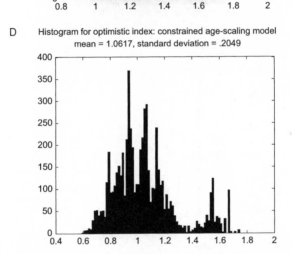

Fig. 12.4   (cont.) Histogram for optimistic indices: *A,* **histogram for optimistic index: unconstrained hazard-scaling model (mean = 0.8229, standard deviation = 0.2956);** *B,* **histogram for optimistic index: constrained hazard-scaling model (mean = 1.0398, standard deviation = 0.3752);** *C,* **histogram for optimistic index: unconstrained age-scaling model (mean = 1.2708, standard error = 0.1855);** *D,* **histogram for optimistic index: constrained age-scaling model (mean = 1.0617, standard deviation = .2049)**

estimated model, we construct several optimistic indexes for each individual and conduct a test that is based on out-of-sample prediction. These optimistic indexes are used to create individual subjective survival curves that have considerable variations and are readily applicable to economic models that require individual subjective survival curves. In a companion paper, we apply these individual subjective survival curves to a life-cycle model of savings and bequests.

Appendix

Mean of the Truncated Normal Distribution

If $x \sim N[\mu, \sigma^2]$, the density of the truncated normal distribution is then

$$g(x \mid e < x < f) = \frac{\frac{1}{\sigma}\phi\left(\frac{x - \mu}{\sigma}\right)}{\Phi\left(\frac{f - \mu}{\sigma}\right) - \Phi\left(\frac{e - \mu}{\sigma}\right)}.$$

The mean is

$$(A1) \quad E[x \mid e < x < f] = \int_e^f xg(x \mid e < x < f)dx = \frac{\int_e^f x \frac{1}{\sigma}\phi\left(\frac{x - \mu}{\sigma}\right)dx}{\Phi\left(\frac{f - \mu}{\sigma}\right) - \Phi\left(\frac{e - \mu}{\sigma}\right)}$$

$$= \mu - \sigma \frac{\phi\left(\frac{f - \mu}{\sigma}\right) - \phi\left(\frac{e - \mu}{\sigma}\right)}{\Phi\left(\frac{f - \mu}{\sigma}\right) - \Phi\left(\frac{e - \mu}{\sigma}\right)}$$

$$= \mu - \sigma\eta(e, f, \mu, \sigma),$$

where

$$(A2) \quad \eta(e, f, \mu, \sigma) = \frac{\phi\left(\frac{f - \mu}{\sigma}\right) - \phi\left(\frac{e - \mu}{\sigma}\right)}{\Phi\left(\frac{f - \mu}{\sigma}\right) - \Phi\left(\frac{e - \mu}{\sigma}\right)}.$$

Mean of the Censored Normal Distribution

If $x^* \sim N[\mu, \sigma^2]$ and $x = e$ if $x^* \leq e$; $x = x^*$ if $e \leq x^* \leq f$; and $x = f$ if $x^* \geq f$, where e and f are constant, then

$$(A3) \quad E[x] = \Pr(x = e)E\lfloor x \mid x = e\rfloor + \Pr(e < x < f)E\lfloor x \mid e < x < f\rfloor + \Pr[x \geq f]E\lfloor x \mid x = f\rfloor$$

$$= \Pr(x^* \leq e)e + \Pr(e < x^* < f)E[x^* \mid e < x^* < f] + \Pr[x^* \geq f]f$$

$$= \Phi\left(\frac{e - \mu}{\sigma}\right)e + \left[\Phi\left(\frac{f - \mu}{\sigma}\right) - \Phi\left(\frac{e - \mu}{\sigma}\right)\right][\mu - \sigma\eta(e, f, \mu, \sigma)] + \left[1 - \Phi\left(\frac{f - \mu}{\sigma}\right)\right]f$$

where $\eta(e, f, \mu, \sigma)$ is defined in equation (A2).

References

Bassett, William, and Robin Lumsdaine. 2001. Probability limits—are subjective assessments adequately accurate? *Journal of Human Resources* 36 (2): 327–63.

Hamermesh, Daniel. 1985. Expectations, life expectancy, and economic behavior. *Quarterly Journal of Economics* 10 (2): 389–408.

Hubbard, R. Glenn, Jonathan Skinner, and Stephen Zeldes. 1995. Precautionary saving and social insurance. *Journal of Political Economy* 103 (2): 360–99.

Hurd, Michael D. 1989. Mortality risks and bequests. *Econometrica* 57 (4): 779–813.

Hurd, Michael D., and Kathleen McGarry. 1995. Evaluation of subjective probability distributions in the Health and Retirement Study. *Journal of Human Resources* 30 (5): S268–S292.

———. 2002. The predictive validity of subjective probabilities of survival. *The Economic Journal* 112 (482): 966–85.

Hurd, Michael D., Daniel McFadden, and Li Gan. 1998. Subjective survival curves and life cycle behavior. In *Inquiries of economics of aging,* ed. David Wise, 259–305. Chicago: University of Chicago Press.

Manski, Charles. 1993. Dynamic choice in social settings: Learnings from the experiences of others. *Journal of Econometrics* 58 (1–2): 121–36.

Comment   Robert J. Willis

Cognitive capacity, personality, physical abilities, motivation, and other factors influence the willingness of individuals to participate in surveys, their willingness to answer any given question, and the quality of the information they provide in their answers to that question. Survey designers attempt to minimize survey and item nonresponse and try to ask questions in a way that will elicit "true" answers. While much progress has been made in increasing the quality of data produced by surveys such as the Health and Retirement Study (HRS) used in the Gan, Hurd, and McFadden (GHM) paper, there remains considerable heterogeneity in the quality of responses across respondents. Because of this, I believe that economists (and other survey users) need to develop theories of survey response that provide a link between observed responses and the underlying true values. It is also important to recognize that many of the factors that influence the quality of an individual's survey responses may also influence his or her behavior in the real world. This suggests that it may be useful to model behavior in the real world and on surveys jointly. The paper by GHM under discussion can be understood as an important contribution to this general agenda.

The HRS has pioneered asking questions about subjective probability beliefs on a wide variety of topics, including survival probabilities. These

Robert J. Willis is a professor of economics at the University of Michigan.

questions depart from the conventional approach to expectations in economics. Specifically, as Dominitz and Manski (1999) argue, "Economists have typically assumed that expectations formation is homogeneous; all persons condition their beliefs on the same variables and process their information in the same way" (Dominitz and Manski 1999, p. 16). Within the conventional approach, probability beliefs are treated as unobservable, and assumptions about beliefs, such as rational expectations, along with assumptions about unobservable preference parameters, such as risk aversion or time preference, are embedded in optimizing models from which (hopefully) testable relations between observable variables may be derived. An important motivation for asking directly about subjective probabilities in a survey is to allow relaxation of the assumption of homogeneous expectations by converting probabilities from an unobservable to an observable quantity that may vary across respondents and thus capture individual heterogeneity in expectations.

Early analysis of the survival probabilities questions in HRS by Hurd and McGarry (1995) showed that, on average, there was (to me, surprising) agreement between these subjective reports and life table estimates of survival, including covariation with health status and health behaviors such as smoking. However, the probability reports are quite "noisy," with a large number of "focal" answers at 0 percent, 100 percent, and 50 percent. In terms of the original purpose of asking these probability questions, this is quite troublesome. On the one hand, there is clear evidence that the survey questions are successful in capturing important information about people's probability beliefs. On the other hand, it is also clear that answers at the individual level do not necessarily measure a given person's probability beliefs.

GHM attempt to clarify the link between survey responses and an individual's subjective survival probability by utilizing three pieces of information: (a) the individual's survey response to a question about the probability of survival to a given age, (b) the life table estimate of the survival probability of a person whose demographic characteristics (age, race, sex) match those of the respondent, and (c) observations of the subsequent mortality experience of members of the AHEAD cohort in the HRS. These three pieces of information are combined in an elegant Bayesian model in order to recalibrate the range of individual answers to conform to a range consistent with the life table, and to estimate an individual-specific "optimism" parameter indicating the degree to which a given person believes that he or she is more or less likely to survive than observationally identical individuals.[1] If this approach is successful, the recalibrated probabilities

---

1. The survival probability questions ask about survival to a given age, which varies with the current age of the respondent. GHM rescale these probabilities to measure one minus the annual mortality hazard.

can be used as direct measures of individual subjective survival probabilities in optimizing models that allow for individual-specific heterogeneity in beliefs.

In my comments, I first use a geometric approach to explain how the GHM model works. I then argue that GHM fail to take into account the uncertainty (or ambiguity or imprecision) that an individual may have about his or her mortality risks and that this may lead to a bias in the estimated probabilities implied by their model. Using a theory of survey response to probability questions developed in Lillard and Willis (2001), I sketch out why the GHM model should be generalized to include the degree of uncertainty about probability beliefs and discuss briefly why heterogeneity in the precision of probability beliefs as well as heterogeneity in optimism may be important for behavior.

One basic problem in relating survey responses on subjective survival probabilities to an objective measure of survival probabilities is illustrated in figure 12C.1. The lower panel of figure 12C.1 shows a histogram of subjective survival probabilities based on responses in wave 1 of AHEAD. The histogram shows that responses cover the entire range from 0 to 100 percent. The histogram shows heaping at focal points of 0 and 100, which GHM regard as improper responses, because it is not possible for probabilities to be truly 0 or 1. There is also a focal response at 50, which produces a larger spike than those at 0 or 100. The focal response at 50 is ignored by GHM, a point to which I return later.

The upper panel of figure 12C.1 depicts a stylized "calibration curve"

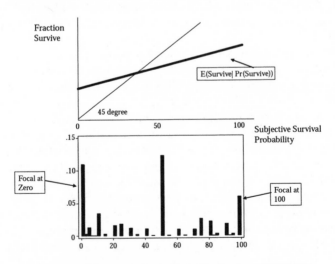

Histogram of Responses to Survival Probability Question, AHEAD-1993

Fig. 12C.1   Calibration of survival probabilities: Histogram of responses to survival probability question, AHEAD 1993

(Camerer 1995), which relates subjective probability reports, measured on the horizontal axis, to relative frequencies such as life table estimates, measured on the vertical axis. If the elicitation of subjective survival probabilities on the survey is completely successful and if respondents have rational expectations, the calibration curve would correspond to a 45-degree line. For example, consider a set of sixty-five-year-old respondents who give the answer 80 percent when asked about their chance of survival to age seventy-five. These respondents would be judged as "well calibrated" if 80 percent of them actually survived after ten years.

In practice, calibration curves usually tend to be flatter than the 45-degree line, like the thick line labeled E(survive | Pr(survive)) in figure 12C.1. In the behavioral economics and psychological literature surveyed by Camerer (1997), this pattern is usually explained by suggesting a cognitive bias. Thus, Camerer (p. 591) states, "In general subjects are overconfident. They are insufficiently regressive in judging the likelihood of events. Events they say are certain happen only 80 percent of the time." Conversely, "Events judged to be impossible happen 20 percent of the time." To an economist reared on Milton Friedman's explanation for a flat consumption function, an obvious alternative explanation for a flat calibration curve is that the survey measure of subjective probability contains measurement error, implying that mean response errors tend to be negative for persons who report relatively low probabilities and positive for people who report high probabilities.[2] Still another possible explanation is that people vary in their degree of optimism or pessimism about their survival chances. On average, the pessimists will be found among the people giving low survival probabilities and the optimists among those with high probabilities. To the extent that optimism or pessimism is unwarranted, this would also produce a flat calibration curve.[3]

These three alternative reasons for a flat calibration curve represent substantively different hypotheses about the nature of subjective probability beliefs. The first suggests that people tend to have biased beliefs, with the bias becoming worse and worse as the objective probability of the event tends toward small or large values. The second is consistent with individuals having rational expectations that are not elicited with complete accuracy on a survey. It is also consistent, as I argue later, with the possibility that people are uncertain about what the true probability really is. The third reason emphasizes the possibility of considerable individual heterogeneity in beliefs that may or may not be warranted by their private information. Obviously, these possibilities are not mutually exclusive. However, it is of interest to know the extent to which each is operative, since they may

2. This possibility has also occurred to psychologists. See Soll (1996).
3. Physicians, including Alan Garber at this meeting, tend to think that optimism is a good trait because they find that among patients who present equivalent clinical data the optimists are more likely to recover than the pessimists.

have different implications for the way in which people behave in the real world.

GHM emphasize the role of focal responses at 0 and 100 in creating a miscalibration of individual responses. They suggest modeling the relationship between the individual's subjective survival probability and his survey response as a truncated normal distribution, with truncation points at 0 and 1. Two versions of this model are considered. The "constrained version" assumes that the mean survival probability across respondents is the same as the life table value, while the "unconstrained" version allows for the average of the survey responses to differ from the life table estimates.

A geometric interpretation of how their model works is presented in figure 12C.2, which replicates figure 12C.1 except for labels and scale. The vertical axis in figure 12C.2 measures survival probabilities by the actual mortality experience of a sample of AHEAD respondents (treated in the diagram as observationally identical) between wave 1 and wave 2, while the horizontal axis represents a recalibrated (or rescaled) version of the subjective probabilities such that the expected fraction of survivors in wave 2, conditional on the rescaled subjective probabilities, falls on the 45-degree line. The mean of the rescaled probabilities may either be constrained to be equal to the life table value or be unconstrained and left to be estimated from the response data. After rescaling, the histogram of survey responses is compressed, as shown in the bottom panel of figure 12C.2, so that persons who answer 0 have a substantial positive probability of survival and

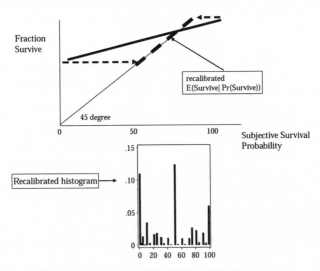

Fig. 12C.2   Recalibration of survival probabilities

those who answer 100 have a significantly positive probability of death. (This histogram is conceptually equivalent to those shown in figure 12.1 of the GHM paper.)

In addition to allowing the population as a whole to be optimistic or pessimistic relative to life table probabilities, GHM also allow for an individual-specific optimism parameter. This is depicted in figure 12C.3 for persons who give survey responses that are above or below the average of the answers given by observationally identical members of the AHEAD sample.

In their empirical work, GHM find evidence that, on average, the AHEAD respondents believe that their survival probabilities are higher than life table estimates and, in addition, that there is considerable individual-specific variation in their degree of optimism or pessimism, based on answers to survival probability questions in wave 1 of AHEAD and observed mortality between wave 1 and wave 2. Using the estimated parameters to make out-of-sample predictions using data on the mortality experience between wave 2 and wave 3 of individuals who survived to wave 2, they find that the unconstrained model is a statistically significant improvement on a model constrained to conform to the life table and that the individual-specific parameters are significant predictors.

These findings suggest to me that it might be better to choose some other term than "optimism" or "pessimism" to describe these parameters. Apparently, individual beliefs contain considerable predictive information that is not contained in the life table. However, as illustrated in table 12.5

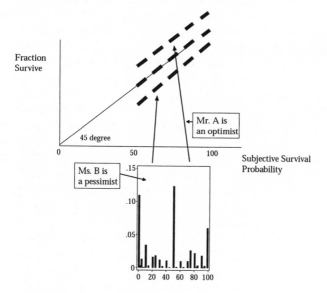

Fig. 12C.3   Optimism and pessimism

of GHM, a significant amount of the heterogeneity in individual beliefs is associated with economic and demographic characteristics of the individual in the same direction that these characteristics are correlated with actual health and mortality. It would be useful to have some additional discussion and, if possible, analysis of the degree to which heterogeneity in subjective beliefs about survival is rational versus the extent to which it is biased in an optimistic or pessimistic direction. It would also be interesting to ask whether the data available in the HRS could be used to address the physicians' hypothesis, noted earlier in note 3, that optimism has a beneficial causal effect on survival.

Although their earlier paper on subjective survival curves (Gan, Hurd, and McFadden 1998) gave equal attention to focal answers at 0, 50, and 100, the current paper ignores focal answers at 50, even though these are more numerous than those at the endpoints of the distribution. In the concluding part of my comments, I briefly describe a theory of survey response to probability questions developed in Lillard and Willis (2001) that attempts to relate the pattern of focal and "exact" responses to an individual's subjective probability beliefs and discuss some possible implications of this theory for the GHM model.

In each wave of the HRS survey, respondents are asked a series of subjective probability questions about the likelihood of a variety of events. Topics range from questions about general events (e.g., likelihood that economy will experience major depression, of an increase in stock prices, that tomorrow will be a sunny day), events with private knowledge (e.g., survival to a given age), and events subject to personal control (e.g., leaving an inheritance, working past age sixty-two). On average, respondents take about fifteen seconds to listen to each probability question and give a response by choosing a number on a scale ranging from 0 to 100.

What is the relationship between the chosen survey response and the respondent's subjective probability belief about the event in question? Lillard and Willis (2001) hypothesize that an individual's subjective belief about the likelihood of a given event is represented by a subjective density function, $g(p)$. If the individual has precise beliefs, this density has a mass point at a particular value of p. For example, the person may believe that the probability that a coin will come up heads is exactly one-half or the probability that a die will come up 5 is exactly one-sixth. For many events, including the chance of survival, it is reasonable to assume that a respondent is not completely sure about the value of the probability. This uncertainty or imprecision is represented by the spread of $g(p)$.

In giving a single number in response to a probability question in HRS, what aspect of $g(p)$ does the respondent report? One possibility is the mean: $\bar{p} = \int_0^1 g(p)dp$. In addition to being cognitively difficult, assuming that an answer to a subjective probability question measures $\bar{p}$ is inconsistent with the evidence that a large fraction of answers are focal, since $\bar{p}$

would tend to have a nonfocal value no matter how uncertain the individual might be. An alternative suggested by Lillard and Willis (2001) is the "modal choice hypothesis." According to this hypothesis, the respondent answers by giving that probability, denoted by p^{mode}, which is most likely among all possible values. This, of course, is the mode of $g(p)$. If the person has relatively precise beliefs, $g(p)$ is unimodal, the value of p^{mode} tends to be close to $\bar{p}$, and we expect the respondent to give an "exact" (i.e., nonfocal) answer. As the person's degree of uncertainty increases, we show that that $g(p)$ tends to become J-shaped with a mode at 0 if $\bar{p} < 1/2$ or at 1 if $\bar{p} > 1/2$. In these cases, the modal choice hypothesis implies that the individual will give a focal answer at 0 or 100. As uncertainty increases still further, $g(p)$ tends to become bimodal at 0 and 1. In this case, the individual is truly ambivalent about the most likely value of the probability and gives a focal answer of 50, reflecting his or her "epistemic uncertainty" (Bruine de Bruin et al. 2000).

One implication of the modal choice hypothesis that is of relevance to the GHM paper concerns the proper treatment of focal answers versus nonfocal or exact answers. As is illustrated in figure 12C.2, the recalibration of the subjective probabilities in the GHM model compresses the range of the subjective probabilities, moving the focal answers at 0 and 1 away from these extremes. Their model also compresses the range of the nonfocal answers so as to maintain the same ordering in the recalibrated probability as in the raw survey answer. Thus, a person who gives a 99 percent chance of survival to the survey question will be assigned a smaller probability of survival by GHM than the person who gives a focal answer of 100 percent. Conversely, a person who gives a very low nonfocal answer will have that answer raised in order to assign a sufficiently positive probability to those who give a focal answer of 0 percent. This is problematic if people who give focal answers are less certain about their beliefs than those who give nonfocal answers.

I examine this issue empirically in a simple regression model relating survival between the first two waves of AHEAD to answers to the subjective survival probability question in wave 1 of AHEAD.[4] The (unweighted) fraction of survivors between waves was 0.917. The implied average subjective survival probability including both focal and nonfocal answers is 0.692, considerably below the actual survival rate.[5] The average excluding those who gave focal answers is 0.894, which is much closer to the actual

---

4. I thank Jody Schimmel for carrying out this analysis.

5. The raw answer to the survival probability question is first rescaled into an annual rate, using the time distance between the individual's age and the target age in the question under the simple but somewhat inaccurate assumption of a constant mortality hazard. (GHM are more sophisticated in their adjustment for time distance.) This rate is then used to form the subjective probability of survival from the date of interview at wave 1 to the date of interview at wave 2. This procedure assigns a probability of 0 or 1 to those who give focal answers at 0 or 100. This rescaled variable is used on the right-hand side of the regressions in table 12C.1.

Table 12C.1   Linear regression of survival to AHEAD wave 2

	Model 1	Model 2
Two-year self-reported survival probability	0.105	0.262
	(0.009)	(0.041)
Focal at 0		0.136
		(0.036)
Focal at 50		−0.008
		(0.009)
Focal at 100		−0.038
		(0.013)
Constant	0.844	0.713
	(0.007)	(0.035)
No. of observations	6,140	6,140
R^2	0.0206	0.0232

Note: Standard errors are in parentheses.

rate. Table 12C.1 reports two regression models. Model 1 simply regresses actual survival on the (rescaled) subjective survival probability. The slope coefficient is only 0.105, indicating that the empirical counterpart of the calibration curve in figure 12C.1 is extremely flat. Model 2 adds dummy indicators for focal answers at 0, 50, and 100. This causes the slope coefficient to increase dramatically from 0.105 to 0.264, which, however, is still far flatter than the 45-degree line in figure 12C.1. The dummy variables for focal answers at 0 and 100 are both highly significant, while the dummy for focal at 50 is insignificant. Model 2 implies that a person who gives a focal answer of 0 has an actual survival probability that is 13 percentage points higher than a person who gives very low nonfocal answer. Similarly, a person who gives a focal answer of 100 has a survival chance that is 3.8 percentage points lower than a person who gives a nonfocal answer near 100.

These results suggest that hetereogeneity across respondents in the precision of their subjective beliefs is important and should be taken into account in recalibrating raw answers to subjective survival probability questions into values that can be treated as a direct measure of individual-specific subjective mortality risk in behavioral models. In addition, Lillard and Willis (2001) argue that imprecision of beliefs is of direct significance for behavior. For example, they show that imprecision of subjective beliefs about rates of return to stocks causes individuals to behave more risk aversely. I would encourage GHM to extend their elegant model of survival probabilities to address this issue.

References

Bruine de Bruin, Wandi, Baruch Fischhoff, Susan G. Millstein, and Bonnie L. Halpern-Felscher. 2000. Verbal and numerical expressions of probability: "It's a fifty-fifty chance." *Organizational Behavior and Human Decision Processes* 81 (1): 115–31.

Camerer, Colin. 1995. Individual decision making. In *Handbook of experimental economics,* ed. John H. Kagel and Alvin E. Roth, 587–703. Princeton: Princeton University Press.

Dominitz, Jeff, and Charles F. Manski. 1999. The several cultures of research on subjective expectations. In *Wealth, work and health: Innovations in measurement in the social sciences,* ed. James P. Smith and Robert J. Willis, 15–35. Ann Arbor: University of Michigan Press.

Hurd, M., D. McFadden, and L. Gan. 1998. Subjective survival curves and life cycle behavior. In *Inquiries in the economics of aging,* ed. David A. Wise, 259–305. Chicago: University of Chicago Press.

Hurd, M. D., and K. McGarry. 1995. Evaluation of the subjective probabilities of survival in the health and retirement study. *Journal of Human Resources* 30: S268–92.

Lillard, Lee A., and Robert J. Willis. 2001. Cognition and wealth: The importance of probabilistic thinking. University of Michigan, Michigan Retirement Research Center. Working Paper no. WP2001-007.

Soll, Jack B. 1996. Determinants of overconfidence and miscalibration: The roles of random error and ecological structure. *Organizational Behavior and Human Decision Processes* 65 (2): 117–37.

Contributors

Axel Börsch-Supan
Mannheim Institute for the Economics
  of Aging
University of Mannheim
Building L13, 17
D-68131 Mannheim, Germany

Anne Case
Woodrow Wilson School
367 Wallace Hall
Princeton University
Princeton, NJ 08544

James J. Choi
National Bureau of Economic
  Research
1050 Massachusetts Avenue
Cambridge, MA 02138

David M. Cutler
Department of Economics
Harvard University
Cambridge, MA 02138

Angus Deaton
Woodrow Wilson School
328 Wallace Hall
Princeton University
Princeton, NJ 08544-1013

Esther Duflo
Department of Economics, E52-252G
Massachusetts Institute of Technology
50 Memorial Drive
Cambridge, MA 02142

Lothar Essig
Department of Economics, MEA
Building L13, 17
Universität Mannheim
68131 Mannheim, Germany

Elliott S. Fisher
Dartmouth Medical School
1 Rope Ferry Road
Hanover, NH 03755

Li Gan
Department of Economics
University of Texas
Austin, TX 78712

Alan M. Garber
PCOR/CHP
Stanford University
117 Encina Commons
Stanford, CA 94305-6019

Jeff Geppert
SPHERE Institute
1415 Rollins Road, Suite 204
Burlingame, CA 94010

Florian Heiss
Department of Economics, MEA
Building L13, 17
Universität Mannheim
68131 Mannheim, Germany

Michael D. Hurd
RAND Corporation
1700 Main Street
Santa Monica, CA 90407

Robert Jensen
John F. Kennedy School of
   Government
Harvard University
79 JFK Street
Cambridge, MA 02138

Arie Kapteyn
RAND Corporation
1700 Main Street
P.O. Box 2138
Santa Monica, CA 90407-2138

David Laibson
Department of Economics
Littauer M-14
Harvard University
Cambridge, MA 02138

Thomas MaCurdy
Department of Economics
Stanford University
Stanford, CA 94305-6072

Brigitte C. Madrian
The Wharton School
University of Pennsylvania
1400 Steinberg Hall-Dietrich Hall
3620 Locust Walk
Philadelphia, PA 19104-6372

Daniel McFadden
Department of Economics
University of California, Berkeley
549 Evans Hall #3880
Berkeley, CA 94707-3880

Andrew Metrick
The Wharton School
University of Pennsylvania
3620 Locust Walk
Philadelphia, PA 19104

Constantijn Panis
RAND Corporation
1700 Main Street
P.O. Box 2138
Santa Monica, CA 90407-2138

James M. Poterba
Department of Economics, E52-350
Massachusetts Institute of Technology
50 Memorial Drive
Cambridge, MA 02142-1347

Antonio Rangel
Department of Economics
Stanford University
Stanford, CA 94305

Joshua Rauh
Graduate School of Business
University of Chicago
1101 East 58th Street
Chicago, IL 60637

Andrew A. Samwick
6106 Rockefeller Hall
Department of Economics
Dartmouth College
Hanover, NH 03755-3514

Jonathan Skinner
6106 Rockefeller Hall
Department of Economics
Dartmouth College
Hanover, NH 03755

James P. Smith
RAND Corporation
1700 Main Street
P.O. Box 2138
Santa Monica, CA 90407-2138

Steven F. Venti
Department of Economics
6106 Rockefeller Center
Dartmouth College
Hanover, NH 03755

John E. Wennberg
Dartmouth Medical School
7251 Strasenburgh
Hanover, NH 03755

Robert J. Willis
Department of Economics
University of Michigan
611 Tappan Street
Ann Arbor, MI 48109-1220

David A. Wise
John F. Kennedy School of
    Government
Harvard University
1050 Massachusetts Avenue
Cambridge, MA 02138

Author Index

Abel, A., 335n8
Adams, M., 208, 213
Adams, Peter, 217n3, 230, 235
Agarwala, S. N., 360n3
Ai, C., 243
Akerlof, George A., 61n5
Altonji, Joseph G., 146, 147
American Association of Retired Persons, 279
Ameriks, John, 54, 56
Anderson, Gerard F., 129
Anderson, Todd, 127
Attanasio, O., 317

Baker, M., 208
Banks, J., 293
Bardhan, Pranab, 365
Barker, David J. P., 234
Barnes, B. A., 157
Bassett, William, 380n1
Baumeister, Roy F., 74
Beltrametti, L., 285
Benartzi, Shlomo, 74
Bernheim, Douglas, 74, 335n8
Bertaut, Carol, 282, 295
Bhat, M., 360n3
Blöndal, S., 284, 286n7
Blundell, R., 293
Bolen, Julie C., 143
Börsch-Supan, Axel, 8, 9, 241, 242, 243, 244, 318, 347
Brennan, M. J., 55, 56

Browning, M., 282, 317
Brugiavini, A., 283, 293
Brumberg, R., 282, 335n8

Cafferata, Gail Lee, 242
Camerer, Colin, 405
Carroll, Christopher D., 294, 314, 335n8, 352
Case, Anne, 6–7, 233n9
Chen, Martha, 357, 358, 358n1, 360, 360n3, 365, 375
Choi, James J., 3, 59, 61, 61n2, 72
Cooper, Megan M., 127, 133, 140, 143
Copeland, Craig, 289
Corder, Larry S., 162
Costa, D. L., 243
Cox, D., 242
Cuerdon, Timothy, 140n10
Cutler, David M., 6, 126, 129n2, 130, 161

Deaton, Angus, 6–7, 143n13, 213, 294, 317, 352, 362
Deri, C., 208
De Vos, K., 285
Dominitz, Jeff, 403
Drèze, Jean, 357, 358, 360n3, 375
Duflo, Esther, 374
Dumont, Louis, 371n18
Dynan, K. E., 293

Elder, Todd E., 146, 147
Ellwood, D. T., 241, 243

Subject Index